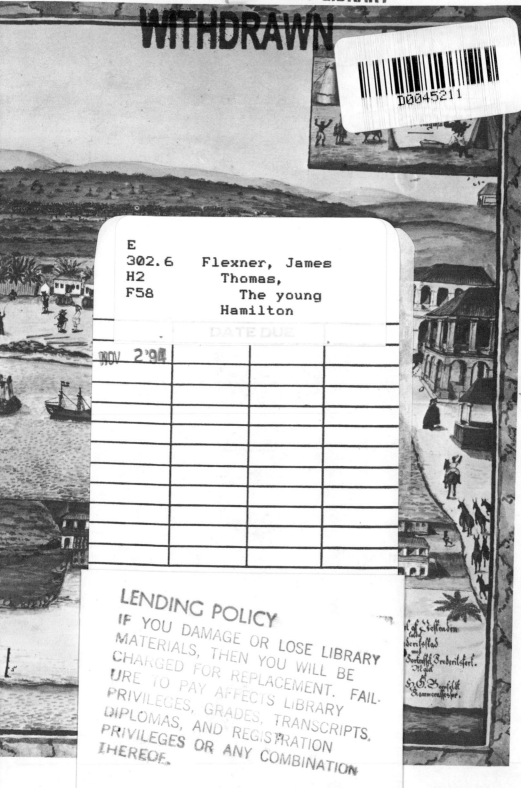

Books by James Thomas Flexner

AMERICAN PAINTING
I. First Flowers of Our Wilderness
II. The Light of Distant Skies
III. That Wilder Image

AMERICA'S OLD MASTERS

THE POCKET HISTORY OF AMERICAN PAINTING
(also published as *A Short History of American Painting*)

JOHN SINGLETON COPLEY

GILBERT STUART

THE WORLD OF WINSLOW HOMER
(with the editors of Time-Life Books)

NINETEENTH CENTURY AMERICAN PAINTING

DOCTORS ON HORSEBACK
Pioneers of American Medicine

STEAMBOATS COME TRUE
(also published as *Inventors in Action*)

THE TRAITOR AND THE SPY
(also published as *The Benedict Arnold Case*)

MOHAWK BARONET
Sir William Johnson of New York

WILLIAM HENRY WELCH AND THE HEROIC AGE
OF AMERICAN MEDICINE
(with Simon Flexner)

GEORGE WASHINGTON
I. The Forge of Experience (*1732–1775*)
II. In the American Revolution (*1775–1783*)
III. And the New Nation (*1783–1793*)
IV. Anguish and Farewell (*1793–1799*)

WASHINGTON: THE INDISPENSABLE MAN

THE FACE OF LIBERTY

THE YOUNG HAMILTON

The Young
Hamilton
A BIOGRAPHY

This miniature by Charles Willson Peale seems
to be the earliest likeness of Hamilton. He wears
across his chest the green sash that identifies an
aide-de-camp, and on his shoulder the epaulettes
of a lieutenant colonel. His hair is cut surprisingly
short for the eighteenth century but it is powdered. Courtesy, Nathaniel Burt. Photograph,
Frick Art Reference Library

The Young Hamilton

A BIOGRAPHY

JAMES THOMAS FLEXNER

LITTLE, BROWN AND COMPANY
BOSTON · TORONTO

FIRST EDITION

T 03/78

LIBRARY OF CONGRESS CATALOGING IN PUBLICATION DATA

Flexner, James Thomas, 1908–
  The young Hamilton.

  Bibliography: p. 460
  Includes index.
  1. Hamilton, Alexander, 1757–1804. 2. Soldiers—
United States—Biography. 3. United States—History—
Revolution, 1775–1783. 4. Legislators—United States—
Biography. I. Title.
E302.6.H2F58 973.4′092′4 [B] 77–13877
ISBN 0–316–28594–3

Published simultaneously in Canada
by Little, Brown & Company (Canada) Limited

PRINTED IN THE UNITED STATES OF AMERICA

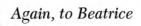

Again, to Beatrice

Contents

CONTENTS

CONTENTS

CONTENTS

Illustrations

ILLUSTRATIONS

The Young Hamilton

A BIOGRAPHY

Introduction

According to Frederick Scott Oliver, one of Hamilton's most admired biographers, "if we seek for a complete presentiment of the man in what he wrote and spoke, we shall not find it. He treats his public ceremoniously and with reserve. . . . Hamilton has left us no record of his private life from which we can construct a human being. His pen was a sacred weapon which, if it had to write of personal affairs, dealt with them as if they had been state papers or a legal précis."[1]

Before I launched on this study of Hamilton I was warned, by scholars more familiar than I was then with the relevant archives, that I should see him flash and achieve, but that his inner feelings would remain hidden. Since I am convinced that no personal documents exist that are not indicative of character, I went ahead anyway. What I found amazed me: it was as if I had stepped under Niagara. In all my career as a biographer I had never come across documents so revealing.

The insights offered by Hamilton's writings were at their clearest during the years with which this book deals. As Hamilton grew older, he became a little less indiscreet, and his personality became somewhat buried under accumulations of financial and political detail. Yet what may be concluded from the papers and events of Hamilton's first twenty-six years—almost half his lifetime—remains applicable to his entire career. The great mind, so precocious at the start, never matured.

The long tradition of Hamiltonian biography has, almost without exception, been laudatory in the extreme. Facts have been exaggerated, moved around, omitted, misunderstood, or imaginatively created. The result has been to depict an almost spotless champion suited to be the national symbol of a capitalism viewed as triumphant and beneficent, a capitalism that in the beginning created the United States and that subsequently produced its strengths, its aristocracy, and its legitimate leaders. Those little satisfied with this reading of American history have struck back by depicting Hamilton as a devil

3

devoted to undermining all that was most characteristic and noble in American traditions and life. Under this controversy, the Hamilton that really lived has been buried.

My biographical technique, as I have practiced it down the years, demands that before I begin my labors I clear my mind, as far as is possible, of every conclusion and prejudice. I do my best to start anew, as if I had never before heard of my protagonist. By studying what he and his contemporaries actually did and wrote, I build the foundations for my narrative and my conclusions. Thus, as I shaped this book on Hamilton, the battle cries of his supporters and their opponents, the Jeffersonians, came only dimly to my ears. And, pursuing as best I could the facts, I reached conclusions that were as surprising to me as they may be to others.

Every man's story begins with his childhood, and here, at the very start, I found myself drawn to new conclusions. Hamilton's experiences on the Leeward Islands, where he was born and reared, have been viewed by his biographers in a distorting light engendered by their affections and their desire to have their hero's career respectable throughout. Around the unavoidable fact of Hamilton's illegitimacy there has been constructed a saga of warm homelife lived out in affluent surroundings. What I discovered turns the accepted story completely upside down. I found not affluence but relative squalor; not warmth but betrayal. Hamilton's home was a shambles. His officially designated role in the world was as an "obscene" child.

A shift in the grounding alters a projectile's flight. As my biography evolved, I was propelled into new skies. It became manifest that the young man who appeared from the West Indian islands to serve the emerging United States was by far the most psychologically troubled of the founding fathers.

In its most visible aspects, the action here recounted plots an amazing trajectory of genius. Although, while not yet in his teens, Hamilton is left almost completely on his own, his mother's death has unencumbered his immediate circumstance, if not his mind, of many fetters. Becoming the clerk of an international merchant, he is soon running the business in his employer's absence. His brilliance shines so clearly that the community of St. Croix subscribes to send him to North America for education.

Like a seed blown by happy chance onto perfect ground, Hamilton finds himself, at the age of sixteen, on a continent, previously alien to him, that is about to explode into a revolution that will create a new nation. Into this process, he throws himself passionately, writing effective propaganda pamphlets when he has not been in America for two full years. He becomes an artillery captain, sees active fighting, and, when still under twenty-one, joins the staff of the Commander in Chief. There his first celebrity blossoms. Becoming rapidly Washington's de facto chief of staff, he is for three and a half years in the pilothouse of the Revolution. As Washington's brilliant and almost unbelievably efficient substitute brain and extra pair of hands, he assists the cause in every capacity into which the Commander in Chief is drawn. And he engages in important activities on his own. Particularly after he has married into a rich and politically important family, he begins to occupy himself with those political and financial matters that are to be the major concern of his more mature years.

At Yorktown, the climactic battle of the Revolution, Hamilton carries through triumphantly a conspicuous assignment: commanding the capture of an enemy redoubt. Back in civilian life, he becomes, as victory nears, a leader of the Continental Congress.

The rise from where Hamilton started to where he stood when only twenty-six is so precipitous, so dramatic, that watchers are impelled to stand up and cheer. But one man does not stand up and cheer. That man is Hamilton himself. The cankers in his spirit have not been assuaged.

Every person is inwardly various, but Hamilton was so divided that he sometimes seemed to be two different men. One was the paragon: visionary, logical, controlled as an expert fighter is controlled. The other was the semimadman who sought from the world an ever-denied release from inner wounds. In an effort to justify one of his wilder drives, his desire to use the army at the end of the Revolution to terrorize the civilian governments, Hamilton explained to Washington: "I often feel a mortification, which it would be impolitic to express, that sets my passions at variance with my reason."[2]

Hamilton had a gift for language that made his selection of words deeply indicative of his feelings. His passions, even on a political matter, were set "at variance" with his reason, not by rage or indignation but by "mortification": a feeling of humiliation, of shame. His childhood had been instinct with humiliation and shame.

As we examine Hamilton's acts, public and private, large and small, we shall find him behaving upon many occasions in ways so extraordinary that they are hard to believe. This difficulty is undoubtedly one reason that so much is noted here that had not been noted before. It is natural for the human mind to discard as accidental and irrelevant what seems to make no sense.

Although Hamilton's aberrations seemed so often (even to him) deviations from the true course of his genius, both sprang from the same source. He carried with him from the Leeward Islands not only his inner problems. He also brought the cast of mind that directed his logical structures, creating his outer solutions.

Once the realities of Hamilton's early years have been allowed credence, we realize to how startling an extent his desperate efforts to handle the situations into which he had been by birth thrown created his adult points of view: his low opinion of his fellow human beings that could mount almost to hatred; his unsympathetic myopia to the loyalties and prejudices of his neighbors, which both freed his mind and earned him enemies; his view of himself as a loner, not expecting to be popular but obsessed with a need to exert power, to demonstrate himself superior to everyone; his conviction that the best way to lead men was not through their affections and virtues but by either persuading their intellects or satisfying their weaknesses; his industry and efficiency, which also served to drive from his mind painful things; his passion for overcoming disorder with order, for building sound institutions, and his belief that order must be imposed on his fellowmen rather than built in cooperation with them; his nationalistic yearning to create a powerful, honorable, and internationally admired state as an object of pure, abstract beauty—he was not inspired by any love for the land or its inhabitants. He was a nationalist, but he never felt that warm springing of the heart which is patriotism.

Fired by genius, this constellation of traits enabled him to recognize in the structure of the emerging United States serious weaknesses which he had the ability and drive to cure. While others cut with the grain, he cut against it. Hamilton's view was always from the outside, and it was this that made him one of the greatest of the founding fathers.

Hamilton's originality of mind, his almost demonic strength of conviction, his ability to strike clean and true as a sword blade strikes, gathered to him a group of idolizing followers. Worshipers of his genius, they ignored as best they could his flaws. They were puzzled and disturbed by unaccountable eruptions too great to overlook: for instance, those that tore into shreds the Federalist Party, which his constructive and rational self had previously created.

The Jeffersonians allowed themselves to be much more conscious of the strangeness in Hamilton. Disagreeing profoundly with what he labored to achieve, they dwelt on his excesses. Since they envisioned a deep-dyed villain nurturing to his advantage desperate schemes, it drove them almost to distraction that they could not catch him in some preconceived, insidious plot.

Neither Hamilton's admirers nor his detractors realized the truth: the accomplished, smooth, and brilliant man of the world could at any moment change hysterically, invisibly, for the time being decisively, into an imperiled, anguished child.

I

Setting a Traumatic Stage

CONCERNING Hamilton's forebears and his childhood much may be induced from his future behavior, but little learned from recorded memories. He himself wanted to forget, and those of his earlier companions who were available when he became celebrated joined the conspiracy of silence. As is usual with the poor and unimportant, what specific facts remain come from legal records. When families have been respectable and have behaved themselves, such documents prove dull and only routinely informing. Not so the records that elucidate the shaping of the career which was to do so much to shape the United States.

Hamilton's mother's maiden name was variously spelled. It may be solidified as Faucett. Because of the name's French sound, the family is supposed to have been of Huguenot extraction. The Faucetts had lived on the British West Indian island of Nevis since the mid-seventeenth century, but had never profited greatly from the vastly rewarding sugar culture. Owning only a few slaves, they obviously belonged, in an outrageously opulent society, to the small bourgeoisie—traders, artisans, overseers for others.[1]

The Hamilton story zeroes in on a John Faucett who seems to have had two wives both named Mary. The first bore him, about 1714, a daughter Ann. When the second Mary, who was to be Alexander's grandmother, appears on the scene the record instantly muddies. We have the notation in the archives of St. George's Episcopal Church in Gingerland, Nevis, for April 21, 1718, of the marriage of "John Fauseet and Mary Uppingham." This is straightforward enough, but we also find noted for two months earlier, the baptism of "John, the son of John Faucett and Mary, his wife." Does this mean that the first Mary died in childbirth and her husband married again within three months? Or was Baby John's illegitimacy covered over by a kind clerk who copied the notation into the register after the parents had gotten around to marrying?[2]

It is assumed that the new wife, who was soon producing a flood of children, was considerably younger than the widower she wed. All the children died in infancy (three in a single month of 1736), all the children except one. The survivor was Rachel, who was to be Hamilton's mother.* The record of her birth is missing, but the year can be reckoned as about 1729. Rachel was a witness to the multiple deaths of 1736.[3]

An item in the Common Records of Nevis, dated February 5, 1740, raises the curtain on the continuing sexual drama that was to cast over the yet-unborn Hamilton a shadow deep enough to darken his entire career. Rachel's mother could no longer bear to live under the same roof with Rachel's father. Having brought property to the marriage, she insisted that she had a right to enough money to set up for herself. The father's refusal filled the home of the eleven-year-old Rachel with "divers disputes and controversies."

Finally, Rachel's mother appealed to the chancellor of the Leeward Islands "to be relieved against the said John Faucett." His Excellency issued a writ, not of marital separation (no such law existed) but of supplicavit (to prevent the petitioner from being injured). Having achieved an agreement that the couple "live separately and apart for the rest of their lives," he ruled that, since the dowry that Mary had brought to the marriage would entitle her to one third of John's property on his death, she was to receive, in return for renouncing any such claim, fifty-three pounds and four shillings annually during her lifetime. The documents then went on at length to bind John or his heirs not to "vex, sue, implead, or cause or promise to be vexed or impleaded the said Mary Faucett."[4]

Mary's annual stipend reinforces the other evidence concerning the financial standing of the family. Although calculated to reflect one third of the couple's combined property, the fifty-three pounds and four

---

* A rumor still goes round the islands that Rachel was part black. The races were strictly segregated in those days and she was treated as a white woman, which makes impossible any black admixture well enough known to start an authentic historical rumor.

shillings would not enable a mother and daughter to live on a level much above poverty.

The records now go blank for six years. When the story reopens, Rachel is with her mother on the Danish island of St. Croix in a wild environment that was to be the background of much of Alexander Hamilton's rearing.

St. Croix had been known to European man since 1493, when, during his second voyage, Columbus had seen it looming from unexplored waters. In the succeeding two centuries, history had flickered over the little island, twenty-two miles long and one to six miles wide. The flags of five nations had been raised only to be torn down violently—not once but again and again—slaughter following upon slaughter. Finally, the embattled hills became quiet. Some squatters appeared and coves became favored havens for pirates, but from 1695 onwards St. Croix was marked on maps as deserted.[5]

Around it, on the dots on the sea that were the other West Indian islands, activity was feverish. The popularization in Europe of three exotics—chocolate from the Western world, tea and coffee from the Eastern—created a sudden, immense demand for sugar. And, about 1650, it was discovered that the West Indies were perfectly suited to the cultivation of sugar. Plants were brought in from Brazil and, to work the fields, thousands of blacks from the Guinea coast of Africa. Perhaps never before had an agricultural innovation engendered such an instant flow of wealth. Planters became rich men in a few years. Soon English upper-class life was fretted by nouveaux riches vulgarians from the Indies, who were as wealthy as the ancient aristocratic families. So valuable were the Indies that the British considered, at the end of the Seven Years War, annexing, instead of Canada, the French sugar island of Guadeloupe, only slightly larger than St. Croix. There are historians who blame the American Revolution on the presence in Parliament of sugar millionaires who had bought their constituencies and had no respect for traditional British liberties.[6]

In 1733, the Danish West India and Guinea Company, needing another outlet for its slave-purchasing depot on the African coast, bought St. Croix with the ambitious intention of creating from scratch a great sugar island. Surveyors sighted through the multicolored foliage to lay out the 381 plantations of from 150 to 300 Danish acres. The best land was assigned to sugar; the hilly eastern third of the island to the less rewarding crop of cotton. As an attraction to settlers whose activities would eventually enrich the company, land was offered at a low price.[7]

Thus was created the weird gold-rush environment that was so to influence Hamilton's beginnings. Since established planters stayed where they were, a flood of speculators crested in St. Croix. The stakes were high and the financial dangers were great. Before a sugar plantation would pour out wealth, a small fortune had to be invested in slaves and equipment. Those who tried to start small and snowball their assets were usually driven to desperate measures.

Calculated into the cost of a slave was the fact that he could only be expected to survive for a few years. Slave insurrections were always to be feared. Destructive droughts were not uncommon, sometimes local ones when rain inundated one plantation but skipped its neighbors. Tropical fevers made the lives even of the planters uncertain and usually short. Hurricanes snatched away all. But if, at the end of the season, a planter's windmills crushed quantities of ripe cane, the white liquid that flowed through lead-coated wooden troughs to the boiling vats might as well have been liquid gold. It was a world of the wildest ups and downs. Next year perhaps an imported coach with footmen in livery blowing arrogantly on trumpets. Or perhaps debtors' prison.

This hectic world, held within its narrow confines by the surrounding ocean, seethed under the most languorous of climates: the sun bright without being dazzling, heat or cold rarely extreme, the air moist without being damp, seemingly clear but softening the distances with haze. The participants in this gold rush were far from being grimy prospectors in rags. West Indian tradition demanded, even when the specter of bankruptcy stood gaunt beside fine doorways, the greatest affectation of nonchalance and elegance. The ladies made calls, played cards, and perhaps sewed a little. The men, socially driven to import fine clothes rather than new sails for the windmill, engaged in every kind of dissipation a slave-holding society encouraged. The Reverend Hugh Knox, who was to befriend the young Alexander Hamilton, thus described his communicants: "young fellows and married men, not only without any symptoms of serious religion and without family religion, but keepers of Negro wenches . . . rakes, night-rioters, drunkards, gamesters, Sabbath breakers, church neglectors, common swearers, unjust dealers, etc." Among Hamilton's relatives as among the others, adultery, theft, suicide, and lawsuits proliferated.[8]

Within three years of the establishment of a government on St. Croix, when the Danish fort was still being built, the Faucett family began moving to the wild island. Rachel's half sister Ann, had married a planter named James Lytton. Although Lytton had achieved no particular success on long-settled Nevis, after he emigrated to St. Croix in 1738 he became one of those pioneers for whom things broke right. His mounting prosperity drew his relations to St. Croix.

In 1745, Mary Faucett reappears in the records. She is on St. Croix, standing as godmother at the baptism of a Lytton child. Probably in the same year and on the same island, the daughter who was to be Alexander Hamilton's mother made her disastrous marriage to John Michael Lavien.[9]

When in the mid-nineteenth century, Hamilton's son John published two books on his father, he placed in both the identical statement that Rachel's "first husband was a Dane named Lavine who, attracted by her beauty and recommended to her mother by his wealth, received her hand against her inclination." This statement has been enlarged and embroidered to echo down the corridors of history. However, there is no evidence that Rachel was beautiful unless we so assume from the highly demonstrable fact that she was sexually wayward. The man involved was not Rachel's *first* husband but her *only* husband; he was not a Dane; and he was not wealthy but rather the opposite.[10]

The keepers of the financial records were imaginative spellers. The first names of Hamilton's malevolent stepfather come through consistently: John Michael or Johann Michael. The last name is written as Lavien, Lovien, Lawine, Levine, Levin, Le Vin, and so on. Hamilton was to recall his name as Lavine, but John Michael himself seems to have preferred the spelling Lavien. No documents in his writing exist in Danish. He wrote his Danish attorney in German, kept his accounts in English, and also wrote Dutch. The presumption is that he was North German. Although even the soberest historians refer to him as a Jew called Levine, he was not legally considered a Jew.[11]

Before 1738, Lavien was a merchant on Nevis who sold clothing and household goods, and already had business connections with the Lyttons. In 1744, he took a bold step to lift his position by making a down payment on a sugar plantation on St. Croix. Before the end of the year he lost his investment. Trying in a more humble way to escape the role of shopkeeper, he bought half a cotton plantation.[12]

Exactly where in this progression Rachel married him is not clear. But it is clear that he was never such a catch as a mother would force her daughter to marry. At his highest, he was a plunger who might or might not make good. It is improbable that Mary was fooled about his position since her brother-in-law, Lytton, was a shrewd man who had long done business with Lavien.

If the attraction was not money, what was it? A strong hint was given when Lavien died a pauper. The old man had recently pawned some gold buttons, and almost the only objects in his estate considered not "trash which cannot be appraised" were a brown dress coat with gold lace, a blue vest with silver lace, a belaced blue dress coat, a green dress coat with lace, a black silk dress coat and a pair of black trousers, three pairs of white trousers, and some silver shoe buckles. Lavien had clearly been such a dandy as attracts giddy young girls. Rachel was probably about sixteen—that being the marriageable age; Lavien was at least twenty-eight.[13]

Ironically, the cotton plantation to which Lavien took his wife was called Contentment. Close to the town of Christiansted, it was in a valley with no view. Here was born Rachel's only legitimate child (or at least the only one who survived infancy). There is evidence that Peter Lavien, who was to have so baleful an influence on his future half brother Alexander Hamilton, was born in 1746.[14]

Documents reveal Lavien as incompetent, his business career moving steadily downward. He was also unimaginative and vindictive toward his wife. As the daughter of a woman who had taken such strong action against an unsatisfactory husband that Rachel had been brought up fatherless, Rachel was not one to submit meekly. She found solace—and perhaps revenge—in the arms of other men. Late in 1749 or early in 1750, Lavien took legal action under a Danish law that was applicable only if he could prove that Rachel had been "twice guilty of adultery" and that he was no longer living with her.

The witnesses to her adultery probably included those Lavien was later to summon when he initiated against her a divorce suit: humble people who in that slave-glutted society owned no slaves. Lavien convinced the judges and Rachel was sentenced to jail.[15]

The center of Danish administration on St. Croix was a fort that still looks out over Christiansted Harbor. It is a hollow square of stone walls around a courtyard, the walls on the sides a single story high, with a raised rampart in front for cannon and at the back a two-story administration building. There remains from Rachel's time a subterranean dungeon, reached by descending stone steps. The one, small high window barely lights a considerable cavern, which may once have been divided into two rooms. If Rachel had been kept in this dismal place, she certainly had every reason to repent her sins. However, imprisoning rebellious or wayward blacks, even those who were caught at night away from their plantations without leave, was a principal use of the fort. It is doubtful that distinctions essential to slavery would have been violated by throwing Rachel in with blacks. She was probably housed where there are now police cells of a later date, in one of the buildings that run inside the lower walls. If she had a window to peek through, she would have viewed the medium-sized central courtyard, which was the busiest area of Christiansted. Here drunken soldiers were kept overnight. Here, in the daytime, officials and their clients bustled; here the little garrison drilled; here stray horses and cattle were impounded; here delinquent blacks were branded or whipped, "without any expense to the owner of such slave."[16]

After Rachel had been imprisoned for an undetermined time, her husband concluded that she had learned her lesson: "that everything would change to the better and that she, as a wedded wife, would change her unholy way of life and as is meet and proper live with him." He let her out of jail. She ran away.[17]

A later legal record reveals that she fled to the mansion of the town captain, Bertram Peter de Nully. This presents three possibilities: first, that the town captain, who commonly put up various people including the minister of the Dutch church, gave her refuge out of charity; second, that he or some other member of his household was or had been among her lovers; or, third, that she was joining her mother. We know that Mary Faucett was living in St. Croix, but had no residence of her own. She might have been living at the town captain's and working there in some capacity, perhaps supervising the labor of the slaves she still owned. Her husband was dead and the annual stipend the court had ordered for her was clearly not coming in. We know that she took in sewing.[18]

Rachel and her mother may well have left St. Croix together. On October 15, 1750, Mary published a notice to her creditors that she was departing. In a few weeks, she raised money by selling a slave. The departure was by no means a triumphal exit. A legal record stated that Mary had "in poverty left the island" and that—this was four years later—her whereabouts were unknown. As for Rachel, her deserted husband asserted that she had "given herself up to whoring with everyone, which things . . . are so well known that her own family and friends must hate her for it."[19]

A fleeting record shows Mary living in 1755 on the Dutch island of St. Eustatius. In 1756, she executed, on the British island of St. Christopher, a legal document which showed that she felt herself failing and implied that she had lost touch with her daughter. Although actual ownership was to pass to Rachel, she stipulated that "to provide for the future of my three dear slaves Rebecca, Flora, and Esther," they were, on her death, to be transferred to the care and service of "my friend Archibald Ham, or his heirs."

In this document, Mary Faucett referred to her daughter as "Rachel Lavien."[20] Rachel was then passing herself off as the wife of a Scot called James Hamilton, to whom she had already borne two sons, one named Alexander.

2

Parental Shadows

[1757–1766   BIRTH TO AGE 10]

JAMES HAMILTON, Alexander's father, was an exile from a wealthy, aristocratic world. Perhaps out of bitterness, perhaps out of shame, he never communicated to his illegitimate son, while they were living together in perpetual financial difficulties, how tremendous was the contrast with his own beginnings. In 1797, when Alexander was trying to claim as much family prestige as he dared, he did not go beyond stating that his father, "as I am informed," had been "a man of respectable connections in Scotland."[1]

The refugee in the Indies named the elder of his and Rachel's illegitimate children James after himself, and the younger, Alexander, after his own powerful father, who had presided over an ancient but lesser branch of the ducal family of Hamilton. His prosperity is testified to by his marriage contract of 1711 with Elizabeth Pollock. Owning estates suitable for raising sheep in the lowland Scots county of Ayreshire, the elder Alexander collected annual rents that by themselves totaled £6,000, more than a hundred times the stipend that Mary Faucett had extracted from her husband. Elizabeth Pollock brought, in addition, a dowry of almost £41,000. Her father, Sir Robert Pollock, had been created Baronet of Nova Scotia by Queen Anne in 1702. The citation referred to the antiquity of his family, going back some six hundred years, and praised Robert's "faithful and zealous service in defending the reformed religion" during the Revolution of 1688. An attitude towards the Catholic chivalry of the Highlands is revealed by the statement that Pollock had been confined, because of his allegiance to King William, "in the most barbarous and uncivilized places."[2]

The James Hamilton who wandered incompetently among the garishly and brutally prosperous West Indian islands, who guided the first steps of a boy over whom the future of a not-yet-existent nation invisibly hovered, had himself grown up surrounded by the Middle Ages. His childhood home, then known as Kary-Lew or Shenistone Castell, was described between 1602 and 1608 as "a fair strong building" that had belonged in "Anno 1191 to ye Lockarts." In 1488, then the property of the Glencairn family, it had been partly burned by the Montgomeries. James Hamilton XIV had bought it in 1685, and changed the name to one associated with his family, the Grange. It was here that James Hamilton, Alexander's father, was born in about 1718.[3]

The Grange was one of those ancient buildings that was partly habitable, partly a ruin. It had been built for defense. Thick masonry, almost hidden by ancient ivy, rose high, light entering the rooms through deep-set arrow slits. However, on one side of an inner square there was an incongruous line of lofty, delicately arched Gothic windows concerning which an Ayrshire antiquary wrote, "No other castle of the thirteenth or fourteenth century has such beautiful windows."

When the young James stepped out the door, he stood on a steep bank overlooking a picturesque glen. An ancient gate gave access to a decorative garden behind high walls. There were other buildings and extensive yards. A short ride away was the homestead of James's mother. Everything here was more up to date. The old fortified tower with its high battlement had by the beginning of the eighteenth century been torn down and replaced by "a large stately house of a new model. 'Tis well planted and hath good orchards and large commodious parks."[4]

That Alexander's father would not come into possession of his childhood world was dictated when he was born as the fourth son. He could not expect every one of his three older brothers to die without issue. However, important families had methods for providing their younger sons with berths suitable for gentlemen in the church, in the military, or in government, and by arranging for them profitable marriages.

Alexander's father could not have been, as Alexander's son stated, "bred a merchant" since engaging in trade was considered in aristocratic circles demeaning. Furthermore, he revealed no skill or aptitude for the pursuit by which he tried to make his living after he had been somehow driven to the Leeward Islands. The clear indication is that, at least by the time Alexander was a small child, James was entirely cut off from his wealthy family. If he had brought with him to the Indies any property or auspices, they had been dissipated. And so the son of an extremely rich family lived out his life with Rachel and her children in relative poverty. After Alexander had earned his own prosperity in America he feared that his father was suffering, somewhere in the Islands form "indigence."[5]

That James Hamilton had broken with his family and was exiled from his birthright seems clear. Did he depart as a gesture of independence that left him subsequently too proud to ask for help? Had he fled from a disastrous love affair, a hated marriage, conduct considered unbecoming a gentleman, an irreconcilable difference with his father and brothers, debts he could not pay, or a yawning of prison gates? If little Alexander was ever told, he never recorded what he knew.

On which island and exactly when Hamilton and Rachel got together is a matter of pure speculation. There is no compelling reason to deny that Alexander, the second of the illicit couple's two sons, was born on the date he himself gave when in the United States: January 11, 1757. This was more than six years after Rachel had left Lavien. That Hamilton was born a British subject on a British island is certain. There is excellent evidence that the island was Rachel's own birthplace, Nevis.[6]

At least in his manhood, Hamilton seems never to have doubted that James Hamilton was his father. But he was so secretive that after his death, Timothy Pickering had felt it necessary to investigate. In 1822, James Yard, who had close family connections with Nevis, confirmed that Alexander had been, as the Hamilton family stated, born on that island. It was on the basis of Yard's information that Pickering jotted down: "Although little if anything was publicly spoken, yet it seems always to have been understood among those who were acquainted with this extraordinary man that he was the illegitimate offspring of a Mr. Hamilton, in the West Indies."

Yet Pickering had his doubts. He remembered that when he had met, in the late 1790's, Hamilton's boyhood friend Edward Stevens, "at the first glance I was struck by the extraordinary similitude of his and General Hamilton's faces. I thought they must be *brothers*." When he mentioned the resemblance, Yard admitted that the similarity of appearance had been remarked upon "a thousand times." Since Yard could give no explanation, Pickering reflected, "In cases of this sort, the possibility of *kindred blood* gives rise to surmises or strong suspicions, of which no proof is attainable."[7]

Edward Stevens's father, Thomas, was among those who most befriended Alexander when the boy was, following Rachel's death, cast loose on the world. That Rachel could, without the knowledge of her husband and son, have had relations with Thomas is chronologically and geographically possible. But there is no evidence that he was Hamilton's father beyond Pickering's statements of a resemblance that does not seem to have bothered the boyhood friends themselves.[8]

Legendary history has given Alexander other fathers. Gertrude Atherton allowed herself to be deflected from her panegyrics about Rachel's sexual purity by the seductive idea that Hamilton was sired by George Washington. This conception naturally appeals to proponents of another aspect of the Hamilton legend: that Washington treated the younger man with the preference and affection of an indulgent father to a beloved son. Atherton was carried away into writing that Lavien's divorce petition "specifically states" that Rachel was in Barbados in 1756; she added that Washington was in that year also there. But the petition states no such thing, and Washington's only trip to the West Indies was in the winter of 1751, several years too early for any fathering of Hamilton.[9]

As the tops of mountains rising from the floor of the Caribbean, the Leeward Islands run to idiosyncratic geography. Nevis is a single volcanic cone that had exploded upward to tower 3,596 feet over the ocean. In a circle around the peak and its shouldering foothills, rolling lowlands extend irregularly for some two miles until they slip underwater. The island measures at its longest nine miles, at its widest five.

The Faucett family's region was Gingerland. Here the central cone leaps dramatically upward from the valley, but without any of the majestic repose exhibited by most mountains. Because the high land intercepts vapors carried by the trade winds, the slope is haunted with what an eighteenth-century writer called "clouds of congregation fantastical." The ever-moving mists descend to the very bottom of the mountain, only to rise in irregular tatters. In Hamilton's time, they revealed intensive sugar cultivation. On up they would go, when the atmosphere so drew them, to uncover forests and then reveal, usually for a moment or two, the high peak of the volcano which seemed, as the clouds streamed away from the crater, to be in eruption.

The triangular valley, which old records identify with the name

Hamilton's probable birthplace, the British Leeward Island of Nevis. *Above:* Ruins of what may have been the house where Hamilton was born. These remains, which are in the region of Nevis known as Gingerland, are traditionally associated with the Faucetts, Hamilton's mother's family. Long hidden by surrounding tropical growth, the ruins were cleared by William Gordon, who undertook the labor as a courtesy to the author and who contributed the photograph. *Below:* Nevis is the upper part of an extinct volcano. Since the peak intercepts vapors being blown along by the trade winds, the volcano appears to be in constant eruption.

Faucett, is too small to have been a full sugar plantation. It is tucked away between hills so low that a small child could climb them, coming closer to the mountain and seeing, in the opposite direction, the sea not far away and everywhere the turning of windmills.[10]

"We had," so wrote a visitor in 1745, "a kind of perpetual spring, for our orange trees, lemon shrubs, shaddocks, pepper, etc., exhibited at one and the same time fruit that were full grown, half grown, a quarter grown, and even flowers and buds, and as for our vegetables of all sorts, they were ever fresh and blooming." He adds sternly that Nevis was nonetheless not an "earthly paradise" because of heat, mosquitoes, hurricanes, and other recurrent travails.[11]

How long the infant Alexander remained in Nevis it is impossible to say. Successful merchants are rooted where their business is, but James Hamilton, so his famous son recalled, "became bankrupt as a merchant at an early day in the West Indies." He was reduced to what Alexander, when a half-grown boy, denounced as a "groveling condition": the aristocrat was serving more successful merchants as a clerk. Nor did he stay long in any one position. Whenever the Hamiltons surface in the record, it is on a different island. "My heart bleeds," the mature Hamilton was to write of his father, "at the recollection" of his "misfortunes and embarrassments."[12]

Homelife was clearly not peaceful. Hamilton later wrote, "It's a dog's life when two dissonant tempers meet."[13] Rachel may have joined up with James Hamilton when he was still in better circumstances. In any case, she did not—as later events make clear—take kindly to the privations and scrounging that grew from the inability of the highborn gentleman to keep from foundering in the money-mad society of the Indies. However, little Alexander concluded that his was a way of life superior to the aggressive, vulgar society in which the aristocrat was failing. This is demonstrated by the fact that the one aspect of those dreadful years that Hamilton was happy to remember was his father.

After Alexander became engaged to Elizabeth Schuyler, whose aristocratic connections in New York ranked high among the charms that attracted him, he wrote her that he had found a new opportunity to write "our father" in the Indies. He was urging James Hamilton to come to America and live with them.[14]

Although James Hamilton never did come to the United States, he was to play an important (and heretofore unrecognized) part in its history. There can be little doubt that Alexander imbibed from his father an aristocratic ideal held the more passionately because in the little household where the statesman spent his most formative years that ideal was so demeaned and imperiled. In 1778 Alexander wrote, "There are men in all countries the business of whose lives it is to raise themselves over indigence by every little art in their power." Not a sin like the misbehavior of the opulent, this was "nothing more than might be expected, and can only excite contempt."[15] James Hamilton undoubtedly found contemptible the little arts to which he was reduced. Alexander Hamilton continued all his life to express contempt for money-grubbing.

Jefferson, that inheritor of wealth and privilege, could find it amusing that such a gentleman as he knew himself to be would condescend to the extent of establishing, for his slave children to labor in, a nail factory. Hamilton could not be thus amused. Although concerned with making the fortunes of others, he left himself often in debt, and died so. He used his marriage into the Schuyler family to raise his station in life to where he felt he ought to be, but with a pride that may have been reminiscent of his own father's, he would only rarely accept more than oblique financial help from his rich father-in-law.

British aristocrats operating on home ground profited almost automatically from the government positions their rank brought them, but the man who had viewed in childhood the aristocratic life as a romantic dream was in his own behavior more nice. Hamilton's statement of 1778 continued: "When a man appointed to be the guardian of the state and the depository of the happiness and morals of the people, forgetful of the solemn relation in which he stands, descends to the dishonest artifices of a mercantile projector, and sacrifices his conscience and his trust to pecuniary motives, there is no strain of abhorrence of which the human mind is capable, nor punishment the vengeance of the people can inflict, which may not be applied to him with justice." This attitude on the part of a financier seemed impossible to the minds of men like Jefferson. They could not believe that Hamilton did not make money out of the speculations which, when he was Secretary of the Treasury, he opened to others.

Why did Hamilton open the way to such speculations? If, as a child, he did not (as there is good reason to adduce) blame the family poverty on his father, he needed an outside explanation, and such outside explanations run to denouncing "the system." The ancient castle in Ayreshire, which figured in his father's memory, was to the son unknown or insubstantial. He wished to bring order to the world as he saw it. The contrast between the West Indian reality in which his father suffered and his aristocratic dream encouraged Hamilton to conclude at the very start that most men were beasts who could be most easily ruled by their appetites. Like a man who trains seals by tossing them fish, Hamilton was glad to use the cupidity of others to create order in the financial affairs of the commonwealth. But he felt himself to be above such paltry rewards.

On West Indian islands where they were not otherwise known, James and Rachel put themselves forward as a conventional couple. During October, 1758, when Alexander was less than two, it was recorded in a church record on the Dutch island of St. Eustatius that "James Hamilton and Rachel Hamilton, his wife," stood at a baptism as godfather and godmother.[16] Very different was the tone of the divorce proceedings initiated some months later in the matrimonial court of St. Croix by Rachel's legitimate husband, Lavien.

The official summons, addressed to "you, Rachel Lavien," describes her husband's efforts to reform her by putting her in jail and his hopes that on her release she would become a good wife. "Instead now for nine years [she] has been absent from him and gone to another place, where she is said to have begotten several illegitimate children . . . which is acknowledged or generally known." The plaintiff, "who has in this manner been insulted," had taken care of Rachel's legitimate child "from what little he was able to earn, whereas she has shown herself to be shameless, rude and ungodly . . . and instead given herself up to whoring with everyone." It would, the plaintiff continued, be "very hard" if, should he die before her, she were able to claim a widow's share and "therefore not only acquire what she ought not to have, but also take this away from his child and give it to her whorechildren what to such a legitimate child alone is due."

The summons then called on Rachel to appear within six weeks, and in describing the projected proceedings prejudged her case. Her evidence plus that of witnesses were to be examined "so that you, Rachel Lavien, shall have no rights whatsoever to the plaintiff's person or means." He "will be free from you in every way and, if he so desires, marry again; whereas you are to be further punished (if seized in this country) according to law and ordinances, in regard to which the plaintiff promises to give the court further demonstrations." The summons was to be posted in the last places where Rachel was known to have resided in St. Croix: the jail and the plantation of the town captain.[17]

23

Whether or not she received the summons on whatever island she then inhabited, Rachel did not come back and make herself liable to be "seized and further punished." The verdict noted her failure to appear and continued, "Not only has the plaintiff legally proved that Rachel Lawin has been absent from him and lived on an English island for seven or eight years, but also that she during that time has begotten two illegitimate children." The court then confirmed the divorce as specified in the summons, remitted the costs "by the plaintiff's plea" (he undoubtedly stated that he could not pay), and further threatened Rachel: "For the rest, his Majesty is reserved the right to Rachel Lewine."[18]

In the midst of the sentimental evasions served up by John Hamilton concerning his father's forebears and childhood, there appears suddenly a sentence that has the ring of truth: "Rarely as he dwelt upon his personal history, he mentioned having been taught to repeat the decalogue in Hebrew at the school of a Jewess, when so small that he was placed standing by her side on a table."[19] Alexander preserved a great respect for the Jews but Hebrew did not become one of his accomplishments.*

The year 1765 was one of the most important in Hamilton's life. Enough documentation remains to permit conjuring up what happened in some detail.

The Hamilton family are on the British island of St. Christopher, where the father is serving as chief clerk for the merchant Charles Ingram. He brings home the news that he is ordered to Christiansted on St. Croix to collect a debt. Going along would carry Rachel to an island concerning which she has memories—many not pleasant—and would enable her to reestablish close connections with her rich relatives, the Lyttons. First, of course, she would have to make sure that she was no longer liable under the threat contained in the divorce decree, that she be "seized" and "further punished" for her sexual misdeeds. When this is satisfactorily determined, Rachel, her paramour, and her two sons, set out for Christiansted.

---

* Among his papers is a fugitive scrap, evidently once part of an essay, which reads, ". . . progress of the Jews and their [illegible] from the earliest history to the present time has been and is entirely out of the ordinary course of human affairs. Is it not then a fair conclusion that the cause also is an extraordinary one —in other words, that it is the effect of some great providential plan? The man who will draw this conclusion will look for the solution in the Bible. He who will not draw it ought to give in another fair solution."[20]

Since James Hamilton must go to law courts that move slowly, the stay on St. Croix becomes a long one. The family arrives in May, 1765; Hamilton does not get his desired legal ruling until January 8, 1766. This allows plenty of time to look around and make decisions.[21]

There is no possibility, here in the community where Rachel has been married, jailed, and divorced, for any polite fictions about "James Hamilton and his wife Rachel." As he walks down the streets, Alex— now about eight years old—is recognized, by those who recognize him at all, as what the Danish courts called an "obscene" child. In his divorce petition, Lavien had stated that Rachel's "whoring with every-one" was "so well known that her own family and friends must hate her for it." But this and the other violent assaults on Rachel's reputation and status had not prevented the Lyttons from remaining on close terms with Lavien.[22]

In the agricultural gold rush that was St. Croix, all of the Lytton children had turned out badly. The daughters' husbands went bankrupt. Matrimonial litigation abounded. James Lytton, Jr., absconded in his father's schooner with slaves belonging to the infant child of his first wife, occasioning great scandal and a lawsuit in which James Lytton, Sr., was involved. Peter Lytton was accused in rumor, if not in law, of bigamy. The elder Lyttons had, by the time the Hamiltons arrived, sold their plantation and slaves, intending to "end their days" on Nevis—but they were still rich.[23]

On August 1, 1765, Rachel receives from her brother-in-law six walnut chairs. Probably with family assistance, she has rented a house. The poll tax reveals that she lives there, with her two children but no adult male, under her maiden name of Faucett (spelled by the tax collector with fine abandon as Fatzieth). Although James Hamilton is to remain on St. Croix, attending to his legal business for more than five months, he is no longer part of the family.[24]

Biographers have almost universally assumed that the noble Rachel was basely deserted, but the evidence goes strongly in the opposite direction. In his only account of what took place, Alexander wrote: "My father's affairs at a very early date went to wreck, so as to have rendered his situation during the greatest part of his life far from eligible. This state of things occasioned a separation between him and me, when I was very young, and threw me upon the bounty of my mother's relatives, some of whom were then wealthy."[25]

Apart from the interesting fact that Alexander describes the separation as being altogether between him and his father (no mention of his "deserted" mother), here is a clear statement that the break was due to

James Hamilton's lack of prosperity. It seems that when Rachel, no longer banned from St. Croix, succeeded in getting under the wing of her rich relatives she saw no further reason to tolerate the paramour who had failed to make her life financially "eligible."

The fear of a comparable fate haunted Alexander. When in 1790 he was engaged to Elizabeth Schuyler he sent her what he called "a set of sober questions of the greatest importance." The question that most concerned him was whether she would be willing to "share every kind of fortune" with him. "Be assured, my angel, it is not a diffidence of my Betsey's heart, but of a *female* heart, that dictated the questions. I am ready to believe everything in favor of yours, but am restrained by the experience I have had of human nature, and of the softer part of it."[26]

We know that Alexander kept in touch with his father. His mother never used the name Hamilton again. After living for two years under her maiden name, she adopted the name of her divorced husband, who was elsewhere on the island, in poor circumstances, and perhaps with a new wife.* The two Hamilton children must have felt in their mother's willful repudiation of their name a repudiation of themselves. Every time Rachel referred to Alexander as a Hamilton she was underlining his illegitimacy.

Rachel was now, as a church record reveals, considered to be in her late twenties, some seven years younger than she actually was.[27] This implies that she had not withdrawn her hat from the sexual ring. It is, indeed, hard to imagine that a woman with Rachel's history would completely alter her proclivities merely because there was not a resident man in her house. Strange males surely invaded Alexander's childhood.

As a member of the New York Senate in 1787 Hamilton demonstrated a lack of sympathy for marital offenders like his mother, even though, in so doing, he supported the type of legislation that had made him illegitimate. He voted against a liberalization of the divorce law by which a person found guilty of "an instance of frailty" would be allowed to marry again.[28]

---

* At the time he had divorced Rachel for adultery Lavien had, as the poll tax shows, a white woman living in his house. Six years later, a "Mrs. Lavien" billed an estate for washing. The new marriage resulted in a son and daughter who died young. Lavien had long since given up trying to be an independent planter. After living on other men's plantations, where he seems to have hired himself out as a captain of a work gang of his own slaves, he became superintendent of the newly erected Frederiksted Hospital. He died there in 1771, leaving behind little except his cherished horde of elaborate clothes.[29]

In no known work that Hamilton ever wrote did he express affection for his mother. Naturally, his son John made, in his defensive biography, an effort to cover up. Rachel, we are told, obtained a divorce from Lavien and became legally married to James Hamilton. Alexander "recollected her with inexpressible fondness and often spoke of her as a woman of superior intellect, highly cultivated, of generous sentiments, and of unusual elegance of person and manner."[30]

Had this statement been factual, had Hamilton possessed an adoring and admirable mother, his character and career would certainly have been very different. A mother's betrayal is the worst blow a child can receive. "You know," Hamilton wrote his friend John Laurens in 1788, "the opinion I entertain of mankind, and how it is my desire to preserve myself free from particular attachments, and to keep my happiness independent on the caprice of others."[31]

Hamilton's low opinion of mankind, his aloofness, his inability to feel with his fellowmen, was to be the great statesman's Achilles' heel.

3

The End of Rachel

CHRISTIANSTED, where Hamilton was to spend more time than in any other place except New York City, filled the end of a descending valley. It was flanked by gently sloping hills on which black men labored amid the light green of growing sugar cane. Finally the valley slipped under water to form St. Croix's most protected harbor. To the west, the hills extended for almost four miles, creating a picturesque headland. In the middle of the harbor there rose a tiny island. Beyond the island was an extensive, submerged coral reef. The water over the coral was lavender. As wind agitated the bay, the delicate color seemed to shred and shift below the bright blue of sky, within the deeper blue of ocean.

The fort, of which Rachel had such unpleasant memories, stood at the end of a peninsula that ran a little way into the harbor. Behind it was a large square flanked by the customs house, a church, and a long, low row of mercantile establishments. Then began the main street of masonry buildings with variously colored façades. All the second stories jutted out over arcades, which made tunnels of shade from the tropical sun and were continuous except for the breaks created by side streets. There were in all twenty streets and six hundred houses.

Christiansted teemed. Sailors were ashore from the many ships usually anchored in the harbor; planters rode by in their fine carriages to disgorge elegantly clothed patrons into the shops. Blacks were everywhere since more than two and a half thousand lived in the town. But despite all this activity, Christiansted was from a social point of view a small town. Only some 850 whites lived there. Presumably many knew about the Hamilton boys.[1]

Writers have contended that in the licentious society of the Leeward Islands the Hamilton–Rachel liaison was so completely regarded as a matter of course that Alexander had no reason to be sensitive about his illegitimacy. This is contradicted by every piece of legal evidence that survives. The court records of St. Croix, indeed, reveal what seems today an almost unbelievably brutal attitude towards Rachel and her "obscene" children. Considering the standard cruelty of small boys to each other, it follows that little Alexander was on the streets an object of public mockery. That this was indeed so is copiously testified to by Hamilton's behavior after he grew up.

Slaves were so common that a Cruxian could possess a goodly number of human bodies and yet not be wealthy. In 1767, Rachel owned three female blacks, perhaps the Rebecca, Flora and Esther who had been willed to her by her mother in 1756. If so, although listed as "capable," they were not young. Rachel also had four slaves under twelve years old. At the time of her death it was stated (perhaps accurately, perhaps to save the child from being seized with the rest of the estate by Hamilton's half brother) that Rachel had given little Ajax to little Alexander.[2]

There is no reason to suppose that Alex, as he was then called, was sent to school. He was needed at home, where he was placed in a situation that offered a temporary escape from his personal anxieties. Rachel had been set up, undoubtedly by the Lyttons, in a little store that was (except for one year when Rachel lived elsewhere) part of the family residence. Customers appeared with whom the "whore child" could have an unequivocal social relationship: they were there to buy, and he to sell. Then there were the two warehouses in the yard where an eager small boy could keep track of stock—salt pork, salted fish, butter, flour, rice, kitchen utensils, and so on—bought from importers to be sold at retail. And there were the ledgers in which the boy could make entries that need not be confused, were not wounding, but which grouped themselves neatly into matching balances.[3]

There is no reason to suppose that Rachel, who had shared James Hamilton's bankruptcy, had any gift for business. Her older son James was to be apprenticed to a carpenter. Thus, although Alex was not yet in his teens, the success of Rachel's store was probably the result of his

29

genius.* The number of female slaves—women could be purchased more cheaply than men and were suitable to storekeeping and could be hired out—rose to five. Accounts were settled with a speed quite unusual in St. Croix, where a year's leeway was commonly allowed.[4]

So matters proceeded for some years until a tropical fever struck.

In February, 1768, Rachel was taken ill. She was nursed for five days by one Ann McDonnell, and then Dr. Heering was called in. He drew blood from her arm and gave her a fever medicine. The next day the doctor continued to try and fight the fever according to the conventions of the time: by debilitating the body, which was considered overexcited. He gave Rachel an emetic along with another dose of fever medicine. Alexander was now also ill. The physician decided he needed to be built up rather than debilitated, as is revealed in a charge submitted by Thomas Dipnall, Rachel's landlord: "a chicken for Elicks."

Rachel became so agitated that she was given a sedative and cooling alcohol compresses for her head. The doctor decided that that the time had come for Alexander to be depleted: he was given a bloodletting and a purgative. "Elicks" was still very ill when on the 19th, at nine o'clock at night, Rachel died.[5]

Within an hour there was a knock at the door and in marched five members of the probate court. As Alex tossed feverishly, perhaps on the same bed with the corpse (there was only one bed in the house), the officials, anxious that nothing should be removed from Rachel's estate and their jurisdiction, gathered her portable effects, her trunk, and so on, into a room which they sealed with the King's seal. They also sealed up an attic storage room and two storage rooms in the yard. "After which," so the official report reads, "there was nothing more to seal up." They excluded objects that would be needed as the body was being prepared for burial, among them six chairs, two tables and two washbowls. When the functionaries had filed out, the woman who had nursed Rachel began "laying out the corpse, etc.," an elaborate process for which she sent a large bill (which was not altogether honored) to the estate.[6]

A strange event then took place. Someone broke the King's seal and entered the room where Rachel's effects had been locked up. When the officials discovered what had happened, they were outraged. Questioning—Alexander was undoubtedly quizzed with the others—elicited no

* There is inconclusive evidence that the little boy was accepted as witness to a legal document in 1766.[7]

clue. The court could do no more than reserve to itself "the right of legal prosecution" against the guilty party should he eventually be identified.[8]

Before the illegal act had been discovered, Alex, still shaky from his illness and peering through the black mourning veil that had been hung over his face, walked behind a hearse to the family burying ground on what had formerly been the Lyttons' plantation. Through the dark cloth he saw, perhaps for the first time, the mansion house that had been the center and symbol of the prosperity to which his mother had been related. The elegantly carved doors and windows, the innumerable indications of rich living were far above his head. They looked down from the blank walls some ten feet high that surrounded the plantation storehouse and made the mansion defensible against a slave revolt. The graveyard was beyond the house, down a little hill.[9]

Although Rachel's grave was not marked—the present impressive monument was placed there more or less at random in the twentieth century—James Lytton had not wished to disgrace the family by having his sister-in-law buried in a poor manner. Besides, the expense could be charged to her estate. A thirteenth of the entire value of that estate was spent on the black cloth that covered the coffin. Rachel, the wayward wanderer beyond conventional limits, went into the earth at last surrounded by respectability. Friends of the Lyttons' served as pallbearers, and the English minister, the Reverend Cecil Wray Goodchild, intoned the service.

The probate court recognized the existence of three possible heirs. There was "Peter Lewine, born of the deceased person's marriage with John Michael Lewine, who is said to have divorced her later for valid reasons (according to information obtained by the court) by highest authority; and also two sons, namely, James and Alexander Hamilton, one fifteen and the other one thirteen years old, who are the same obscene children born after the deceased person's divorce." Peter, it was noted, was in South Carolina. He was not represented, although James Lytton was there for the Hamilton boys.[10]

The discovery of this document in 1930 set historians by the ears because the age given for Hamilton—thirteen—seemed to demonstrate that he had been two years older than he had encouraged people to believe. It was contended that the statistic, being part of a legal paper, was obviously correct, and the conclusion was drawn that Hamilton had dishonestly bamboozled his American associates into thinking him more of an infant prodigy than he actually was.[11] But in fact no one

present at the legal proceedings, except the boys themselves, had any
way of knowing for certain when Alexander and his brother were born.
It seems fair to assume that Alexander, wishing to escape from dependence on reluctant relatives, realized that he could more easily find
employment if he were considered thirteen rather than eleven. His
brother, facing an apprenticeship until he was twenty-one, was undoubtedly also glad to up his age.

The inventory of Rachel's estate revealed modest prosperity. She
owned five adult blacks and four black children. Effects still in place
included six silver spoons, seven silver teaspoons, one pair of sugar
tongs, fourteen porcelain plates, eleven cups and saucers, three stone
platters, two metal candle holders, and a mirror. There was only one
porcelain basin. Rachel's clothes worth listing were four dresses, one
red and white shirt, and one black sun hat. There was a chest of
drawers and an ordinary chest. That there was only one bed implies
that Alex and his brother slept on the floor. Also recorded was the
stock of the store: pork, flour, and so forth. Rachel had owned a goat.
There were thirty-four books which were probably Alexander's, since
at the sale of Rachel's effects they were bought, presumably for the
boy, by his guardian.[12]

The court gave the usual notice that bills for the estate would be
received for a year and a day. Half this time had passed when the
blow fell. John Michael Lavien appeared to make the assertion, which
was not contested, that the Hamilton boys, having been born in
"whoredom," could not inherit. Rachel's whole estate, including everything that the young Alexander had worked so hard to achieve, belonged to her one legitimate son, who had surely not been in touch
with her for eighteen years.[13]

The future financial statesman was left destitute. His father was far
away and indigent. His mother's rich relations were neither generously
disposed nor stable. James Lytton's oldest son, Peter, had been appointed the boys' guardian. After a little more than a year, Peter was
found dead in his room, covered with blood. He had, so the legal
record ran, "stabbed or shot himself to death." The nature of the strain
under which he had shattered was revealed by his will. He tried to
establish as his heirs Ledja, a black slave, and a mulatto child named
Don Alvirez Velesco. He made no provision for his wards, James and
Alexander Hamilton.[14]

Since Peter had died a suicide, his estate was claimed for the King.
James Lytton protested bitterly that as the deceased's father he should

be the heir, and then he himself died. His will also contained no mention of the Hamiltons.[15]

With nothing behind him that he wished to preserve except the bittersweet memory of his father, with no legacy of property or name or influence, Alexander was thrown into what he described a few years later as "this selfish, rapacious world." If he had not been uneasy for the remainder of his life, that would have been a miracle. He had much—even if it was not of his own volition or doing—to live down. He did not face what modern terminology calls an "identity crisis." His need was to smother an identity that was too clear, along with the mean destiny it presaged, under a new identity that would have to be altogether of his own manufacturing. Alexander Hamilton was eleven when, completely by himself, he launched out on this stupendous adventure.

4

Explosion Outward

[1768–1772   AGES 11–15]

S URELY Alexander had wept, behind the black veil that darkened the world, as his mother was lowered into the ground. But
when the veil was removed, and the sun shone clear, he must
have felt relieved—even if he did not exactly admit it to himself—that
the nightmare of his childhood was over.

Rachel had bought much of what she sold at retail from the import-
export house just established on St. Croix by two young men from
New York City: David Beekman (also spelled Beckman) and Nicholas
Cruger.[1] The bright little boy who handled Rachel's affairs was a
prodigy to catch the eye, and after Rachel's death, Cruger, who was
operating on his own, employed him as a clerk.

There is evidence that Alexander stayed in the house of Thomas
Stevens, whose son, Edward, was later said to look so like Hamilton
that they could have been brothers. Perhaps for the first time in Alexander's life, he was part of a household where order reigned and
there was no worry about paying bills. Alexander and Edward
Stevens, who was almost two years the senior, got on famously.
Stevens was to write of "those vows of eternal friendship, which we
have so often mutually exchanged."[2]

Roughly a year after Rachel's death, Edward sailed off to New York
to complete his education. Hamilton's first known composition is a
letter to Stevens, dated November 11, 1769. Hamilton was then going
on thirteen.

Stevens seems to have written Hamilton that he hoped soon to be

34

again at St. Croix. Hamilton replied: "I wish for an accomplishment of your hopes, provided they are concomitant with your welfare, otherwise not; though doubt whether I shall be present or not, for to confess my weakness, Ned, my ambition is [so] prevalent that I contemn the groveling and condition of a clerk or the like, to which my fortune, etc. condemns me, and would willingly risk my life, though not my character, to exalt my station. I'm confident, Ned, that my youth excludes me from any hopes of immediate preferment, nor do I desire it, but I mean to prepare the way for futurity. I'm no philosopher, you see, and may be justly said to build castles in the air. My folly makes me ashamed, and beg you'll conceal it, yet Neddy we have seen such schemes successful when the projector is constant. I shall conclude saying I wish there was a war. . . .

P.S. . . . Am pleased to see you give such close application to study."[3]

There is an extensive character sketch in those few hundred words.

Hamilton felt that he had been "condemned" to his current position by "my fortune, etc." The word "condemn" reveals resentment, and he was clearly using "fortune, etc." to indicate matters—the nature of his birth and childhood—outside his control. His statement that being a merchant's clerk was a "groveling" condition gave, of course, an involuntary comment on the experiences of his father. He had learned from the exiled aristocrat that engaging in trade was unworthy of a gentleman. But this was not all. Some years later, when sons of patricians were clamoring to become General Washington's aides, Hamilton felt that his de facto position as chief of staff was, most disturbingly, "a kind of personal dependence." He was oversensitive about engaging in any activity that could conceivably be considered menial.

Psychologically fascinating is Hamilton's feeling that it was "folly" for one in such a fortune-blasted station as his to dream of great achievements. If people knew of his "castles in the air," they would laugh at him. He begged his friend "to conceal it." The phrase that he would risk his life but not his reputation sounds like empty rhetoric, but his career, including its tragic end, was to reveal its sincerity.

He urged on his friend "close application to study." No man ever applied this advice to himself more passionately than did Hamilton. How a half-grown youth, with no family to bring him rank, could earn glory if "there was a war" is hard to visualize, yet he was again pointing in future directions. He always yearned to be celebrated as a soldier.

Hamilton dreamed of getting away from St. Croix; hoped indeed to be off before Stevens returned. Although he does not state why he saw his destiny elsewhere, there was a cluster of important reasons. By leaving, he would cast off all his past that he could disentangle from his own nerves. The lack of educational opportunities in the Indies had sent Stevens and many others to North America for an education. And, although there was money to be made in the lush, sugar-fueled environment of the Indies, there were surely wider (and less distasteful?) opportunities in a larger world.

Most interestingly, Alex expected to advance by receiving "preferment." He was expressing an aristocratic conception, all the more clearly because of his resentment of what he considered "groveling." Gifts, if exalted enough, were not gifts but honors. Hamilton was not to spurn as charity the subscription that was eventually taken up on St. Croix to send him to New York.

In middle age, Hamilton remembered that he had "always had a strong propensity to literary pursuits." The future financier made his first public bow in the guise of a poet.[4] During April, 1771, exaggerating his age to seventeen, he sent to St. Croix's English-language newspaper, the *Royal Danish-American Gazette*, two linked effusions. These verses are the first of many revelations that the misfortunes brought on him by Rachel's propensities had not turned her son against sexuality—rather the opposite.

Within the eighteenth-century convention of innocent shepherds and shepherdesses, Hamilton celebrated matrimony not for its virtuousness but as a source of greater physical pleasure:

> *And hymen join'd our hands.*
> *Ye swains behold my bliss complete;*
> *No longer then your own delay;*
> *Believe me love is doubly sweet*
> *In wedlocks holy hands.—*
>
> *Content we tend our flocks by day,*
> *Each rural pleasures amply taste;*
> *And at the suns retiring ray*
> *Prepare for new delight;*
> *When from the field we haste away,*
> *And send our blithesome care to rest,*
> *We fondly sport and fondly play,*
> *And love away the night.*

In the second poem, Hamilton is lightheartedly amused by a wanton:

> *Coelia's an artful little slut;*
> *Be fond, she'll kiss, et cetera—but*
> *She must have all her will;*
> *For do but rub her 'gainst the grain*
> *Behold a storm, blow winds and rain,*
> *Go bid the waves be still.*
>
> *So stroking puss's velvet paws*
> *How well the jade conceals her claws*
> *And purrs; but if at last*
> *You hap to squeeze her somewhat hard,*
> *She spits—her back up—prenez garde;*
> *Good faith she has you fast.*[5]

Fortune, having frowned on Hamilton's beginnings, had turned a beneficent face in arranging for the countinghouse where he secured his first job. His employer, Nicholas Cruger, was descended from important merchants in New York—Cruger's father and uncle had been mayors—who had intermarried with the Dutch aristocracy. Nicholas had come to St. Croix as a semi-independent operator in a family mercantile network. Only twenty-five when Alex entered his employ, he was young enough to be accessible to a brilliant youth. And his closest business connections on the island, David Beekman and Cornelius Kortright, belonged to merchant families as important as the Crugers' in the politics and trade of New York City.[6]

Ships, letters, and men shuttled between St. Croix and New York. Fortune had placed Hamilton in an outpost of the world where he was to play so great a role. On his little island he stood out in isolation. Probably in New York City itself no brilliant but impoverished boy was so conspicuously placed within the view of influential New Yorkers as was Hamilton at a distance of fifteen hundred miles.

Hamilton's resentment of his "groveling" situation was an aspect of his long-range ambition rather than an impediment from day to day. His son tells us that despite his "aversion" to mercantile pursuits, he often referred to his work with Cruger "as the most useful part of his education." It had imparted "method and facility."[7]

"Ham," as he was now called, was by no means a cog in a big

machine. The usual trading operation was then conducted not by a company but by an individual. When the husband was away, his wife handled his affairs (girls' finishing schools taught accounting). Cruger being unmarried, Hamilton quickly became his employer's backstop, involved in every aspect of the business. And he was not serving, as he had in his mother's store, a narrow enterprise.

Although each family member was more or less on his own, the Cruger operations were international and on a large scale. In New York, they had their own wharf that extended Pearl Street into the East River. Nicholas's brother, who operated the English end, became important enough there to be a close associate of Edmund Burke's in Parliament. Other brothers were stationed on British Jamaica and Dutch Curaçao. Since the reigning "cold war" made it hard to conduct trade with French possessions from British territory, many of the Cruger operations with France passed through Nicholas's counting-house. He was also concerned with purchases on the Spanish Main (the mainland of South America) and from the slave pens in Africa.[8]

The countinghouse in which Ham worked served what was in effect an ocean-girt factory town. He was to remember that what arable land there was on the tiny West Indian islands was so valuable for sugar and to a lesser extent cotton that almost none was used for any other purpose. "There is seldom or ever in any of the islands sufficient stock of provisions to last six months, which may give an idea of how great the consumption is." This consumption was due to the island's being made "very populous" by the industrial demands of the cash crops.[9] In Hamilton's time, St. Croix swarmed with twenty-four thousand people.

The work force was a ruthless capitalist's dream. More than ninety percent of the population were slaves. Because mortality among these involuntary workers was high, they were mostly recent arrivals from Africa. They had been sold by black chiefs to white traders. The brand of the importing company on the slaves' shoulders mingled with tribal tattoos and slashes. Intelligent purchasers studied the markings in an effort to establish on their plantations a mixture of tribes and languages that would discourage concerted action. There were usually few representatives of the more warlike tribes since these were more likely to capture slaves for sale than to be themselves sold. Yet the basic statistic of more than ten blacks to one white indicated continual danger, and there had been enough slave rebellions on other islands— cane fields and mansions burned, whites slaughtered—to encourage extreme precautions. By law, every white man had to be armed with a gun, sixteen cartridges with balls, and a sword or cutlass. When alarm guns were fired from the fort or certain drumbeats were sounded, all were to appear in the field, each carrying at night a lantern that was to be always ready. To keep terror perpetually alive among the blacks, it was legislated that if a slave struck a white man, he would lose the hand he struck with. If he drew blood, he could be executed.[10]

Among the commodities that Hamilton, as Cruger's clerk, helped import and sell were slaves. In January, 1771, some "300 prime slaves" were crowded for vendue in "Cruger's Yard" outside Hamilton's office door. The purchasers were not allowed in until the merchandise had been well rubbed with oil "in order to make them look sleek and handsome. As they can with a small comb curl one another's hair in inimitable knots, like ropes, etc., it gives a much further addition to their beauty."[11]

A year later, Hamilton saw an even more pitiable sight. Cruger was selling the cargo of a Dutch Indiaman named *Venus,* which had had a poor passage from the African Gold Coast. Cruger complained that the 250 slaves were "very indifferent indeed, sickly and thin." They brought on an average about £30, which was less than the value of a healthy mule.[12] The clerk executed with his usual efficiency his tasks concerning this aspect of Cruger's business.

Hamilton's political and emotional heirs go to great lengths to demonstrate that he was a stalwart opponent of slavery. However, his later life reveals that his heart was not seriously wrung by the plight of the human merchandise in which he dealt. During the Revolution, it is true, he had written (under the influence of his friend John Laurens, who was passionate on the subject) that the blacks' "natural faculties are probably as good as ours." Yet when a citizen of New York after the Revolution had been won, he never went beyond what was expected of a member of his circle in that vaguely abolitionist city. As secretary of the Society for the Promotion of the Manumission of Slaves, he signed a petition urging manumission, but he himself owned, bought, and sold house slaves for himself and his friends. Writing in 1789 that the slaves in the South were "bound by the laws of degraded humanity to hate their masters," he scratched out "degraded" and substituted "injured," which he underlined. When a national leader, he did not hesitate to annoy the South in many ways, yet he deplored as divisive the injection of slavery into the debates of Congress. He was willing to let the southerners profit from their slaves in the population count that determined representation in the House. His opposition was, in sum, extremely mild for a man of his combative temperament. Hamilton actively crusaded for many things in his life; abolition was not one of them.[13]

On the islands, Hamilton was less concerned with the sufferings of the blacks, which did not impinge on him except when the merchandise proved to be sickly or had died, than he was with the effect of slavery on the society in which his desperate childhood had been passed. A youthful propaganda pamphlet written shortly after he reached America made the usual contention that the British were trying to reduce Americans to a state of slavery. Slavery, he argued, "relaxes the sinews of industry, clips the wings of commerce, and introduces misery and indigence in every shape."[14]

Supplying the needs of the St. Croix population was the bread and butter of the Cruger operation; the gambler's excitement was serving the sugar factories. Unlike nonagricultural manufacturing, in which seasonal variations can be accurately foreseen and gradually provided for, the timetable of sugar culture depended on the weather and reached a peak that suddenly demanded extensive resources unnecessary during the rest of the production year. When the cane was perfectly ripe, it had to be cut at once by squads of blacks wielding knives in a jungle of lush green plants that towered above their heads. Then the long leaves were cut from the tubes which contained a sweet liquid that would ferment if not instantly processed. Most plantations had their own windmills—there were sixty-three on St. Croix in 1766—each a handsomely crafted tower of stone capped by a wooden dome which had, with every change of wind, to be revolved into a new position by straining blacks. If there was no wind, catastrophe was averted by activating auxiliary mills, which were turned by horses or mules that the planters kept in reserve.[15]

After the cut cane had been hurried to the mills, rollers crushed out juice that was conducted by hollowed logs to boiling houses. In huge iron vats, perpetually skimmed by sweating slaves, the precious liquid was reduced to sugar or to a thick liquid, which was, in expensive equipment also belonging to the planters, fermented and distilled into rum. Barrels were hammered together from imported staves and bottoms. Rum barrels by the thousands were rolled behind mules or horses to Christiansted, where they piled up in places like Cruger's Yard until they could be transferred to the ships that filled the harbor with sails.

Prices for all the needs of the sugar industry rose as harvest approached, and then, the harvest over, collapsed. Hitting the market on the head was made doubly difficult by the fact that, while the perfect moment varied from year to year and island to island, shipments had had to be dispatched months in advance. The merchandise came in vessels that sailed at the mercy of wind and calm over vast expanses of ocean: New York was 1,500 miles away; the African slave coast, about 3,000; the Spanish Main, 500.

When the ships finally came among the Leeward Islands, space reversed itself; the vast became miniature. Wealthy communities, legally parts of nations that were in Europe widely separated, were in the Indies within easy sailing distance of each other. It was simplicity itself to shuttle back and forth between different economies and customs systems. This fostered aboveboard manipulation of currencies and prices. It also made the West Indies the world's greatest paradise for smugglers.

No one on the islands was deeply moved by customs regulations. When temporarily running Cruger's business, Hamilton reported that there was a shortage of wine on St. Croix. Danish officialdom was thirsty. If wine could be quickly imported, officialdom would look the other way, but once the first arrivals had satisfied exalted thirsts, importing wine would become "impracticable."[16]

The precocious youth already gave off a charismatic glow. He was noticeably Scottish in appearance: his skin fair and ruddy, but given to freckling; his hair sandy; his eyes of a blue that his admirers later described as almost violet. Yet he was to mourn, "I am not handsome." There was a major clumsiness in his features.

At the bottom of his protruding forehead there was a vertical drop to the almost nonexistent bridge of his nose. Starting from the level of his eyes, which emphasized the conformation by being set unusually close together, the nose jutted forward at a very sharp angle. His lower face was long, narrowing as prominent jawbones descended to the powerful knob on his chin. That his peculiarity of feature (which portraitists in oil and marble could not gloss over) created no written comment is an indication of how greatly his personality overwhelmed the details of his appearance.

Hamilton touched emotions by communicating a sense of physical frailness electrified by a gallant spirit. There is a strange contradiction between the statements, regularly accepted by his biographers, that he was conspicuously small and five foot seven. In that epoch, five foot seven was more than average height. It is hard to believe that he was not in actuality shorter than that, but there is another explanation. Written documents indicate that he was slight; his full-length portrait by John Trumbull shows him delicately made, with shoulders surprisingly narrow.[17]

Hamilton's St. Croix friends were during the Revolution to express amazement that a man of such "delicate" health could survive as a soldier. It may well have been to compensate for weakness—as he always tried to compensate—that his favorite vision of himself was as a warrior. Typically, he collapsed into what could seem a very serious illness after the completion of a task that had profoundly strained his energy and nerves. He was from time to time incapacitated while working for Cruger—"it is with difficulty that I make out to write these few lines"—yet when Cruger was forced to seek medical attention in New York, he left the fourteen-year-old boy in complete charge of his business.[18]

The excitement of Hamilton's independent tenure was the sloop *Thunderbolt*. Cruger had paid a third of the construction costs, but neither he nor his clerk had ever seen her. When in November, 1771, the ship appeared in Christiansted Harbor, Hamilton did not emphasize, in reporting to his employer, what was pleasing. Rather the opposite. She was, he wrote dubiously, "a fine vessel indeed, but, I fear, not so swift as she ought to be. However, the captain said he has never had an opportunity of a fair trial, and consequently could form no right judgment yet of her sailing."[19]

Speed was of the essence if the *Thunderbolt* were to complete her present voyage and then carry out her next assignment: bringing from the Spanish Main a cargo of mules that would arrive on the very eve of harvest. Hamilton rummaged passionately in the hold, extracting what merchandise could be reached without too much unloading and which he judged would do well in the St. Croix market: 23 hogsheads of Indian meal, 6,469 barrel staves, 20 barrels of apples, 300 inch-and-a-half boards, 21 kegs of bread, and 646 ropes of onions. After the *Thunderbolt* had been only two and a half days in port, he sent the ship and the remaining cargo on to his employer's brother Tileman Cruger at Curaçao.[20]

In the accompanying letter he informed Tileman that he was writing "in behalf of Mr. Nicholas Cruger, who by reason of a very ill state of health went from this to New York." With no further explanation, he gave Tileman some instructions for the disposal of the cargo. Although he admitted in another letter that he suspected Captain William Newton of exaggerating the matter *"by way of stimulation,"* he stated to Tileman that "reports here represent matters in a very disagreeable light with regard to the Guarda Costos [Spanish customs officials] which are said to swarm upon the coast. . . . Captain Newton must arm with you as he could not so conveniently do it here." The inexperienced boy added: "Give me leave to hint to you that you cannot be too particular in your instructions to him. I think he seems rather to want experience in such voyages."[21]

When writing Tileman and his employer's other equals, Hamilton was formal, efficient, just adequately respectful. To Cruger, he was frank, intimate, sometimes jocose, but still the perfect assistant: "If I have neglected anything material, I beg you will excuse me." To those who were under Cruger's command, he assumed the authority and voice of the employer whose name he signed. As he explained to Cruger, "I am convinced [that] if you had been present you would have done just as I did."[22]

The captain of the *Thunderbolt* might well have expected deference from the fourteen-year-old clerk. If so, he soon learned otherwise. As the ship was about to sail from St. Croix, Hamilton ordered, "I . . . desire you will proceed immediately to Curaçao." Newton should be "very choice" after he had proceeded to the Spanish Main in purchasing the best quality of mules and bringing "as many as your vessel can conveniently contain. . . . Remember you are to make three trips this season and unless you are very diligent, you will be too late as our crops will be early in." Newton was to beware of the Spanish customs guards. "I," so Hamilton ended conventionally, "place an entire reliance upon the prudence of your conduct."[23]

The *Thunderbolt* departed. Hamilton reported to his employer on his handling of cargoes that came in from other ships. He collected bills: "Believe me, sir, I dun as hard as is proper." Yet his heart was with the *Thunderbolt* and her cargo of mules. He examined the cane growing on the inland fields to prophesy the moment of the harvest; he scanned the ocean, studying each incoming sail. When in mid-November a large sloop of rival ownership appeared from the Spanish Main with seventy mules he hoped that, the time being too soon for top prices, the mules would be carried to another island. Then the perfect time arrived. No *Thunderbolt!* He became increasingly nervous as reports came in that pirate cutters were operating off the South American coast. Had Tileman Cruger armed the sloop as he had been urged? Or was the *Thunderbolt* now tied up in some pirate cove?[24]

On January 29, 1772, she made her belated landfall. How eagerly Hamilton hurried on board! How taken aback he was by what he saw! Yet his account to his employer communicated not chagrin but rather exhilaration at the way he had handled the disaster.

Hamilton had found on the sloop "forty-one more [mere] skeletons. A worse parcel of mules never was seen. She took in at first forty-eight and lost seven on the passage. I sent all that were able to walk to pasture, in number thirty-three. The other eight could hardly stand for two minutes together, and in spite of the greatest care, four of them are now in limbo. . . . I refused two great offers made me upon their first landing, to wit 70 pence a head for the choice of twenty, and fifteen pence a head for the aforementioned invalids, which may give you a proper idea of the condition they were in." He was feeding up "those now alive" and hoped in the end to get a good price.

Hamilton did not blame the sloop—"'tis now known that she sails well"—or Captain Newton—"no man can command the winds"—for the castastrophe, but he did not hesitate, in writing to Nicholas Cruger, to blame his employer's brother. Tileman had deigned to write the clerk "only a few lines." Having made no sales from the cargo Hamilton had sent on to him, Tileman "excused himself being sick." Hamilton was enraged that, because the request had come from the clerk rather than the master, Tileman had risked the *Thunderbolt* by refusing to hire a few guns. The clerk had now ordered Captain Newton, who was going to Curaçao and then to the Main for more mules, to disobey Tileman if necessary and "hire four guns himself."[25]

Hamilton's instructions to Newton were again written as if in Cruger's voice: "I trust I may rely on you to perform your part with all possible diligence and dispatch. Reflect continually on the unfortunate voyage you have just made and endeavor to make up for the considerable loss therefrom accruing to your owners." Newton was to prepare for the worst by laying in at least a month's supply of food for the new mules. "This," the boy concluded, "is all I think needful to say, so I wish you a good passage."[26]

The most amazing thing the youth did during the some six months of his master's absence was to fire the company attorney and hire another. After Nicholas Cruger returned from New York in March, 1772, he wrote one Hans Buus that he was "glad to find my clerk . . . has desired you to take all my affairs in your hands that was in Mr. Hassells', who I am confident has been very negligent in them, and trifled away a good deal of money to no purpose."[27]

But such is the way of the world that, with the return of his employer, Hamilton sank again to the role of employee. There was, of course, no room to rise in a one-man business, and although he did make some "small" purchases at St. Eustatius on his own account, he lacked the capital effectively to start out for himself. At the moment, he could see no way of escaping from his "groveling" situation.[28]

5

Springboard

[1770–1773   AGES 13–16]

I N his farewell letter on the eve of his fatal duel with Aaron Burr, Hamilton urged his wife to take care of his first cousin, Ann Venton, "the person in this world to whom as a friend I am under the greatest obligations."[1]

Ann, who appeared on St. Croix when she was twenty-seven and Hamilton was thirteen, seems to have been the only one of his mother's relations who befriended the boy. Her life had been a continual disaster. At sixteen, this daughter of the James Lyttons had married a merchant, John Venton, who had quickly gone bankrupt. He had taken her with him on his flight to New York, although this involved leaving their infant daughter behind with her parents. The Ventons were soon on such bad terms with each other that Ann's father made extraordinary provisions in his will to keep the husband from grabbing the money he was leaving to her and the child.

In 1770, shortly after Lytton died, Ann returned to Christiansted to reclaim her daughter, who was then six or seven, and try to collect James Lytton's legacies. Like a bird of prey, her husband followed. He settled in St. Croix's other town, Frederiksted, whence he started a lawsuit to get for himself the money Lytton had left to Ann and the child. Since all the Lyttons had characteristically sprung like tigers at each other's throats, this was only one of the many litigations that made it impossible to settle the will. After Ann had waited more than two years, she decided to return to New York. But her husband tried to hold her captive within the jurisdiction of the Danish courts. He advertised that he would take legal action against any shipowners who gave his wife and daughter passage.

During Ann Venton's stay of more than two years in Christiansted, she found solace in befriending Hamilton. The strength of the emotion he later expressed for her, which so contrasts with his silence concerning Rachel, implies that his cousin gave him the motherly affection he craved.[2]

The other major influence on Hamilton's youth was, like his father, a misfit spun by society off to an incongruous place. The Reverend Hugh Knox was a theological controversialist, brilliant and unconventional. The son of a Scotch Presbyterian minister, he had emigrated to New Jersey as a young man and tried almost instantly to be ordained in his father's faith. When he was refused, he turned to "a life of worldly gaiety." Typically, he was not reconverted but reconverted himself. Having listened with derision to a sermon by the august Presbyterian divine John Rodgers, he undertook to amuse his drinking companions with a parody. But when he was on his feet, repeating to the laughing tipplers what Rodgers had said, the words assumed for him so deep a meaning that he was shocked and horrified by the laughter. Tears streaming from his eyes, he fled from the community, abandoning all his possessions. In shame, he vanished.

Knox reappeared some months later at the College of New Jersey (now Princeton) seeking instruction from the Reverend Aaron Burr. This son-in-law of Jonathan Edwards had a son whom he had named after himself. It was undoubtedly amid the lush vegetation of St. Croix that Hamilton first heard the three syllables that were to end his existence.

Burr received Knox, who was in due course ordained. But the synod did not want the firebrand flaming under their noses. They sent Knox to what they admitted was "so distant a part of the Lord's vineyard": to Saba, a tiny volcanic cone that rose from the Caribbean some thirty miles northwest of Nevis. A village of 180 dwellings nestled in the crater of the extinct volcano, one thousand feet up. The village could only be reached by tortuous, craggy paths; and the island itself, having no anchorage, was accessible only by surfboats.

In this isolated spot, Knox stayed seventeen years—but not obscurely. The surfboats brought him hundreds of books on theology and carried out thousands of letters through which Knox communed with the leading Presbyterian divines of the English-speaking world. The sermons he preached to his minuscule congregation were gathered into tomes—usually two-volume sets—that were published in America or London or Edinburgh (and which continued to be republished by radical Presbyterians into the nineteenth century). Knox argued for free will against the Calvinist doctrine of predestination. Since Christ had died for the sins of all mankind, how could most men be automatically condemned to eternal damnation? Had Christ commanded "nonelect sinners to believe a lie," when he called on all men to come to him?[3]

Although Knox complained of a lack of association with his "ministerial brethren" who would "warm my devotion and quicken my zeal," he stayed on Saba until a personal squabble, undefined by history, forced him to leave the island. In the summer of 1771 (when Hamilton was about fourteen) he moved to the Presbyterian Church at Christiansted.[4]

What could be more delightful for a shy man, who seems to have shuddered away from direct contact with his peers, than to guide a brilliant mind that because of its youth offered him no threatening competition? And how exciting for that youth, whose previous connections had included no person with mental depth, to hold discussions with a mentor of profound intellect! Knox's library must have been to Hamilton a cascade of possibilities and ideas.

Alexander's son John wrote in one of his most believable passages, "The little leisure he could command from his mercantile duties was devoted to study. His knowledge of mathematics was enlarged. He became fond of chemistry and, although his proficiency in it was small, he often urged it as a pursuit well adapted to excite curiosity and create new combinations of thought. Among the books to which he had access, he preferred those which treat of some branch of ethics. His favorite authors were Pope and Plutarch, on the latter of which there remain several curious observations from his youthful pen; but even these were often laid aside for the more profound researches of severer writers."[5]

Knox doubled as a doctor, which may be where the chemistry came in. The "severer writers" were, of course, ecclesiastical. Under the influence of his teacher, Hamilton became extremely religious. Knox, whose own powers as a writer were admired even by those who considered him theologically unsound,[6] encouraged Hamilton in literary ambitions.

In the religious field Knox was such a thinker and polemicist as Hamilton was to become in the political. Hamilton's mature prose style was, in its clarity, pugnacity, and legalistic reasoning, much in Knox's manner. But, for the moment, Hamilton's style was very different.

During August 31, 1772, St. Croix suffered a devastating hurricane. On the following Sunday, Knox delivered a sermon in which he pointed out, with scriptural quotations and theological reasoning, that God had spoken from the whirlwind and that the cataclysm was a warning to sinners. Deeply impressed, Hamilton wrote an essay pursuing the same theme. It was published in the *Royal Danish-American Gazette* on October 3.

An introductory paragraph stated that the text had fallen "by accident" into the hands of a gentleman (generally assumed on no evidence to have been Knox) who showed it to others. They "all agreed that it might not prove unentertaining to the public. The author's modesty in long refusing to submit it to public view is the reason for its making its appearance as late as it now does."

The author is described only as "a youth of this island," yet surely all Hamilton's connections knew that he was the author. There on St. Croix, where Rachel had repudiated his father and the name Hamilton, Alexander published his first important appearance before the world as a letter to his father.

"Good God!" wrote the youth. "What horror and destruction! . . . It seemed as if a total dissolution of nature was taking place." He envisioned "fiery meteors flying about it in the air" to mingle with "almost perpetual lightning, the crash of the falling houses, the ear-piercing shrieks of the distressed. . . . My reflections and feelings on this frightful and melancholy occasion are set forth in the following self-discourse:

"Where now, O vile worm is all thy boasted fortitude and resolution? What is become of thine arrogance and self-sufficiency? Why doest thou tremble and stand aghast? How humble, how helpless, how contemptible you now appear. And for why? The jarring of the elements—the discord of clouds? O impotent, presumptuous fool! how durst thou offend that Omnipotence, whose nod alone were sufficient to quell the destruction that hovers over thee—or crush thee into atoms? See thy wretched helpless state, and learn to know thyself. . . . Despise thyself and adore thy God.

"How sweet, how unutterably sweet were now the voice of an approving conscience." Possessing that, one could say, "Let the earth rend. Let the planets forsake their course. Let the sun be extinguished and the heavens burst asunder. Yet what have I to dread? . . .

"But alas!" so Hamilton continued, "how different, how deplorable, how gloomy the prospect. Death comes rushing on in triumph veiled in a mantle of ten-fold darkness. . . . On his right hand sits destruction, hurling the winds and belching forth flames; calamity on his left threatening famine, disease and distress of all kinds. And O thou wretch, look still a little further; see the gulf of eternal misery open. . . . Thou canst not call upon thy God; thy life has been a continual warfare with him."

Hamilton then specified that he himself was not suffering from "a conscience over-burdened with crimes of an uncommon cast. . . . The scenes of horror exhibited around us," he explained, "naturally awakened such ideas in every thinking breast."

This consideration of his own situation led him onto a more rational plane and into a less stern theology: "That which in a calm unruffled temper we call a natural cause seemed then like the correction of the deity. Our imagination represented Him as an incensed master, executing vengeance on the crimes of his servants. The father and benefactor were forgot, and, in that view, a consciousness of our guilt filled us with despair."

Hamilton then interpreted the ending of the storm as God hearing "our prayer." He urged his own soul "to rejoice at thy deliverance and humble thyself in the presence of thy deliverer.

"Yet hold, O vain mortal! Check thy ill timed joy. . . . Art thou incapable of the soft pangs of sympathetic sorrow? Look around thee and shudder at the view." Hamilton described the "pale and lifeless" bodies of fellow creatures whose souls were "snatched into eternity unexpecting. Alas! perhaps unprepared." He described the sick exposed to the "wind and water." He described the infant starving while the mother's poverty "denies relief. Her breast heaves with pangs of maternal pity, her heart is bursting, the tears gush down her cheeks. O sights of woe! O distress unspeakable! My heart bleeds, but I have no power to solace. O ye, who revel in affluence, see the afflictions of humanity and bestow your superfluity to ease them."*

A final sentence, thanking the governor general for efficient management of the crisis, seems to have been added for prudential reasons, whether by Hamilton or the editor.[7]

Hamilton's son, fixing on the hurricane letter perhaps because it was available to him, asserted that the attention it attracted among leading Cruxians, from the governor general down, was the cause of Alex-

---

* It is a tantalizing question whether Hamilton had been reading Shakespeare's *King Lear* (Act III, Scene 4): "Take physic, pomp; expose thyself to feel what wretches feel, that thou mayst share the superflux to them."

ander's being sent to North America to be educated.[8] Although this has become one of the "facts" embedded in American history texts, documents make clear that those responsible for Hamilton's departure had been familiar with him long before the letter was published. The most it could have done was to solidify ideas already in the minds of his associates.

Nowadays, scholarships are a standard part of American higher education: a quite impersonal exchange between the affluent and the needy. In those days, neighbors came to the aid of individuals they admired. Thus two of America's four old masters in painting, Benjamin West and Charles Willson Peale, were sent to study in Europe by local subscriptions. No one who had much contact with Hamilton could have doubted that he would profit immensely from the educational opportunities that came automatically to sons of the well-to-do.

Though Knox in one of his sermons praised the patron who draws genius from obscurity, he had little money to contribute. He later spelled out his role: "I have always had a just and secret pride in having advised you to go to America and in having recommended you to some of my old friends there."[9]

The records of the Lytton executors reveal that between May 3 and June 3, 1773, they honored three drafts that Ann Venton had sent from New York in favor of Hamilton. But the major support for his hegira came not from the Lyttons but from the merchants in whose midst Hamilton had worked since a small boy.[10]

Not only had Nicholas Cruger's business prospered with Hamilton as clerk, but Cruger had just made a rich marriage. His father-in-law, Town Captain Peter de Nully, had longtime memories, since it was to his plantation that Rachel had first fled when her husband had released her from jail. The family firm of Cruger's close business associate Cornelius Kortright was entrusted with handling Hamilton's assets at the American end. Kortright and Company received, so the brother of a partner remembered, "from time to time, the first shortly after his [Hamilton's] arrival, West India produce to be sold and the proceeds to be applied to his use."[11]

Everything was arranged that could be arranged, but destiny would not allow Hamilton to escape into a new world and a new life without visiting upon him one of the most terrifying of dangers. The little wooden vessel in which he was making his voyage caught fire as it approached the North American coast. We can envision Hamilton standing in an anguished line of sailors and other passengers who

An immigrant's first view of America. The New York City skyline, from Liberty Street to the Battery, as it appeared when Hamilton sailed in after the long journey from the Caribbean. Courtesy, Museum of the City of New York

handed buckets from where they were lowered into the ocean to where the water could be thrown on the blaze. Overhead, smoke billowed. Finally, the crackling ceased and the smoke faded. Hamilton was on his way again.[12]

The muse of history is by no means always present at world-shaking events. We do not know for certain when Hamilton first reached American soil or where he landed. However, the chances are that the place was New York Harbor, and the time, June, 1773.*

---

* See Appendix A, pp. 455–456.

6

Schoolboy in a New Land

[1773–1774   AGES 16–17]

ALEXANDER HAMILTON was a changeling. He had entered a new world free at last. The brightly colored, steaming Caribbean islands where he had been reared, with their eternal grinding out of sugar from the lush soil and the helpless bodies of kidnapped blacks, had receded into the past never to be resurrected in actuality, to be struggled with only in memory and dream. At St. Croix, the scandals involved in his upbringing had been available to anyone who was interested. Here, they were known only to a very few old friends, who admired him the more for what he had overcome—and who were not likely to reveal his secrets.

Hamilton found already resident in New York two of the people who were closest to him: his substitute mother, Ann Venton, and his dear friend Edward Stevens, now a student at the forerunner of Columbia University, King's College. And letters he had brought opened to him agreeable worlds.

The business representatives in New York of Hamilton's patrons in the West Indies observed the boy with a semipaternal eye. The shipments consigned to his account were part of an extremely prosperous trade. Thus, the youth was able to pursue his education (and, when the Revolution broke out, his nascent military career) with fine indifference to how much he spent.[1] But this was only the underpinning. More important were the contacts made for him by Knox. The heterodox recluse carried sufficient prestige with America's Presbyterian

53

leaders to open doors for his young disciple, and once Hamilton was inside those doors, his own character and appearance inspired confidence.

Knox's letters introduced Hamilton to the two leading Presbyterian clergymen in New York City: John Rodgers and John Mason. Rodgers's son had roomed at the College of New Jersey with Aaron Burr, a youth almost exactly Hamilton's age. Burr, who belonged by birthright in the group Hamilton was beginning to frequent, was even more of a prodigy: he had graduated from college with high honors at sixteen. The West Indian needed to travel a long distance if he were to catch up. His mentors agreed that, because of his utter lack of formal education, he would require preparation before he could enter college. He was sent to the Presbyterian academy at Elizabethtown, New Jersey.[2]

The Swedish traveler Peter Kalm described Elizabethtown as "a small place. . . . Its houses are for the most part scattered, but well built, generally of boards, with a roof and walls of shingles. There are likewise stone buildings. A little rivulet passes through the town from west to east. . . . There are two fine churches, either of which makes a better appearance than any in Philadelphia." The Anglican church "is built of brick, has a steeple with bells and a balustrade around it from which there is a view of the country. The meeting place of the Presbyterians is built of wood, but has both a steeple and bells." The town hall also had a belfry. "In and about the town are many gardens and orchards, and it might be said that Elizabethtown is situated in a garden."

It was only a few steps to the country, where wooden farmhouses were flanked by large orchards. Ovens, usually of clay, stood at a distance from the houses. The landscape had "a charming appearance, some parts high, others forming valleys, and all of them well cultivated. . . . You have a prospect of houses, farms, gardens, tilled land, forests, lakes, islands, roads and pastures." Kalm noted that the geese had foot-long sticks fastened around their necks crossways to prevent them from creeping through fences. "They look very awkward, and it is very diverting to see them in this attitude."[3]

The Elizabethtown Academy, a "commodious" two-story building with a cupola, stood close to the Presbyterian church. It had a fine reputation in the middle colonies. An announcement stated that it would instruct youth in the several branches of mathematics, both theoretical and practical, "without detriment" to the teaching of Latin and Greek. Elocution was also taught. The scholars trooped regularly to the church, which claimed to be the oldest congregation organized in New Jersey for the worship of God in English. The Reverend James Caldwell rarely preached without weeping and sometimes melted the whole congregation into tears.[4]

The principal of the school, Francis Barber, was only four years older than Hamilton; he was (perhaps partly because of Hamilton's machinations) to lead a battalion under his pupil's command in the celebrated attack on a redoubt at Yorktown. Barber was a specialist in Greek. However, Hamilton was more interested in a more practical language. He somehow managed to teach himself French so well that even Frenchmen thought he spoke it "perfectly." Folk memory has it that Hamilton was seen pacing the graveyard, hour after hour, mumbling to himself with a book in his hand.[5]

Although Hamilton was trying to gulp down years of education in a few months, he was no restricted pedant. He is said to have made friends with the officers of a military company stationed near Elizabethtown. When they presented a play, he wrote the prologue and epilogue, usually composed in couplets and of local import, with which performances were then conventionally opened and closed.[6]

More importantly, Elizabethtown, once the capital of New Jersey, supplied him with associations that were to remain with him for the rest of his career. He presented letters from Knox to Elias Boudinot and William Livingston.[7]

Hamilton is believed (and it is quite possible since intimacy existed) to have lived in Boxwood Hall, the just-completed spacious mansion of Elias Boudinot. A successful lawyer, Boudinot was to become the most celebrated philanthropist of his generation and also a President of the Continental Congress. There the youth undoubtedly met Boudinot's brother-in-law, Richard Stockton, who was to sign the Declaration of Independence, and Mrs. Stockton, a poet, who was to flirt with General Washington. The Boudinot children were too young to become Hamilton's companions.

William Livingston was the most impressive member of the community. A son of the lord of Livingston Manor, he was as highborn as was possible in the aristocratic colony of New York. He had added to hereditary wealth by marrying a wife who owned extensive properties in New Jersey, and by a successful law practice in New York City. He was also a writer: not only like Knox a polemicist but—this must particularly have pleased Hamilton—a poet of considerable reputation in the American colonies. He was famous for his cantankerousness. After suffering a political defeat in the dynastic politics of New York, he had "retired" at the age of fifty to Elizabethtown, where he was seeking "philosophic solitude" by clearing "pretentious grounds" and erecting a great mansion. As he awaited completion of what he called "Liberty Hall," he lived in the village. After New Jersey declared its independence, he became the first governor of the state.

When Hamilton visited Livingston's house, he found a squad of children—eight born between 1751 and 1758—with whom he could cavort. He flirted with several of the daughters, and they may well have introduced him to their cousin, Elizabeth Schuyler, who did not particularly interest him at the time but whom he was some years later to marry. Sarah Livingston, almost exactly Alexander's age, was engaged to John Jay, ten years Hamilton's senior. A serious, self-righteous, and extremely able New York patrician, Jay was to be a major founding father of the United States and a lifelong colleague of Hamilton's. A brother, Henry Brockholst Livingston, who was Alexander's fellow pupil at the academy, became an important Revolutionary officer and a justice of the U.S. Supreme Court.[8]

It was only a short ride to Basking Ridge, the home of William Livingston's rich brother-in-law, William Alexander, who claimed an extinct Scottish earldom and in America called himself Lord Stirling, although the British House of Lords refused to take him in. He was to be one of Washington's important generals. At Basking Ridge, Hamilton may well have met William Duer, who was to marry one of Lord Stirling's daughters. Duer eventually became Hamilton's second-in-command at the Treasury and brought disgrace on his patron by dishonest dealings.

By the time Hamilton had reached North America, the drift towards revolution was flowing but not yet in flood. The fundamental issue was, of course, whether America could and should be ruled from overseas. Although by no means extremists, almost all of Hamilton's Elizabethtown associates were deeply disturbed by the English claims. As a newcomer to American soil, Hamilton could not see what the fuss was all about. And, having no intention of "groveling" to anyone, he was surely argumentative at the homes of Livingston and Boudinot about what he later called his "strong prejudices" for the British point of view.[9]

Most of the issues were of no immediate concern to Hamilton, but one had particular connections with his future plans. William Livingston's favorite cause, which had induced him to subsidize the newspaper in which he published his polemics, was to ward off what he

Lord Stirling's mansion, which Hamilton often visited when he was a schoolboy in Elizabethtown, New Jersey. Stirling, who had flirtatious daughters, became one of Washington's important generals. He tried to induce Hamilton to become his aide-de-camp. The location of this needlework is unknown.

considered a British plot to force the "establishment" of the Church of England in New York. All citizens, whatever their beliefs, would then have to pay taxes for the support of the official religion. The major bone of contention came to be whether money raised by a public lottery should be used to found an Anglican college. Assisted by Hamilton's other neighbor, Boudinot, Livingston succeeded in having half the money assigned to a jail and a pesthouse; but the other half was used to finance King's College. It was to be primarily Anglican, an adjunct of Trinity Parish. The college was now exemplifying what the Presbyterians had feared: it was serving as a center for the support of English rule over America.

The Presbyterians had their answer to the Anglican college: the College of New Jersey (now Princeton University). That was where Hamilton should obviously go. But he announced to his Elizabethtown friends that he would go to New York City and King's.

The universally accepted explanation comes from an account written four decades later by Hercules Mulligan, a brother of a member of the company that was administering the funds sent Hamilton from the Indies. He claimed to have acted *in loco parentis* to Hamilton. When the boy informed Mulligan, so the story goes, that he was now ready for college, he added that his preference was the College of New Jersey "because it was more republican" than King's. Being "well acquainted" with President Witherspoon of the college in Princeton, Mulligan "introduced" Hamilton, who requested "to be permitted to advance from class to class as rapidly as his exertions would enable him to do so." Witherspoon was sympathetic but, after consultation with his trustees, refused. Hamilton thereupon entered King's "in the spring of 1775 in the sophomore class on the terms proposed at Princeton."[10]

Mulligan's reminiscences, when checkable, almost always prove wrong, and this account is no exception. Hamilton entered King's well before 1775. He would not have preferred the College of New Jersey because it was "more republican" since he himself was still pro-British. It is furthermore inconceivable that Hamilton needed the Anglican New York City tailor to introduce him to Witherspoon. For Witherspoon, himself a Presbyterian minister, had long been a correspondent of Hamilton's sponsor, Knox. The Elizabethtown Academy was in effect a preparatory school for the College of New Jersey. Several of Hamilton's connections, including Rodgers and Livingston, were trustees of the college, which made it probable that, if an exception to the rules were made for anybody, it would have been for Hamilton. We know that a boy from distant Virginia named James Madison had in the autumn of 1771 been graduated from the College of New Jersey after completing the four-year course in two.

The situation was much more interesting and significant than the acceptance of the Mulligan story has permitted writers to realize. Hamilton's choice of King's over the College of New Jersey was his first recorded major independent decision. He had stepped naturally after his mother's death into the employ of Cruger, who had supplied his mother's store. His friendship with the Reverend Knox and his resulting adherence to somewhat evangelical Presbyterianism had been dictated by his need to escape from what had been an intellectual vacuum into association with the first man he had ever met who possessed considerable intelligence and learning. No ambitious youngster could possibly have refused the opportunity to study in North America. The choice of New York as a base and Elizabethtown as a preparatory school had been dictated by the connections of his patrons. But his selection of a college was in opposition to the pressures around him.

Hamilton, who was still in practice a devout Presbyterian but who was soon to lose all religious faith, quietly ignored the religious issue. Politically he was, of course, drawn to King's. But an even greater attraction, so Hamilton's future life indicates, was the environment. Princeton and Elizabethtown were very close to each other in the same landscape. One might well assume that the immigrant from those lush and brutal agricultural factories that were the Leeward Islands would not wish to leave what was by contrast so Arcadian an agricultural scene. But Hamilton's months in Elizabethtown were to remain his entire peacetime experience of rural America. He never wished to return to that environment which his Jeffersonian enemies regarded as a political ideal and accused Hamilton of trying to destroy. Hamilton, when he reached New York, had seen his first city. It was a case of love at first sight.

Hamilton's departure from Elizabethtown broke no friendships. Although he was, throughout his career, to accumulate a stunning crowd of enemies, he had an equal gift of inspiring loyalty. The circle of able and powerful men he had come to know as a teen-age schoolboy in Elizabethtown remained with him down the years as a center of affection and a source of power.

The population of New York, some twenty thousand, seems tiny to us today but would then have been considered large anywhere in the world. New York had all the bustle of St. Croix without the unpleasantness. The streets were just as crowded, but not with pitiful blacks and despicable planters. Instead, free men and women pursued their personal tasks. There were a hundred times as many shops—infinitely more various than at St. Croix; the proprietors stood firmly on their feet and looked customers cheerfully in the eye. Hamilton's own pace was in tune here, even if he thought and sometimes moved more quickly.

Almost due west of the present City Hall Park, King's College was then on the outskirts of the city. Surmounting a grassy hillside that sank gently down to the Hudson, it was called "the most beautifully situated college in the world." The president during Hamilton's time, Miles Cooper, boasted of "the commanding eminence on which it stands." Hamilton could see, as he paused in his studies, "the most extensive and beautiful prospect," not only of the New Jersey country-side he had deserted and the rocky, wooded upper stretches of Man-hattan Island, but of the whole city to the south. It was surrounded at the tip and along both flanking rivers with what looked like a dead forest that sometimes blossomed with white foliage. The trees were the masts of moored ships. Beyond was an expanse of water that made St. Croix's vaunted harbor look like a puddle: "New York bay with its islands, the Narrows forming the mouth of the harbor, etc., etc." A perpetual shifting of commerce moved over this inland sea. The college, so Cooper's ecstatic account continued, "being totally unen-cumbered by any adjacent buildings and admitting of the purest cir-culation of air from the river and every other quarter, has the benefit of as agreeable and healthy a situation as can possibly be conceived."[11]

King's College was housed in a single large building: high basement, three full stories, each with a twenty-window front, a cupola on top. Here were contained the president's quarters, accommodations for twenty-four students, a chapel, a library, steward's quarters, a kitchen, a dining hall, and some classrooms. Although the rules stated that students must live in, there were not enough beds. Those who lived out had the most freedom, since the gates that gave access to the "college court" were locked at nine in winter and ten in summer.

Hamilton boarded, at least for some of the time, with Hercules Mulligan, who lived over his tailor shop next to Philip Rhinelander's china store, somewhat downtown from the college and all the way. across to the East River.[12] Towards the end of his fifteen-minute walk to his studies, Hamilton had to pass an enticement. A Scottish visitor noted: "One circumstance is, I think, a little unlucky; the entrance to the college is through one of the streets where the most noted prosti-tutes live. This is surely a temptation to the youth." John Adams, who

A South East View of the City of New York, in NORTH AMERICA. Vue du sud Est de la Ville de New York, dans L'AMÉRIQUE SEPTENTRIONALE.

Drawn on the Spot by Cap.ᵗ Thomas Howell of the Royal Artillery. Engraved by P. Carnot.

1 New College. 2 Old English Church. 3 City Hall. 4 French Church. 5 North Rever. 6 Staten Island. 7 The Prison.

King's College, where Hamilton studied. The building is shown as dominating New York City. Engraved in England during 1768 from "drawings made on the spot" by Captain Thomas Howell, this view reveals that the engraver, P. Carnot, was not one to allow his creativity to be extinguished. He enlarged the building in relation to its surroundings and, a little confused about geography, embellished New York with a palm tree. Courtesy, Library of Congress

was to attribute what he considered Hamilton's villainy to his having "a superabundance of secretions which he could not find whores enough to draw off," would undoubtedly have believed that the undergraduate succumbed.[13]

After Hamilton reached the college, he had to change into academic dress since Cooper was determined that his "diminutive Oxford" should be just as formal as its prototype. Nonattendance at classes, meals, prayers, or study hours, dozing over your book, or climbing over the gate after it was closed, made you subject to fines. The book recording the fines still exists, but is innocent of Hamilton's name.[14]

A fellow student, Robert Troup, tells us that "part of the time" he and Hamilton "occupied the same room, and slept in the same bed." Troup's further statement that he had met Hamilton at King's during 1773 has been taken to mean that Hamilton started studying there in that year. However, Hamilton might have been visiting their mutual friend Stevens. The only official record of Hamilton's presence at King's is his inclusion in the list of those who matriculated in 1774.[15]

Troup remembered that when Hamilton "entered college, he did it as a private student and not by annexing himself to a particular class. The president and the professors instructed him at their leisure hours. He was studious, and made rapid progress in the languages and every other branch of learning to which he applied himself. He had originally destined himself to the science of physic, and with this in view, he was regular in attending the anatomical lectures then delivered in the college by Dr. Clossey."[16]

One record remains of his private instruction: Professor Robert Harpur noted on September 20, 1974, that Hamilton "entered with me this day to study mathematics, at three pounds four shillings a quarter." The youth's interest in medicine could have been inspired by the Reverend Knox, who doubled as a doctor, but Hamilton was not officially a medical student, as the 1774 matriculation list reveals.[17]

He had not abandoned his literary ambitions. A poem he wrote in 1774 on the death of Elias Boudinot's daughter continues the tendency, already revealed when he was Nicholas Cruger's clerk, to write in other people's voices. Here it is the bereaved mother who speaks:

> *But what, alas, availed my care?*
> *The unrelenting hand of death,*
> *Regardless of a parent's pray'r*
> *Has stopped my lovely infant's breath.*

Then comes a verse that most incongruously escapes from pious rhetoric into amused observation:

> No more thy self-important tale
> Some embryo meaning shall convey,
> Which should th'imperfect accents fail,
> Thy speaking looks would still display.

The poem ends correctly:

> Let reason silence nature's strife
> And weep Maria's fate no more.
> She's safe from all the storms of life
> And wafted to a peaceful shore.[18]

Troup remembered that Hamilton "now and then paid court to the muses and, as a pledge of friendship, presented me with a small manuscript of fugitive poetry, the amusement of his leisure hours." Mulligan describes a domestic scene: Hamilton "used in the evening to sit with my family and my brother's family and write doggerel verses for their amusement. He was always amiable and cheerful and extremely attentive to his books."[19]

According to Troup, Hamilton "was attentive to public worship; and was in the habit of praying on his knees both night and morning." Listening as Hamilton's roommate, Troup was "often powerfully moved by the fervor and eloquence of his prayers." Hamilton "had read most of the polemical writers on religious subjects; and he was a zealous believer in the fundamental doctrines of Christianity. And I confess that the arguments with which he was accustomed to justify his belief have tended in no small degree to confirm my own faith in revealed religion."[20]

Five students, including Stevens, Troup, and Hamilton, formed "a weekly club for our improvement in composition, in debating, and in public speaking; and the club continued until we were separated by the Revolution. In all the performances of the club," Troup continued, "the General [Hamilton] made extraordinary displays of richness of genius and energy of mind." When the debate was political, he argued for the British position. According to Troup, Hamilton was "originally a monarchist. He was versed in the history of England and well acquainted with the principles of the English constitution, which he admired."[21]

7

A Teen-aged Propagandist

[1774–1775   AGES 17–18]

T
HE toboggan that was to speed down the winding route to
independence was given its irreversible push by the Boston
Tea Party. All Americans except the most radical viewed the
event with alarm. King's College was shocked.

To the British and to unsympathetic observers in America, this
reaction against (as Hamilton put it) "the petty duty of threepence on
a pound of East India tea," seemed so irrational that it could only be
explained as the insanity or the villainy of the most extreme agitators.
His Majesty's government was so satisfied with this same conclusion
that they sent no royal commission, not a single person, across the
Atlantic to find out what was really going on. But Hamilton sensed the
existence of forces he did not understand. Troup tells us: "Soon after
the destruction of the West India tea . . . when the public mind was
in a state of violent fermentation," he journeyed to Boston to determine what his opinions should be.[1]

Since he was neither hesitant nor shy, Hamilton undoubtedly found
his way to the revolutionary leaders. We can see an Adams or a Warren
viewing with surprise the slight, intense college student, sixteen years
old and looking younger, recently from the Indies and now from New
York, who considered it to be a matter of importance what conclusions
he came to. Hamilton had not been moved by the contentions of the
staid patriots who had surrounded him at Elizabethtown. But listening
to the New England firebrands, he felt "the superior force" of their
"arguments in favor of the American claims." He now agreed that the

issue was "whether the inhabitants of Great Britain have a right to dispose of the lives and properties of the inhabitants of America."[2]

As soon as he was convinced, Hamilton sat right down and wrote his "first political piece," which was published in a Boston newspaper. He carried a copy back with him to New York, where his arguments to demonstrate that the destruction of the tea was "both necessary and politic" convinced Troup, although, as his friend remembered, "I was prejudiced against the measure."[3]

The reaction in London to the Tea Party was much more Draconian than even the most apprehensive Americans had foreseen. As Hamilton put it, "An act was passed to block up her [Boston's] ports and destroy her commerce, with every aggravating circumstance that could be imagined."[4] Massachusetts implored the other colonies to establish a boycott of British goods. This resulted in the calling of the illegal convention that has gone down in history as the First Continental Congress.

For a whole series of reasons, New York was of all the major colonies the least anxious to get in trouble with the British. To begin with, the city was disunited: its population was the most diverse, both in religion and national origins, in America. Its economy was highly dependent on mercantile connections with England, and it did not, like New England, have its own fleets with which to trade elsewhere. Albany, at the upper end of the Hudson navigation, enjoyed a profitable fur trade with Canada. The land in between was so dominated by great families that local self-government was rudimentary. Because of Long Island Sound and the configuration of rivers, almost all the colony's well-settled areas were vulnerable to British naval attack.

New York had in effect two governments: the legally elected Provincial Assembly, which was extremely conservative; and the illegal Committee of Safety, which was extremely radical. The assembly voted against participation in the Congress. Lest the committee take over and then go too far, the moderates, such men as had been Hamilton's Elizabethtown associates, infiltrated the radical body. Establishing a middle ground, they resolved to send delegates to the Congress but refused to support a boycott of British goods.

The radicals thereupon called a mass meeting in "The Fields," now City Hall Park, where the Liberty Pole stood. Years later an old gentleman told Hamilton's son that on this occasion Hamilton made his first public address. The episode, which may or may not be grounded on actual fact, was thus reconstructed by the son:

The youth had attracted attention on the streets by indulging in what was to be his lifelong habit of talking to himself as he walked along, "apparently engaged in deep thought." Passersby had stopped to converse with him. Remarking the vigor of his thoughts, they had suggested that he address the meeting. He had recoiled with modesty, but when he concluded that the speakers were not making the necessary points, he stepped forward. "Breathless silence" reigned, and after he had concluded, the murmur "It is a collegian! It is a collegian!" was lost "in loud expressions of wonder and applause at the extraordinary eloquence of the young stranger."[5]

In urging nonimportation, Hamilton again revealed that he had swung passionately from the pro-British position he had supported in Elizabethtown to the opposite extreme. His arguments, with those of the other speakers, persuaded the mass meeting but not the moderates, who now dominated the Committee of Safety. When the committee refused to go along, the radicals could do nothing but resign.

Despite New York's hesitations, the Continental Congress, which met at Philadelphia in September, 1774, voted to bind the colonies into an "Association," which would not import or consume British goods or export American goods to any British possession. The lieutenant governor of New York, Cadwallader Colden, reported to the government in London that fostering "disunion" between the colonies was the best way to defeat the Congress, and that lukewarm New York was the obvious colony to pry loose from "the Continental Association."[6] Towards this end, a major gun was fired during November, 1774, in the form of a pamphlet entitled (in part) *Free Thoughts on the Proceedings of the Continental Congress.* Aimed at persuading New York's agriculturalists, the pamphlet was signed "A. W. Farmer."[7]

The Continental Association was, so the Tory propagandist argued, a plot of American merchants to bleed the farmers. The merchants had laid in great stocks of English goods, which they could, if further importations were stopped, sell at high prices. Having to buy, while nonexportation kept them from selling, the farmers would be caught in an inescapable squeeze. The writer pictured noble tillers of the soil shivering without warm clothes as they were driven from their lands in midwinter because of debt. If they tried in any way to protect themselves, they would be tarred and feathered by radical committeemen.

Reveling in confusion, anarchy, and violence, the committeemen wished to impose on their fellow Americans "vile, abject slavery. . . . Can men defend rights who act in open defiance of our laws?" He urged the farmers to restore peace by renouncing all usurpers in favor

66

of their elected, sensibly moderate New York Assembly, which would achieve redress for grievances through petitions.

Although no patriot actually knew who "A. W. Farmer" was, he was assumed to be one of the Anglican ministers who were the most articulate of the Tories. (He is now known to have been the Reverend Samuel Seabury, an Episcopal rector in Westchester County.) Hamilton may well have believed, as did others, that the author was the president of his own college, the Reverend Miles Cooper. However, the undergraduate determined to take up cudgels in reply. It took him three weeks to write and get published a thirty-five-page pamphlet entitled *A Full Vindication of the Measures of the Congress from the Calumnies of their Enemies; In Answer to A Letter, Under the Signature of A. W. Farmer. Whereby His Sophistry is exposed, his Cavils confuted, his Artifices detected, and his Wit ridiculed* . . . . It was printed in mid-December, 1774, and signed "A Friend to America."

Light flowing backwards from Hamilton's later career has dazzled away the recognition that, although it shows energy, audacity, and the ability to write clearly, the seventeen-year-old's pamphlet is immature, helter-skelter, and hodgepodge. There are bursts of eloquence* and also of humor, as when he stated that the British might eventually "find means to tax you . . . for every kiss your daughters received from their sweethearts, and, God knows, that would soon ruin you."[8]

Hamilton had obviously started scribbling before he had thought out his arguments. It is always a problem in such essays that the ideas do not fall naturally into a consistent progression (as in a chronological narrative); each point assumes and underlies many others. Instead of trying by careful outlining to achieve a step-by-step progression, Hamilton accepted confusion, repeating contentions over and over again as they reappeared in new contexts. And his contentions were often more emphatic than logical.

* "And first, let me ask these restless spirits whence arises that violent antipathy they seem to entertain, not only to the natural rights of mankind, but to common sense and common modesty. That they are enemies to the natural rights of mankind is manifest because they wish to see one part of their species enslaved by another. That they have an invincible aversion to common sense is apparent in many respects: They endeavor to persuade us that the absolute sovereignty of Parliament does not imply our absolute slavery; that it is a Christian duty to submit to be plundered of all we have, merely because some of our fellow subjects are wicked enough to require it of us; that slavery, so far from being a great evil, is a great blessing; and even, that our contest with Britain is founded entirely upon the petty duty of three pence per pound on East India tea; whereas the whole world knows, it is built upon this interesting question: whether the inhabitants of Great Britain have a right to dispose of the lives and properties of the inhabitants of America, or not?"[9]

A
FULL VINDICATION
OF THE
Measures of the Congress,

FROM

The CALUMNIES of their ENEMIES;

In ANSWER to

A LETTER,

Under the Signature of

A. W. FARMER,

WHEREBY

His *Sophistry* is exposed, his *Cavils* confuted, his
Artifices detected, and his *Wit* ridiculed;

IN

A GENERAL ADDRESS

To the Inhabitants of America,

AND

A Particular Address

To the FARMERS *of the Province of New-York.*

Veritas magna est & prævalebit.
Truth is powerful, and will prevail.

NEW-YORK:
Printed by JAMES RIVINGTON. 1774.

Hamilton joins the propaganda war. The title page of the
pamphlet that in one burst made its author, the seventeen-year-
old college student who had been in America only two years,
stand out among the New York patriots. Courtesy, New-York
Historical Society

To Seabury's statement that the Continental Congress and all the committees set up by the protesters were impertinent usurpers, Hamilton answered that the groups were made up of leading citizens and had been chosen—this was untrue—by the entire population. Since, when they were elected, no limit had been placed on their powers, whatever decisions they considered the crisis required were binding on all the people.

The crisis was caused by an effort to reduce the American people to slavery. Hamilton's definition of slavery would have pleased the most extreme anarchist. Since the "law of nature" presented no reason why one man should exercise preeminence more than any other, any man who was governed by another without his consent was a slave.[10]

Hamilton did not follow this contention to the logical conclusion of denouncing monarchy, for he had a contradictory point to make. The American refusal to accept the rulings of Parliament was not, he argued, opposition to the British Empire, since the sovereign was George III. Under the beneficent all-over surveillance of the Crown, each region within the empire should elect its own legislature. If Hamilton thus foreshadowed what was to be the organization of the British Commonwealth, the idea was not original with him. During the first months of actual fighting, the British army was referred to as the "Ministerial Army," to indicate the colonists' conviction that the invaders represented only Parliament and its ministers.

Seabury's argument that the proper policy was to send further petitions of grievances, was easily answered; all previous petitions had been spurned. It was more difficult to demonstrate that England, not America, would be hurt by mercantile reprisals. The man who was to see a national debt as an engine for prosperity, now pictured England as extremely vulnerable, tottering on the verge of bankruptcy, because she had such a debt.[11] He had worked up facts and figures, not particularly convincing (except for the West Indies, which he knew about), to show that the whole British Empire would suffer from an American boycott. He believed that the boycott would be tremendously effective because of a principle that was always to lie at the base of his political thought: "The vast majority of mankind is entirely biased by motives of self-interest."

To demonstrate that America herself would not be bankrupted, Hamilton argued that the widely diversified economic potentials of the various colonies could be welded into a self-sufficient economic system. Like many another patriot writer, he urged that America make her own manufactures rather than import them. There was much here that foreshadowed his later economic conceptions, but Hamilton did not visualize any of the complicated expedients—credit, capital, banks—that would be needed to make his dream come true. The teen-ager saw economic institutions rising from mere acts of will.*[12]

Seabury had written his whole pamphlet as if it were a personal exhortation to an audience of farmers. Hamilton wrote the first two thirds of his reply largely as an impersonal argument, and then went over the whole ground a second time, now in his own voice. He mocked his opponent's pretense to be a farmer—he was "some ministerial emissary that has assumed the name to deceive you"—and went on to say: "I despise all false pretensions and mean arts. . . . 'Tis my maxim to let the plain, naked truth speak for itself; and if men won't listen to it 'tis their own fault; they must be contented to suffer for it. I am neither merchant nor farmer."[13]

The cockiness Hamilton had shown as a small boy in lecturing Cruger's sea captain reappeared as the teen-ager lectured the farmers of New York. When writing of the patriot leaders, he slipped into the pronoun "we."

Seabury had planned three pamphlets. The second, which came out almost simultaneously with Hamilton's, was a special plea to the merchants of New York. By the time he brought out the third, Hamilton's *A Full Vindication* had attracted so much attention that Seabury presented his *A View of the Controversy* as "A Letter To the Author of A Full Vindication."

The mature debater pounced on such gaucheries as Hamilton's contention that the Continental Congress had a right to demand unquestioned obedience. The Congress, Seabury pointed out, was "founded in sedition," and in any case an Englishman had a right to criticize any governmental body. He challenged "A Friend to America" to define what he meant by natural rights. "In a state of nature," Seabury argued, "the weak must submit to the strong. Justice, liberty are created by political institutions." The right to legislate for yourself was not a natural right. It was not an inherent right of colonies. He quoted from various American colonial charters to demonstrate that no such privilege had been granted by the British government. As for New York, it had no charter and was thus completely excluded from making any legal claim against British prerogatives.

---

* Modern admirers of fur coats may be interested by Hamilton's argument concerning the advantages of the fur trade: "A suit of skins would not be quite so elegant as one of broadcloth, but it would shelter us from the inclemency of the winter full as well."[14]

Hamilton, Seabury continued, was unjustified in trying to make a distinction between King and Parliament. The Crown, the Lords, and the Commons were indivisible, a single government. They fostered and protected the colonies, and had a right, in return, to fealty. To deny this fealty was an effort to break the bonds of the empire and was thus, whatever the professed intention, a move towards independence, a move that every loyal British subject must abhor.[15]

For an eighteen-year-old immigrant, who had been on the American continent less than two years and had been a convert to the cause for less than one, Hamilton's *A Full Vindication* had been an amazing example of audacity. However, the evidence indicates that he had undertaken the task in high spirits, with no sense of inadequacy. The studies he had made to determine what was his own position had shown him that, although the other colonies teemed with anti-British publications, no adequate answer had appeared in lukewarm New York to such Tory sallies as the Farmer's. There was a vacuum to be filled. Surely, if Hamilton put down on paper the points that had convinced him, he would convince others! He did not hesitate to entitle his essay a "full" vindication, and went on glibly page after page. Having overcome so many obstacles just to be sitting at the table where he was writing, he could not, as a rational human being, feel any need for modesty.

But when the appearance of the pamphlet showed his face before the public, he was bothered by faults. His publisher, James Rivington, doubled as editor of the *New York Gazette;* Hamilton induced him to run in the newspaper an errata list.[16] Rivington was also Seabury's publisher. He may have leaked to Hamilton that the Farmer's new blast was going to be an attack on his publication. In any case, Hamilton now dived into the first of those Herculean periods of preparation that were, as the years passed, to precede his major state papers. He made a more intense study of the publications of other revolutionary pamphleteers, examined what relevant books he could find in the King's College library, reconsidered and sorted out his arguments. When, only eighty days after the first, he brought out his second pamphlet, it shows an increase in maturity that could, for an ordinary man, have taken years.

On February 23, 1775, Rivington published *The Farmer Refuted: or A more Impartial and Comprehensive View of the Dispute Between Great Britain and The Colonies, intended as a Further Vindication of Congress; in answer to a Letter from A. W. Farmer,* and so on. It was signed "A Friend of America."

Seabury had accused the author of *A Full Vindication* of lacking that eighteenth-century desideratum, wit. Hamilton was determined to answer this insult at the very start. "Sir," he began, "I resume my pen in reply to the curious epistle you have been pleased to favor me with; and can assure you that, not withstanding I am naturally of a grave and phlegmatic disposition, it has been the source of abundant merriment to me. The spirit that breathes throughout is so rancorous, illiberal, and imperious; the argumentative part of it so puerile and fallacious; the misrepresentation of facts so palpable and flagrant; the criticisms so illiterate, trifling and absurd; the conceits so low, sterile, and splenetic that I will venture to pronounce it one of the most ludicrous performances which has been exhibited to public view during all the present controversy."[17]

When Hamilton got down to his arguments, he did not wander with his previous discursiveness. The text, although more than twice as long as *A Full Vindication*, advances with almost no backcurves or repetition. Its resemblance is to a lawyer's brief. Propositions are clearly stated and discussed, the conclusions then summarized. Determined to refute every one of the Farmer's points, he concocted in each case the best argument he could summon. In answer to the Farmer's sneer, "If you seldom sink into meanness of diction, you never soar into . . . brilliancy of thought," Hamilton stated that brilliancy came most easily to writers like the Farmer, who pursued not fact but fancy. He himself appealed to "judgment."[18] But when, on specific points, fact and reason failed him, Hamilton did not hesitate to take metaphorical leaps. As he paraded historical research to demonstrate that the colonies' charters did not place them under the jurisdiction of Parliament, he found himself confronted by the incontrovertible fact that New York had no charter. Borrowing a metaphor the Reverend Knox had used in one of his sermons, he jumped into the air: "The sacred rights of mankind are not to be rummaged for among old parchments or musty records. They are written as with a sunbeam in the whole *volume* of human nature by the hand of divinity itself, and can never be erased or obscured by mortal power."[19]

Hamilton lectured his opponent: "The fundamental source of all your errors . . . is a total ignorance of the natural rights of mankind." His own backup argument was always "natural rights." Accepting Seabury's challenge that he define these rights, Hamilton cited the supporting authorities to whom revolutionary pamphleteers commonly appealed: Grotius, Pufendorf, Locke, Montesquieu, Blackstone, and the like. He himself had completely discarded the slapdash contention that any exterior interference with the individual was "absolute slavery." Now, his argument was that of the most eloquent patriots: the "Supreme Being" had given every man "an inviolable right to personal liberty and personal safety." Government had grown up as a voluntary compact between the ruler and the ruled "for the security of the *absolute rights* of the latter." Thus, to usurp rule away from the people to their own despite "is to violate that law of nature."[20]

This line of thinking led the future conservative to advocate world revolution: "The nations of Turkey, Russia, France, Spain, and all other despotic kingdoms in the world, have an inherent right, whenever they please, to shake off the yoke of servitude (though sanctified by the immemorial usage of their ancestors) and to model their government upon the principles of civil liberty."[21]

The Farmer's trouble was that, being a disciple of Hobbes's, he contended that Natural Man was a savage and that moral obligations were created by civil institutions, by government. The youth charged his opponent (possibly the Anglican minister who was president of his own college!) with, in effect, denying the existence of God. "To grant that there is a supreme intelligence who rules the world and has established laws to regulate the actions of his creatures; and still to assert that man in a state of nature may be considered free from all restrictions of *law* and *government* appear to a common understanding altogether unreconcilable."[22]

Hamilton was not only taking for granted what his mentor Knox argued—the falsity of the Presbyterian conception that only a small minority were endowed with God's grace—he was denying original sin. Indeed, his contention that a state of nature was a state of virtue because a beneficent deity willed it so, reflected the heretical romantic thinking that we today associate with the French philosopher Rousseau. Hamilton even appealed for the highest wisdom not to trained intelligence but "a common understanding." However, the young man was far from consistent. In arguing that Parliament would not beneficently give the welfare of America equal weight with the interests of its own constituents, he quoted Hume's contention that, for the purposes of government, *"every man must be supposed a knave."*[23]

Hamilton, of course, cited examples of British "tyranny" and drew the conclusion that they "revealed an inveterate design to extinguish the liberties of America." He argued again, although now with more information to display, that a boycott of trade with British possessions was an effective weapon, not a boomerang. He wrapped himself in the British flag as a defender of the British constitution, while standing up, as before, for the revolt's illegal governing bodies. All these points were not original with him, but the standard rhetoric of the time.

Hamilton followed the others in repeating his denial that America was aiming at independence, yet he recognized deep-seated causes of conflict between America and England. Parliament, ever jealous of the rising power of the colonies, had to be opposed to keep her from clipping America's wings. But if America's wings were not clipped, the colonies would become richer and more powerful than the mother country. What then? Hamilton did not go beyond warning England to behave herself now, since she would eventually need American friendship more than America needed hers.

Hamilton's preview of what would happen if fighting broke out was uncannily prophetic. Recognizing that Spain and France could find "no more desirable object" than that England should lose her colonies, he stated that even if these powers avoided an open rupture with England, they would "undoubtedly take very clandestine methods to introduce among us" the supplies most needed. If, as was barely possible, such action proved contrary to existing treaties, that would make little difference: "The promises of princes and statesmen . . . never bind them longer than till a strong temptation offers." And America might well "throw itself into the arms of its [former] enemies."

Although Hamilton did not foresee the Hessians, he recognized (although his estimate of fifteen thousand men was low) that the manpower England could send to America was limited, and would be tremendously inferior to American possibilities. The British had, it is true, professional officers but many were "effeminate striplings . . . who are better calculated to marshal the forces of *Venus* than to conduct the sturdy sons of *Mars*." America had veterans of the French and Indian War and, in any case, men of "sense and courage" would soon make excellent officers.[24]

Most amazingly, Hamilton outlined the strategy it would take General Washington two years of bitter defeat to work out, the very strategy that was to establish Washington's military fame and win the war. "The circumstances of our country," Hamilton wrote, "put it in our power to evade a pitched battle. It will be better policy to harass and exhaust the [English] soldiery by frequent skirmishes and incursions than to take the open field with them, by which means they would have the full benefit of their superior regularity and skill. Americans are better qualified for that kind of fighting, which is most adapted to this country, than regular troops. Should the soldiery advance into the country, as they would be obliged to do, . . . their discipline would be of little use to them." Furthermore, "there is a certain enthusiasm in liberty that makes human nature rise above itself in acts of bravery and heroism. . . . We have a recent instance in Corsica to what lengths a people will go in defense of its liberties, and if we take a view of the Colonies in general, we must perceive that the pulse of Americans beats high in their country's cause. . . . Superior numbers joined to natural intrepidity, and that animation which is inspired by a desire of freedom and a love of one's country" might well, Hamilton concluded, overbalance all British advantages.

Concerning matters for which he was later to become most famous, Hamilton was now the least prophetic. He foresaw none of the difficulties which America's diffused agrarian economy would suffer in trying to concentrate into the single area the supplies needed to support a large army. "Our country," he stated, as if that solved the matter, "abounds in provisions."

The greatest danger in case of war, Hamilton wrote (as Washington was to write again and again), was not British action but disunion among Americans: "It is more than probable," he concluded, "that America is able to support its freedom, even by force of arms, if she is not betrayed by her own sons."[25]

The Reverend T. B. Chandler, the rector of the Episcopal church at Elizabethtown, who, of course, knew Hamilton, did not know that the youth had written the pamphlets, as his annotated copy of *The Farmer Refuted* reveals.[26] Mulligan tells us that the pamphlets were generally attributed to Hamilton's Elizabethtown patron William Livingston. However, there could have been no purposeful conspiracy of silence since Troup tried to inform the president of Hamilton's college who was, of course, suspected of being "the Farmer." Cooper refused to believe that his pupil was the author. He insisted that John Jay must be responsible, "it being absurd to imagine that so young a man . . . could have written it."[27]

The actual "Farmer," Seabury, seems to have known the truth. He laughed at his opponent for "the airs and importance you give yourself," as if he were "a man of consequence," at least a committeeman. And in mocking Hamilton's use of the expression "sweet sir," Seabury asked, "Pray was you in the nursery, where the whole conversation turns on *sweets* and *goodies* when you happily lit on that expression?"[28]

That the political ideas Hamilton expressed were not consistent was a reflection of his reading; the pamphlets of the American polemicists were a grab bag of many mutually inconsistent ideas. As a group, the

Americans had been washed out of their normal mental habitations as by a river that had overflowed. They were found clinging to all kinds of solid objects and driftwood all along the stream—some moored, some rushing by on a rapid current, some spinning in whirlpools, some almost motionless in backwaters. Except for those dedicated to one or another extreme, it was a period of expediency, anger, worry, fear, excitement, belligerence, compromise. Hamilton, a newcomer who had picked up a cause that had fortuitously been thrown into his path, who had never previously concerned himself with such considerations, was less deeply involved than the others, but he caught from them their emotional tone.

Although his effusions, which were never picked up for reprinting in other colonies, struck a minor note in the Continental cacophony of pamphlets, his were the principal documents on the patriot side specifically addressed to New York. When the colonies tended to feel themselves separate from their neighbors, this was a considerable distinction that surely impressed those who knew he was the author. Marius Willett, an outstanding Son of Liberty and a leader of the New York City radicals, remembered (or so Gertrude Atherton would have us believe) that "Hamilton, after these great writings, became our oracle."[29]

8

The War Tunes Up

[APRIL, 1775–JANUARY, 1776   AGES 18–19]

AFTER the battles of Lexington and Concord had brought war to the Continent, Lieutenant Governor Colden complained to his masters in London, "The spirit of arming and military parade still runs high in the city."[1]

With his King's College companions Troup and Nicholas Fish, Hamilton joined what seems to have been the most elite of several volunteer companies. It certainly had the most experienced commander. Captain Thomas Fleming had been the adjutant of a regular British regiment. He had married into the De Lancey family, important in New York, and was now, Troup remembered, "ardently attached to the American cause."[2]

The "young gentlemen" who had banded together to practice under this "excellent disciplinarian" seemed to have called themselves the Corsicans in memory of the guerrilla activity on that island. Every morning, Hamilton donned a short green coat; pinned over his left breast a tin heart on which was written "God and our Right"; put on his head a small, round leather hat, cocked on one side, which bore the legend "Liberty or Death." He hurried, musket in hand, to St. George's churchyard, where he maneuvered among the graves for "a considerable time." His companions remembered that he became "exceedingly expert" in marching, ramming powder and shot down his gunbarrel, and pretending to fire. His excitement and passion revealed that "the military spirit" infused his "heart."[3]

The population of New York remained divided, not only between loyalists and rebels, but within the rebel cause itself. Gentlemen like Livingston and Jay remained moderates who wished to proceed cautiously. The extremists, known as "the Liberty Boys," were frequenters of the waterfront taverns and often possessed too little property to vote. They were eager to hurry things along. Anglican clergymen suspected of being in secret Tory propagandists were among their principal hates.

In late April, 1775, the New York press carried a letter, signed "Three Millions," which accused the president of King's College, Miles Cooper, and four other "obnoxious gentlemen" of responsibility for the blood being shed in Massachusetts. The "parricides" were warned that patriotic Americans could no longer satisfy their resentment by hanging villains in effigy: "Fly for your lives or anticipate your doom by becoming your own executioners." Cooper fled to a British frigate in the harbor but returned after a few days to his college.[4]

On the night of May 10, Hamilton and Troup were awakened in their college room by shouts. Hurrying to a window, they saw a "pale moon" above and below a moving forest of torches. Some two hundred Liberty Boys had broken down the outer gate of the college yard and were advancing with cudgels and roaring mouths. Hamilton and Troup, having ascertained that Cooper had been warned, dashed downstairs. Hamilton stood between the mob and the door. "He proceeded," Troup remembered, "with great animation and eloquence to harangue the mob on the excessive impropriety of their conduct, and the disgrace it would bring on the cause of liberty, of which they avowed themselves to be the champions." Thus Hamilton "arrested, for a little while, the proceedings," thereby enabling Cooper to get away.

Cooper fled to England, never to return.[*5]

On June 25, 1775, Hamilton saw for the first time the man who was to be, as he himself stated, the "aegis" of his great career.

The Continental Congress, after much hesitation and with perturbation of spirit, had finally adopted the army that was fighting in Massachusetts—but not by a direct vote. They sidled into the decision by electing a Virginian commander in chief. George Washington was to

---

* That a rhymed account of this adventure, which Cooper published in the *Gentleman's Magazine,* does not mention Hamilton's intervention has worried scholars, but need not. Cooper was undoubtedly too busy getting out the back way to observe what was happening on the other side of the large building.

pass through New York on the way to his command in Cambridge. The date of his expected arrival was unfortunate, since the royal governor of the province, William Tryon, was expected back from England on the same day.

Although New York's Provincial Congress had illegally displaced the more conservative Assembly, such was the state of public opinion that the congressmen did not dare show a preference for Washington. It was ruled that the patriot commander, who was approaching through New Jersey, should cross the Hudson to the edge of the city furthest from the harbor. A company of militia would await him. Another company would await Tryon at his harbor landing. The remaining six companies, stationed halfway between, would hurry to greet whichever man landed first.

Wishing to calm rather than encourage controversy, Tryon stayed on his ship, allowing Washington the honor. Hamilton had no official position that entitled him to be among the group who greeted the Commander in Chief's party as they stepped off the Hoboken Ferry, and then went for lunch to the nearby mansion of a brewer. However, he was certainly present at the parade, which went downtown along the bank of the Hudson and by King's College.

Past the watching youth there first moved several hundred militiamen, many of whom Hamilton knew, marching sloppily to fifes and drums. They were followed by the members of the Provincial Congress and various committeemen, all familiar faces. Then there loomed on horseback the man Hamilton most wanted to see. General Washington's head towered above the other horsemen since he was, for the time, very tall. His body was heavy, yet he rode with a surety and grace that, in a generation when everyone rode horseback, attracted admiration wherever he rode. His face was massive, sober, and benign. His response to the cheers was as restrained as perfect courtesy would allow.

Behind Washington rode two other major generals. Charles Lee was a scarecrow figure, almost as tall as Washington but very thin. He gestured to the crowd frenetically and his horse was followed by several dogs. To the third general Hamilton probably paid less attention because he had surely seen him before. General Philip Schuyler was an extremely ugly man—tiny, beadlike eyes under shaggy brows, a bulbous nose in a red face—but his uniform was perfect and he hardly deigned to notice the crowd. The possessor of huge estates near Albany, he was one of the richest and most powerful men in the colony of New York. The refugee from a demeaning West Indian childhood would have leapt with joy had he realized that this aristocrat would one day be his father-in-law.

After the generals came some staff officers and then some young men in bright uniforms: the Philadelphia Light Horse, who had served as an escort across New Jersey. Making up the rear was a crowd of spectators who had fallen in behind the parade. Hamilton undoubtedly joined this crowd. With the others, he turned into Broadway and advanced down that handsome, tree-lined boulevard to Hull's Tavern, on the west side of the street not far north of Trinity Church. The officials all crowded into the tavern.

Word came out that the General was receiving. In those days, there were no invitation lists for such receptions. Those who felt themselves entitled to appear, automatically did so, while others did not presume to intrude. Hamilton certainly considered himself entitled. Someone who knew about his propaganda activities may well have called him especially to the attention of the Commander in Chief. He would have been greeted with a bow, an affable smile, and a few words that were friendly without in any way inviting intimacy.

The occasion was in full swing when a whisper went around that Tryon was arriving a few blocks away, at the foot of Broad Street. It was amusing to see which of the guests, wishing to hedge their bets, slipped as inconspicuously as they could out of Washington's presence. Hamilton must have been torn between his loyalty to the patriot cause and his natural curiosity. History does not report which impulse triumphed.[6]

Shortly after Washington had moved on towards Boston, an effort was made to recruit the four regiments in the Continental service that Congress had demanded of New York. Alexander McDougall, who had presided at the meeting in The Fields, where Hamilton is reputed to have spoken, became colonel of the first regiment. Hamilton's drillmaster, Fleming, was nominated lieutenant colonel of the second. Hamilton's collegemate Fish went in as a lieutenant. There was much beating of drums and shouting of recruiting officers, but the results were disappointing. The New Yorkers were extremely slow to enlist.

One would expect that Hamilton, who had as a boy yearned for a war and was always to visualize himself as a warrior, would have been among the first to seek a commission. Why he did not can only be presumed. For one thing, he was following the fashion. The rich and socially prominent New Yorkers stayed in their volunteer companies, early in 1776, until their own colony was seriously threatened.[7] Troup, who was to become a colonel in the Continental Army, did not enlist at the first call, and Fleming refused his Continental commission. He continued, so one gathers, to drill the Corsicans, which meant that Hamilton could go on with his training as an infantryman. However, the studious and ambitious Hamilton had already concluded that he could serve more effectively and more conspicuously if he used his studies with Harpur, the professor of mathematics, to acquire, with the help of special manuals, complicated skills which the fledgling American military greatly lacked. He would become an artilleryman. Hamilton was furthermore engaged in essential nonmilitary service. He was to remember that at "early periods of the war near half of them [the New Yorkers] were avowedly more attached to Great Britain than to their liberty."

Here was the basic problem. Colonel McDougall did not join his regiment. It was considered more important for him to exert, as a member of the Provincial Assembly, his influence with the class of self-made merchants to which he belonged. Hamilton was continuing his propaganda activities. Just before Washington passed through the city, the youth had published in *Rivington's New-York Gazette* a two-part attack on the Quebec Act. This British ruling granted the French Canadians free exercise of the Roman Catholic religion and reestablished French civil law in "Quebec," which was extended to include the territory between the Ohio and the Mississippi. Hamilton protested the resulting denial of English civil liberties, argued that Catholicism had been made the established religion of Canada, and reasoned that, since no Protestants would submit while Catholic immigrants would be drawn in from all over Europe, a Papist state was being created to encompass Protestant America "with innumerous hosts of neighbors, disaffected to them both because of religion and government. How dangerous" this would be, "let every man of common sense judge."[8]

In presenting this argument Hamilton, unlike many other patriot propagandists, limited himself to political considerations, making no religious slurs against Catholicism.[9]

Patriot ardor was dampened by a high, floating wall, bristling with cannon, forever visible in New York Harbor. The *Asia* was a major British warship carrying sixty-four guns. That she could, at any moment, loose a salvo of fire shells that would burn the city down presented an inescapable problem to all Revolutionary activity. How far could the tail of the British lion be twisted before the captain of the *Asia* decided to intervene? Naturally, the most extreme Revolutionaries, including the Liberty Boys who had little property to lose should the city burn, were the most willing to take the risk. Their leader was Isaac Sears.

Originally from Connecticut, Sears exemplified in lukewarm New York the extremism of New England,* and he used his control of the mob as a goad to push ahead his more moderate fellow members of the Provincial Congress. After it had been decided to close the Hudson to British shipping by constructing forts, Sears put through a motion impowering a subcommittee to procure cannon. In the middle of the following night, August 23, he led a motley group of patriots in an effort to carry away the British cannon from the old Grand Battery, which looked out over the harbor and was itself surveyed by the more numerous, more modern, and more effective guns that in three tiers protruded from the *Asia*.

If Mulligan's testimony is to be believed, Hamilton could not resist taking part in this caper. Heavy physical labor was required because the cannon, weighing more than a ton apiece, were naval guns mounted on tiny wheels unsuited to cross-country hauling. It was particularly difficult to manhandle them up the hill between Bowling Green and Wall Street. As Mulligan tugged, Hamilton appeared, asked his friend to hold his musket, and then took the older man's place on the rope.

The noise—the rumbling and squeaking of the little wheels, the shouting of men—was considerable. Soon the Liberty Boys espied only a little way out in the bay one of the *Asia*'s boats, on the watch with its sails down. The two groups of armed men stared at each other across the slightly glistening water, and finally they fired. The sloop raised its sail and vanished with on board a mortally wounded man. Soon isolated bursts of fire lighted the dim shape of the *Asia*. A few solid shots were released, and then several cannon loads of grape sped over the heads of the toilers.

Hamilton was pulling away on a rope in a street back from the waterfront when the explosions out in the harbor kindled, as if by magic, lights in the windows around him. Alarm drums sounded and there was a great running of persons. But Hamilton and his companions continued to drag away their cannon.

After a pause, which implied that the captain was waiting to see if the Liberty Boys would desist, the *Asia* let go with a full broadside of thirty-four guns. As the sounds echoed and reechoed, Hamilton ap-

* While New York dawdled, Connecticut had filled its quota for the Continental Army in ten days.

peared beside Mulligan, who was hurrying towards safety. Hamilton asked for his musket. When Mulligan acknowledged that he had dropped it behind him, Hamilton "went for it, notwithstanding the firing continued, with as much unconcern as if the vessel were not there."

The *Asia's* captain had wished to frighten the inhabitants but to avoid supplying the patriot propagandists with an "atrocity." He therefore aimed the shots above the houses and little damage was done. Hamilton was not touched. And the matter soon took on an element of farce.

The Provincial Congress regretted the incitation that had been given the British, but could not hide the evidence. The eleven stolen cannon were, in the words of Bruce Bliven, Jr., "as conspicuous in the main public square as a herd of elephants." To put them back on their emplacements would be humiliating and extremely difficult. To move them to any fort on the Hudson without further British intervention would be impossible. Governor Tryon, still conciliatory, agreed that the cannon could stay where they were. There they stayed.[10]

The stranded guns, pointing aimlessly at nothing, which Hamilton passed daily as the rope burns on his hands healed, were symbolic of the stagnation into which New York had fallen.

Citizens who were rich enough to do so—even members of the Continental Congress—had moved their families to the country. The areas usually most elegant and gay were dreary: doors locked and windows boarded up. Many of the younger men were absent, fighting in Canada. When October came around, the extent to which life had changed became doubly clear. October was the time for the autumn importation from London, when luxuries had crowded the stores and the newest fashions in furniture and clothes were unveiled to eager colonial eyes. But now there were no imports from London. Ladies did not come sailing down the Hudson from their manor houses; rural storekeepers did not crowd in to replenish their stocks. Hamilton saw a sight he would normally have regarded as inconceivable: the Coffee House, where wine was drunk and business done and news exchanged, where in November no seats could usually be found, remained dark at night because there was not enough business to pay for the candles. Perhaps there sank deep down in the mind of the young man who had championed nonimportation the contrary conception: trade with England was the lifeline of agreeable aristocratic living in America.

An effort of the Provincial Congress to expand its franchise through a new election boomeranged. New Yorkers were so confused that few voted, and many counties did not even bother to hold the election. Not enough members were chosen for the new congress to make a quorum. And Governor Tryon, who had moved onto a merchant vessel under the guns of the *Asia,* allowed royal authority to lapse. The colony was drifting without any government.[11]

Sears decided to take matters into his own hands, with the assistance of zealots from the colony in which he had grown up. He led some hundred men across the New York border from Connecticut. Having arrested Seabury and two other Westchester leaders considered Tories, Sears's men advanced into Manhattan Island, where they were joined by about a hundred Liberty Boys. Their objective was now Rivington's printing establishment. Although Rivington had published Hamilton's pamphlets, the burden of what the printer brought out was considered to be Tory, and he had personally insulted Sears by hardly ever mentioning the radical without commenting on the size of his ears.

The printer was not available for capture, but the mob set to work spilling his files, wrecking his presses, and carrying away his type. On a raised platform in the middle of Wall Street, which was the site of an outdoor market, a crowd gathered to cheer. According to Mulligan, Hamilton found a conspicuous position from which he shouted admonitions against such lawless action. If so, he did not succeed in making himself heard. Contemporary accounts state that no one made the least effort to intervene.[12]

After the event, the City Committee, which was as much government as New York had, protested what they called an unprovoked "hostile" invasion of New York from another colony. Hamilton took it upon himself to write directly to Jay, who was representing New York in the Continental Congress: "I like not to see potent neighbors indulge in the practice of making inroads at pleasure into this or any other province." New England was "very populous and powerful." Fear of New England's domination was, as Jay knew, a principal reason for New York's "disaffection" to the patriot cause. These "ancient animosities" should not be encouraged, nor should the idea be allowed to circulate that New York was so lukewarm that there was a need for interference from outside. Such interference could only "breed division and quarreling."

Hamilton made no mention of the kidnapping of his polemical opponent, Seabury, or the other Westchester worthies. He did not refer to freedom of publication. He denounced his former publisher as a "detestable" character, whose press had been "dangerous and pernicious."*

What worried Hamilton was the "great danger" that the commotions would lead to "fatal extremes." When "the due medium is hardly to be found among the more intelligent," he commented, "it is almost impossible among the more unthinking populace." Also, "the same state of passions which fits the multitude, who have not sufficient stock of reason and knowledge to guide them, for opposition to tyranny and oppression, very naturally leads them to contempt and disregard for all authority. . . . When the minds of these are loosened from their attachment to ancient establishments and courses, they seem to grow giddy and are apt more or less to run into anarchy. These principles, too true in themselves, and confirmed to me both by reading and my own experience, deserve extremely the attention of those who have the direction of public affairs." He himself was "always more or less alarmed at everything which is done from mere will and pleasure, without any proper authority."

In a forecast of his long-range view, Hamilton called for intervention from the center. Although Jay was his elder and a member of the Continental Congress, the youth fell naturally into a didactic, preaching tone: "Many ill consequences will be prevented if your body gently interposes a check for the future. . . . A favorable idea will be impressed of your justice and impartiality in discouraging the encroachments of one province on another. . . . Believe me, sir, it is a matter of consequence and deserves serious attention."

Hamilton admitted that the Tories were growing "insolent and clamorous. . . . Let your body station in different parts of the province most tainted . . . a few regiments of troops" raised anywhere but in New England. "The pretense for this would be plausible" since there was reason to believe that the British ministry might soon attack New York. Then Hamilton propounded a concept that was to make him trouble throughout his entire career: because there would be "some order and regularity" in such action, there would be no grounds for objection.[13]

Although Jay's convictions were close to Hamilton's, he realized that Congress would be accused of encroaching if it made any effort to intervene between one colony and another. Ignoring the suggestion that outsiders should curb New York's Tories, he wrote McDougall

---

* Only in the twentieth century has it been discovered that Rivington was a secret patriot who spied for Washington.

that New York herself would have to make the protest against Sears's invasion.[14]

Jay probably wrote Hamilton in much the same vein. The letter is lost, but we know that the congressman asked the youth to keep sending him "information concerning the state of the province or any matters of importance that may arise." Hamilton "gladly" agreed.[15]

During December, 1775, more than six months after Hamilton's second attack on the Farmer had been printed, Jay wrote McDougall, who was still acting as a leader of the New York Provincial Congress, "I hope Mr. Hamilton keeps busy. I have not received Holt's newspaper these three months and thus cannot judge of the progress he makes."[16]

Troup tells us that Hamilton wrote many "political tracts," some published as pamphlets and others as articles in newspapers, "particularly the newspaper edited by John Holt [*The New York Journal or General Advertiser*]. . . . This printer, by his zeal for the American cause, drew upon himself all the invectives of the ministerial writers." Hamilton defended Holt (whose newspaper had a "poet's corner") "by burlesquing his antagonists in doggerel rhyme with great wit and humor."[17]

The publications Troup mentions are unidentifiable in the welter of printed controversy. Although in mocking Seabury's pretense at being a farmer Hamilton had written that he despised all such "false pretensions and mean arts,"[18] he was clearly publishing over a variety of noms de plume. This was the propaganda practice of the time; it enabled a writer to pretend to be whatever variety of citizen would most effectively espouse certain ideas, and would also make one man appear to be many acting in concert.

An aspect of Hamilton's practice is revealed in a letter to Jay. "I have much reason to suspect that the Tories have it in contemplation to steal a march upon us." They intended inconspicuously to hold an election for the legally established but presently sidetracked New York Provincial Assembly, hoping that the patriots were too concerned with their own institutions to notice, thus permitting them to slip in their own candidates. "I have thrown out a handbill or two to give the necessary alarm, and shall second them with others."

Hamilton wished that Jay and the other Continental congressmen from New York would come back and stand in the election, thus attracting attention to it.[19] Four days later, he wrote Jay again to emphasize his advice. "I shall be glad to see you here with all convenient dispatch."[20]

These communications, written as 1775 gave way to 1776, bring to an end existing records of Hamilton's activity as a youthful propagandist—and also as a student at King's College. He is to reappear as he changes his pen for a sword—or rather for the cannon's mouth.

9

At Last, a Soldier

[JANUARY–MAY, 1776   AGE 19]

THE war in Massachusetts—Washington encircling Boston and the British fortified within—was a stalemate that rendered the British army useless. However, employing their available ships, the enemy could sail without challenge (the patriots had no navy) to any part of America the ocean touched. During December, 1775, they seemed to be preparing for a move. Both logic and rumor indicated that they would come to New York which, because of its tremendous harbor and deep surrounding rivers, was the perfect base for a power that controlled the waters.

Frantic efforts were taken for defense. Washington sent down from Cambridge his second-in-command, Charles Lee, who brought with him some Connecticut soldiers. Hamilton did not object to their presence because they had been sent by what he approved of: official orders. A regiment also came in (as he had suggested) from New Jersey. It was under the command of his old Elizabethtown patron, Lord Stirling.

When the streets filled with troops, when earthworks were going up everywhere, when danger actually threatened, civilians seemed out of place. Recruiting for the Continental Army picked up. On January 6, 1776, the Provincial Congress decided to create an artillery company, not in the Continental service but in their own. They commissioned a lieutenant to start recruiting, but were at.a loss for an officer well enough versed in artillery to serve as captain. Hamilton returned with redoubled ardor to his studies. In about seven weeks, he considered himself ready.

It was February 23, 1776, when McDougall recommended to the Provincial Congress Hamilton's appointment as captain. If he were approved, Hamilton would be New York's top artillery officer. The Congress postponed his election until he could be examined by Captain Stephen Badlam, Lee's artillery expert.[1]

In the meanwhile, what would normally have been considered a better opportunity opened. Stirling, who was residing in his own extremely elegant New York town house, had been elevated to brigadier general and appointed to succeed Lee as commander of New York. He offered Hamilton, whom he had known since shortly after the boy had appeared from the West Indies, the post of brigade major. Not only did a major outrank a captain but, as chief of Stirling's staff, Hamilton would be associated with the top command. Furthermore, he could continue his political and propaganda activities; Stirling could only be pleased by his closeness to the New York civilian regime, with which Lee had got into hot water. True, Stirling would probably be superseded by a more experienced general if New York actually were attacked, but he would surely continue to play important roles in which Hamilton would share.[2]

Explaining that he was committed to the artillery captaincy (for which he had, in fact, not yet been qualified), Hamilton turned Stirling down.[3] This could hardly have been due to any deep-seated personal objection to the man who would have been his superior. Stirling was a patrician, a breed Hamilton liked; as a governor of King's College he must have approved of Hamilton's untrammeled admission there; concerned with mathematics, he had written a report on the transit of Venus; far from being an overbearing martinet, he admitted himself in military matters an "amateur." What if he drank too much? Hamilton was no prude.

The young man's motivation was clearly pride. He wanted to find his own glory on the field of battle. The decision was all the more remarkable because Hamilton had in his own right no auspices. He had no important relative in all North America. He still had some money in reserve, but the dislocations of war would surely bar his receiving any further funds from the West Indies.

A few days after he had turned Stirling down, Hamilton appeared for his examination. Captain Badlam's source of artillery information was the same as Hamilton's—books. He was impressed with the youth, but could not realize that this interrogation would remain the most conspicuous act of his life, to be mentioned at his funeral, thirty-nine years later. Having received Badlam's certification, Hamilton was commissioned.

McDougall, in his role as provincial congressman, agreed to handle the payroll of what was designated "the artillery company of this colony." No higher officer stood between the youth and the legislature. It was within Hamilton's character to insist—perhaps when he held the alternate offer from Stirling—on independent status. He was as free of superiors as any captain could hope to be.[4]

Biographers have endlessly repeated Mulligan's statement that Hamilton's commission depended on his raising thirty men: "I went with him that very afternoon and engaged twenty-five," Hamilton offering to equip them "with his own funds." But muster roles reveal that there were already some fifty men in the company when Hamilton took over and that only five were added at that time.

At the first drill, the new captain was revolted by the sounds emitted by the fife and drum corps. After the drummer, Robert Finton, was persuaded "voluntarily" to enter the ranks, Hamilton enlisted James Galloway to strengthen the fifes. He had been in command less than a week when he discharged Lewis Ryan for "being subject to fits." The boyish commander discharged another Irishman, Matthew O'Hara, "for misbehavior."[5]

The military vehicle that Hamilton intended to use for the first stage of his trip to reknown as a soldier was discouragingly shabby. Most of his company wore coarse blue coats over whatever trousers they had brought with them when they enlisted. Hamilton purchased heavily: seventy-five buckskin trousers; sixteen gross and eight dozen buttons (probably brass); quantities of various colors of fabrics for coats, waistcoats, linings; shoes and hats. An advertisement for the return of a deserter from Hamilton's company stated that he was wearing "a deep blue coat turned up with buff, a pair of leather breeches, and a new felt hat."[6]

Charles Lefferts, the pictorial historian of Revolutionary uniforms, synthesized the evidence concerning Hamilton's company to draw a most stylish figure in a gracefully molded three-cornered hat with a cockade; stock and boots black; a blue coat with long swallowtails; a buff collar merging into a lapel of the same color that extended down to the waist and was copiously decorated with brass buttons. The white with which the coat was lined reappeared in the shoulder belts that crossed over the chest and descended to the hips. Equipment dangled from these, and a musket hung from a separate shoulder strap of leather.

The captain bought for himself more elegant materials at several times the cost. His trousers were made of a white fabric rather than the tougher buckskin needed for troops who would actually labor.[7]

As an officer, Hamilton paid in cash for his own uniform, but the cost of his men's clothes was by regulation to be stopped from their wages. Either because they protested their captain's extravagance or because he himself realized that it was unfair to charge them in full for what went so far beyond necessity, Hamilton absorbed the large sum of £76 18s. We are told (believably) that his expenditure exhausted what remained of his most recent and surely final remittance from his West Indian sponsors. It was not in his temperament to hold back anything when ambition and enthusiasm called.[8]

Since there was still no fighting, a corps could be most conspicuous through their appearance in drill. Troup remembered that Hamilton "with indefatigable pains" made his company perfect "in every branch of discipline and duty; and it was not long before it was esteemed the most beautiful model of discipline in the whole army."[9]

As an artillerist, Hamilton had more to offer the spectator than did infantry officers. The refinements of marching were the same, but instead of the simultaneous handling of muskets he could display the much more various and complicated service of cannon, impressive even if, powder being in short supply, there was no culminating flash and boom.

Hamilton's elite corps was exempt from the common occupation of digging. They were assigned to guarding the colony's records.

When Hamilton had served only a month, he had a second opportunity to see George Washington ride into town. But this time the Commander in Chief stayed. Menaced by guns which the Continental Army had placed on Dorchester Heights, the British had evacuated Boston. They had vanished into the ocean, no one knew with certainty whither. Washington's spies reported (as it turned out correctly) that the enemy's immediate intention was to refit at their base in Halifax, yet it seemed certain that their ultimate objective would be New York. The Continental Army flooded in around Hamilton's corps.

There was also an influx of militiamen. Indifferent to the commands of their officers, whom they had often elected in the first place, these temporary soldiers did pretty much what they pleased. Washington perpetually complained that their example undermined the discipline he had painfully inculcated in the Continentals. It is impossible to doubt that Hamilton wished to make clear to the regular officers that his independent company, so conspicuous in its bright and tidy uniforms, was not, like the other non-Continental troops, laxly commanded. He found himself doing this not positively but negatively.

After some undefined dispute with his enlisted men, Hamilton had a sergeant, two corporals, and a private arrested for the serious crime of "mutiny." The court-martial that heard the charges was unimpressed, dealing out very minor punishments. But on what was the very first recorded occasion—April 20, 1776—when Washington mentioned Alexander Hamilton, he supported the artillery captain. Overruling the court, he ordered that the two principal offenders be discharged after they had been "stripped" of the uniforms for which they had not yet paid.[10]

Washington's general orders for May 15 directed Hamilton to muster his company "at ten o'clock next Sunday morning upon the Common."[11] Such musters, held on Sundays when many officers were free to come and watch, were intended to put the various units of the army on public display, for praise or criticism. Washington commonly added weight to the occasions by being present. Since Hamilton had been preparing for such an opportunity with so much expenditure of energy and money, we can visualize the impressiveness of the drill, the almost histrionic snap and elegance of the nineteen-year-old commander.

If Hamilton had no more trouble with his soldiers than most officers, he surely did not have much less. On May 8, John Reling, who had been "confined" for desertion, was caught after having broken from his confinement and was sentenced to six days on bread and water.[12]

On May 9, Hamilton advertised in Holt's newspaper for the return of a deserter called Uriah Chamberlain. Chamberlain had been bred a farmer in New Jersey, was twenty-one years old. He was "nearly five feet eleven inches, a well-set, likely fellow, of a ruddy complexion and usually wears his hair carefully tied." He had departed wearing his company's conspicuous uniform. Whoever brought Chamberlain or effective information to Hamilton's quarters on Chapel Street would be "handsomely rewarded." A week later, the deserter was back. He was stripped to the waist before the company and given thirty-nine lashes.[13]

The same punishment was meted out to another deserter; to a soldier who struck an adjutant; and to still another of Hamilton's men found guilty of stealing.[14] As soon as the Continental Congress agreed to countenance privateering,* the gunners Hamilton had trained slipped away to this more lucrative service in such numbers that the New York Congress authorized Hamilton "to go on board any ship or vessel in this harbor" and take "such guard as may be necessary," to find and reclaim his vanished soldiers.[15]

With Washington's arrival, Hamilton's company had been attached to the Continental artillery regiment commanded by Colonel Henry Knox, but it remained administratively independent. When the Continental pay and rations were raised, Hamilton's men were left out of the order. There were other problems. Hamilton, who had fitted out his company so elegantly, was now either unwilling or unable to pay for "frocks" (long hunting shorts worn outside the trousers) that would enable the uniforms to last longer in actual service. Such difficulties involving a force of less than a hundred men elicited petition after petition from their captain to the Provincial Congress. The legislators, having a thousand larger matters to attend to, eventually became annoyed and insisted that they had voted (which they had never done) that Hamilton's company be administered as part of Colonel Scott's militia regiment. Hamilton had no desire to extend this arrangement to an interference with his command. He kept his company so separate that when in March, 1777, he resigned to become Washington's aide, the New York legislature recognized that the company was now floating in limbo. They then merged it with the Continental service.[16]

After one of his lieutenants had been promoted to the captaincy of a row galley, Hamilton urged the New York Congress to breach the unbroken wall that separated enlisted men from officers. Pointing to the scarcity of artillerymen, he urged that his first sergeant, Thomas Thompson, be elevated to fill the vacancy. "He has discharged his duty in his present station with uncommon fidelity, assiduity, and expertness." He was a good disciplinarian, had seen a good deal of service in Germany, and had, so wrote Hamilton, "a tolerable share of common sense." Social proprieties would not be outraged since the sergeant "is well calculated not to disgrace the rank of an officer and gentleman." Furthermore, "his advancement will be a great encouragement and

---

* Privateering was piracy legalized as an act of war. Vessels commissioned by a belligerent government could capture merchantmen belonging to the other belligerent. The value of the ship and cargo was divided among the privateer's owners and crew. There was no quicker way to get rich.

benefit to my company in particular and will be an animating example to all men of merit to whose knowledge it comes."[17]

Although many ranks in the brand-new patriot army had been granted in the most haphazard manner, the effort was being made to solidify the organization according to the practice of long-existing hierarchical armies. Puzzled about how to proceed, the Congress appointed the patrician Peter R. Livingston to confer with Hamilton. Livingston's report persuaded the Congress. To their acceptance of Thompson's promotion, they added the statement that they would "exert themselves in promoting from time to time, such privates and noncommissioned officers in the service of this state as shall distinguish themselves by their sobriety, valor, and [so it was added lest bumptiousness be encouraged] subordination to their officers. Ordered this resolution be published in the newspapers."[18]

Thus Hamilton's first recorded active effect on legislation favored the upward mobility of the able.* This accorded well with his own past history and his future career.

* Hamilton subsequently recommended Thompson's further promotion. Captain Thompson was killed fighting valiantly at the Battle of Springfield.

IO

Towards Danger and Opportunity

[FEBRUARY–JULY, 1776   AGE 19]

RECEIVING his orders from Colonel Henry Knox, Hamilton came into close contact with the second of the truly major founding fathers—the first had been John Jay—with whom he was to collaborate closely down the years.

Knox, who was only seven years Hamilton's senior, had been almost equally precocious. His father had died in the West Indies, and he became at the age of twelve the sole support of his mother. He worked for a Boston bookseller and at the age of twenty-one started his own bookstore. This was a year after he had intervened in the confrontation that led to the Boston Massacre: he had tried to restrain the British captain from firing on the mob. While, as the Revolution approached, he had drilled in the crack Boston Grenadier Corps (as Hamilton had drilled with Fleming), he caught the eye of Lucy Flucker, daughter of the royal secretary of the colony. The resulting marriage enraged her prosperous Tory family.

Like Hamilton, Knox studied artillery from books, becoming during the siege of Boston (and, as it turned out, for the duration of the war) the commander of that service. Weighing almost three hundred pounds, high-spirited, given to gobbling food and guzzling wine, he was considered by proper Bostonians a "Bacchanalian character," but he was one of those fat men whose weight seems only to contribute to their activity. It was he who had supervised a masterpiece of heavy transport with sledge and horse: the bringing from distant Ticonder-

95

oga of the cannon which Washington had mounted on Dorchester Heights to drive the British from Boston.[1]

Compared to Henry Knox, Hamilton seemed a lath, but he too had a natural flow of high spirits. Knox was impressed into giving Hamilton one of the most important of all the artillery commands.

The fundamental fact that America had no navy but was fighting the world's greatest naval power, made New York a very dangerous berth for Washington's army. On the tip of Manhattan Island, the city faced a perfect anchorage for ships, one of the world's greatest harbors. To make matters worse, the two flanks of the island were washed by deep, tidal rivers. The Hudson (or, as it was then called, the North) River was navigable to large ships all the way up to Albany and the brink of the northern wilderness. Along this river, the Manhattan shoreline was high and rocky, not suited to a waterborne invasion, yet ships that penetrated further up the Hudson could block the city's major avenue for supplies. Along the East River, which flowed into Long Island Sound, were low lands, ideally suited to landing parties. And Manhattan was too long—twelve and a half miles—to be well protected in its entirety by any force Washington could collect. It was, furthermore, so narrow that a successful landing party would not have to march far to draw a line across the island, thereby trapping any patriot garrison in New York City. Neither river could possibly be blocked without putting cannon on the far as well as the near bank. This meant that contiguous areas on Long Island and New Jersey would have to be held, although both land masses were too extensive to be defended in their entirety.

The obvious strategy was for Washington to abandon New York and do what the British had refrained from doing with fire bombs from the *Asia*. He should burn the city. An intact New York would make for an invading sea power an ideal military and naval base. But such purposeful destruction of a major center was not practical politics when the Tory propagandists claimed that the patriot leaders were bloodthirsty zealots who did not care how much the people suffered as long as they could rule. Washington and his army had somehow to hold New York.

The patriot soldiers, most of them farmboys, were at their best wielding shovels. Innumerable earthworks had been thrown up. Many were intended to block streets against invaders, but the all-important first defenses, which might keep the invaders from landing, were

Knox's cannon. To house and protect these, many sod forts were built. In a comprehensive report to Washington, dated June 10, 1776, Knox specified the guns and artillerymen in thirteen forts.

Only the fortifications at the tip of the island, which the patriots had inherited, were built of stone. Fort George, as it was now called (it had borne the names of many kings), had been first built in 1624 by the Dutch authorities of New Amsterdam. For generations, it had filled the function of the fort Hamilton had known at St. Croix: partly defense against invaders, partly a center of civil authority containing such a prison as Hamilton's mother had occupied when jailed by her husband for adultery. When New York grew, administration had expanded out of the fort, but the governor's mansion had remained behind the walls until all the interior buildings had burned in 1773. They had been replaced only by a barracks which, as it pressed against the west wall, was dwarfed by the huge interior courtyard. In February, 1776, General Lee had torn down the entire wall that overlooked the end of Broadway lest "Mr. Tryon and his myrmidons" try to use the fort to terrorize the populace.[2]

Knox entrusted to Hamilton the immediate command of the artillery in Fort George. This fortification was a conventional "star-shaped redoubt": a square that had protruding from each of the four corners a bastion, shaped like the head of a lance, from which marksmen could "enfilade" (sweep with fire) the outside of the adjoining walls. The square was angled so that one side was parallel to the shore of the harbor, the other to the east bank of the Hudson. To this fort Knox assigned some of the patriots' biggest guns, four thirty-two–pounders (they could fire balls of that weight) and two twenty-fours.

Closer to the waterfront there ran across the whole tip of the island and somewhat back along each river a masonry esplanade known as the Grand Battery. This had for generations been the city's principal defense. Here Knox had placed a considerable portion of his cannon, including thirteen thirty-two–pounders and a variety of mortars—the largest of brass with a thirteen-inch barrel—designed not to fire balls a long distance but to lob shells at close range. The command of this fortification, which extended for about a third of a mile, was entrusted to three captains. Hamilton's share was the part of the Grand Battery closest to Fort George and connected to it with a "covered way" (a corridor with bombproof roof). The entire complex was under the top command of Captain John Pierce, who had come down from Boston with Knox and was Hamilton's senior.[3]

97

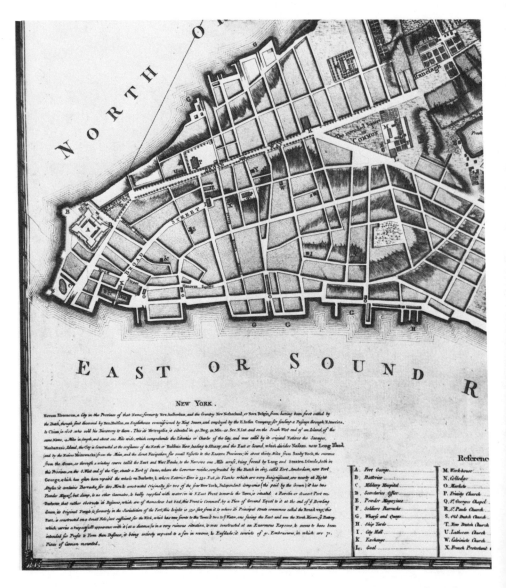

Lower Manhattan: detail of "A Plan of the City of New York" (1775) by John Montresor. At the southwest tip of the island, fronting both the harbor and the North (Hudson) River, is Fort George (marked A), the star-shaped redoubt where Hamilton was artillery commander. B–B is the Grand Battery, which ran across the whole end of the island. The western section, where Hamilton also commanded, was joined to Fort George by a covered way. Courtesy, New-York Historical Society

Washington regarded Fort George and the Grand Battery as the keys to New York. This was because of his conviction, which he assumed the British shared, that the efficient way to take the city was not to nibble in from the edges but by a surprise frontal attack. The enemy fleet would appear suddenly from the ocean and, having sailed at full speed down the harbor, draw up in battle line, using superior fire power to silence the shore guns. Then the infantry would land and complete the conquest.

The shore batteries, behind their ramparts of stone, were less vulnerable than the wooden ships, yet a single ship of the line carried more armament than the whole patriot defense. The best hope was to take advantage of the crucial minutes—if lost never regained—when the invading fleet of square riggers, not yet in a position for effective firing, had to slow down and turn their ships sideways, so that they could bring in play their murderous broadsides.

Never did a man naturally a perfectionist have more actual need to be a martinet than did Hamilton. Theoretically, he would receive some advance warning since Washington had stationed lookouts on the peripheries of the long harbor and on the New Jersey Highlands. During the day, a procession of cannon shots from hilltop to hilltop would carry the alarm with the speed of sound. After dark, there would be the speed of light as a succession of beacons flared. Yet the British effort would be to fool the lookouts, and every kind of slipup was possible. Never was perpetual alertness and inexorable preparedness more required. Hamilton had not been able to fill more than two thirds of his quota of one hundred men. The other artillery companies being similarly undermanned, Washington ordered that they be reinforced from the infantry regiments. The influx of greenhorns into Hamilton's fortification—they made half his force—sent him into paroxysms of drilling.[4]

There were lookouts stationed at Fort George, yet the perfectionist had little faith in anyone else's efficiency. If he were relaxing in the town while the wind blew down the bay, part of his mind would always be on watch for a change of wind. The worse the weather the greater the danger. When a black night or a fog or a heavy rain put sooty hands over telescopes everywhere, Hamilton would stand on his fortification staring out for the appearance, beyond the very edge of his vision, of almost imperceptible shadows.

Before 7 A.M. on June 29, 1776, a relay of signals resulted in Hamilton's cannons alerting the city. The alarm seemed at first false. Hamilton could see no alien sails. Then news came in by mounted messenger that enemy shipping was gathering behind Sandy Hook directly outside the harbor. By evening there were 110 battleships and transports, and as darkness closed in, more sails had been described approaching from the distance. Identification of individual British ships revealed that this was Sir William Howe's force, which Washington had driven from Boston more than three months before.

As New York sweltered under one of her heat waves, the bay was uncannily empty. The American ships recently anchored there had fled up the Hudson and no new ones came in. The British were reported to be still receiving reinforcement, but not so much as a boatswain's barge came in sight. Then, on July 2, 1776, the pageant began.

First—it was the very early morning—three British warships steered through the Narrows (the present site of the Verrazano Bridge). A small patriot battery on the Long Island shore roared and puffed smoke, but the ships sailed smoothly on, not even deigning to fire back. After this prelude there came a procession of tall vessels, as endless as if all England were moving miraculously on New York. The little Long Island battery kept firing, but was utterly ignored until the very last ship, the *Asia,* responded with a few shots that made a discouragingly louder boom than the American cannon.

As Hamilton stared hour after hour through the summer haze, his men standing around the cannon with their matches ready, no ships came directly towards him. The long line veered west to move along the Staten Island shore and then turned at the bottom of the island into Kill Van Kull. Since the sails soon were brailed and furled it was impossible to doubt that the enemy were attempting to land on Staten Island. Although the inhabitants were notorious for Tory leanings, the watching patriots listened eagerly for some sounds that indicated opposition. The hot afternoon was quiet. As the steaming night came down, the British had established possession of a large and fertile land mass, bursting with provisions, that dominated New York Harbor and was separated from the New Jersey mainland by only a narrow channel.

Spies reported common talk among the British officers that this terrifying armada and the troops it had brought were only the lesser part of the British expeditionary force. A larger fleet, commanded by Sir William's brother, Admiral Lord Howe, and a larger army, including German mercenaries (they came to be known as Hessians) were daily expected to appear directly from England.

The present force, so the intelligence reports continued, would make no further moves until the reinforcements arrived. But this might well be false information, circulated to lull American fears, and Hamilton could no longer hope for advance warning from distant lookouts. Whenever, as the days passed, a raised British sail came into view, his heart pounded. Whenever visibility vanished and the wind was right, British ships could be momentarily expected.[5]

The political situation had raced ahead during the eight months since Hamilton had argued, in reply to the Westchester Farmer, for nothing more violent than nonimportation. War has, of course, its own momentum. There had been bloodshed not only in Massachusetts at Bunker Hill and thereafter, but a patriot force had captured Ticonderoga and Montreal, failed in an assault on Quebec, and been driven out of Canada into northern New York with the British in pursuit. George III, to whom the pamphleteer Hamilton had appealed to stop the encroachments by his Parliament, had proved instead the most violent enemy the Americans had. He had gone to the lengths of hiring German mercenaries to kill his transatlantic subjects.

In denying the charge of the Westchester Farmer that America sought independence, Hamilton had spoken for most of his compatriots. Now independence was very much in the air. Hamilton, who had staked his future so unreservedly on the rebellion he had found fermenting in America, surely wished that Congress would stop dawdling and take the step necessary for securing French aid, the possibility of which he had early foreseen. But on July 5, 1776, the news had not yet reached New York that independence had in fact been declared.

On that day, Hamilton was most concerned, when he took his mind off the English ships and his own cannon, with a lost pocketbook. Since he had no relations to trust, no home where he could stow things, it contained a surprisingly large sum of money for a young subaltern to carry around: seven guineas, two eight-dollar bills in Continental currency, and in New York currency, one dollar, one half dollar, and one shilling bill. There were also, "a few papers of no service to any but the owner."

Hamilton persuaded Nicholas Fish, his college friend who was brigade major to the New York Militia General John Morin Scott to advertise the loss in Scott's general orders. Scott seems to have been annoyed, since the notice ended, " 'Tis ordered for the future that no advertisement be sent to headquarters to be inserted in the general orders except very extraordinary." But the offer was there that Hamilton would give the reward of a guinea (today more than fifty dollars)

Above: The British fleet gathers off Staten Island in New York Harbor, menacing the city and the battery Hamilton commanded at the lower tip of Manhattan. Watercolor by Archibald Robertson. Courtesy, Spencer Collection, New York Public Library. *Below:* The British warships that give Hamilton his first taste of actual warfare. The *Phoenix* and the *Rose* are shown under attack further up the Hudson, after they have passed unscathed through a barrage from Hamilton's artillery. The British did not return Hamilton's fire, but his company suffered several casualties because their own guns burst. Courtesy, I. N. Phelps Stokes Collection, New York Public Library

The PHŒNIX and the ROSE Engaged by the ENEMY'S FIRE SHIPS and GALLEYS on the 16 Aug.t 1776.
Engrav'd from the Original Picture by D. Serres from a Sketch of Sir James Wallace's.

to "any person delivering the same to Captain Hamilton's head-quarters."[6]

Whether the pocketbook was ever recovered remains a mystery. As it was awaited, momentous news was moving across New Jersey.

On July 6, Hamilton was, with other New Yorkers, greatly excited by a sentence inserted on page three of a little biweekly newspaper, *The Continental Gazette*: "On Tuesday, last, the CONTINENTAL CONGRESS declared the UNITED COLONIES FREE and INDEPENDENT STATES." Since "Tuesday last" was July 2, whoever had sent the news in from Philadelphia had exaggerated an early vote.

There was no further printed information for two days. On the 8th, a major newspaper, Hugh Gaines's *New York Gazette and Weekly Mercury* printed, also on page three, a single sentence, no more detailed than that previously published. It had been so hastily inserted at the head of a column labeled "PHILADELPHIA," that Gaines had not changed the old dateline, June 3.[7]

Also on the 8th, a printed copy of the Declaration reached Washington's headquarters. He instantly set his aides to work making longhand copies to be distributed to brigadier generals and colonels of regiments. On July 9, Washington's general orders stated: "The Honorable the Continental Congress, impelled by the dictates of duty, policy and necessity, have been pleased to dissolve the connection which subsisted between this country and Great Britain, and to declare the United Colonies of North America free and independent states: The several brigades are to be drawn up this evening on their respective parades, at six o'clock, when the declaration of Congress, showing the grounds and reasons of this measure, is to be read with an audible voice." Copies of the Declaration were to be picked up at The Adjutant General's office.

"The General hopes this important event"—so Hamilton read aloud or heard read aloud—"will serve as a fresh incentive to every officer and soldier to act with fidelity and courage, as knowing that . . . he is now in the service of a state, possessed of sufficient power to reward his merit, and advance him to the highest honors of a free country."[8]

II

Defeats

THE morning of July 12 brought to Hamilton and the whole city of New York the news that the anticipated second British fleet, larger than the first, was emerging into the telescopes of lookouts on the Jersey Highlands. The weather could not have been more propitious for the tactic Washington foresaw (and was later to urge on his French allies): a rush down the harbor by an armada that appeared suddenly out of the ocean. The necessary wind was blowing briskly down the bay, enlarging the tides that were about to flow in from the sea to the estuaries that surrounded Manhattan Island. At Fort George and the Grand Battery, Hamilton attended to, checked, rechecked all preparations.

With amazing, almost frustrating quietness, the hours moved by. Not until between one and two in the afternoon did starers from the waterfront see any confirmation of the new arrivals. Then a brace of warships—no more!—sailed through the Narrows. They joined the ships anchored off Staten Island and furled sail. Did this mean that no sudden attack was after all intended? Or was it a ruse to lull patriot preparations?

At about three o'clock, sails did rise at the anchorage, but they were not many. Finally a major battleship, the *Phoenix* (forty-four guns); a frigate, the *Rose* (twenty-eight guns); and three small tenders came out into the open water. As the *New York Gazette* put it, "They stood for the town." Their course soon indicated that they wished to enter the mouth of the Hudson. Sped on by wind and tide, they would dash by the protecting batteries and mount the river to the rear of the American position. The first and heaviest guns they would meet would be Hamilton's. The young captain saw hurrying towards him his first combat.[1]

When the flotilla came within cannon range, the ships did not fire: they were concentrating on speed. Hamilton's guns let go with great explosions of sound. The captain, who had never before heard his batteries go off in concert, may not have realized that the sound was much louder than it should have been. Despite the absence of enemy fire, lethal metal was flying among his men. Men fell to lie motionless; others were wounded. William Douglass had a mangled mass where his arm should have been. Several of Hamilton's cannon had responded to their charges of powder by bursting.

The British flotilla passed rapidly by. Further up the Hudson, they were shot at by a battery on the Jersey shore. The British responded with salvos aimed at both banks of the river. Then the two tall ships and the three smaller ones vanished triumphantly into the upper Hudson.

Although several houses and some trees in the suburb of Greenwich Village had been damaged, the British fire created no casualties. (One ball burst through a brick wall and skimmed over the bed of a Miss Clark, but she was not in bed.) The American losses—six dead and four or five wounded—were all attributed to the bursting of cannon where Hamilton commanded.

That evening, the dead were, with much ceremony, buried in Bowling Green. Bowling Green was right outside Fort George, where the separating wall had been torn down by General Lee. As Hamilton watched (perhaps officiated) his thoughts could not have been solely concentrated on mourning for the dead. Popular rumor blamed the deaths on the inadequate training of the company he had commanded with such conspicuous zest.

The cannon, it was said, had exploded because of the carelessness of the gunners, who had not effectively swept the leftover sparks from the barrels before putting in powder for a new shot. The chances were just as good that the cannon, mostly antiques pulled in from old fortifications and not fired since the French and Indian War, had burst because of interior weaknesses. But there was no way to be sure.

The failure of Hamilton's guns that did discharge their balls to hit anything put them in unanimous agreement with the rest of the American cannon. The enemy had been a fast-moving target, and all the patriot cannon were firing scrounged-up ammunition that did not really fit. Yet Hamilton was not inclined to accept liabilities or excuse himself on the grounds that he had done no worse than the others. He could only regard his first military engagement as a humiliating failure.[2]

However terrifying in its implications, the appearance in the harbor of British reinforcements became almost commonplace as lines on lines of fighters and transports sailed through the Narrows. Although Hamilton could not have realized this, he was witnessing the gathering together of the greatest expeditionary force sent out by any power during the eighteenth century. The British force now numbered forty-two thousand men, including some ten thousand sailors and eight thousand German mercenaries. These fighters were all professionals, while Washington's force, less than half the size of the invaders', was a conglomeration of amateurs.[3]

Having given this disproportion time to sink into American consciousness, the British dispatched an elegantly appointed barge, with two lines of oars one above the other. It came down the bay under a white flag of truce and was met at some distance offshore by an everyday, utilitarian row barge carrying some of Washington's aides. Soon each boat returned to its own base.[4]

This was the beginning of negotiations that passed before Hamilton's eyes. Eventually the British barge actually landed near the fortifications Hamilton commanded. A colonel in dress uniform was blindfolded and led to a house on the waterfront where Washington waited.

The British had managed by now to spread the information that the Howe brothers had been ordered to use force as a last resort. They were doubling as emissaries, bringing from His Majesty liberal offers of conciliation that would lead to peace. The future of the West Indian immigrant who had cast his lot with the Revolutionary cause might well be drastically changed by the words General Washington was speaking. But Hamilton could not hear them. He was not one of Washington's aides. He could only watch as the British colonel reappeared with his eyes again covered and was led to his barge, which then grew smaller as it moved across the glistening water.

Finally, word came out that all the British offers added up to little more than that rebels who sued for forgiveness would be pardoned. Hamilton's chances for glory would not be taken from him. The war, the founding of a new nation, would go on.

On August 20, Captain Nathan Hale wrote his brother from New York: "For about six or eight days the enemy have been expected

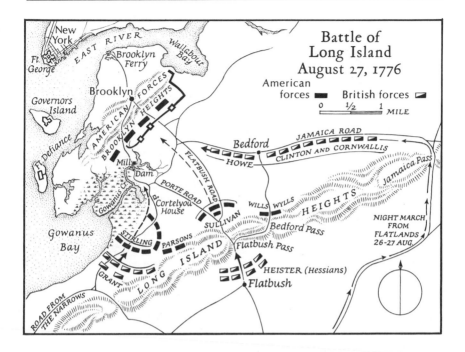

hourly, whenever the wind and tide in the least favored. We kept a particular look out for them this morning. The place and manner of attack time must determine."[5]

On the 22nd, the British anchorage whitened with sails. Warships and transports began to move, but not towards Hamilton's batteries. They sailed in the other direction, out through the Narrows. Eventually, word came that a considerable British force had landed from Gravesend Bay onto the southern tip of Long Island. A few patriot militia had fired and then run, but the beachhead had been too far away from the American position on Brooklyn Heights to be seriously defended.

The next days saw a buildup of British force on Long Island until about half the army was there. The obvious interpretation: the enemy intended to march up the island and capture the major American fortifications on Brooklyn Heights which, as its cannon looked across towards the tip of lower Manhattan Island, cooperated with the Grand Battery to keep the East River closed. If the East River were thus opened, the gently sloping shore of Manhattan Island would be vulnerable to British invasion at any point on its length.

Although what seemed probable was a very practical strategy for pinching off the city without undertaking a frontal attack, head-quarters warned that the Long Island invasion might well be a ruse. All temptations to handspike the guns from Hamilton's side of the Grand Battery over to the East River must be resisted. Washington still expected the British to come down the bay.

At one o'clock on the morning of August 27, the city was awakened by cannon fire on Long Island. The news was that the British were advancing in force against Brooklyn Heights. The main thrust seemed to be along the East River, where the British navy would be able to cooperate if it could get past the batteries and the various impediments—mostly boats filled with rocks—which had been sunk in the channel. Sure enough, when dawn dissolved the darkness, British warships were descried heading for that sector under full sail. Although one of the vessels exchanged shots with the fortifications on Brooklyn Heights, none came within range of the Grand Battery. The wind came ahead, and after tacking several times, the ships gave up and returned to their anchorage.

The change in the wind made it manifest that the British could not combine the action that had started on Long Island with an immediate frontal attack on the city. Washington led reinforcements across the East River to Brooklyn Heights. But the wind might change again. It would have been foolhardy in the extreme to weaken in any way the batteries Hamilton commanded. Although much has been written making him a hero in the battle, he certainly took no part in the Battle of Long Island.

After the enemy thrust along the riverbank had died away, Hamilton could see little from the Manhattan waterfront. But at about 9 A.M. he heard for the first time the multiple, the terrifying, the exhilarating sounds of a major battle. From a short distance inland on Long Island, clouds of powder smoke billowed into the sky.

After an hour or so, the clouds diminished and the sounds frayed off into semisilence broken by random musket fire. Some conclusion had clearly been reached. It was impossible to hope that the British had surrendered: they had all of Long Island to retreat into. Nor could they be thus retreating, since the patriots would certainly follow, creating sounds that Hamilton did not hear. Washington's army could hardly have withdrawn into the fortifications since the British surely would have attacked him there with audible cannon and musket fire. Had Washington, pinned with his back to the river, surrendered? It seemed impossible, but then the silence seemed impossible.

How much time dragged by on the parapets of Fort George and the Grand Battery before speculation and rumor were supplanted by informed reports it is hard to guess. Probably by nightfall Hamilton knew at least the bare bones of what had happened.

Before the British had attacked, half the patriot army of some seven or eight thousand had been within the extensive fortifications on Brooklyn Heights. The other half had been drawn up at the top of a rocky ridge that ran far inland. So far indeed, that it could not be defended along its whole length. Conscious that his eastern flank hung in the air, Major General John Sullivan had dispatched five officers to patrol Jamaica Road, which offered easy access to the ridge beyond the American defenses. That this patrol vanished was doubly shocking to Hamilton: one of the lost officers was his intimate, Lieutenant Robert Troup.

The action along the East River which had been visible to Hamilton had been a ruse to distract attention from the opposite side of the American line. A major British force—ten thousand men and fourteen field pieces—emerged without warning from Jamaica Road. As they sliced through the unprotected American left, Hessians wielding bayonets had come charging up on the front. Caught in a pincers, only few of the patriots had paused to make a stand. Those who were not killed had either surrendered or had by fast running pelted to the fortifications, where they spread consternation among the greener troops who had been watching in horror over the walls.

General Howe's decision to stop the battle at this point, to camp outside the forifications, rather than attack while all within was confusion, puzzled strategists then as it has thereafter. Hamilton would not have been Hamilton had he not tried to fathom this decision, and his brilliant mind may well have drawn the correct inference. While the American army potentially possessed the manpower of a continent, any British loss had to be expensively and slowly replaced from overseas. The enemy generals needed to achieve their results with the fewest possible casualties. The earthworks on Brooklyn Heights were formidable, and, as Bunker Hill had demonstrated, the Americans who fled like rabbits in the open were deadly when they had something to crouch behind. Furthermore, the British high command could see no need for hurry. Was not Washington trapped in his fortifications? He would have to sit there while the British engineers employed their skills to bring down the fortifications without the need of an assault.

Patriot anxiety was concentrated on whether Washington could escape by getting his army back across the East River. This would, of course, be impossible if the British fleet could pass the defenses at the river's mouth. Every care had to be taken to keep in perfect preparation the cannon at the other end of the battery from Hamilton's command lest the wind change. But hour after hour it remained a patriot wind, blowing towards the ocean.

The other necessity, and this seemed the impossible one, was for Washington to find some way to get his army away without tremendous loss. The problem was that, when part of the force was on the water, the rest, unable adequately to man the fortifications, would become easy prey for the enemy. Unless he could somehow slip secretly away, Washington would have to sacrifice half his army.

The Commander in Chief fed to British spies the story that the shipping he was gathering on the Manhattan shore opposite Brooklyn Heights was intended to ferry over fresh troops to replace exhausted regiments. Then, on a rainy night when visibility was zero, Washington removed his endangered men in unbroken darkness and so silently that the enemy got no hint until it was too late.* British suspicions had not been active because what the Continental Army had achieved would have been impossible for European regulars. Correctly trained soldiers and sailors needed to move at command and in formation, but the Americans had trickled self-reliantly to the landing places to be picked up by river captains who had always taken personal responsibility for their little boats. Since utter secrecy had lain at the bottom of Washington's plan, Hamilton could not have been aware of the rescue until it was almost completed, or until dawn revealed to him the presence of the regiments from Long Island.

Although Washington's achievement was to be praised as a near miracle by European military writers, it was regarded in New York as only the aftermath to a most discouraging defeat. The patriots, who had triumphed at Lexington and Concord, had done tremendous execution on Bunker Hill, and had maneuvered the British into evacuating Boston, had been cocky. They were cocky no longer. In this, their first full-scale battle, they had found themselves almost as helpless as a rabble of boys. Laid out everywhere on the streets, the wet clothes, accouterments, and tents of the rescued regiments "dampened," so a diarist tells us, "the spirits of the army. . . . The merry notes of fife and drum" were heard no more.[6]

The capture by the British of the Brooklyn Heights fortifications, with all their artillery, opened the East River to enemy shipping. British troops could be landed anywhere on Manhattan above the

* Mulligan's often-repeated story that credited this maneuver to a message from Hamilton to Washington is obviously false.[7]

city. Continued occupation of New York had become doubly hazardous. Hamilton undoubtedly puzzled his brain to determine the correct American strategy, but he was not consulted. With the rest of the army, he learned of decisions from Washington's general orders.

To the north, Manhattan narrowed until the entire top of the island became an extensive, defensible rocky spur called Harlem Heights. Washington ordered to this natural sanctuary nine thousand men. Still reluctant to abandon the city, he left five thousand there. The remaining troops, about another five thousand, were to guard the intervening ten or so miles of East River shore. They were to prevent invaders from establishing a beachhead until reinforcements could arrive from the city or, if that were nearer, from Harlem Heights.

The heavy guns remained at Fort George and the Grand Battery. Since Hamilton and his company were experienced there, it stands to reason that he should have been left in command. He was not idle. To impede the ferrying to Harlem Heights of what military equipment and stores could be spared from the city, British warships made several dashes into the Hudson, which because of its width and depth, had never been as effectively blocked as had the East River. If the defensive batteries, as they banged away with their antiquated guns and ill-fitting ammunition, did little damage, they did contribute to preventing enemy vessels from attempting more than a series of sudden raids.

Having achieved their victory and endangered the whole New York position, the Howe brothers sent out another peace feeler. But the Americans proved not yet scared enough to give up. On September 15 Hamilton was awakened at dawn by firing well above the city.

The inference that naval cannon, roaring from the East River, were softening up a landing place was verified when the louder noise gave way to the crackling of muskets. The hope was that the sound of muskets would not spread. But the crackling moved inland. It should have been augmented as defending reinforcements appeared. Instead, it shredded away into silence. The silence not only indicated that patriot resistance had collapsed, but made it impossible for listeners in the city to determine how far across the island the enemy was penetrating. Was there still a corridor up the western side of the island through which the troops in the city, including Hamilton's company, could escape?

The certainty of danger, the uncertainty of its extent and how to cope with it, threw into turmoil the armed forces below the British landing. Passionate patriot diggers had thrown across the island just above the city a rampart that was crowned (at the present junction of Grand and Centre Streets) with a dirt fort that had been named Bunker Hill. Troops made for this fort and then, recognizing the hopelessness of undertaking a defense there, hurried away. According to Mulligan, Hamilton's company made an appearance. Before moving on, the captain abandoned his personal baggage and a cannon that had broken down.*[8]

Somehow, news came through that the British had not cut off escape up the Hudson shore.† The patriot forces, including Hamilton's company, set out at a run to traverse the ten miles of rough wilderness (most of it devoid even of assisting cart tracks) that separated them from the safety of Harlem Heights. They could not conceivably drag along their heavy cannon. All the men, or almost all, arrived safely at their rocky sanctuary. Hamilton's account book testifies to the arduous footwork of his company. He had to procure for many of his men new shoes.[9]

---

* Aaron Burr was to claim that through his superior judgment and knowledge of the terrain he had saved Colonel Knox and a considerable force from capture at Bunker Hill. If this incident ever took place, it must have been at a time when Hamilton was not there: Burr would not have missed a chance to state that he had nobly saved Hamilton's life.[10]

† Having landed in Kip's Bay (which then extended almost to Third Avenue), the British had advanced to the present site of the Public Library (Fifth Avenue and Fortieth Street). There they waited for their landing craft to cross the East River and return with the second wave of the invasion. It has seemed quixotic to many writers that the first troops landed did not immediately seal up the island, but the British strategy made sense. The remaining half of the island was a wild terrain—small fields, thick woods, rocky outcroppings—particularly hostile to European regulars and particularly suited to American irregulars. Furthermore, the force that would seek escape by coming up from the city greatly outnumbered the original landing party, which had, indeed, achieved its function: to establish and hold a firm beachhead.

12

Blackness

HAMILTON could easily discover what had happened as the British landed at Kip's Bay. The raw recruits who had from skimpy trenches first faced the enemy had, without attempting any resistance, fled from the cannon fire before the enemy even landed. This was unfortunate but under the circumstances understandable. The truly terrifying fact was that experienced regiments had, after being hurried to the rescue, at the mere sight of enemy infantrymen jettisoned their arms and fled. In his dismay, Washington had sat stunned on his horse, and would have been killed or captured had not his aides pulled on his bridle.

On the day following the loss of New York City a skirmish developed in the woods during which some of the troops who had turned tail the day before showed ability to drive back a small British force when they had rocks and trees to maneuver behind. In what is known to history as the Battle of Harlem Heights, the artillery (and thus Hamilton) had no part. It had been a victory, but not a sufficient victory to counteract the discouragement spread through the army by the abject defeats that had been suffered at Long Island and Kips Bay, the only two occasions when Washington's soldiers had been faced with true British might. As morale plummeted, desertion and looting became so common that Washington expressed utter despair.

The almost immovable heavy cannon Hamilton had commanded had, of course, been left behind on the city's waterfront. His battery now consisted of two fieldpieces. They belonged to the state of New York and were capable of being pulled either by horses or men. His company serviced them during the rest of the campaign.[1]

Although one of Hamilton's soldiers was sentenced to thirty-nine lashes for "plundering and stealing,"[2] the captain kept up discipline so remarkably that he attracted the attention of General Nathanael Greene, who invited him to his marquee for dinner.

Greene was only thirty-five. Although he had never known poverty, being the son of a rich Rhode Island ironmonger, he too had had a severe handicap to overcome. His lame knee had prevented his neighbors from granting him even the lowest rank as a militia officer. But that had been a few years ago; now he was one of Washington's most trusted generals. He was a robust man, whose conventionally handsome features were small in his fleshy face. As compared to the ever-active Hamilton, he seemed controlled, the fires of his temperament only showing in the intensity with which he stared from his long narrow eyes. The two men who had brilliant futures before them instantly found themselves, as Greene's son wrote, "strangely drawn to each other."[3]

When he summoned Hamilton, Greene was just moving from brigadier to major general. Hamilton was to remember that two generals had offered him the post as aide before he succumbed to Washington's desire. We know that McDougall was the first; Greene probably was the second. Although he had the highest opinion of Greene, Hamilton preferred to remain in his tiny but independent command.[4]

During the black autumn at Harlem Heights, when gloom haunted the camp, Hamilton diverted himself by setting up an elaborate ledger. With a broad pen he drew up a calligraphic title page: "Pay Book of the State Company of Artillery Commanded by Alex.ʳ Hamilton."[5] Subsequently, he lettered elaborately on each of sixty-six pairs of pages the name of an officer or soldier. Done with an obvious eye to elegance, all the lettering proved—as did a doodled-in drawing of a head—that the young officer was completely lacking in any innate feeling for design. There is not one glint of attractive shape, harmony, or balance.

Absence of esthetic sense need not bother a future financier. What is truly amazing is the carelessness with which the accounts were kept. No aristocrat trained and enabled to ignore pounds and pence could have created greater confusion.

As commander of an independent company, Hamilton was its

The title page Hamilton lettered and the head he doodled further in the same account book exemplify his lack of any aesthetic sense. Courtesy, Library of Congress

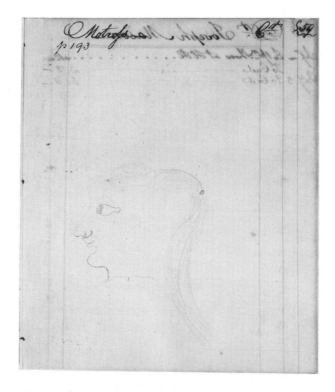

banker. At the end of each month, he submitted a bill for the amount New York State owed his men for the total number of days they had served, each at his particular rate of compensation. When the money came in, Hamilton distributed it, deducting what he had advanced to each man in anticipation of pay. Hamilton's intention was to enter, on the left-hand sheet of each opening, what the soldier owed him, and on the right-hand sheet the payments he received.

The routine debits charged to the men were for clothes: mostly the shoes and stockings (they wore out the fastest), sometimes for a blanket, a greatcoat, a pair of breeches. But Hamilton, who in imagining an ideal wife wrote that he desired "a great deal of generosity," and hated an "economist," was perpetually advancing cash to his soldiers for no stated purpose.[6] He normally gave six or seven shillings to the sick as they departed for hospitals, and sometimes paid directly the cost of nursing. He recorded one payment for a funeral. Several sums credited to wives—a bombardier's widow did washing—revealed that Hamilton suffered from a problem of which Washington also complained. When New York City had fallen to the British, the families of various soldiers were dispossessed, and had no recourse but to march, often dragging along children, beside their husbands so that they could live off army rations.

There are entries in the Pay Book up to the end of Hamilton's artillery command, but although there were plenty of extra pages, he never added the names of soldiers who joined his company after the doldrums on Harlem Heights. Many of the personal accounts remained completely blank. What accounts do exist, are spasmodic and obviously incomplete. A scrambling of dates, earlier entries following the later, demonstrate that many notations were made long after the expenditures. He seems to have had bursts—the most extensive was in January, 1777—when he tried to complete his records, but the bursts soon faded. Often he noted down what he admitted was an incomplete memory or inscribed a question which he hoped he would eventually be able to answer.

Some of the sixty-six accounts were marked formally with signatures, as being settled—but only a very few. When billing New York State after the war for sums he contended were still owed him, Hamilton referred to "memorandum book No. 3."[7] This must have contained notes he never got around to transcribing into his formal Pay Book.

Hamilton often specified in the book where purchases had been made. Since his company was too insignificant to be featured in other records, the resulting information is extremely useful. It reveals that, throughout the rest of 1776, Hamilton belonged to that part of the army which was under the direct command of General Washington.

After delaying for a month to consolidate their hold on New York City, the British sailed up the East River and landed on the New York mainland at Throg's Neck, where the river enters Long Island Sound. If the enemy were to establish a line from there west to the Hudson, Washington would, unless he hurried off Harlem Heights, be separated from New England. Parting from his new friend Greene, who was left behind to defend the Heights, Hamilton marched with Washington to high ground, north of the British, at White Plains. There the army awaited an enemy advance.

The state of Hamilton's company is revealed by a return he submitted on October 25. Present were sixty rank and file (there were supposed to be one hundred), including Hamilton himself, five junior officers, two sergeants, three corporals, two bombardiers, seven gunners, and thirty-nine of those common soldiers who were known in the artillery as matrosses. The band of music was crippled unless the one man listed under "fifers and drummers" had four hands. Three men were sick, two were still on the roll though they had deserted, and two were listed as "prisoners."[8]

On October 28, 1776, Washington's army, as they looked down from their hillside over a long field, were given their first panoramic view of a beautifully trained and equipped European force. There emerged from the distant forest large oblongs of red and blue. The angles were sharp because there was no straggling; bayonets glistened above, and the geometric shapes advanced with an even undulating motion as all the men in each regiment kept perfect step. Officers and cavalrymen glittered on fine horses in the bright sunlight, the officers moving sedately with the importance of command, the cavalrymen dashing around, their sabers upraised. The perfectly accoutered artillery came in at a trot. To music played, not by fifes and drums but by many bands, the procession traversed the mile-long field, the head of the line disappearing into the nearby flanking woods while the rear was still emerging from the distant forest.

The contrast between this richly dressed and lavishly supplied human machine and the men who waited to fight it struck every American breast. Even the few corps who had been, like Hamilton's company, well uniformed and disciplined, were now ragged and disheartened.

More and more British cannon were being brought into closer range.

American field artillery: such guns as Hamilton's company dragged, by horse or by hand, from Harlem Heights to White Plains, across New Jersey, and to the battles of Trenton and Princeton. Drawings in Charles Willson Peale's military diary. Courtesy, American Philosophical Society

"The scene," a Pennsylvania soldier wrote, "was grand and solemn.
. . . The air groaned with streams of cannon and musket shot; the
hills smoked and echoed terribly with the bursting of shells, the fences
and walls were knocked down and torn to pieces, and men's legs,
arms, and bodies were mangled with cannon and grape shot all around
us."9

The British attack developed against Chatterton's Hill which, although only lightly fortified, commanded Washington's main encampment that was below it. To get there involved crossing the Bronx
River. This situation inspired Hamilton's son to cast his father as an
intrepid warrior. According to John Hamilton, the Hessians ordered to
the attack "loudly refused" to ford the river, which was alive with
driftwood. British engineers began a temporary bridge.

Hamilton "forthwith descended the hill," planted his two field
artillery pieces on a rock where they were screened from the enemy
artillery by trees, and "poured his fire on the bridge. The effect was
instantaneous. The bridge was repeatedly struck. Several of the work-
men, killed, fell headlong into the rapid stream. The Hessians were in
great disorder."

In this crisis of German cowardice, the British general Alexander
Leslie called on British regiments. They crossed the river by another
ford, and rushed up the hill towards Hamilton with bayonets fixed.
"Again and again Hamilton's pieces flashed, driving the ascending
columns down to the river's edge." But now the bridge was completed.
Hessians swarmed and Hamilton had to retreat.10

A report written a few days after the battle by Colonel Charles
Hazlet states that only one American fieldpiece was ordered to protect
the stream crossing. It was "so poorly appointed that myself was
forced to assist in dragging it along the rear of the regiment. When so
employed, a cannonball struck the carriage, and scattered the shot
about, a wad of tow blazing in the middle. The artillerymen fled. One
alone was prevailed on to tread out the blaze and collect the shot. The
few that returned made not more than two discharges, when they
retreated with the field piece."11

It is amusing to think how vociferously John Hamilton, had he
known of Hazlet's letter, would have insisted that his father had nothing to do with the attempted artillery defense of the Bronx River
crossing. It seems, indeed, highly improbable that a captain whose
prestige continued to rise in the army could have been responsible for
such conspicuous incompetence.

The entire engagement, which history refers to as the Battle of

White Plains, was from the American point of view another discouragement. The Americans had had no time to dig fortifications on Chatterton's Hill. Protected only by permeable clothing from British and Hessian bayonets, the defenders ran. And once the enemy controlled the height, Washington's encampment was outflanked. All he could do was demonstrate again the American skill at retreat. He managed to get his army away from what could have been a trap and up on higher hills a short distance northward at New Castle.

At New Castle, Hamilton advanced some cash to several of his soldiers who were sick.[12]

From the American position, the British encampment was plainly visible, only a little more than a cannon-shot away. At night, Hamilton looked out over a vast number of campfires. At dawn on November 5, his blood was set pulsing by a general alarm. Men rushed to their battle positions as the augmenting light revealed a great stirring in the British camp. Tents came down, the enemy mustered in formation, but then amazingly, they made no move towards the American position. They marched off to the left, towards the Hudson.

What was the enemy about? If, as was the case when Hamilton last heard, his friend Greene was still occupying Harlem Heights, the British might, by descending upon him from the north, surround that position except for the Hudson shore. Or, the British might cross the Hudson and hurry (the season was late) through New Jersey to capture the patriot capital of Philadelphia. Or the entire maneuver might be a ruse: if Washington followed the enemy, they might double back and advance unimpeded into New England.

Washington's orders revealed that he hoped by dividing his already weak army to bar the British in all directions. He reinforced the forts in the Hudson Highlands lest Harlem Heights, further down the river, should have to be evacuated. He left the lion's share of his force at New Castle, under General Lee, to keep closed the way to New England. And he himself marched, keeping north of the British advance, for the Hudson. The detachment he had allowed himself was so small—only a quarter of the army—that it was clear that he expected to meet, after he had crossed the river, reinforcement from the states to the west and south. The actual ferrying was done at King's Ferry, where Hamilton bought clothing for some of his men.

Since the British remained on the New York side of the river, Washington's column met no opposition as it marched down the west shore to Fort Lee which, with Fort Washington directly across on Harlem

Heights, seriously impeded British movement up and down the river. Since Fort Lee was Greene's headquarters, Hamilton may well have learned more than had previously been confided to him about the general situation.

What observation had made him suspect was confirmed: the reinforcements Washington had counted on had proved illusory. This was considered the more serious because headquarters was convinced that the main British thrust would be against Philadelphia. Washington intended to hurry with what troops he had to the plains of southern New Jersey, where the roads to Philadelphia lay. A debate raged on what to do about Harlem Heights. Many of Washington's advisers urged that, although this meant abandoning the effort to block the river, the Heights should at once be evacuated in boats: on all land sides the rocky spur was surrounded and liable to assault. Greene insisted that, since the British intended for Philadelphia, the Heights would be menaced only by a secondary British force. The fortifications, which were under his command, were very strong, and if any major menace developed, he could then get his men and supplies back across the river.

Washington expressed a wish to be ferried over to the Heights so that he could see for himself. But, if he were to block the road to Philadelphia, he did not have time. He decided, to Greene's great satisfaction (which was to turn into immense regret) that since Hamilton's friend knew the situation, his advice should be accepted.

After a day at Fort Lee, Hamilton marched with Washington down the river to Hackensack. If he had been watching at the right moment, he would have seen Washington and his staff galloping hell-for-leather back upriver. Then there came the sound of distant guns. Eventually, rumor hardened into definite intelligence that, as Washington looked on helplessly from the west shore, the main British army had stormed and taken Harlem Heights, capturing some two thousand prisoners and a quantity of artillery.

This was the worst defeat the patriot cause had so far suffered. Criticism of both Washington and Greene buzzed around Hamilton.

Soon there was further disastrous news. The British had surreptitiously crossed the Hudson and marched down on Fort Lee. Washington managed to get his troops out—they came panting and terrified into the camp where Hamilton was—but the fact remained that a second fort had been captured, and with it all its supplies and artillery. A cry went up that Washington was indecisive to the point of incompetence. The only hope, it was argued over every campfire, lay in hurrying General Lee from New Castle to take over the command. There is no evidence concerning Hamilton's reaction at this time, although he was later passionately to support Washington against Lee.

Now Hamilton took part in the most abject retreat of the American Revolution. Washington's shadow of an army fled like a shadow across New Jersey, pursued by a larger British force, a force bountifully fed and beautifully equipped as compared to the American soldiers who ate what they could get their hands on, and had already lost most of their baggage, sometimes even their muskets. The terrain was a flat "champaign country" devoid of all those lifesavers for untrained American fighters: anything—stone walls, cliffs, thick vegetation—to hide behind. Depressed by the series of defeats the Continental Army had suffered, many of the soldiers could not bear to serve any longer, and no one was willing to take their places. That Hamilton's company was not immune to desertion is revealed by the large bill he sent in 1784 to the state of New York for sums, advanced to individual soldiers, which could not be stopped from their pay because they had absconded.[13]

The only two impediments to the British advance were the narrow Raritan River at New Brunswick and the broad Delaware, which flowed between New Jersey and Pennsylvania. On November 30, Washington drew up his army on the far side of the Raritan. The enlistments of more than half of his feeble force were to expire the next day. When the enemy came in sight Hamilton must have hoped—as did Washington—that the men would stay to meet the crisis. Hamilton's independent company had been assigned to a brigade of three Maryland militia regiments, whose period of service was lapsing. We can visualize the passion with which he sought to inspire the Maryland officers with a zeal to remain, but as the British appeared on the far side of the river, the Marylanders gathered up their belongings and vanished. Hamilton undoubtedly had to look to his own men: although their own enlistments had not expired, many could hardly have been happy to stay behind.[14]

The river passed through a deep cut, the crossing being possible only at one bridge. Patriot soldiers had succeeded in tearing the bridge halfway down when they were driven back by Hessian Jaegers, the enemy's partial equivalent of the American riflemen. The riflemen then prevented the British engineers from repairing the bridge. The two armies watched from their respective heights. "We had," Washington reported to Congress, "a smart cannonade whilst we were parading our men, but without any or but little loss on either side."[15] Evidence exists concerning Hamilton's role in this engagement.

George Washington Parke Custis, Washington's step-grandson, wrote in his *Recollections* that at New Brunswick Washington had been "charmed by the brilliant courage and admirable skill displayed by" Hamilton, "who directed a battery against the enemy's advanced columns." In his own *Memoirs*, Captain James Wilkinson noted laconically, "Our battery was served by Captain Alexander Hamilton."[16]

Washington could not hope to hold the Raritan with his depleted force. His flight from what was the only defensive line in one state spread panic through the civilian population of New Jersey. The terror was further incited by former soldiers who justified their personal departure from the fighting with horrendous tales of Washington's incompetence and the helplessness of his army. Hamilton could not possibly have missed the news—it was repeated by every mouth and caused further desertions—that the whole state was returning to its allegiance to the Crown. Even former militiamen lined up to take the oath that, it was hoped, would protect families and farms from enemy violation and looting.

The prevailing vision of Hamilton at this time comes from Washington Irving's life of Washington, published some seventy-five years later: "A veteran officer of the Revolution used to speak in his old days of the occasion he first saw Hamilton. It was during the memorable retreat through the Jerseys. 'I noticed,' he said, 'a youth, a mere stripling, small, slender, almost delicate in frame, marching beside a piece of artillery with a cocked hat pulled down over his eyes, apparently lost in thought, with his hand resting on the cannon, every now and then patting it as he mused, as if it were a favorite horse or pet plaything.' "[17] It is more likely that he looked around him with anxiety grounded in disgust. There could hardly be a greater object lesson in human frailty.

13

Resplendent Luster

[DECEMBER, 1776–JANUARY, 1777   AGES 19–20]

WASHINGTON'S fleet-footed troops dashed to reach a viable defensive position by getting across the Delaware River. Although the British followed with what their officers praised as exemplary speed, they never came close enough to fire a shot. And when they reached the east side of the river, which Washington had crossed, they proved to have brought with them none of the transportable boats that would have enabled them to continue the chase and take Philadelphia. In a short time the main British force returned to their New York base, leaving behind a series of garrisons to hold down their conquests. The nearest garrison to Washington—some two thousand Hessians—was directly across the Delaware at Trenton.

Washington was puzzled. We have no record of whether Hamilton understood the basic explanation: regular armies did not tear their expensive selves apart in winter campaigns. Having started into New Jersey so late in the season, Howe had intended to go as far as Philadelphia only if no impediment appeared. That Washington had sequestered from possible capture all the boats that normally plied the Delaware was enough to stop the advance.

The British were delighted with what they had accomplished. They believed that the majority of the American colonials continued to love the Crown, but were prevented from giving rein to their loyalty by armed radicals. What had happened in New Jersey seemed to demonstrate that if you drove away the radicals, the love for the Crown would well forth. And the augmenting group of American loyalists would, of course, fight for their loyalty if the odds were changed from unfavorable to favorable. It followed that the Revolution could be extinguished by capturing successive areas, which would then be held down by such protective garrisons as the one at Trenton.

Washington was going to have something to say about this.

As December, 1776, moved towards the Battle of Trenton, Hamilton's company encamped, with the main body of Washington's army, in Upper Wakefield Township, Bucks County, across the Delaware from Trenton. Hamilton seems to have been with his company. The second-in-command, Captain Lieutenant James Moore, suffered in that township from what Hamilton described, in words which implied his presence at the bedside, as an "excruciating illness." Moore was to die of "camp fever" at the very moment of the battle.[1]

Hamilton was short of officers. Lieutenant James Gilliland had resigned early in December, so the captain reported angrily, "from domestic inconveniences and *other motives*." Another lieutenant, James Bean, seems to have had a passion for alcohol. Hamilton wrote that, although a brave man, he was "incurably addicted to a *certain failing*." Hamilton's mainstay was Thomas Thompson, the lieutenant whose precedent-making promotion from sergeant he had procured. He still had two cannon but his company had dropped to less than thirty men.[2]

Peter Cattell, who lived on the farm adjoining the house in Upper Wakefield Township identified as Knox's headquarters, remembered in the mid-nineteenth century that the artillery general had occupied the east portion of the first floor. In a back room, Hamilton lay sick. But, so Cattell stated, he rose to take part in the Battle of Trenton.[3]

This was Hamilton's typical pattern of behavior. After a period of great strain had been eased, he fell sick. But, when a new necessity arose, his nerves carried him again into action. In expressing amazement that Hamilton's "delicate health" was able to "sustain the hardships and fatigues of a winter campaign," his friend Stevens commented that this would only be possible if Hamilton were inspired by "something extraordinary."[4]

Because of his closeness to Knox, Hamilton may have understood what was planned, when, at about three o'clock on Christmas afternoon, a large part of the army was routed out of its quarters. As the men lined up in frigid dampness that presaged snow, they could foresee some extensive operation since they were issued three days' cooked food. Most of the soldiers could not help being sadly conscious of the contrast between their plight and the domestic celebrations they would have shared on this Christmas Day had they been home with their families. No such contrast bothered the homeless captain while he made sure that the horses were soundly hitched to the cannon and that all the supplies necessary for combat were in place.

The artillery company joined the long column—the untrained Continental Army marched single file—that moved upriver behind hills which shielded them from enemy lookouts across the Delaware. They came to a halt at a road that led, at a distance of a mile and a half, to McKonkey's Ferry.

Since campfires, if permitted, would throw a visible glow into the lowering skies, everyone ate a cold supper. When darkness was complete, battalions began to march off, one by one, towards the river. Orders revealed that they were to cross into British-held territory. The artillery was to go last, at about midnight.

At about eleven o'clock, the wind that had been steadily building rose to a shriek. A heavy snow began to fall. The men huddled together. Detachments were being ordered with increasing slowness to march off towards the ferry. When Hamilton's watch said midnight, many regiments were still waiting. Information may have trickled back from the riverside that the trouble was not only snow and wind, but in the river: swollen current and floating ice. The maneuver was falling dangerously behind schedule.

According to the reliable historian William S. Stryker, it was well after one o'clock in the morning when Hamilton's company got their call.[5] The rumble of artillery wheels was deadened by the snow on the ground and in the air. The road sank downhill towards the ferry. After marching in complete darkness, Hamilton saw ahead a dim glow. Soon, shielded torches threw just enough light to make barely visible the silent bustle of the embarking place.

An aide, speaking in a whisper, led Hamilton and his company onto the ferry slip, where they found waiting what looked like an oversize canoe: sixty feet long by only six wide. On the gunwales stretched narrow wooden platforms. Along these, men would walk from stern to bow, pressing poles against the bottom of the shallow river, thus propelling the vessel across. The gunwales were, like every other surface, slippery with ice. It was difficult to keep the guns, as they were hoisted and shoved aboard, from slipping into the shallows, where they would crash through the thin ice. The horses were frightened by the rocking decks. Unable to get footholds, they scrambled and neighed. Any clothing that was splashed, instantly froze as hard as armor.

In the river, Hamilton saw jagged chunks of ice that seemed to increase in size even while the swift current swept them momentarily into and out of his field of vision. After the Durham Boat got under way, the poles being used to stave off the ice got entangled with the poles being pushed against the bottom of the river. The Durham Boat veered, almost unmanageable in the swift flow. But the crossing was not more than a thousand feet. Then came the unloading, as time-consuming and hazardous as the loading had been.

Hamilton's company was led by a staff officer to its position in General Greene's division. The Pennsylvania artillery of Hamilton's superior officer, Captain Thomas Forrest, was further ahead, separated from Hamilton by a column of infantry.[6] The whole formation was drawn up aiming downriver. At about 3 A.M., explanatory orders finally came. The army was to march some eight miles to Trenton and attack the Hessian garrison there. Since the object was to surprise the enemy, no unnecessary sound was to be made, no light shown.

Snow continued to pour down, driven by a high wind. Horses and soldiers were hardly able to advance as they slipped perpetually on snow over ice. At the crossroads hamlet of Birmingham, there was a pause while cold rations were distributed. The men ate standing up. Those who sat down were in danger of freezing to death.

At Birmingham, about half the army filed off to the right on a road that would enter Trenton close to the river. Hamilton proceeded directly ahead with Greene's division, which was under the personal command of General Washington. In about half an hour, the first signs of daylight appeared. The intention had been to attack in the dark, but the snow was as good a cover.

It was about quarter of eight when firing sounded ahead. Hamilton could not see what was happening. As the line of infantry with which he was moving advanced rapidly, the firing became both louder and more distant. Clearly the enemy pickets were being strengthened but were nonetheless still being driven back. Soon firing sprang up on the right; the division that had veered off at Birmingham had arrived, and was now involved.

Hamilton reached the hill where the two main streets of Trenton abutted, one a short distance beyond the other, against the road on which the army was advancing. Captain Forrest's cannon were firing or preparing to fire down the further of these roads. Hamilton was ordered to aim his guns down the nearer.[7]

The town was echoing with musket shots. As Hamilton stared along

King Street through the falling snow, the road with its flanking houses became in the unnatural twilight increasingly dim, shredding at last into complete obscurity. Sounds indicated that the patriot forces were operating between or behind the buildings on the left side of the street. The street was empty except when an occasional Hessian wandered confusedly into view. He was likely to make a dramatic fall and leave his body to be quickly covered with snow.

Hamilton's cannon were placed and ready to fire when a considerable Hessian detachment appeared in parade formation from an alley on the right. Their metal helmets and upraised bayonets gleamed against the grayish-white of air and ground. Unable to see Hamilton's battery because of the snow blowing into their eyes, they advanced up the street towards the cannon. The two guns spoke. While Hamilton's men reloaded with all possible speed, augmented musket fire sounded from the houses on the left. What Hessians were still upright wheeled in parade-ground formation and disappeared into an alley on the left, leaving behind more bodies to be covered with snow.

Shapes approaching from the edge of vision sharpened, as they came closer, into eight horses drawing two cannon. The horses circled in the street, pointing the cannon at Hamilton's battery. Both sets of guns fired almost simultaneously. Balls whistled in the air around Hamilton, but did no damage. Whether because of Hamilton's cannon or the flanking muskets' fire, Hessian artillerymen and horses were going down. The battery fired once again, this time with grape, and then those Hessians who could still do so vanished at a run. Americans came dashing from between the houses, their cheers dully audible through the deadening snow. They turned the Hessian cannon down the street towards the enemy.[8]

What was Hamilton's first experience of combat at close quarters came suddenly to an end.* As the news spread that the Hessian commander had surrendered, a milling crowd of shouting soldiers filled King Street. Discipline, always a scarce commodity in the Continental Army, went to the winds. Whatever orders Hamilton shouted surely could not keep his men from joining their gesticulating companions. The Hessian store of rum was quickly discovered and even more quickly tapped.

---

* The Hessians, recovering from the celebrations of Christmas Day, had been caught completely by surprise. Their commanders had, it is true, been warned of patriot activity, but regular officers could not believe that any army would operate in such a blizzard. Since the German soldiers, trained to fight only in formation, achieved as a group no opportunity to form, defeat was inevitable.

As saturnalia developed in the town, the American officers and what men they could collar gathered up captured ordnance, herded and counted prisoners. It eventually developed that the Americans had captured about 920 men, some thousand stands of arms, and six pieces of brass artillery, the best-appointed cannon Hamilton had ever been able to examine closely. The American casualties were two killed, four wounded.

The troops felt at the moment strong enough to devour any enemy anywhere. Washington considered beating up the next Hessian post, downriver at Burlington. But the men were soon in no condition to undertake a further offensive. As for staying at Trenton, that would invite reprisal by some major enemy force. The booty was loaded into captured wagons, the prisoners lined up. A march back to the boats at McKonkey's Ferry was ordered. Since the storm had not abated, the return was just as strenuous as had been the advance: the crossing of the Delaware was no more easy; the men were exhausted and many had hangovers. Yet hearts were high.*

On December 29, Washington's troops, after being issued two days' provisions, recrossed the Delaware and returned to the scene of their victory at Trenton. The nearby garrisons of Hessians had all retreated from their exposed positions. Although a major British force, bent on revenge, was to be expected, the most serious menace was that the enlistments of most of Washington's army would expire in forty-eight hours, at the end of 1776.

Washington had begged Congress to enlist men for three years, but this had been strongly opposed on the grounds that it would create an army independent enough to establish a military tyranny. There was also the desire of the states, each a separate political entity, not to become committed, during the waging of the war, to a permanent interrelationship closer than mutual cooperation and friendship. It was feared that if men were allowed to stay too long away from home in service with men from other states, they might lose their local allegiances.

Hamilton's own convictions concerning long service being so strong, he persuaded himself that the New York Convention had originally ordered his company to be enlisted for the duration of the war, a term almost unheard of before the Declaration of Independence, and not included in the recorded votes for setting up the company. When his men were able to demonstrate that they had been enlisted only for a

* See Appendix B, p. 457.

year, Hamilton blamed what he insisted was an error on the lieutenant who had gathered the company together before he came in as captain. But the issue was not for him immediately crucial since, at any calculation, his men had at least a month to serve.[9]

Bringing the troops back to where they had triumphed had been a psychological maneuver of Washington's. He now rode from regiment to regiment, begging the men to stay for another six weeks, offering a bounty of ten dollars. About half agreed. Washington's total force, which included many raw militiamen, entered the year 1777 at about five thousand men.

The British general Lord Cornwallis came storming across New Jersey with an army only slightly larger than Washington's but much better trained and equipped. Washington sent out skirmishers to harry the enemy advance, and withdrew the rest of his army onto a hill at the opposite end of Trenton from where the previous battle had been fought. Between Trenton and the hillside flowed a minor watercourse, Assunpink Creek. The position was extremely dangerous: the creek could be forded at many places, and the unfordable Delaware was not far behind Washington's back. If Washington were driven against the Delaware he would be trapped because his boats were elsewhere. It was necessary not only to defend the bridge across the Assunpink at Trenton but various shallows up and down the stream.

Slowed by the skirmishers, who eventually came scrambling into the American camp across the Assunpink, the British did not arrive until dusk. They probed the American defenses, stirring up cannon fire in which, so an officer who was present tells, Hamilton took part.[10] When it became clear that they could not cross the river without fighting in the dark, Cornwallis encamped—confident that he could destroy the American army in the morning.

Since Washington had no boats with which to retreat across the Delaware, he could not evade Cornwallis without going deeper into British-held territory. Thus, he was, according to strategical axioms, in a hopeless situation. There were no principles more basic than that an army defended its supply lines and never allowed an enemy to interpose between its position and its base. What Cornwallis did not realize was that the Americans, being in any case rarely supplied, would not miss their supply line. Furthermore, they could put the enemy between them and patriot-held territory. They moved so much faster than regular troops that they could count on somehow extricating themselves.

The Battle of Princeton. Detail from a full-length portrait of Washington by Charles Willson Peale. Patriot soldiers are deploying before the college building where the British made their last stand. Hamilton may have fired through a window the cannonball that decapitated a painting of George II. Courtesy, Scott and Fowles

Leaving behind, to soothe Cornwallis, lighted campfires and one artillery company to fire at any enemy who appeared near the bridge, Washington marched around the British left and advanced on the enemy base at Princeton. The appearance of the Continental Army where according to accepted strategy it could not possibly be, caught three British regiments by surprise. Two were on the march to join Cornwallis at Trenton. After a stiff engagement, the Americans, for the first time in a pitched battle on open fields, put enemy regulars to flight. The third British regiment occupied the large brick building of the College of New Jersey. They were too flabbergasted by their unaccountable plight to put up much resistance, but before they surrendered, a cannonball passed through a window and decapitated a portrait of George II.

Such a happening seems so much more suited to legend than sober history that the event has been doubted. However, the records of Princeton University present proof. The frame was not damaged, and the trustees, refusing to be outdone in symbolism by an uneducated cannonball, commissioned Charles Willson Peale to replace the destroyed portrait with his now-famous *Washington at the Battle of Princeton.*[11]

It has often been assumed that Hamilton fired the cannonball. Since we know that his company was marching with Washington's army shortly after the battle, the chances are good that their captain, whether or not he decapitated George II, took part in the engagement.[12]

Coming on top of the victory at Trenton, this second achievement of the Continental Army made the British abandon their hope that the rebellion could be stifled piecemeal by holding down conquests with scattered posts. It was shattering that the inhabitants had not, like loyal Britons, risen to the defense of their defenders; it was even more shattering that those who had sworn allegiance to George III when they were menaced by his troops, now took down their guns and went hunting redcoats. The invaders retired from New Jersey except the area contiguous with their stronghold on Staten Island.

After the firm establishment of independence, Hamilton described "the enterprises of Trenton and Princeton . . . as the dawnings of that bright day which afterwards broke forth with such resplendent luster."[13]

When the Princeton campaign was over, the bulk of the Continental Army went into winter quarters at Morristown, three fourths of the way back across New Jersey. However, notations in the papers of the artillery commander Knox reveal that Hamilton's company was stationed on the Pennsylvania side of the Delaware, in Bucks County. Indications in the official records that the captain was not with his men are confirmed by Hamilton's Pay Book, which shows money advanced to the soldiers by subalterns. When Hamilton himself handed out money, it was in Philadelphia, where some of his men lay sick and others, it may be assumed, were on leave from their nearby cantonment and needed cash with which to have a good time. Hamilton himself was sick. In answering a letter (now lost) which Hamilton had written on February 14, 1777, the Reverend Hugh Knox congratulated him on his recovery from "a long and dangerous illness."[14]

While Hamilton was ill, his whereabouts were not as easily discovered as if he had been on active duty. The *Pennsylvania Evening Post* published on January 25 the following notice: "Captain Alexander Hamilton of the New York Company of Artillery, by applying to the printer of this paper, may hear of something to his advantage."[15]

What the editor had for Hamilton could well have been the most important communication he received during his whole career.

14

A Disturbing Letter

AFTER an extended campaign during which Washington had faced crisis after crisis, quiet now descended. Since his encampment at Morristown was too formidable to be attacked even if the enemy broke their rules by operating during a winter; since the enemy were behind their New York defenses where Washington could not get at them, he found leisure to attend to neglected matters including the weakness of his own staff. He had been in Morristown only three days when he wrote his senior secretary, Robert Hanson Harrison, asking whether Harrison's brother-in-law, Major George Johnston, would make "a good aide de camp to me." Education and good sense Washington considered "necessary qualifications, but how is his temper? As to military knowledge, I do not expect to find gentlemen much skilled in it. If they can write a good letter, write quick, are methodical and diligent, it is all I expect to find in my aides." Should Johnston also have "a good disposition," Harrison should send him on. Harrison sent him on.[1]

In a later letter, dated January 20, 1777, Washington asked about Caleb Gibbs, whom he was to appoint captain of the headquarters guard. He also requested Harrison to "be so good as to forward the enclosed to Captain Hamilton." A comparison of dates makes it reasonable to suppose that Harrison's efforts to find Hamilton inspired the notice published on January 25 in the *Pennsylvania Evening Post*.

Washington's letter to Hamilton was almost certainly an invitation to join the headquarters staff.[2]

Why did the Commander in Chief choose the young artillery officer? Although Hamilton always liked to think of himself as a warrior, he surely had not stood out in battle. The captain of one artillery company among many can only thus shine if chance places him in a crucial place at a crucial time. Had this happened to Hamilton it would, since he so soon became an object of general attention, surely have been recorded. Nor was he, as innumerable writers would have it, conspicuous because he was young and frail. The captain was not younger than many an officer of higher rank in that hastily improvised army, and many a soldier collapsed, as he never did, by the wayside.

Hamilton's company had once been a crack outfit, impressing viewers with uniforms and parade-ground discipline, but that situation lay far behind. After Hamilton had joined Washington's staff, he advised the New York Convention to give up (as they did) their artillery company, offering the remnant to the Continental service. The junior officers had all resigned or died or proved incompetent. Most of the men had refused to continue when their year's enlistment was over; only twenty-five remained. Hamilton was able to report this failure so baldly, without explanation or apology, because the story was a usual one. However, it cast no special light on his gifts as a commander.[3]

Surely information concerning Hamilton's propaganda activities in New York, which were known to various of Washington's associates, reached the General, whose aides spent so much of their time drafting letters and other documents. But Hamilton's current reputation was not dependent on his publications. The pamphlets and newspaper pieces had never penetrated beyond New York, and even mere knowledge of his authorship was restricted and unclear. Yet Pickering, who came from Massachusetts, remembered that he had already been told—he believed by the Massachusetts general Lincoln—"that Hamilton was a very extraordinary young man."[4] The explanation of why such a rumor moved through the army lay in the air, in that series of little actions that lead up to an impression, those indefinable symptoms which speak from minute to minute of greatness like a candle steadily burning. Hamilton had already interested two of the generals who were among Washington's closest intimates: Greene and Knox. He was the obvious staff officer. It was inevitable that he should receive a call from headquarters presided over by so perceptive a general as Washington.

When Washington's invitation came to him, Hamilton was recovering from his "long and dangerous illness." Since he could not ride at once to headquarters (he was not to do so for about a month) there was plenty of time for him to ponder the question whether he should lay aside in relation to the Commander in Chief the objection to what he considered "a kind of personal dependence," which had made him refuse similar requests from lesser generals.[5]

Now that his artillery company was on the verge of collapse, his military position was equivocal. Eager for personal independence and perhaps because of a then-exclusive loyalty to the adopted colony of New York, Hamilton had placed himself outside the regular line of command and promotion. Although he had functioned as part of Knox's continental regiment, his was a state commission. He could not change to the Continental service without probable loss of rank, certain loss of seniority. And his attitude towards the various states and their local troops had undergone a great change.

As Washington was later to argue, the mingling in the army of men from every one of the thirteen states had been the original seedbed of a continental point of view. Hamilton was on the way to becoming one of the most passionate of continentalists. And he had imbibed the disdain of the Continental soldier for those shifting, disciplineless, amateurish forces, the state militias.

True, being Washington's aide would not altogether repair Hamilton's original mistake. The Continental Congress, ever confused about military organization, had failed to regularize the position of staff officers. They did not, like officers of the line, receive congressional commissions. Hamilton would have the brevet rank of lieutenant colonel—quite a raise from captain!—but only as long as he served as Washington's aide. It was far from clear how this could be translated into what Hamilton's vision of himself demanded: an important command in the fighting line. Yet having the ear of the Commander in Chief should somehow enable him to make, when the time arrived, a shift to the line in which, at the moment, he had no rank whatsoever. So he hoped, as later actions made clear. But it must have given him a queasy feeling when the general orders that announced his appointment as Washington's aide referred to him not as Lieutenant Colonel (or even Captain) Alexander Hamilton, but "Alexander Hamilton, Esq."[6]

In considering whether to accept Washington's offer, Hamilton could conclude that his role in combat would not be greatly reduced. As an artilleryman, he fought only at long range. Although generals' aides were forbidden, so that they would stick to their correct duties, to carry arms, Hamilton had seen members of Washington's staff ride on their missions through the greatest danger, directing the bloody movements that followed their orders.

There was another aspect of service with Washington that appealed to Hamilton mightily. Basic to his mind was a passionate need to achieve a panoramic view. In his adolescent pamphlets, he had tried to examine the controversy between the colonies and England from every angle. To the end of his life he was impelled, even if this exercise were unnecessary for what he wished to achieve, to deal with subjects as he envisioned them completely, from the ground up. For a man thus disposed, the outlook of an artillery captain seemed almost blindness. But a member of the Commander in Chief's staff would stand on the highest lookout tower. Surely he could help determine events—and Hamilton suffered from no modesty, false or otherwise.

For Hamilton, the decision he faced was more determining than it would have been for almost any other man. With no childhood he chose to remember, no family to sustain him, no place (as he later commented) to go when other officers went home on leave, his total position in the world at any moment was the position he at that moment occupied. How completely his role in the army was synonymous in his mind with his own personal value was revealed when he wrote that having officers achieve rank without merit "in some degree makes me contemptible in my own eyes."[7]

If, after he had joined Washington's staff, his dignity were somehow violated to a point where his honor would force him to resign, he might well, having no other foothold in the Continental Army, become an outcast indeed. Thus, responding to Washington's call would profoundly shatter what he defined as "my desire . . . to keep my happiness independent of the caprices of others."[8]

It was the usage in the American as well as the English army to refer to a general's aides as his "family." What a poignant word! Did Hamilton, with all his fears, wish again to subject himself to family life, even in a simulated form?

In the "family" he had been asked to join, Washington would obviously play the role of father. His estimate of "the General's character" was therefore the key to Hamilton's decision.[9]

There is no reason to suppose that Hamilton had ever experienced more than the most casual association with Washington. Artillery captains neither transact business with top commanders nor are socially entertained by them. Yet, since such was Washington's habit as he rode around encampments, he had undoubtedly sometimes paused to exchange a few words with the eager captain.

The first thing that would have been obvious was their difference in bulk. From his height of over six feet, Washington, even if he dismounted, looked down on the top of Hamilton's head. And in every other dimension he seemed twice as large. While Hamilton talked with an eagerness and vivacity that made his words trip over each other, Washington listened with grave courtesy and, when he made smiling responses, he made them slowly. When he remounted and rode off, he left behind him the indelible impression of individual strength greater even than the powerful rank he held. As Abigail Adams wrote, "Not a king in Europe but would look like a valet de chambre by his side."[10]

Washington had led through the wilderness an official British delegation to the French in Canada when he was little more than a year older than Hamilton was now. His genius for command had accompanied him visibly since he was a stripling. It had solidified into an assumption, of which he was no more conscious from day to day than he was of his physical strength. Hamilton was a respecter of power, and he had the highest opinion of Washington's leadership. He had admired the way "His Excellency" had inspired the troops by "putting on the face of fortitude and resolution . . . while our affairs in this department were at the lowest ebb and the continent almost in a state of despair."[11] But what of Washington's "delicacy and good temper"? Basing his judgment on the high esteem in which Washington was held by all, Hamilton assumed that here there would be no problem.

Shooting up almost miraculously from the squalor of his childhood, Hamilton had never associated with any human being whose abilities might well top his own. Certainly not his father, that lovable weakling. If in some parts of his nature he yearned for a powerful father figure to serve as a bastion of the stability he had never known, he was also afraid of being overwhelmed. When he finally resolved that he would accept the possibilities—and take the risks—of joining Washington's staff, Hamilton also resolved that, should Washington make to him any "advances" of personal friendship, he would receive them "in a manner which showed at least I had no inclination to court them, and that I wished to stand rather on a footing of military confidence than of private attachment."[12]

15

New Father, New Family

[MARCH—MAY, 1777   AGE 20]

T HERE is evidence that Hamilton reached headquarters at Morristown shortly before his appointment as aide—undoubtedly he and Washington wished to have a closer look at each other. His position was formally announced to the army on March 1, 1777. Hamilton drafted a letter for Washington on that day, and soon had the pleasure of riding out with the Commander in Chief as one of those envied young men who were visibly and actually at the center of things.[1]

Hamilton instantly found himself at home. He had not been a member of the Family for two weeks before he extended, quite naturally, the regards of the group to a mutual friend. Even earlier in his service, he intercepted and himself answered a letter to Washington from his original military patron, General McDougall. Lest the older man, who had secured for him his first commission, think that he had reached out to show off his new power, Hamilton specified that the letter had by chance fallen into his hands. He was undertaking the reply since Washington was not well: "I conceive the only answer he would give may be given by myself." Hamilton refused the brigadier general's request that the post on the Hudson highlands he commanded be reinforced. Headquarters, he explained, had received what "I think" was decisive evidence that the British intended to go into New Jersey, not up the Hudson. Hamilton had, indeed, expressed what Washington would have wished.[2]

The conventional assumptions about a general's being father to his military "family" were a pale shadow in relation to a headquarters presided over by a parental figure so stupendous that he came to be regarded not only as the father of the whole army but of the nation that emerged. "Your Excellency"—for it was always thus formally that Hamilton addressed the General—seemed a stunning contrast to the incompetent exile whom Hamilton had as a child loved and pitied. Or perhaps it was not a contrast at all but a completion.

Washington exemplified in many ways the aristocratic ideal Hamilton had nurtured during his battered years with his father. That veteran aide Tench Tilghman had written some two months before Hamilton came to headquarters, "If it pleases God to spare the honestest man that I believe ever adorned the human race," the Revolution would be won. "I think I know the sentiments of his heart and in prosperity and adversity I never knew him to utter a wish or drop an expression that did not tend to the good of his country regardless of his own interest. He is blessed wherever he goes for the Tory is protected in person and property equally with the Whig. And, indeed, I often think more, for it is his maxim to convert by good usage not severity."[3]

A resemblance to James Hamilton would have been more difficult to recognize had Washington not been embattled with very similar difficulties—but now not personally, not meanly. There was in the Continental Army a perpetual need to scrounge for food and clothing, not for two sons and a complaining wife, but for men by the thousands. All the pettiness of an imperfect world impinged on headquarters as it had on James Hamilton's ever-shifting residences, but Washington, although he complained mightily—more perhaps than the declassed Scot who had his pride so carefully to tend—managed always, somehow, to overcome. Not a half-swamped small boat in a stormy sea, he rose like a great cliff against which the waves shattered. Above all, Washington had what Hamilton most yearned for: grandeur both in the world's attitude towards him and in his demands on himself.

Hamilton's dread that Washington would try to possess his soul passed quickly. His Excellency was not given to personal confidences nor did he desire them. Hamilton commented that "from the moderation and caution with which the General usually expresses himself" a letter praising a French officer "means a good deal." After Hamilton had been a member of the Family for more than three years, Lafayette felt it necessary to write: "I know the General's friendship and gratitude for you, my dear Hamilton. Both are greater than you perhaps imagine."[4]

Despite what has been written ten thousand times, there can be no doubt that Hamilton did not now become—he was never to become—a particular object of Washington's affections. If we are to diagnose for Washington a substitute for the son he never had, that individual would be Lafayette, concerning whom Washington's emotions were so strong that they often brought tears to his eyes. Lafayette's closeness did not inspire jealousy in Hamilton, who was indeed glad to make use of this relationship in an effort to further his own requests from Washington. Does this fact militate against the conception that Hamilton saw in Washington a superfather? Or can we assume that Hamilton was glad to have Lafayette between them as an emotional lightning rod?

Hamilton, as we shall see, found it extremely difficult to talk to Washington about matters that concerned him personally. Although he conferred with his chief many times a day, when he wished to raise affairs of his own, he would write Washington a letter. Eventually, after three and a half years of service, largely motivated by a passion to achieve independence, he was to break away from Washington. He acted in a sudden rage and then refused any discussion of the matter. If, after this declaration of freedom, he was extremely critical of Washington, before it he could not have behaved as a more loyal subordinate. Indeed, during the three and a half years, he made only one recorded criticism of his chief. Moved by his emotion for the accomplished John André, who had been convicted as a spy, Hamilton denounced privately to his fiancée Washington's decision that the charming young man be hanged not shot. Hamilton's perpetual attitude towards His Excellency was thus expressed: "I cannot forbear being uneasy lest my conduct prove displeasing to you."[5]

Hamilton had carried from his blighted childhood two opposite desires. One was to prove himself completely self-reliant, proudly independent of the outside world. The other was to merge his identity with some potent force outside himself. We have seen that from Cruger's countinghouse he wrote letters in his employer's very voice. We have seen the passion with which the recent immigrant threw himself into the patriot cause, and we shall see how completely he came to envision that cause and his personality as one. Time will show that he clasped to his bosom a federal constitution that he had opposed and that he continued, in one part of his nature, deeply to distrust. Our immediate concern is with how, as a youthful aide, he subordinated his personality to Washington's.

When he felt at last free to denounce his general, Hamilton wrote, "The truth is, our own dispositions are the opposites of each other."[6] In actuality, Washington had been, when himself a young man, very like his aide. Washington too had been what is to modern eyes an infant prodigy.* When Hamilton joined Washington, he was twenty. At twenty-one, Washington had led a royal mission to the French. Shortly thereafter, he became, during the French and Indian War, colonel of the Virginia regiment and commander in chief of the Virginia forces. In those years he had been pugnacious, wild, and uncontrolled, as Hamilton was inclined to be.[7] But there was a fundamental difference: Washington had another, stronger side to his nature, one that enabled him to combat those destructive tendencies. By the time the younger man came into his orbit, he had almost conquered them.

Washington imposed the results of this conquest on his aide. Left to himself, Hamilton regarded all human disagreements—indeed, most human relations—as a fight in which one individual won and the other lost. Washington had become a conciliator, deeply dedicated to healing all wounds within a cause that could be defeated only if the people were divided. Hamilton did get into some brawls when he was Washington's aide, but only in his private activities. Acting in his official capacity, he was as conciliatory as his master. Although temperamentally one of the most indiscreet of men, he became a model of discretion. The French general and philosopher Chastellux observed that Hamilton had "developed those talents which the General had known how to discover and put into activity, while the young soldier, by a prudence and secrecy still more beyond his years than his information, justified the confidence with which he was honored."[8]

Hamilton brought to every problem a set of preconceived conceptions which, like a template, determined his decision. Washington's fundamental effort was becoming more and more to dig so deep into a situation that he reached the bedrock, where opposition had to cease because here was where all attitudes were grounded. To achieve immediate decisions, Hamilton, marshaling only those facts that accorded with his temperamental leanings, moved fast. Washington was much slower. Seeking a comprehensive view, the General set up, sometimes in facing columns on paper, more often in his own mind, a mental

---

* In those days people, who died so much younger, were encouraged to mature much more rapidly. The star-crossed Juliet was twelve. Pitt became prime minister of England at twenty-four. A Renaissance Italian artist normally made his mark by the time he was fifteen. John Keats died at twenty-six, two years before this volume leaves Hamilton.

balance, on the opposite sides of which he piled information and opinions until the beam tipped in one direction or another. For this process, Hamilton's contributions were very valuable: the more brilliant the statements of points of view available to Washington, the more effective his method of decision.

Washington was to write of Hamilton as being "enterprising, quick in his perceptions, and his judgment intuitively great."[9] Hamilton had to be conscious that his mind moved with much greater speed. It was disappointing when, after he had put forward what seemed to him an incontrovertible argument, Washington decided otherwise. But nonetheless Hamilton found himself, if only through his chief, in a position of power.

In degrees varying with the extent of their pro-Hamilton infatuation, writers have claimed that the aide controlled the Commander. Atherton has Washington admit that Hamilton was "my brain," and tell the young man, "You are my good genius. Take care of yourself. . . . I believe I am not lacking in courage, but I always have most when you are close by."[10] This is, of course, an extreme example, but similar contentions are made in innumerable volumes. They are all poppycock.

Washington was, in areas he considered his province and responsibility, among human beings one of those most unwilling to be led. Furthermore, Hamilton came to him in 1777 with extremely limited experience. The promising youth was caught up in a phenomenon that applied as well to most of the army's top command, and that underlay the loyalty which made Washington's position as commander in chief unassailable. Like the others, Hamilton was educated on the job by Washington. This was done with suitable respect, since His Excellency, one of whose great gifts was to recognize ability, realized almost instantly that he had found a jewel. It took only a few months for Hamilton to become, as Washington put it, "the principal and most confidential aide of the Commander in Chief."[11]

However, Hamilton was never designated chief of staff. If he were not off on a mission, he shared the work of the other aides. Washington has been accused of being a poor organizer, and, indeed, when Commander in Chief as when President, he made little effort to diversify activities.*

It is often claimed that whenever Hamilton drafted a letter for

---

* That Secretary of the Treasury Hamilton interfered in foreign relations and Secretary of State Jefferson interfered with Hamilton's financial programs seemed to President Washington a reasonable offshoot of their both being in his cabinet.

George Washington: life mask taken at Mount
Vernon in 1785. Courtesy, Morgan Library

Washington's signature, he was expressing his own ideas. This would be easier to contend if Hamilton handled largely by himself specific aspects of headquarters policy. It is true that his knowledge of French made dealing with the French officers in the American army his province, but for the most part the hundreds on hundreds of letters he drafted were parts of sequences in which the surrounding letters were in the handwriting of other aides. Some documents were begun by Hamilton and then—presumably because he was called away—finished in another hand. The aides seem to have functioned as a unit, tasks being handed to whoever was not occupied at the moment.

Another contention is that Hamilton taught poor, backwoods Washington how to write. In this epoch, Washington wrote much better than did Hamilton, and in any case their natural styles were very different. Hamilton was by far the more verbose, intellectual rather than imaginative, given to arguing matters out as in a legal brief. Washington sought conciseness, often achieving synthesis through the use of metaphor. All of Washington's aides, including Hamilton, when they wrote for Washington approximated his style.

Washington upon occasion jotted down or dictated for his aides "heads," that is, main points he wished a letter to cover, but as a general rule, a few words of instruction sufficed. This was because the staff operated as an adjunct to Washington's brain: they knew what he knew and understood his policies.

The Continental Army was by no means a professionally organized military establishment, and what organization there was often broke down. It was Washington's fate, and thus that of his staff, to fill in for all lapses. If, for instance, the adjutant general was away or proved incompetent, his duties were handled by headquarters. This meant that headquarters had always to be prepared, to some extent at least, to take anything over.

When, later in the war, French allies encamped next to Washington's army, the Gallic officers were amazed at how little informed gossip concerning present and future operations circulated in the American camp. Since the war was in part a civil war, in which the loyalties of many persons were torn, Washington was forever fearing leakage of information to the enemy. He played his cards close to his chest, but headquarters could not operate unless the young men around him were encouraged to look over his shoulder.

Washington was to comment that during the Revolution Hamilton had been afforded "the means of viewing everything on a larger scale" than generals, "whose attentions were confined to divisions or brigades."[12] In talking to generals, Hamilton could sometimes gratify their curiosity, but it was perhaps a more enchanting role to preserve his superiority with silence. His highest hopes of omniscience were more than realized.

But omniscience had its price: except when the army was in winter quarters, headquarters was awash with business. Washington wrote: "I give in to no kind of amusement myself, and consequently those about me can have none, but are confined from morning 'till eve hearing and answering the applications and letters. . . . To have the mind never unbent, always on the stretch, makes material odds."[13]

For most people, those odds would be materially negative—but not so for Hamilton. All his life long he sought masses of detail as an anodyne: they filled his mind to the exclusion of unwelcome horrors. "Details of every kind, political and military," so Chastellux remembered, were entrusted to Hamilton.[14] Washington could rejoice that too many could not be poured on the brilliant young man: he always had an appetite for more. And, as good luck would have it, he had no family in America: no aged parents to comfort, no wife and children to lure him home. Year after year, day after day, he was eagerly at Washington's service. Furthermore, Hamilton became so sensitive and effective an instrument for communicating and implementing the needs of his commander that he could, as we shall soon see, be entrusted with the most delicate missions.

How valuable Washington considered Hamilton's help will be made manifest when we examine His Excellency's reiterated efforts to keep, even if unfairly, his hold on the brilliant youth. Yet, when Hamilton did go, there was no significant change in the command. His Excellency had lost an extremely valuable coadjutor, one who had helped clarify his thinking and who had taken off his hands innumerable tasks, large and small—but headquarters operated, if less efficiently, less excitingly, basically as before.

Hamilton's closest day-by-day associations now were in a semi—boarding school atmosphere with his fellow aides, who normally fluctuated between three and five. He regarded "the lads" as "friends and brothers," sending them "love" at the end of high-spirited letters. (He typically signed himself to Washington more soberly: "With the warmest esteem and respect.") Until the group was joined by the Marquis de Lafayette, who was eight months Hamilton's junior, Hamilton was the youngest. And he remained physically the smallest. Harrison, aged all of thirty-two, was the senior and much teased by his juniors because he sat so interminably at his desk that he was often troubled with piles.[15]

The aides always lived and worked under the same roof with their general in whatever building became Washington's headquarters—on the march sometimes for a single night, in the winters for months. The structures varied from mansions to mean farmhouses, but in eighteenth-century America even mansions were small. Since Washington had an objection to displacing families, the owners often continued to occupy several of the rooms, two sets of servants commingling in the kitchen. The aides usually slept two or more to a bed in rooms filled to the walls with beds. Sometimes Hamilton and his companions stretched out on the kitchen floor, and lucky he who could get a berth closest to the fire.

At the very best, working quarters were cramped. Tables were gathered from around the building and borrowed from other houses to be placed so close together that the aides had to keep their elbows hugged to their sides. Everyone knew in general what everyone else was doing: laughter or indignation would spring up to fly across the room. The best toy the aides had to play with—the subject of their most delightful gossip and their best strokes of wit—was the conduct of the entire war.

The esprit de corps of Washington's family was remarkable. Under the benign and sometimes terrifying—His Excellency was given to herculean rages—leadership of their chief Hamilton associated with his companions in harmony greater than he was ever, in the hurly-burly of men and affairs, to know again. Thinking in terms of military honor and gentlemanly "delicacy," the aides were exquisitely careful of each other's feelings. There is no evidence that Washington's gift of the greatest responsibility to the youngest incited any jealousy. According to the Hamilton family tradition, Harrison dubbed Hamilton "the little lion." He was also called, as was to be expected, "Ham," or "Hammie." Soon after his arrival he began referring to Washington's headquarters by a word that his previous experience made poignant: "home."[16]

Even in the middle of strenuous campaigns, Washington's headquarters was a social center. The various officers of the day were automatically asked to dine, as were officers and civilians who appeared on business or had any claim to be entertained. When the situation permitted, everyone sat long over their wine, cracking walnuts in season.

Hamilton's own social position had leaped upward. As the Commander in Chief's aide he could fraternize on a basis of equality with anyone. General Greene told his son that he found Hamilton's entry into headquarters "a bright gleam of sunshine, ever growing brighter as the general darkness thickened." No longer separated from Hamilton by considerations of rank, Greene established a close friendship with the graduated artillery captain.[17]

The possibilities of relaxation were, of course, greatly increased when, fighting having come to a virtual standstill, the army was in winter quarters. Then the purely masculine society was varied with wives—Martha Washington appeared each year from Virginia—and young ladies from the leading neighborhood families. Hamilton joined Washington at such a time. No one knows what house was headquarters at Morristown during the winter of 1776–1777, but we do have an account, written when spring was on its way, of the life Hamilton shared. The Virginian wife of Colonel Theodorick Bland described Morristown as "a very clever little village situated in a most beautiful valley at the foot of five mountains. It has three houses with steeples, which give it a consequential look. . . . It has two families [who are] refugees from New York in it, otherwise inhabited by the earnestest rustics you ever beheld. You cannot travel three miles without passing through one of these villages. All of them have meeting houses and court houses, etc., etc. decorated with steeples which give them a pretty, airy look, and the farms between the mountains are the most rural sweet spots in nature, their meadows of fine luxuriant grass which looks like a bed of velvet interspersed with yellow, blue, and white flowers. They present us with just such scenes as the poets paint Arcadia: purling rills, mossy beds, etc., but not crying swains and lovely nymphs, though there are some exceeding pretty girls, but they appear to have souls formed for the distaff rather than the tender passions. . . .

"Now let me speak of *our* noble and agreeable commander [Washington], for he commands both sexes, one by his excellent skill in military matters, the other by his ability, politeness, and attention. We visit them twice or three times a week by particular invitation. He is generally busy in the forenoon, but from dinner [at about 4 P.M.] till night he is free for all company. His worthy lady seems to be in perfect felicity when she is by the side of her *Old Man* as she calls him. We often make parties on horseback . . . at which time General Washington throws off the hero and takes on the chatty, agreeable companion. He can be downright impudent sometimes—such impudence, Fanny, as you and I like."

"The General's family," who took part in the outings, were described by Mrs. Bland as "all polite, sociable gentlemen who make the day pass with a great deal of satisfaction to the visitors." Fitzgerald was "an agreeable, broad-shouldered Irishman. . . . Johnston is exceedingly witty at everybody's expense, but won't allow others to be so at his own." She described both Tilghman and Harrison as "worthy," adding for Tilghman the word "modest." As for "Captain Gibbs of the General's guard," he was "a good-natured Yankee who makes a thousand blunders in the Yankee style and keeps the dinner table in a constant laugh." Mrs. Bland did not select out for particular comment Colonel Hamilton, whom she described as "a sensible, genteel, polite young fellow, a West Indian."[18]

Colonel Alexander Graydon, a young Philadelphia merchant-turned-soldier, who visited headquarters in the summer of 1777, saw Hamilton in altogether different colors. It was Washington's habit to sit to one side at the dinner table. By rotation, an aide occupied the position of host. When Graydon dined, the turn happened to be Hamilton's. "In a large company in which there were several ladies, among whom I recollect one or two of the Miss Livingstons and a Miss Brown, he acquitted himself," so Graydon recorded, "with an ease, propriety and vivacity, which gave me the most favorable impression of his talents and accomplishments." In the evening, Hamilton and Tilghman took the visitor to drink tea "with some of the ladies of the village, where were also those with whom he dined."

The Philadelphian, who liked to boast of his own dissipations and considered himself much of a rake, did not, as he later recalled, then see in Hamilton "the solid abilities his subsequent career unfolded." Instead, Hamilton's behavior "announced a brilliancy which might adorn the most polished circles of society, and fitted him for the part of Algarotti and the court of a Frederick:

> 'Vous que les grâces et les ris
> Formerent pour flatter et plaire,'

to borrow the words of the king in an address to his favorite."[19]

Hamilton had known the "Miss Livingstons" since his schooldays at Elizabethtown. Susanna (Suky) encouraged Hamilton to write her sister Catherine, a flirt who at twenty-six was considered, according to the ideas of the time, too old to remain unmarried. She belonged to one of the richest and most powerful clans of New Jersey and New York.[20]

Suky, Hamilton wrote, had stated that Catherine had displayed "a relish for politics. . . . Though I am perfectly willing to harmonize with your inclination in this respect, without making cynical inquiry whether it proceed from sympathy in the concerns of the public or merely from female curiosity, yet I will not consent to be limited to any particular subject. I challenge you to meet me in whatever path you dare; and, if you have no objection, for variety and amusement, we will even make excursions in the flowery walks and roseate bowers of Cupid. You know, I am renowned for gallantry, and shall always be able to entertain you with a choice collection of the prettiest things imaginable. I fancy my knowledge of you affords me a tolerably just idea of your taste," but he wished she would give him "such intimations of it as will remove all doubt." Otherwise, "I should have a most arduous task on my hands, at least, if connoisseurs in the sex say true, according to whose representations, contrary to the vulgar opinion, woman is not a *simple*, but a most complex, intricate, and enigmatical being.

"And knowing exactly your taste, and whether you are of a romantic or discreet temper as to love affairs, I will endeavor to regulate myself by it. If you would choose to be a goddess and to be worshipped as such, I will torture my imagination for the best arguments the nature of the case will admit, to prove you so. You shall be one of the graces, or Diana, or Venus, or something surpassing them all. And after your deification, I will cull out of every poet of my acquaintance the choicest delicacies they possess, as offerings at your Goddesship's shrine. But if, conformable to your usual discernment, you are content with being a mere mortal, and require no other incense than is justly due to you, I will talk to you like one [in] his sober senses, and, though it may be straining the point a little, I will even stipulate to pay you all the rational tribute properly applicable to a fine girl."

He had little news to send, except that he hoped the ensuing campaign would mark the defeat of British hopes. "You and I, as well as our neighbors" should "pray for victory . . . and peace; as . . . they would remove those obstacles which now lie in the way of that most delectable thing called matrimony;—a state which with a kind of magnetic force attracts every breast . . . in spite of the resistance it encounters in the dull admonitions of prudence, which is so prudish and perverse a dame as to be at perpetual variance with it. . . ." He signed himself "Your assured friend and servant, Alexr. Hamilton."[21]

The general tone of this epistle is in keeping with the flirtatious idioms of the time. A parody of pretentious metaphors, it makes fun both of the writer and the recipient. When Hamilton speaks of himself as being "renowned for gallantry," it is part of the game, as is his suggestion that referring to Catherine as "a fine girl" might be "straining the point a little." As for the bantering generalizations concerning the opposite sex, they were an accepted convention, perhaps because they served as a nonphysical and impersonal way of keeping in the foreground that the communication was a sexual one. Both women and men teased each other with presumably witty allegations unflattering to their correspondent's gender.

Yet Hamilton's letter, despite its superficial subtlety, is at base far from subtle. Unless we assume a previous heavy flirtation, which the entire context of Hamilton's communication seems to exclude, the young man is trying to pounce on the older woman with the suddenness of a tiger: "I challenge you to meet me in whatever path you dare." This is aggressive, yet within the bounds of rational behavior. But, as the letter continues, Hamilton allows his determination to come clear in a quite irrational nakedness. Although he has not included one word of affection for her but has regarded her only as an adversary he wished to conquer, he now indicates that his thoughts are running to marriage. Such a hint might conceivably have been viable had the possible match been dynastic—one great family, one great fortune joining with another—but for a Livingston and a nobody from the Indies! His closing comment about marriage being contrary to prudence may have been intended as a cover for the highly prudential implication of his letter—but did it suffice?

Hamilton eagerly expected a quick and encouraging reply. Eventually Catherine Livingston did write to him. The letter is lost, but Hamilton's response reveals, under a pretext of banter, hurt feelings and resentment:

"When I was almost out of patience and out of humor at your presumptuous delay in not showing yourself duly sensible of the honor done you by me, your epistle opportunely came to hand, and has put all matters tolerably to rights.

"As I thought it well enough written and no discredit to you, I ventured to show it to a gentleman of our family. He was silly enough to imagine that I did this through vanity and a desire to display my own importance in having so fair and so sensible a correspondent, as he indulgently called you; but I hope you will not be so vain as to entertain a single moment the most distant imagination of the same kind. It would be paying yourself too high a compliment, and give room to suspect you are strongly infected with that extreme self-complacency commonly attributed to your sex."

He then stated that his friend had described her as a "divine girl," a "goddess," but he was sure that Catherine was too averse to flattery to take this seriously. "I am," he went on, "glad you are sensible of the obligations you are under to me for my benevolent and disinterested conduct in making so courageous an effort, under all the imaginary terrors you intimate, without any tolerable prospect of—compensation." He was, however, willing to continue their correspondence despite running the risk of being, on the one hand, "anathematized by grave censors for dedicating so much of my time to so trifling and insignificant a toy as—woman," and, on the other, "of being run through the body by saucy inamoratos who will envy me the prodigious favor, forsooth, of your correspondence. . . . But ALL FOR LOVE is my motto. . . . Now for politics."

Having written a short paragraph on that subject, he said that he agreed with the antipathy she had expressed for war. "Every finer feeling of a delicate mind revolts from the idea of shedding human blood." Were it not "in defense of all that is valuable in society, I could never be reconciled to a military character."[22]

This, as far as the records go, brought his correspondence with Catherine Livingston to an end. Some years were to pass before Hamilton succeeded in marrying her even more importantly placed cousin.

16

Thoughts During Doldrums

[MARCH–MAY, 1777   AGE 20]

T HE encampment Hamilton had joined at Morristown represented a new strategic concept, one of Washington's greatest
contributions to winning the war. Hamilton was to remember
"the *almost magic operations* of the remainder of that winter," which
offered "the extraordinary spectacle of a powerful army [the British]
straitened within narrow limits by the phantom of a military force, and
never permitted to transgress those limits with impunity, *in which*
skill supplied the plan, and means of disposition was the substitute for
an [American] army."[1]

The basic principle was drawn from the example of Bunker Hill on
the one hand, Trenton and Princeton on the other. The Americans had
first considered Bunker Hill a defeat, since they had in the end been
driven from their fortifications. But Washington had come to realize
what the enemy had recognized from the start: the action was a
precedent-making victory. The British could not again risk such heavy
losses. Achieving manpower was for the Americans only a matter of
national morale, but the enemy, who were neither able nor eager to
arm many Tories, had to import their men from Europe. Not only was
this operation slow and complicated, but for the Crown to procure
men to send was extremely expensive. The Hessians were rented at so
much a head, and the price went up tremendously for every mercenary
wounded or killed.

Bunker Hill taught both armies that, however vulnerable the Americans might be on flat terrain, where they were accessible to the exertion of European skill, they might not be dislodged from strong positions. Washington established strong posts blocking each of the three directions along which the British might advance by land from New York City. Fortifications in the White Plains–New Castle area overhung the direct road to New England. Fortifications in the highlands of the Hudson, by blocking that waterway, protected Upstate New York, the back door to New England, and the wilderness that led on to British-held Canada. And the hills around Morristown overlooked the flat New Jersey plain, across which Washington had been sent scuttling the previous fall.

Since professional troops fought to earn their livings, they could not be expected to put up with poor rations which, like all the powerful equipment of a sophisticated army—cavalry horses, well set up artillery—depended on a continual flow of supplies. In Europe a prized tactical maneuver was to make an enemy army wither by cutting the stem that connected it with its supply base. Any British advance had to dangle behind it a supply line that would continue to function. The British could not leave any American strong point at their rear. Thus, as long as Washington could hold Morristown in any considerable force, the British could not repeat their advance overland towards Philadelphia.

The flaw in this strategy was created by the British fleet. Since the patriots had only the most rudimentary navy, enemy transports and supply ships protected by warships could carry troops to any point on the long seacoast of the thirteen states. There was no important city which was not vulnerable to troops landed nearby. But during Hamilton's first months on Washington's staff, no such action was to be feared. Sailing ships did not venture out on winter seas.

Ever since the army had started its peregrinations by leaving Harlem Heights, the New York Provincial Congress had desired a direct line to headquarters that would keep them informed on "military operations." They had requested Tench Tilghman to write them "daily." Tilghman had done his best, but as soon as Hamilton became Washington's aide, the congress decided to pay Tilghman off with a present worth £80 and substitute for the Marylander the West Indian who had put his roots down in New York. This served Hamilton's future career by restoring contact with the political leaders of the state that was to remain his political base.[2]

Hamilton undertook the task "cheerfully," and then put the situation, as he had done in offering to flirt with Catherine Livingston, on an advisory basis. He accepted the congress's "challenge" to meet it "in the epistolary field." He had no intention of being, like Tilghman, a semiofficial channel from headquarters. The opinions he expressed were not, he warned, to be considered as an "echo" of Washington's, but as his own "private sentiments," which would "probably differ widely" from the General's "in many respects." He on at least one occasion quoted his personal sources of information.[3]

Washington, who was informed, surely approved of his aide's insistence that he was not writing officially. Not only did this remove from the General the necessity to supervise, but it gave him a means of disseminating from headquarters ideas and information that he did not wish officially to sponsor.

There was an amazing difference between the pessimistic reports Washington sent to the Continental Congress and Hamilton's optimism to the New York legislature. Washington wrote that the shortage of supplies was "almost incredible." He suffered "the most painful anxiety when I reflect on our situation and that of the enemy." Unless the recruits promised for the Continental Army arrived soon, "we must, before long, experience some interesting and melancholy event." Towards the end of the month, when the recruits had not materialized, he stated that he had "no men with which to oppose the enemy's designs on any quarter although called on from every quarter."[4]

Hamilton wrote that the many deserters coming in from the enemy showed them to be in desperate straits. Since the possibility that the French might enter the war in Europe would disincline the British from sending reinforcements overseas, Howe's force would be, during the next campaign, disastrously inferior in numbers to the Americans, who were being steadily reinforced. Hamilton even brought himself to the point of speculating that the enemy would skulk behind their fortifications during 1778, "confining themselves to guerrilla activity. . . . It would be madness in them, weak as they are, to risk all in a capital attempt." Howe would be unable to take the field with more than eight thousand men. Considering "the increase in strength of our army . . . let him go where he will, the probability of defeat will be strong."[5]

The discrepancies between Hamilton's and Washington's reports were partly inspired by an irreconcilable dilemma. Unless military weaknesses were called forcibly to the attention of the national legislature which was managing the war, they would never be remedied. But if they became common knowledge, they would discourage support for the patriot cause. As Washington put it in one of his devastating reports: the "melancholy truths" were "necessary to be known to Congress, however prudent it may be to conceal them from the observation of others."[6] The leaders, and through them the population of that lukewarm state New York, could be considered among the "others."

Hamilton wrote that a true patriot "would not expose the weak side . . . to find opportunity of displaying his own discernment." When Robert R. Livingston complained that the strength of the enemy was underestimated in Hamilton's reports, the lieutenant colonel replied that to overestimate "is of infinite determent to our affairs." He cited the lesson supplied by the drop in patriot ardor during Washington's ignominious flight through New Jersey and the rise after the successes at Trenton and Princeton.[7]

Despite a basic faith that everything would turn out for the best in the long run, Washington viewed events from day to day with a gnawing apprehension, partly nervous and partly based on a determination always to be prepared to deal with the worst. Hamilton (perhaps because he had succeeded in leaving so many dreadful things behind him) tended to ignore obstacles: "It is a maxim of my life to enjoy the present good with the highest relish, and to soften the present evil by a hope of future good." Even when he wrote Hugh Knox in faraway St. Croix, where there was no propaganda end to be gained, he gave an amazingly rosy picture—rosier than he truly believed—of the Continental Army.[8]

Despite Hamilton's suggestions that the British might be too scared to move out of New York, much of his early correspondence with the New York legislature was an exchange of speculations on where they would move. The two main possibilities were that they would advance on Philadelphia—by water, by a march across New Jersey, or both—or that they would try, by an amphibious attack, to capture the Hudson River Valley. The second possibility most bothered New York officials, and it also bothered Washington.[9]

The Commander in Chief wrote lugubriously that having the British control free navigation on the Hudson and being thus enabled to prevent American movement up and down or across, "would prove fatal to us." Not only would it cut the eastern and southern states from each other, but the defenses in northern New York against invasion from Canada would have to be evacuated because of lack of supplies.[10]

Hamilton's more cheerful view of the situation was, in fact, more realistic. Any advance up the Hudson to cut the nation in half, he wrote, would "do better in speculation than in practice. Unless the geography of the country is far different from anything I can conceive, to effect this would require a chain of posts" that could only be protected by "an immense army." If Washington hung on the British rear and seized every opportunity for skirmishing, "their situation might be rendered insupportably uneasy." Even after word came that General Burgoyne was advancing down from Canada with a second large force, Hamilton refused to agree with those who postulated that Howe would march north to achieve a rendezvous at Albany. Yet the aide urged that as a precaution all the small boats on the Hudson, which would be essential to American movement across the river, be prepared to flee, at any alarm, up inlets where British warships could not follow.

Hamilton was becoming ever more convinced that Philadelphia must be the objective. The city "has all along been the main source of supply towards the war and the getting it into their possession would deprive us of a wheel we could very badly spare in the great political and military machine. . . . It is also a common and well-grounded rule in war to strike first and principally at the capital towns and cities in order to [achieve] the conquest of a country."[11]

The knowledge of French, which had been part of Hamilton's self-education—the Marquis de Chastellux soon testified that he spoke fluently[12]—came as a welcome addition to headquarters, where the language was haltingly spoken if at all. (Washington knew no French.) The aide's proficiency involved him in trying to handle situations that were highly irritating to the upper officers of the army. At the same time it established his first close contact with members of the nation he was subsequently (during Washington's presidency and thereafter) so conspicuously to dislike and distrust.

The American war against the traditional enemy of France had seemed to innumerable French soldiers of fortune an opportunity for employment and for achieving rank in a foreign army that would further their military careers in Europe. Loud with boasts and pretensions, they grandly offered their services to the American diplomatic representatives in Paris. Since the diplomats were seeking a French alliance, they were eager to be agreeable, and they assumed that professional European soldiers would be enthusiastically welcomed in the amateur American army. Now possessed of letters and promises, the French officers crossed the ocean, descended in droves on the Continental Congress. The legislators supinely gave them major commissions, and shipped them on to Washington. Coming in, as if from another planet, over the heads of the American veterans, they made no secret of their disdain for such self-trained soldiers. Surely their own European experience entitled them to determine the discipline and strategy of the Continental Army. Hamilton spent many long hours trying to mediate between angry soldiers orating in two languages.

The insistence of François, Marquis de Malmady, that he be made a brigadier general inspired Hamilton—he had been at headquarters a little more than two months—to his first effort to advise Congress on military matters. He warned the New York representative, William Duer, that agreeing to Malmady's request would raise the ambitions of all the French officers "already too high, to a pitch which it would be impossible to gratify or endure. . . .

"We are already greatly embarrassed with the Frenchmen among us, and from the genius of the people shall continue to be so. . . . Their ignorance of our language, of the disposition of the people, the resources and deficiencies of the country, their own habits and tempers—all these are disqualifications that put it out of their power to be of any real use or service to us."

Congress, Hamilton complained, had at the start made a general out of "every adventurer that came, without even the shadow of credentials." This, seconding "the aspiring disposition natural to those people," encouraged the expectations of those Frenchmen who actually did have credentials to exceed all bounds. Then, the situation having become impossible, Congress closed its ears to all foreign officers, thereby creating among soldiers "much addicted to national punctilio . . . a general clamor and dissatisfaction." The resulting "united voice of complaint" could cross the ocean to make an unfortunate impression in France, one "which it is not our interest should exist." But Hamilton had a solution.

A few of the most deserving French officers should be advanced "beyond what they can reasonably pretend to." Such "extraordinary marks of favor" conferred on some, would make it easy to persuade French opinion that all the others had failed from lack of merit. This would enable Congress "with safety" to keep the French flood within bounds.[13]

Hamilton carefully disassociated these "sentiments" from Washington's. The Commander in Chief, who was to write in a moment of passion that he wished there were no foreign officers in the service except Lafayette, would have agreed with what his aide was trying to achieve. However, Washington would never have urged a solution that cynically ignored the effect of general policy on individual qualifications, feelings, careers.

In taking it upon himself to advise the New York legislators concerning the treatment of suspected Tories, Hamilton urged what was also Washington's policy: as many should be pardoned and won over as possible. But where Washington liked to emphasize that tolerance and personal kindness created effective policy, Hamilton wrote in terms of expediency. It was impolitic to apprehend persons who would escape ultimate conviction because on being released they would, by expatiating on their sufferings, excite "pity towards themselves" and abhorrence towards their persecutors. And waverers would, after prosecution, "return home worse than they were."

A certain general, Hamilton continued, had advised his son either to destroy the Roman army utterly or dismiss them with every mark of honor and respect. "So with respect to Tories: I would either disable them from doing us any injury, or I would endeavor to gain their friendship by clemency." Either give complete pardons or "inflict capital and severe punishments."[14]

Yet Hamilton enunciated, at almost the same moment, extreme egalitarian principles.

New York, now an independent state if for the moment allied with the others, was drawing up a constitution, and Hamilton's fingers itched to get in on the drafting. However, no one consulted him. When he was finally sent a printed copy, he expressed admiration, but stated to Gouverneur Morris that he saw certain defects, which he would have pointed out were it not "too late." Morris's reply projected as the principal defect a "want of vigor" due to the weakness of the executive. The older Hamilton would have agreed passionately, but the younger Hamilton was more concerned with supporting a political philosophy that would make his older self sputter in outrage. The youth came out in favor of "representative democracy." In the eighteenth century the word "democracy" carried such connotations of unchecked popular rule that even Jefferson was to repudiate it, insisting that he was that less wild creature, a "republican."

Hamilton explained to Morris that, although "unstable democracy is an epithet frequently in the mouths of politicians," if democratic governments failed, it was because they had been "compounded with other principles." All the checks and balances in the New York constitution Hamilton attacked on the ground that they encouraged "distinct interests," which would clash and produce chaos.

The New York constitution graded the vote according to wealth. Only the well-to-do could vote for the governor and the senate, the franchise of men with little property being limited to the lower legislative house, the assembly. Hamilton feared that under this arrangement the senate would "degenerate into a body purely aristocratical." He supported a constitutional conception dear to the radical wing of the patriot party. The basic governmental power should rest with the popularly elected assembly, which would, by majority vote of its members, select the governor, the senate, and even the judges. "The danger of an abuse of power from a simple legislature would not be very great," Hamilton pontificated, when the legislature was created by "equality and fullness of popular representation."[15]

Thus, for all his aristocratic instincts, Hamilton expressed himself, in May, 1777, as a democrat indeed. We can only conclude that the very young man whose political activities had so far been as a hand-to-mouth exponent of a cause to which he had just been converted, and who had since then been busy as a soldier, had not given himself an opportunity to revise the radical conceptions that he had picked up at the same moment as he had picked up the propagandist's pen.

17

Blindman's Buff

[MAY–AUGUST, 1777   AGE 20]

AT the very end of May, 1777, when greening trees presaged bloody fighting, Washington moved his headquarters to Middlebrook, at the very edge of the New Jersey hills. "Our family," Hamilton explained, "seems desirous of cultivating a closer acquaintance with the enemy."[1]

Livingston had been correct when he guessed that Hamilton had underestimated both the force already in New York and the possibility that Howe would be reinforced from overseas. The eight thousand enemy soldiers Hamilton had foreseen turned out to be twenty-seven thousand. In mid-June, General Howe marched onto the plains below Washington's encampment.[2]

To his official New York correspondents, Hamilton echoed the conviction at American headquarters that the British would not, by advancing on Philadelphia, leave dangling behind them a vulnerable supply line. Their object was to lure Washington down from his heights onto fields suited to the skills of a regular army. Since Washington had no intention of obliging, the only possible British victory was on the propaganda front.

"I know the comments some people will make on our Fabian conduct," Hamilton wrote.* "It will be imputed either to cowardice or to

---

* Fabius was a Roman general celebrated in history for avoiding the main Carthaginian army while skirmishing on its flanks. He was removed from his command to make place for a more aggressive general who was defeated by the Carthaginians.

weakness. But . . . the liberties of America are an infinite stake. We should not play a desperate game for it, or put it upon the issue of a single cast of the die." Since "the loss of one general engagement may effectively ruin us," a major battle was to be hazarded only if "our resources for keeping up an army were at an end, and some decisive blow was absolutely necessary; or unless our strength was so great as to give certainty of success. Neither is the case.

"America," Hamilton continued, "can in all probability maintain its army for years," while the British force would shrink. The situation in Europe, where all "maritime powers were interested for the defeat of British arms," boded well. A war of attrition would favor the United States.

"In the meantime, it is painful to leave a part of the inhabitants a prey to [the enemy's] depredations; and it is wounding to the feelings of a soldier to see an enemy parading before him and daring him to a fight which he is obliged to decline. But a part must be sacrificed to the whole and passion must give to reason."

It would be unwise, so Hamilton closed his letter, to publish such "sentiments" as coming from him: that would tip off the enemy to the views of headquarters. Yet it might be well for the New York authorities to circulate what "ought to govern the conduct of the army, in order to prepare the minds of the people for what might happen, and take off the disagreeable impressions our caution may make."[3]

Hamilton's rising position at headquarters was being revealed by the frequency with which he was empowered to communicate the Commander in Chief's orders over his own signature. He no more hesitated to take a high tone with high officers than, when a juvenile clerk, he had hesitated to tick off a sea captain. He wrote Major General John Sullivan laconically and without a word of civility, that the reinforcements Sullivan desired would be forthcoming when and if headquarters concluded that he needed them. "The information contained in your last . . . is not well founded. . . . I am with regard, Sir, your most obed. servant, A Hamilton ADC."[4]

Hamilton had reported British intentions correctly. Having failed to entice Washington down into the plain, they evacuated altogether their posts in New Jersey. Then they busily fitted up their ships to accommodate troops and horses. Since Washington was in no position to attack them in their base, the next move was irrevocably theirs. This grounded the thinking at headquarters on speculation: Were the British going to sail up the Hudson or to Philadelphia, or further south, or north again to Boston? A new and frightening weight on the balance was added by news from up north. The American block against a strong army's coming down from Canada under General John Burgoyne was the fort at Ticonderoga. To the amazement of the entire Continental Army—Hamilton suspected "cowardice and treachery"—the American defenders had abandoned Ticonderoga without attempting any defense. They disappeared, from patriot as well as British eyes, into the wilderness.*5

The New York authorities expressed to Hamilton horror at having the northern part of their state left, as it seemed, defenseless. Hamilton admonished them: "The worst we have to fear is that a panic will seize the people. . . . It behooves their leaders to put on a cheerful countenance."6

Hamilton was, himself, not panicked. In sending the news to Hugh Knox, he wrote that the Revolutionary cause was "too well matured and has too great stability to be shaken by an accident." True, "a new and easy door" had been opened to northwestern Connecticut and Massachusetts as well as northern New York. However, the door could only be used effectively if Howe took the bulk of his army up the Hudson to cooperate with Burgoyne. Such a move would call for all the Continental Army's "efforts to counteract them." But if Howe were "fool enough" not to abandon his manifest intentions against Philadelphia, Burgoyne "will either be obliged to content himself with the possession of Ticonderoga and the dependent fortresses, and with carrying on a partisan [guerrilla] war the rest of the campaign, or he must precipitate himself into certain ruin by attempting to advance in the country with a very incompetent force."

Should the British sail for Philadelphia, Washington would, of course, march to oppose them. Yet, so Hamilton continued to Knox, "I would not have you to be much surprised if Philadelphia should fall." Howe could only be stopped by a general action, which Washington would not risk unless he were heavily reinforced by a "spirited" militia.7

Three months before, Hamilton had expressed the conception, based on European books on strategy, that the fall of Philadelphia, like that of any conventional capital city, would disastrously upset "the great political and military machine." Now he wrote that the principal effect would be psychological, manifesting itself most seriously in a loss of confidence that would cause further depreciation of the currency. Hav-

---

* The explanation was the Americans' ignorance of military engineering. They had failed to build adequate defenses on a hill that dominated the fort, and found that, when the British put cannon there, the fort was commanded.

ing turned away from books to the reality around him, he had come to take into account how decentralized American society was. To Knox, he outlined with approval what was one of Washington's conceptions: "Our hopes are not placed in any particular city or spot of ground, but in preserving a good army furnished with proper necessities, to take advantage of favorable opportunities and waste and defeat the enemy by piece-meal. Every new post they take requires a new division of their forces, and enables us to strike with our united force against a part of theirs." Then Hamilton added with an optimism quite un-Washingtonian, "Such is their present situation that another Trenton affair will amount to a complete victory on our part, for they are at too low an ebb to bear another stroke of the kind."[8]

Washington and his staff sat on the Jersey hills like subalterns await-ing direction from seemingly addlepated superiors. Wherever the enemy went, the Americans would have to go. But where were the British going? Intelligence reports from both New York City and Philadelphia (where pilots were being secretly approached to steer a British fleet the some fifty miles up the Delaware from the sea to the city) continued to point Howe towards the capital in Pennsylvania. Yet Washington could not believe that Howe would be so quixotic as not to support Burgoyne by proceeding up the Hudson. "We are," Hamilton wrote in a masterpiece of understatement, "rather in the dark. . . . This occasions some embarrassment."[9]

Eventually, Washington took his army into the Clove. This was a "very difficult and rugged gorge," surrounded with "the wildest and most deserted country," and because it cut through the Jersey High-lands to the west bank of the Hudson, it supplied a barely passable connection between the routes to Albany and Philadelphia. For ten days the high command kept the Continental Army in the moun-tainous pass. Headquarters was a single room in a log cabin, Washing-ton slept on the only bed, while his Family, including Hamilton, lay "on the floor around him."[10]

On July 24, 1777, there came solid news. Occupying "170 topsail vessels and about 50 or 60 smaller ones," the lion's share of Howe's army had sailed out of New York Harbor and disappeared into the ocean.[11] The implication was that Howe was off for Philadelphia. Since the Continental Army could not risk the disgrace of making no effort to save the capital, they were obliged to march across New Jersey. But headquarters was wracked with anxiety lest the British move were a ruse: having forced Washington to abandon the Hudson,

the enemy could double back in their ships and dash unimpeded up
the river to meet Burgoyne.

For all their weight of hulls and guns and men, the British ships had
vanished like nebulous flying Dutchmen. It was a relief when they
were finally sighted off Egg Harbor, on the sea-lane to Philadelphia.
The next landfall would be the Capes of the Delaware, only sixty miles
away. But day after day, the enemy did not appear. Hamilton rode out
with orders that stopped the troops on the Jersey side of the upper
Delaware, whence they could dash for the Hudson should word come
that the British had doubled back.[12]

On July 31, the fleet finally came in view off the Delaware. Since the
river was blocked by American fortifications for a considerable distance below the city, it was assumed that Howe's army would advance
overland, leaving the fleet to batter its way to join them. Washington's
men hurried across the Delaware. As they marched south, Hamilton
galloped ahead with his general to locate advantageous ground, between the sea and the capital, on which to make a stand. However, the
exhilaration of purposeful action was soon shattered by the news that,
instead of turning into the mouth of the river, the enemy had
again vanished out to sea.[13]

The implication was that Howe, having finally lured Washington
across the river into Pennsylvania, was now speeding for the Hudson
River and Burgoyne. Washington had to admit that, if this were the
case, the enemy strategy had succeeded. The Continental Army was
too exhausted by marching and countermarching in midsummer to
undertake a new trek across New Jersey. The troops were allowed to
collapse at the Falls of the Schuylkill, five miles above Philadelphia.

Washington and Hamilton rode into the city and lodged at the City
Tavern.[14] Their object was to confer with Congress and its many
committees, but their ears were forever cocked for the sound of
unusual galloping in the street. They dreaded word that Howe was
indeed sailing up the Hudson.

When a week had passed with no news of the enemy whatsoever,
Hamilton began to breathe easier concerning New York. Since Howe
had had "the fairest wind to carry him there," his failure to appear
indicated that he had gone somewhere else. But where? "There is no
object, it is thought, further to the southward." New England? Some
thought the enemy would establish a base on Rhode Island, in
preparation for an attack on Boston. Others argued they were heading
directly for Boston. Others thought it more likely that Portsmouth was

the objective. "For my own part," Hamilton continued, "I am weary of conjecture." He reported to Robert R. Livingston that Washington intended, as the best guess, to start the army eastward again.[15]

Livingston did not need the threat of a reappearance of Howe's army to make each of his letters to Hamilton more despairing than the last. His effort was to persuade Hamilton and through Hamilton Washington that the rescue of New York should be the Commander in Chief's primary concern. Livingston's contention was that after Burgoyne had reached Albany—there was at present no way to stop him— he would be joined by the New York Tories and every Indian warrior from the forests between Canada and the northern frontier (the Indians liked to be on the winning side). Should Howe actually join Burgoyne, the only difference would be that the total subjection of New York State would come more quickly—that is, unless Washington appeared at once with the Continental Army.[16]

Hamilton insisted that, as things were, Burgoyne would not be able to reach Albany. The New York legislator and the headquarters aide were soon in a continuing argument over the size of Burgoyne's army. Using information given by prisoners of war, Livingston placed it at an overwhelming ten thousand. Hamilton replied that the testimony of prisoners should be regarded as enemy propaganda, since "great care is taken by the British officers to give the men their lesson, and the dogs are accurate enough to profit by it." At Washington's headquarters, "we compare and compound circumstance, use different calculation, and from the whole deduct [deduce] a pretty accurate judgment." They concluded from a complication of information how many men were in actuality (not officially) in each British or Hessian regiment, and checked the sum with Intelligence on how many troops had been shipped to the American continent. They also tried to determine, and then discount, the number who were out of service because of sickness and wounds, the number previously lost in battle, and the number that would have to be left behind to defend stationary positions. The conclusion was that Burgoyne had between five and six thousand men. This estimate was a source of mounting resentment to Livingston, but it proved in fact more accurate than the New Yorker's. (Burgoyne had marched from Canada with fewer than seven thousand men.)[17]

While Hamilton was with Washington in Philadelphia, Philip Schuyler was replaced as commander in New York by Horatio Gates.

The two generals had long been rivals in that part of the world. Gates, who had bluff, democratic manners and supported the New England settlers against New York landlords in the Hampshire Grants (now Vermont), was New England's favorite. Rich and aristocratic, a leader among the agrarian elite who ruled that state, Schuyler was passionately supported by New York. Hamilton of course did not know that Schuyler was to be his father-in-law. But since he was trying to build his base in New York, which he considered "in a great measure my political parent,"[18] prudence urged that he either support Schuyler or remain silent. However, he penned to Livingston, who was Schuyler's cousin, a violent diatribe which followed the New England contention that the crisis was the personal fault of the New York patrician.

The gravity of the threat, Hamilton insisted, was due not to British strength but to the cowardice of the defense. "I have always," Hamilton wrote, "been a very partial judge of General Schuyler's conduct and vindicated it frequently from the charges brought against it, but I am at last forced to suppose him inadequate. . . . The reason assigned for his last retreat is panic among the army." Armies took "their complexion from their commanders."

Hamilton did not really like Gates either. His nomination for the savior of New York was a man who was to become his and Schuyler's inveterate political enemy: General George Clinton. He considered Clinton "an excellent officer. The people have confidence in him" and would serve with zeal and perseverance under him.[19]

Livingston's next extant letter to Hamilton stated that despair so gripped New York that once Burgoyne got to Albany he would not need to go any further: the Tories would take over the state. They were already committing "depredations on the Whigs in the heart of our settlements." And Hamilton was maundering around with his ridiculously low estimates of Burgoyne's army![20]

Reacting to Livingston's obvious anger, Hamilton replied with the most lugubrious sympathy for the dangers faced by "those for whom I feel the warmest regard. . . . I wish anything in my power could contribute . . . relief." No longer criticizing New Yorkers for pusillanimous hysteria, he wrote of "your most strenuous exertions which to the honor of your state are justly admired as far surpassing what might naturally be expected from you under so many discouragements."

Two regiments had been sent from Peekskill to reinforce the northern army. Taking what credit he could to himself, Hamilton added that he had "for some time past" been urging that Daniel Morgan's regiment of Kentucky riflemen be sent. This was now being done. The "picked corps," well used to "wood fights . . . will soon chastize the forwardness of the Indians. . . . It would be well to propagate . . . such ideas of this corps as will tend to revive spirits of both inhabitants and soldiers. If their numbers, which is about 500, were magnified, it would do no harm."

Howe's fleet, Hamilton reported, had at last been sighted: they were some distance south of the Delaware. If they continued in that direction, Washington might well do what New York wanted: join the fight against Burgoyne. "I have communicated your letter to His Excellency," the aide wrote, and then added in a postscript, "His Excellency desires particular respects to you, and assures you that nothing in his power will be left undone for your assistance."[21]

The sighting of Howe's fleet, which had disappeared again, merely added to the confusion at headquarters. Washington could not believe that Howe intended for Charleston, which was, so Hamilton wrote, the only object south of Philadelphia that "is supposed at all worthy of his attention." The situation made so little sense that Washington decided to halt his army where they were: near the village of Hartsville in Bucks County, Pennsylvania. The General and his Family occupied "one of the best furnished houses in the neighborhood"; it measured twenty-five feet by twenty-seven.[22]

At this place, Washington was joined by a tall French youth, with prominent eyebrows and a long, pointed nose. His reddish hair had prematurely receded up his forehead, which sloped surprisingly to a peak at the very back of his head. Hamilton had been displaced as the youngest man in Washington's circle: he was senior by several months to the Marquis de Lafayette.

The French youth wore the epaulettes and the ribbon across his chest of an American major general. He was so highly placed in the French aristocracy that his volunteering in the American army had created a diplomatic incident with the British, and Congress had wished, through honoring him, to encourage cooperation with France. Yet Lafayette, who had no military experience whatsoever, could not be given any command. He moved in with the headquarters Family.

The Marquis already knew a little English, but he labored—a compliment rarely paid to their hosts by foreign volunteers—to acquire more. He never for a moment forgot his high birth and he admitted that he looked forward to a commensurate opportunity to win the war; yet, when consulted on tactics, he replied, "It is not to teach but to

The Marquis de Lafayette, by Charles Willson Peale. On his arrival from France, Lafayette replaced Hamilton as the youngest man in Washington's circle. The two were fast friends, although Lafayette, being so great an aristocrat, became a major general while Hamilton remained a lieutenant colonel. Courtesy, Henry Francis du Pont Winterthur Museum

learn that I come hither." In conversation at headquarters, he revealed a surprising modesty as well as a warm and engaging friendliness. There is no evidence that Hamilton was ever jealous of the prodigy. It is abundantly clear that they soon became intimate companions.

As part of the honors accorded the newcomer, Washington staged for him a review of the army. Lafayette saw, so he remembered, about eleven thousand "ill-armed" men. "Their clothes were parti-colored and many of them were almost naked. The best clad wore *hunting shirts:* large, gray linen coats which were much used in Carolina." Since the only method they knew of turning when "ranged in order for battle" was to wheel, if the right moved forward, the left had to go backwards. "They were always arranged in two lines, the smallest men [so that others could shoot over their heads] in the first line. No other distinction of height was ever observed. In spite of these disadvantages the soldiers were fine and the officers zealous. Virtue stood in place of science."[23]

Lafayette noted that "the Americans amuse themselves by making many jokes" about the way the British army and fleet kept disappearing, yet the suspense remained unpleasant.[24] Late in August, headquarters was informed that the enemy had again been sighted, this time bearing down on Chesapeake Bay. Washington ordered his troops to move in that direction and then, unable to credit what he had been told, countermanded the order. Soon, the news was conclusive: the British were actually sailing up the Bay. This could only mean that Howe intended to land at the head of the Chesapeake and march from there the forty-odd miles to Philadelphia.*

The problem was now at hand to which Hamilton and everyone at headquarters had long been nervously addressing themselves. The British were about to advance across a flat countryside ideally suited to their equipment and training. How far should the Continental Army be risked, at such great disadvantage, in an effort to save the capital?

---

* When Howe discovered how strongly the lower Delaware had been fortified, he had decided to outflank the American defenses. He had not foreseen that contrary winds would so slow his voyage to the Chesapeake.

18

Fooled Again

WASHINGTON determined that he would insert his men between the British and Philadelphia. To do this, the army had to get to the other side of the city. Why not try to inspire the citizenry by mounting the Continental Army's first parade?

Every effort was made to spruce up the ragged troops as much as possible and arrange them for maximum effect. The army's women were sent around the city by a different route. Each marcher wore in his hat (or his hair if he had no hat) a leafy sprig to signify hope.

Washington led the parade on horseback with beside him that symbol of French cooperation, Lafayette. Next came the headquarters Family.[1] As Hamilton rode, almost at the head of a large army, conspicuously and to cheers, through the streets of the second largest city in the English-speaking world, the youth recently arrived from a distant land may well have marveled at the ways of fate and where they had carried him.

The army soon found itself in a part of the continent (Delaware and Maryland) where it had never seemed probable that they would have to operate. As the British established a beachhead at the Head of Elk (Elkton), ponderously landed from their ships, and cautiously moved inland, Washington stationed his force near Wilmington and rode out every day to study the terrain. Hamilton, who in five months had become de facto chief of staff, stayed behind to handle whatever crises might arise.

Dispatches revealed that Hamilton and the Commander had been right to discount the despairing pleas from New York for extraordinary assistance. A British thrust into the Mohawk Valley had been turned back by Benedict Arnold, the brilliant combat general whom Washington had sent north to second Gates. And at Bennington, a British foraging party in force had been bloodily beaten up by backwoodsmen adept at frontier fighting. To his New York correspondents, Hamilton commented jubilantly that "as General Howe is now fairly sat down to the southward," the northeastern states could "exert their whole force and, if they do, I shall wonder at it if Mr. Burgoyne advances with impunity."[2]

When the matter was still abstract, Hamilton had written that the Continental Army should not be risked to save Philadelphia. Now he reversed himself. He admitted that the landscape was "intersected by such an infinity of roads and is so little mountainous that it is impossible to find a spot [make a stand] not liable to capital defects." However, "the enemy will have Philadelphia, if they dare make a bold push for it, unless we fight them in a pretty general action. I opine we ought to do it, and that we shall beat them soundly if we do. The militia seem pretty generally stirring. Our army is in high health and spirits. We shall, I hope, have twice the enemy's numbers. I would not only fight them, but I would attack them; for I hold it an established maxim, that there is three to one in favor of the party attacking."[3]

Washington suspected (correctly) that Howe had undertaken his Philadelphia campaign in part to force the Continental Army into a disadvantageous battle. The American Fabius was in truth trapped. He could not, without seriously wounding the prestige of the Revolutionary cause, supinely abandon the capital. With none of Hamilton's enthusiasm, he picked out what he considered the least unsatisfactory battleground: low hills rising from Chad's Ford, where the British were likely to wade across the unbridged Brandywine River.

The subsequent American defeat was the direct result of a failure accurately to gather and assess intelligence. In the fatal confusion, Hamilton undoubtedly played his part, although Washington was in the last analysis his own intelligence chief and Hamilton was less familiar with the terrain than those who had ridden out from headquarters to explore.

With Washington's overall plan Hamilton was, as a matter of course, familiar. The Commander in Chief recognized the similarity of the American position to that at Brooklyn Heights. They were again drawn up behind a geographic barrier—in this case a "creek" fordable at many places—which extended beyond the army's flanks. The chances were that Howe would try to repeat his successful maneuver. He would make a show at the center, while his main army undertook a circuitous march. As this party entered by surprise from one flank into the American rear, the force in the center would attack across Chad's Ford. The Continental Army would thus be caught between two fires.

Washington hoped to turn the tables. Howe, by sending off the flanking detachment, would so greatly weaken his center that it could be destroyed if the whole Continental Army charged across Chad's Ford. But this stratagem depended on determining with absolute certainty that a flanking party had indeed marched. It would be suicidal to face the entire British army as his men waded across a river.

Headquarters made every preparation time permitted and their ingenuity could devise for securing at the necessary moment the all-important information. No adequate maps existed. Local inhabitants were interrogated concerning roads and shallow places. Washington with his aides explored personally to chart the possible lines of march that would have to be kept under surveillance. (As it turned out, headquarters remained grievously uninformed concerning fords on the upper river.) Patrols were assigned to prowl on both sides of the stream; they were accompanied by couriers on horseback who could gallop intelligence to headquarters.[4]

As light seeped in on the morning of September 11, a crackle of small arms drowned out the choir of waking birds. American skirmishers fell back across Chad's Ford. Then the enemy appeared on the far side of the river. Cannon were unlimbered and fired while the British flanks fanned out from the narrow road into the forest, where foliage made their subsequent movements invisible.

We know that Washington and Lafayette rode among cheering troops on the slopes that overlooked the river.[5] Hamilton had probably remained at headquarters. That farmhouse was too far back for the present action to be visible. His function would be to correlate dispatches and give any instructions immediately required. The battle was still too embryonic to inspire major orders.

At about eleven in the morning Washington returned. Reports that the troops stationed at the upper fords were observing considerable enemy action across the river, induced a dispatch to Colonel Theodorick Bland, the cavalry commander, ordering him to "send up an intelligent, sensible officer immediately with a party to find out the truth." So that the expected enemy flanking party would not find a vacuum on the American rear, Washington ordered Stephen's and Stirling's divisions to go back three and a half miles onto the low hills near Birmingham Meeting House.[6]

A confirming dispatch: five thousand men with sixteen fieldpieces had been seen proceeding towards the upper Brandywine crossing. Out from headquarters came orders for Greene and Sullivan to prepare their divisions for a forward rush across Chad's Ford. But a warning then came in from Sullivan that militiamen who were local inhabitants had patrolled from Martin's Tavern to Welch's and heard nothing of the enemy. They were convinced there was no British action along the upper Brandywine. Sullivan concluded that Washington's previous "information must be wrong."

This was the moment on which the battle turned. The report of the militiamen gave no indication of when their observations had been made, and headquarters was devoid of accurate information on the location of the taverns. But Washington could not risk his army. He countermanded his orders to Greene and Sullivan.

It was now well past midday. Suddenly the door of headquarters burst open and in rushed a tremendous stranger so dark in countenance that he looked like an Indian. He was unwilling to speak to any aide, shouting that he must see Washington. When admitted to the General's presence, he bellowed that if the army did not flee, it would be surrounded. Riding up a hill on the American right, he had found himself face to face with a horde of redcoats. Only the speed of his horse had saved him.

Faced with the necessity to decide on the spot whether the stranger was in the British pay or a true patriot, Washington stated fiercely that what the man reported was contrary to known fact and that spies were hanged. The man stuck to his story. Washington ran out to investigate for himself. He had hardly mounted, when dispatch riders came in from several directions. A strong British force had indeed crossed the Brandywine high up and was advancing behind the American right. It was now too late for Washington to initiate the cartwheel action he had intended. The approaching British column could fall on his rear as he tried to cross the river.

More troops were ordered back to repulse the enemy advance. Hamilton was undoubtedly as eager as Washington to go where the most fighting portended, but the established headquarters remained the place where dispatches that would reveal the whole operation would be received.

At about 4:30, heavy firing sounded from the direction of Birmingham. And the desultory sounds that had for hours been echoing from Chad's Ford lifted to a roar of cannon fire. On the rear and the front, Hamilton could see when he stepped out of headquarters, rising clouds of powder smoke.

The defenders of Chad's Ford, having the river in front of them, were holding, but both sounds and dispatches revealed that the defenders of Birmingham were being driven back in a manner that endangered the rear of the entire army. Washington decided to lead Greene's division to the rescue. Hamilton, Lafayette, and other members of the Family rode with him.[7]

When Hamilton reached the battlefield, he saw a horde of brilliantly uniformed enemy advancing with smoking muskets and shining bayonets to the constant roar of cannon. The patriot artillery had for the most part been silenced. As the pressure became too great on one part of the line or another, the American infantry was moving clumsily, irregularly, doggedly backward. The left, when Hamilton made his entrance, seemed about to shatter. However, Weedon's brigade of Greene's division moved in. Hamilton, who had no particular respect for General Sullivan, was pleased to see him efficiently take advantage of the reinforcement, "animating and encouraging the men" both by "words and example." The enemy tide was slowed—yet it still came on.[8]

Quickly accepting the inevitable, Washington labored to achieve an orderly retreat. If Hamilton accompanied his general, he assisted in reorganizing companies that had become ragged and in placing them on partially wooded hillsides from which they could slow the enemy. While carrying out such duties, Lafayette was wounded in the leg, but no bullet touched Hamilton.

Word was distributed that the army was to reassemble some ten miles to the rear at Chester. Headquarters was reestablished there. It was a gloomy gathering. As far as the world would see, the command had been fooled a second time, as at Brooklyn Heights. True, there were important differences. This time the British stratagem had been foreseen and a brilliant riposte planned. Furthermore, the American troops had not fled in panic but stayed in orderly retreat. Yet the undeniable fact was that the Continental Army had been defeated and the central command—Washington, Hamilton, and the others sitting there glumly—had been labeled before the whole world as fools.

19

A Wild Warning

[SEPTEMBER, 1777   AGE 20]

PHILADELPHIA occupied the point of land at the confluence of the Schuylkill and Delaware rivers. The Delaware was on the far side, away from the military action. The Schuylkill, a not inconsiderable stream which flowed southeast from the Allegheny Mountains, was the last bulwark between the enemy and the capital. Washington dodged behind the Schuylkill to refit, and then returned to the western shore.

The British made no effort to brush him aside. The capture of Philadelphia could wait until they achieved what their Brandywine victory had not achieved: the destruction or neutralizing of the Continental Army. They marched north, hoping either to pin Washington against the Schuylkill or make him flee from the theater of war into the southern states. Keeping north of the enemy, Washington marched parallel to them and closer to the river. He hoped to find a favorable opportunity to isolate and smash, before the British could bring up their total force, a part of their army.

On September 16, he saw a chance. He issued to his men almost all the army's horded ammunition. This proved a disaster. The skies opened; the American canisters (unlike those of the well-supplied British) leaked; the ammunition was soaked; the Continental Army was disarmed. Washington fled not only north but west. He ended up at Warwick Furnace (now Reading), in the foothills of the Alleghenies, further from the Schuylkill than the British position, and forty miles from Philadelphia.

A quantity of flour stored in a mill on the west bank of the Schuylkill had long been an object of patriot attention. The Board of War had urged that the Pennsylvania authorities release from the militia six bakers to transmute the flour into "hard biscuit" for the army. The bakers had not materialized.[1] Since the flour was now ripe for British capture, Washington deputized Hamilton to destroy it. He was to have an escort of eight cavalrymen commanded by Captain Henry Lee, soon to be known as "Light-Horse Harry" and eventually as the father of Robert E. Lee.

The little cavalcade had ridden fifteen miles when Hamilton saw at the bottom of a long slope and close to the river the mill it was his mission to burn. Moored to a ferry slip on the left were a pair of large flat-bottomed scows. To the right was the millowner's house. Hamilton could not foresee that this building was to be his residence, as a member of the Family, during many anguished months. The name of the settlement that now quietly lay beneath him in the autumn glow was Valley Forge.

Leaving behind two horsemen as lookouts, Hamilton cantered downhill with the rest of the party, crossed a little bridge over a millrace, and prepared to set fire to the mill. As a precaution, he ordered that one of the scows be brought around to offer a means of escape in case of attack.

The mill had not yet been set afire when shots sounded. Hamilton looked upward to see his lookouts aiming at something invisible. Then they came down the slope at a gallop. Over the crest appeared the heads of British dragoons: more and more helmeted heads. An overwhelmingly stronger force came pounding down towards Hamilton's little posse.

Lee and a pair of his horsemen were still mounted. They spurred across the millrace. Joined by the two lookouts, they dashed away. The dragoons gave chase. Then the enemy became conscious of easier prey. They thundered back over the millrace. Hamilton and those of his men who had dismounted were at that moment climbing into the scow Hamilton had ordered around.

The Schuylkill was swollen with the rains that had previously destroyed the patriot ammunition. Despite the frantic efforts of the ferrymen assisted by Hamilton and his soldiers, the scow refused to be driven into midstream. Following alongshore the course of the boat, the dragoons fired round after round. Hamilton's horse sank to the ground with a grotesque scream. One of his men fell dead and another cried out wounded. There was nothing for the survivors to do but jump overboard and swim.[2]

Looking up from the vexed water that was dashing at his eyes, Hamilton saw a sight that horrified him. Not only the scow he and his men had abandoned but the other, which had somehow got adrift, were falling into the hands of the British dragoons. Hamilton struck out as fast as he could for the far bank. Passionately securing a piece of dry paper, he scratched down the missive to the President of Congress, John Hancock, that was to give him his first starring role in the Revolutionary drama:

> Sir,
> If Congress have not yet left Philadelphia, they ought to do it immediately without fail, for the enemy have the means of throwing a party this night into the city. I just now crossed the valley-ford, in doing which a party of the enemy came down and fired upon us in the boat by which means I lost my horse. One man was killed and another wounded. The boats were abandoned and will fall into their hands. I did all I could to prevent this but to no purpose.
> I have the honour to be wth. much respect Sir Your mo. obedt. Servt.
>
> *A. Hamilton*[3]

Hamilton yearned himself to carry this warning to Philadelphia, but decided that "the most cogent reasons oblige me to join the army this night." He procured a horse and sent a messenger galloping for the capital. Then he found a safe way to recross the river, and set out for headquarters.[4]

During the long ride, there was every reason for Hamilton to become increasingly worried about the message he had so excitedly sent. During the previous campaign Congress had fled the capital when the British were no nearer than Trenton on the opposite side of the Delaware. But this year, although the danger was much more immediate, the legislators decided to bolster morale by remaining in the city as long as they possibly could with relative safety. Had Hamilton's sudden reaction needlessly scuttled a statesmanlike policy?

He could not deny to himself that the British had for some days controlled access to Schuylkill crossings closer to the city than Valley Forge. In a highly populated area, they could surely, if they wished, secure other boats than those Hamilton had seen fall into their hands. Hamilton had, in fact, encountered only a small detachment of horse some twenty miles from Philadelphia.

When at last he rode anxiously up to headquarters, he was greeted with a jubilation that he could not at first understand. Then laughing and almost weeping members of the Family told him that Captain Lee had already come in to report that he had probably been killed or captured.[5]

Now Hamilton received further intelligence which, whatever its import for the cause, was for him reassuring: Philadelphia was in greater danger than he had known when he wrote his rash message. The main British army, having seemingly abandoned its pursuit of Washington, was on the march to a Schuylkill crossing, Swedes' Ford, which was some four miles closer to the city than the place where Hamilton had had his adventure with the dragoons. Although headquarters had not yet moved, the bulk of the Continental Army had set out after them.[6]

In his own report to Hancock that the British were advancing on Swedes' Ford, the Commander in Chief had made no suggestion that Philadelphia was no longer safe for patriots.[7] But Washington seems not to have been at headquarters. When the lieutenant colonel again wrote the President of Congress, he made no mention of his general and refrained (as had been the case with the dispatch from Valley Forge) from adding to his signature the letters "ADC." This indicated that he was not writing in his official capacity as Washington's aide-de-camp, but on his personal responsibility.

In the new communication, Hamilton repeated the news about Swedes' Ford and then described in more detail than before his experience with the dragoons. The captured scows, he stated, "will convey fifty men across at a time so that in a few hours they may throw over a large party, perhaps sufficient to overpower the militia between them and the city." But he went on to tone down his warning. No longer stating that the congressmen "ought" to leave "immediately and without fail," he merely urged them to "be on their guard. . . . My apprehensions for them are great, though it is probable they may not be realized."[8]

Congress had been resting far from easy. The question of quitting the capital had been "daily agitated," and all kinds of preparatory votes had been taken: where the legislators would rendezvous if forced to flee (Lancaster, Pennsylvania); special powers for Washington while they were dispersed; and so on and so on. But on the night of September 18, they adjourned at 10 P.M. without any extra concern. What happened then was summarized in the formal congressional *Journal:* "During the adjournment, the President received a letter from Colonel Hamilton which intimated the necessity of Congress removing immediately from Philadelphia. Whereupon the members left the city."[9]

John Adams remembered that the first dispatch from Hamilton (the one he had written as he dripped on the river bank) was so vague and urgent that it inspired double terrors.[10] By the time further reports, including Hamilton's second letter, came in, hysteria had taken over, and the news, as it flew from tongue to tongue, became, at each transfer, more menacing. The whole British army had leapt across the Schuylkill with a speed that only a heated imagination could credit. The regulars were now in full advance down the east bank of the river. An irresistible force was to be expected momentarily at the very outskirts of the city!

Not only congressmen were driven to convulsive action, but every patriot who considered himself subject to British wrath. Sarah Fisher, whose pacifist Quaker husband had just been exiled from the city, wrote: "Had I not my spirits too much depressed with the absence of my dear companion, the scene would really have diverted me. . . . Wagons rattling, horses galloping, women running, children crying, delegates flying, and altogether the greatest consternation, flight, and terror that can be imagined." Thomas Burke, congressman from South Carolina, noted that the legislature made no effort to depart together in a dignified manner. Every member consulted, as he thought most expedient, his own safety. Congressman Nathaniel Folsom of New Hampshire, too hurried to saddle his horse, disappeared bareback.[11]

John Adams, knowing that Hamilton was Washington's aide, attributed the warning to the Commander in Chief, of whom he had a low opinion. Preparing to avoid capture by taking a particularly circuitous route to Lancaster, Adams cried out, "Oh! Heaven grant us one great soul. . . . One active, masterly capacity would bring order out of this confusion and save this country."[12]

After the rushing in the streets was over, the citizens who had stayed behind listened for the sound of firing or the music of some triumphant British band. They heard no unusual sound. September 19 dawned as an ordinary Philadelphia day, and soon the news spread that, although the British had indeed marched to Swedes' Ford, they had encamped there, making no move to cross the river. As for the dragoons who had so excited Hamilton, they were not heard from again. Sarcastically, the Quaker lady, Mrs. Fisher, commented, "Behold, when morning came, it proved a false alarm!"[13]

Surely the impetuous warning Hamilton had dispatched after he had pulled himself out of the Schuylkill would have opened him to the most serious criticism had not the enemy done him the courtesy of marching on Swedes' Ford. Even as things turned out, it seems surprising that his impulsive behavior, by which he personally drove Congress from Philadelphia, did not bring upon him a personal attack. Of course, his hair-trigger reaction to a minor incident had been an authentic response to the larger situation. The patriots who stayed in Philadelphia were from hour to hour in serious danger, not so much from the main British army, which of its inherent nature moved ponderously, but from a gallop of just such horsemen as had induced his warning. (Later in the war, similar cavalry overran the Virginia capital, captured some legislators, and sent Governor Jefferson fleeing into the mountains.) The Philadelphia patriots, who were making what they knew was a foolhardy stand, were seemingly relieved to have had someone create a situation that would permit them to dash legitimately for safety.

Washington, who mentally weighed all alternatives with enough deliberation to permit each to tip the beam, was not a quick decider. He surely recognized that there were situations that required more impetuosity. Hamilton's behavior upset him so little that almost instantly he sent the aide into Philadelphia on a most ticklish mission, which required mobilizing the support of the patriots still in the city.

After failing to cross at Swedes' Ford, the British had marched so far north that Washington was afraid they were aiming for the Continental Army's major supply depot at Reading. He hurried his men north also, leaving Philadelphia further and further behind. If the British made a quick countermarch, the patriot army would be in no positon to respond. The soldiers were underfed, had jettisoned their blankets and packs at Brandywine, had completely worn away the soles of their shoes.

Philadelphia was full of supplies that seemed about to fall to the British. Among the dictatorial powers Congress had voted to Washington, as they prepared for flight, had been authorization to seize, in return for certificates of indebtedness, goods the army required. Three days after Hamilton's warning had upset the city, Hamilton drafted at headquarters, for Washington's signature, a letter to himself: "Painful as it is for me to order, as it will be for you to execute the measure, I am compelled to desire you immediately to proceed to Philadelphia and there procure from the inhabitants blankets and clothing and materials . . . in proportion to the ability of each. This you will do with as much delicacy and discretion as the nature of the business demands, and I trust that every person well affected to the American cause . . . will cheerfully afford assistance to the soldiers" who were suffering in defense of "everything Americans ought to hold most dear." A further paragraph stated that Hamilton was to remove any horses, whether public or private property, which would be useful to the enemy should they "by accident" capture Philadelphia.[14]

Washington's scruples about requisitioning from civilians were so great that only after Hamilton had actually departed on his mission did the General decide to seize also the stock of merchants. Since this action might be resisted by force, Washington ordered a party of twelve or fifteen light horsemen to hurry to Philadelphia, "there to enquire for Colonel Hamilton and give him assistance." Someone then told Washington that Hamilton planned to stay at the City Tavern, and Washington added the information.[15]

Writing Hamilton the next morning, Washington informed him about the horsemen and added that if necessary he might call on fifty or sixty dismounted South Carolinians available in Philadelphia. "I have just now been informed that there are not less than 3,000 pairs of shoes in the hands of three or four persons." Hamilton—"you know our distresses"—was to find them. He was furthermore to requisition "every other article you know to be material for our army. Your own prudence will point out the least exceptional means to be pursued . . . but remember that delicacy and a strict adherence to ordinary modes of application must give place to our necessities."[16]

Hamilton's task was made the more difficult by his previous warnings, which had emptied the city of convinced patriots. Left behind were mostly Quaker pacifists, secret Tories, and (at best) individuals inclined to be neutral. Even the men whom Hamilton was able to persuade to knock on doors were lukewarm.

The diarist Robert Morton noted concerning Hamilton's first morning in town that the seekers for blankets and clothes received "a little" from some; from most, nothing. Two men, with both of whom she was acquainted, appeared at Mrs. Fisher's house to demand blankets and old carpets. "I told them," she noted, "I had none but they had robbed me of what was far dearer than any property I had in the world, that is my husband; and that I could by no means encourage war of any kind. This they treated very lightly, and said they must search the house and desired me to send some person with them. This I positively refused, upon which they both went upstairs and, though there was a carpet on every floor and a blanket on every bed, they came down and in a complaisant manner told me they had had the pleasure of viewing my rooms and saw nothing that suited them."[17]

Collecting private donations was a multitudinous and miniscule task that Hamilton had to leave to others. It was surely to deal with merchants that he wrote, whether before or after he knew that Washington had ordered horsemen to join him, asking Governor William Livingston of New Jersey to send a hundred or so militiamen (they would presumably have no Philadelphia connections) to assist him "on some business of great importance."[18]

During September 23, the British army finally crossed to the Philadelphia side of the Schuylkill north of the city. Early on the following morning, Mrs. Fisher saw "a distressing scene." Under the command of Colonel Hamilton "armed men" forcibly broke down the door of a shop and took away "a large quantity of goods." The shopkeeper pleaded that he needed the clothes for "family use," but he was allowed to keep only a trifle. How mild the Revolutionary War was, compared to other such upheavals, revealed by Mrs. Fisher's exclamation: "This arbitrary conduct of theirs is believed unprecedented before in any age or country whatsoever!"[19]

Hamilton had been ordered to send what shoes and blankets he procured "by some interior middle road, so that they will be secure," and "not to delay a moment in getting them to the army." They did not arrive in time to enable the shivering and shoeless men to descend on the British rear and attempt, at the last breath, to save the capital. Abandoning at long last the hope that they would somehow be able to trap Washington's army, the British, on the 24th, marched into Philadelphia without having to fire a shot.[20]

20

Desperate Measures

O N New York's northern frontier, the tables had turned completely around. Hamilton had diagnosed Burgoyne's principal enemy as "the forest." The British general was, indeed,
a tightrope walker, balanced on a thin line of road and supply which
was attached on one end to the urban bastion of Montreal and presumably on the other to Albany. As long as the line remained taut
and he kept up his momentum, all was well, but the instant the line
slackened or he was slowed, a terrible wobbling began. The encouragement given to patriots by the victories on the Mohawk River and
at Bennington, combined with the replacing of the aristocratic
Schuyler by Gates, who so appealed to New Englanders, brought
militia flocking to the American standard. Burgoyne's supply line to
Canada was cut. His efforts to reach Albany were stopped by battles
at Freeman's Farm and Bemis Heights, in which British advance
parties were smashed back. Halted at Saratoga, Burgoyne seemed
about to pitch from his loosened tightrope into a forest already
touched with premonitions of winter.

The progressively favorable news coming down from the north
penetrated into the heartlands of the Revolution at the time when
Washington was being brushed bloodily aside at Brandywine, and
then so outmaneuvered that Philadelphia fell without his attempting a
defense. Those were dark days in the various farmhouse-headquarters
that the Family temporarily inhabited. It was impossible to overlook

the contrast between the successes up north and the failures of the army Hamilton was helping to command.

Legislators and other civilians had a way of visiting Washington's camp and looking around sniffily at an army that gave off so sordid an appearance in its lack of nourishment and clothing. Then they would drop seemingly ingenuous remarks about the triumphant efficiency of Gates. In denouncing "disorders" among Washington's men, the radical Pennsylvania congressman Dr. Benjamin Rush accused the Commander in Chief of permitting himself to be "governed by General Greene, General Knox, and Colonel Hamilton, one of his aides, a young man of twenty-one years."[1]

Washington himself was greatly perturbed. When announcing another of Gates's victories, he exhorted his troops that they would suffer "disgrace" if they continued to be so "outdone by their northern brethren."[2]

Hamilton took part at headquarters in plans to repeat the success at Trenton, but this time against the main British army. The possibility existed, since Howe had sent only a detachment under Cornwallis to occupy Philadelphia. He was encamped with most of his forces at Germantown, some five miles up the Schuylkill towards where the Continental Army tented. The Briton was expressing his scorn for the rebels by not bothering to fortify his camp. He clearly regarded as past belief any possibility that the underfed and undersupplied army he had defeated and then so outmaneuvered would suddenly throw itself into his jaws.

Germantown was shaped like a cross: the main street, which, a short distance inland, paralleled the Schuylkill was intersected at right angles by a major east-west road. The British outposts and light infantry were encamped on Washington's side of the intersection; Howe's main army beyond.

The strategy developed at Washington's headquarters provided that the American soldiers take off from encampments too far away from Germantown for the enemy to foresee any attack. Getting into motion at one in the morning, showing no light, making no sound beyond the inevitable multitudinous footfalls, the troops would advance with such speed that they would appear out of the darkness into the British encampment at 5 A.M.

Hamilton drafted Washington's general orders, which set the groundwork for the simultaneous use of four entries into Germantown. The main division under General Sullivan (with which Washington intended to march) would go down the main road into the main street. After traversing a secondary road, a strong division under Greene would enter the east-west street inland from the intersection, and, by striking the British right, pin the surprised and disrupted enemy against the Schuylkill. Militiamen moving down lanes at the extremes of the two flanks would further confuse the enemy and perhaps come together beyond them in a pincers movement.[3]

On October 4, 1777, Hamilton set out for Germantown with Washington.[4] This departure was exactly on schedule, but the army was soon entangled in impediments as delaying as the blizzard and floating ice had been before Trenton. Discretion prevented showing enough light to make landmarks easily identifiable: every considerable crossroads was thus a source of confusion. We can visualize Hamilton groping along a dimly looming structure to determine whether it was a dwelling with a portico, a dilapidated farmhouse, an inn, or a mill. All hope of attacking before daylight vanished. However, nature again created an unforeseen disguise: not driving snow but encompassing fog. Daylight drew up a mist so thick that to the eye it seemed palpable.

When the outskirts of Germantown were finally reached, the advance guard ran ahead through the blanched glimmer to raise a sound of firing that moved rapidly forward as the enemy pickets fell back. Washington ordered Sullivan to advance with most of the column, but himself stayed behind, holding several regiments in reserve.

We do not know whether Hamilton remained at Washington's side or galloped off to reconnoiter or carry orders. Wherever he rode, he listened eagerly for sounds which would indicate that Greene was coming in according to plan on the left. There were no such sounds. Finally, as Sullivan's force receded further and further into the distance after the fleeing British, Washington decided to lead his rear guard forward.

Hamilton, it is clear, also advanced into a morning darkness that became increasingly eerie. The British had set fire to a field of buckwheat and the smoke from that burning joined in the net of the fog with the smoke of black powder to reduce light until the eye could only register dim black and white. But the monochromatic picture made the young aide's heart leap: on both sides of the road were deserted tents, motionless wagons, all the paraphernalia of a sophisticated British camp from which the regulars had fled. The firing continued to move away as Hamilton galloped forward—and then surprisingly shots exploded directly in front of him.

Riding ahead he sees through the unnatural darkness a brick mansion, the home of Samuel Chew. It has become, by the simple act of being occupied by British soldiers, a fortress. The enemy are firing from behind heavy shutters almost closed over second-story windows. On the front lawn are piled the contorted bodies of what the British officer John André is to describe as "a prodigious number of rebel dead."[5]

Knox's cannon hurry into position. They enunciate an impressive crashing but the balls bounce off the thick walls. The shot that successfully rushes through a shuttered window makes little contribution towards clearing away the impediment.

The younger officers, of whom Adjutant General Pickering remembered he and Hamilton were at "the head," urge that the house be sealed off by a surrounding battalion while the rest of the force proceed onward to the main battle. But no one knows how many English soldiers are in the improvised fortress, and Knox insists that it would be "unmilitary to leave a castle in our rear." As Washington hesitates, William Smith, assistant to Adjutant General Pickering, offers to advance with a white flag and urge surrender. According to Pickering, he and Hamilton object that Smith will be killed. But the young soldier goes forward and sinks in blood to the ground. Hamilton's intimate and fellow aide, John Laurens, tries to fire the house with straw from the stables and is wounded, although not seriously, in the shoulder.[6]

Finally, Washington orders that a detachment keep the house surrounded, and the rest of the rear guard advance. He himself gallops rapidly towards the very front. If, as seems probable, Hamilton accompanies him, it is despite the acrid air, an exhilarating ride. There can be no doubt that the Continental Army has for the first time driven a major British force. And, to cap the happy climax, sounds on the left indicate that Greene's division has arrived and is now engaged.

British resistance becomes first noticeable, then sporadic, and then active as the riders approach the crossroads. Behind one house after another, American soldiers are firing from behind hedges, ornamental trees, stables, outbuildings. They are driving the redcoats. Washington is so excited that he exposes himself "to the hottest fire of the enemy."[7] Hamilton may well be among the aides who pulls him back. But he does not stay back for long.

Now the crossroads can be descried through the gray glimmer. And from beyond there come the most encouraging conceivable sounds: sounds which reveal that Greene's detachment is advancing from the left into the main British camp. A wild joy sweeps through the Family.

The General himself concludes, so Hamilton will summarize later, that "victory was declaring herself in our favor. The tumult, disorder, and even despair which it seems had taken place in the British army was scarcely to be paralleled." It is even visualized that, once Howe's army has been smashed, Cornwallis will abandon Philadelphia. Reports circulate that the defeated British have been ordered to reassemble at Chester, where Washington's battered army had reassembled after Brandywine.

Then to the horror of the group around Washington, Greene's men begin to appear on the far side of the crossroad, retreating on the run. In terrified flight they shed their weapons. More and more flood back, rushing with warning cries past Washington's advancing corps. At almost the same moment, a sound of firing breaks out on the American rear, implying that the American army is being surrounded.

Washington's men no longer advance. They stand still, and then turning, join the flight. Surely Hamilton is among those officers who, "in chagrin and mortification," shout and flail with the flats of their swords at the fleeing men. It is useless. Into the acrid mist, the army vanishes. There is nothing for Washington and his staff to do but ride after them.[8]

At the time, Washington and his staff could not imagine what had happened. Eventually, it became clear that Greene's troops, who had started the stampede, had been fighting confidently until they suddenly found themselves disarmed. They reached into their canisters to discover that they had no ammunition left. As for the firing in the rear, this was a result of having left behind the occupied "castle" at Chew's house. A part of Greene's army, hearing shooting there, had hurried over, and, mistaking in the fog the patriot troops guarding the house for an enemy detachment, had engaged in a small but noisy fratricidal battle.

When the news of the Battle of Germantown reached Europe, foreign commentators, who appreciated the power of European regular armies, were deeply impressed by the patriot dash into the heart of a major professional military force. The French foreign minister, Vergennes, stated, "To bring an army, raised within a year, to this, promised anything."[9] But in America, the battle was chalked up as another defeat for Washington. And the record of the headquarters in which Hamilton served seemed all the blacker because it was now silhouetted against a very bright light: reports, convincing although not yet official, that Burgoyne had surrendered his entire force to General Gates. Queries so unsubtle as to be audible to the Family and its military father asked whether the contrast between victory and defeat did not dictate that Gates be brought down from the north to replace Washington as commander of the Continental Army.

Never did the need to achieve a victory weigh more heavily on a group of men than on Washington and his Family—for their own sake as well as for the cause. But how? The British had responded to Germantown by withdrawing all their outposts behind the fortifications they had erected at Philadelphia, which Washington's engineers insisted were too strong to assault. However, the occupying army was separated from its fleet, and from every other bit of ground that flew a British flag, by American forts on the shores of the Delaware and cooperating obstructions underwater that kept enemy shipping from coming up from the ocean.

Hamilton had his part in the effective blocking of the river. His general, having pondered the lesson offered by Fort Washington concerning amateur fort building, had entrusted the fortifications of the Delaware to the trained French engineers who were volunteers in his army. With these, Washington usually communicated through his French-speaking aide.[10] The resulting forts were so well designed that they could not be reduced by naval action only. Howe would have to send infantry detachments overland. And meanwhile, what necessary supplies he had not brought with him from the head of the Chesapeake had to be transshipped overland.

This situation opened to Washington opportunities for action, but the risks were great. The countryside along the Delaware was flat, favorable to British arms, and any patriot force could be, if defeated, pinned against the wide river or the ocean below it. Before anything major could be undertaken, the Continental Army needed reinforcements—and it was obvious where they should come from. Having won his victory, Gates needed only a garrison for Albany. He could obviously spare not only the troops Washington had sent north during the crisis (to the weakening of the Continental Army), but large numbers of other troops as well. Probably he had already dispatched them. Word was surely on the way that they were coming.

Messages of many sorts poured into headquarters, but none from the north. Although it was Gates's manifest duty to make his first report to the Commander in Chief, no confirmation came in that Burgoyne had surrendered. The Family, as they talked at night in a crowded bedroom, speculated whether the rumors had not been pre-mature or altogether false, whether Burgoyne and his army were not still on the march.

Eventually, a copy of the surrender terms appeared at headquarters, but indirectly, not from Gates. A disturbing conclusion became clear: Gates in his triumph was refusing to acknowledge Washington as any longer his superior officer. Did it follow that Gates, pushing to replace Washington as commander in chief, was denying, and would continue to deny, the Continental Army the troops that would enable Washington to achieve a victory that might match Gates's own?

On October 29, 1777, sixteen days after Burgoyne had given up, Washington summoned his general officers to a Council of War. Hamilton acted as secretary, keeping the minutes.

Headquarters was able to present solid information on the strength of Howe's army. After the British had voluntarily retired from Germantown, the Americans had found in the village "an almost infinite number of scraps and bits of paper . . . which, being separated and arranged with great industry and care, bear the marks of genuine and authentic returns at different periods. The manner in which they were destroyed and disposed of give no room to suspect" that this was a ruse aimed at fooling the Americans.[11]

On this basis, Washington reported to his Council of War that the British force in the Philadelphia sector was about ten thousand fit for duty. The countering American forces included eight to nine thousand Continentals and 2,717 militia, of whom 1,986 were about to come to the end of their service. Although Washington had in "the strongest terms" requested Pennsylvania and New Jersey to replace the parting militia, he was "uncertain what degree of success these different applications might have." Clearly, the army would not be strong enough to make any aggressive move unless troops were "drawn from the northern armies."

The Council of War decided to send a representative northward to determine whether any reinforcements had already been dispatched and, if it developed that none or not enough had been relinquished, to force from Gates the needed troops.[12] That made obvious sense, but who could carry through such a mission? Gates, ranking second among the officers in the army, could be commanded only by the Commander in Chief. However, a commander in chief does not chase around after a subordinate, and in any case Washington could not be spared from his own troops. If any other general tried to control Gates, he would be exceeding his authority. Washington himself would have to be present in another form.

It was accepted for aides, during crises in battle, to exert, since they were more familiar with headquarters strategy than any division commander, the authority of the commander in chief. Could this convention be extended, at a time when no momentary decisions were required, across several hundreds of miles into another military sector? The bare fact was that the effort had to be made. And fortunately Washington had an aide to whom he felt the extremely important and extremely ticklish mission could be entrusted.

21

The First Major Mission

[OCTOBER, 1777–JANUARY, 1778   AGES 20–21]

O N October 30, 1777, Washington wrote Hamilton a letter
(drafted by Tilghman) that was intended to serve as official
credentials. It was indicative of the difficulty of the situation
that Washington did not count on Gates accepting his unsupported
authority as commander in chief. Hamilton, he stated, was being dispatched in accordance with the decision of a Council of War that
included all the high officers of the Continental Army. Hamilton's
mission was to "point out" to Gates "the absolute necessity" of his
detaching a very considerable part of the army that was "at present"
under his command. This would, by enabling Washington to keep the
British fleet and army apart, "in all probability reduce General Howe
to the same situation in which General Burgoyne now is."

(Whatever Washington's intention, these sentences were not likely
to please Gates. The phrase "at present" was a quiet insistence on
Washington's superior authority, and Washington made no secret of
his desire to use Gates's troops to match Gates's triumph in a way that
would shine even brighter.)

The Council of War, so Washington continued, "judged it safe and
expedient to draw down at present" the three New Hampshire and
fifteen Massachusetts regiments, with Lee's and Jackson's additional
regiments. Should Gates have plans to recapture and hold Ticonderoga, the exact reinforcement Washington required might be different,
"but, if possible, let it be made up to the same number out of other
corps."[1]

General Henry Knox. From the time the Continental Army marched into New York City until Hamilton's appointment as Washington's aide-de-camp, the young artillery officer was under the command of Knox, who became his friend. Courtesy, Independence National Historical Park Collection

The two major generals, one scheming, one stubborn, to whom Lieutenant Colonel Hamilton gave orders in Washington's name. *Above:* General Horatio Gates. Engraving after Pierre Eugène du Simitière. Courtesy, Library of Congress. *Below:* General Israel Putnam. Drawing by John Trumbull. Courtesy, Wadsworth Atheneum, Hartford.

In drawing up the instructions to Hamilton, Tilghman had written, "you are to bear in mind that the demand for the above number of troops is more in the nature of a requisition than a command." Washington scratched this out as too namby-pamby. The finished letter stated that should Hamilton discover an intention of Gates's to employ the troops on some expedition "by which the common cause will be more benefited . . . it is not my wish to give any interruption to the plan." But Washington went on to give the young aide what was in effect authority to supersede anything Gates proposed, as if it had already been considered and vetoed by the Commander in Chief. If Gates, so ran the instructions, "should have nothing more in contemplation than those particular objects which I have mentioned to you and which it is unnecessary to commit to paper, in that case you are to inform him that it is my desire that the reinforcements before mentioned, or such part of them as can be safely spared, be immediately put in motion to join this army."

Hamilton was also given orders in relation to the American commander on the Hudson highlands, General Israel Putnam. Before Burgoyne had surrendered, Sir Henry Clinton, whom Howe had left in command in New York City, had menaced Gates's rear by sending a detachment up the river that had demolished the Highland forts. Gates had responded by reinforcing Putnam with Poor's and Learned's brigades of Continentals. Washington noted in his letter to Hamilton a report that the British detachment had returned to the city. If this actually proved to be the case, Hamilton was to make sure that Putnam sent the two brigades on to Pennsylvania "with the greatest expedition." If Gates had already sent Morgan's riflemen to Washington, and Hamilton met them on the road, he should hurry them on.[2]

In total effect, Hamilton was given the widest possible discretion. He was empowered to overrule Gates concerning any operation the twenty-year-old considered unimportant. Hamilton could, by draining Putnam's command of all troops not needed for local defense, prevent that general from undertaking anything on his own. But all that was on paper. Gates in his pride and Putnam in his stubbornness might deny or evade Hamilton's authority. The embassy was basically a diplomatic one.

Washington added to his instructions letters directly addressed to Putnam and Gates. That to Putnam reinforced his instructions to Hamilton. Having congratulated Gates on Burgoyne's surrender, Washington reproved his titular subordinate for not having sent to headquarters a report of the victory: all that would have been needed was "a line under your signature stating the simple fact." Having announced that Hamilton "will deliver my sentiments on the plan of operations to be pursued," Washington justified his being so unspecific on the grounds that the letter might fall into the hands of the enemy.[3] Actually, he was carrying out his principle of avoiding specific orders when he was unfamiliar with the immediate situation. Usually, he trusted immediate decisions to the regional commander. Since he did not trust Gates, he had to empower the brilliant young aide to determine, after searching the situation out.

Thus instructed and countenanced, Hamilton set off, one must assume with interior jubilation, on the first destiny-shaping mission of his career. He was accompanied by Caleb Gibbs, the humorous Yankee who was captain of the headquarters guard. Speed was of the essence. By 5 P.M. on the day after he had received his instructions, he had ridden the 150 miles to the Hudson shore. The next morning, he crossed the river for his confrontation with General Putnam.

Putnam's head resembled a gnarled apple still hanging on its tree in midwinter. It was amazingly round, not only because of the width between the ears, but because his mouth and chin were so cramped that the bottom of his face seemed to stop at his nose. Although almost sixty, very old for a combat general, Putnam had more physical vitality than judgment. The anecdote that he had strayed into a wolf's den and then captured the wolf with his bare hands is probably legendary but summarizes his character well enough. As one of Rogers's Rangers during the French and Indian War, he had been rescued when, as an Indian captive, he was already tied to the stake for burning. After the death of his first wife, who had borne him ten children, he had made a socially influential second marriage. He had risen high in the governmental and militia politics of Connecticut without bothering really to learn how to read and write. He exuded to Hamilton, as to all he met, the joviality of his sometime trade of tavernkeeper, so much so that Hamilton failed to realize that Putnam was as open to suggestions as the Biblical deaf adder.

The military circle Hamilton now invaded had, since Burgoyne's surrender, developed its own strategies that were entirely independent of the problems, possibilities, and needs of Washington's army. Hamilton was told that the British had indeed withdrawn down the Hudson. Putnam's spies reported that Sir Henry Clinton had pulled the troops back because he had been ordered to lead a large detachment to Pennsylvania for cooperation with Howe.

Putnam's intention was to keep hold of the reinforcements Gates had sent him when the Hudson Highlands were in danger, and also to stop any troops who, as they moved along the prevailing roads along the banks of the river, were on the way to join Washington. He had a great coup in mind. When the reinforcement to Howe had departed, he would overwhelm the weakened garrison left in New York City. Gates had forbidden the attempt as insane—New York was too strongly fortified—but the old general was not listening.[4]

Hamilton now came in with so much energy and panache and show of Washington's authority, so much valuable information on the importance of keeping Howe from being supplied up the Delaware or along its banks, that Putnam was dazzled, as one of his aides wrote, into accepting the orders Hamilton delivered in Washington's name. He agreed to give up Poor's and Learned's Continental brigades along with a brigade of militia which Hamilton had demanded for good measure, although that was not in his instructions. For the moment, Putnam comforted himself with the thought that New York would probably become so weakened that he could take it with what militia was left or he could raise.[5]

After the quartermaster department had impressed from a local inhabitant two fresh horses,[6] Hamilton rode off with Gibbs, satisfied that the first step in his mission had been successfully accomplished. He did not realize that all he had said and all that had been agreed to had only penetrated the outside of Putnam's apple-like head. The core of the old man's determination and stubbornness had not been touched. Hamilton was, in fact, so pleased with what he considered his success that he wondered whether he could not get from Gates more than the three Continental brigades it was in his orders to procure.

But Hamilton was to confront a very different man from Putnam. Although the youth could not know it, Gates's life and character had, like his own, been influenced by illegitimacy. The son of a duke's housekeeper and presumably the duke, he had flickered on the edge of the British ruling class. In the manner of a gentleman, he had received a commission in the British army. Proving an able soldier, he had risen to the rank of major but there, despite his skills, he stuck. His equivocal position in the social world did not justify a higher rank. Washington, who had served with him during the French and Indian War, had persuaded him to settle in Virginia and, feeling the need of such expert advice when elected Commander in Chief, had persuaded Congress to appoint the British refugee his adjutant general. Thence Gates had risen to his present height.

Gates was so hearty with the men of low degree who had been

thrown upward by the Revolution that he had become a favorite of egalitarian New England. Yet much of his pleasure at the Saratoga victory was a snobbish satisfaction at evening the scores with the aristocrats who had failed to accept him: "Major General Phillips, who wrote me that saucy note last year . . . is now my prisoner with Lord Petersham; Major Ackland, son of Sir Thomas and his lady, daughter of Lord Ilchester, and sister to the famous Lady Susan; and about a dozen members of Parliament, Scotch lords, etc." Lady Ackland was part of the bag: the "most amiable, delicate piece of quality you ever beheld."[7]

Gates's character had become an uneasy mixture of push and cringe. When he got into a controversy with his subordinate, General Benedict Arnold, he had removed Arnold from all command—but had not banished him from the encampment. He had watched inconclusively while Arnold, with no authority whatsoever, led the battle that precipitated Burgoyne's surrender. But, believing that Burgoyne, trapped in the forest, would have had to surrender anyway, Gates gave Arnold no credit.

Gates was far from pleased to have the diminutive young aide of a general he had decided to push aside, march efficiently into his office and present orders. "I was sorry," Hamilton reported to Washington, "to find his ideas did not correspond with yours for drawing off the number of troops you directed. I used every argument in my power . . . but he was inflexible in the opinion that two brigades at least of Continental troops should remain in or near this place."

Gates argued that Clinton might not go to Philadelphia after all. Since the demolished Highland forts no longer blocked the Hudson, the British general might sail suddenly to Albany, capturing invaluable artillery and stores. Furthermore, if the troops Washington wanted were to march, Gates would be prevented from recapturing Ticonderoga. "The New England states would be left open to the depredations and ravages of the enemy."[8]

Temperamentally, Hamilton had no hesitation about booming at Gates in Washington's voice, but as he moved around the encampment he became frightened. One of Gates's principal aides was his old college friend Robert Troup. They had not met since Troup had been captured at the Battle of Long Island (he had subsequently been exchanged), and they renewed their friendship, so Troup remembered, "with ardor." He introduced Hamilton into the inner circle of the officers of what was primarily a New England army. Hamilton was careful to be tact itself. Jonathan Trumbull, Jr., wrote to his father, the governor of Connecticut, that Washington's aide had reported that "the General and the army below are exceedingly pleased with our exploits, especially as, our own work being done, they expect some assistance from the northern heroes." But the northern heroes made little effort to hide the fact that they were looking down on Washington.[9]

As Gates's aide, Troup knew much that he may have confided to Hamilton. The victor at Saratoga was receiving, from the sphere where the central government was and where Washington commanded, letters signed by congressmen, by influential citizens, and even by high officers in Washington's army. These communications were highly critical of Washington and called on Gates to take over as the necessary savior of the American cause. Of particular interest to history is a letter which a Franco-Irish soldier in the Continental service, Brigadier General Thomas Conway, had written and entrusted to Troup for delivery. Conway's attack on Washington had been too inflammatory to be sent to Albany in mails that might be intercepted.[10]

In whatever manner he was informed, Hamilton sensed so much danger that when Gates refused to send off more than one brigade, he reported to Washington: "I found myself infinitely embarrassed and was at a loss how to act. I felt the importance of strengthening you as much as possible, but on the other hand I found insuperable inconveniences in acting diametrically opposite to the opinion of a gentleman whose successes have raised him into the highest importance. General Gates has won the entire confidence of the eastern states. If disposed to do it, by addressing himself to the prejudices of the people, he would find no difficulty to render a measure odious which it might be said, with plausibility enough to be believed, was calculated to expose them to unnecessary danger, notwithstanding their exertions during the campaign had given them the fullest title to repose and security. General Gates has influence and interest elsewhere [in Congress]; he might use it, if he pleased, to discredit the measure there also." Should some accident happen as a result of insisting that Gates relinquish troops he did not want to give, "there would be too fair a pretext for censure, and many people are too well disposed to lay hold of it. At any rate, it might be considered as using him ill to take a step so contrary to his judgment."

These considerations and others that Hamilton did not consider it wise to commit to paper, "determined me not to insist upon sending either of the other brigades remaining here. I am afraid what I have done may not meet with your approbation as not being perhaps fully warranted by your instructions; but I ventured to do what I thought right, hoping that at least the goodness of my intention will excuse the error of my judgment."

To ameliorate matters, Hamilton continued to his commander, he had written General Putnam to "forward with all dispatch" two thousand militia and a thousand Continental troops "out of those proposed to be left" with him. These troops, Hamilton reasoned, would not be needed in the Highlands because of the stronger force to be left in Albany. In his confidence that Putnam would obey, Hamilton assured Washington that he would receive a stronger reinforcement than he had expected. But admittedly there would be more unreliable militiamen, fewer trained Continentals. Again Hamilton expressed uneasiness "lest my conduct should prove displeasing to you; but I have done what, considering all circumstances, appeared to me most eligible and prudent."[11]

Hamilton had hardly dispatched this report to Washington when he discovered that the brigade Gates was intending to send in riverboats that had already been prepared was not the one that had been agreed on, but General Patterson's, the very weakest, being made up of only six hundred men. Hamilton decided that he had no choice but to speak up resolutely, be the danger what it might. He wrote to the all-too-influential major general that his instructions from Washington would not permit him to "consent. . . . I am under the necessity of requiring, by virtue of my orders from him," that either Nixon's or Glover's brigade be substituted, "and that you will be pleased to give immediate orders for its embarkation."

Like David swinging his slingshot, Hamilton went on to tell the Goliath that, because Washington "wished me to pay great deference to your judgment," he had consented to Gates's keeping two brigades, although "I am not myself sensible" of any need, nor were various gentlemen [unnamed] he had consulted who were familiar with the situation. "When I preferred your opinion to other considerations, I did not imagine you would pitch upon a brigade little more than half as large as the others." In Hamilton's opinion, Glover's brigade would best serve Washington's purposes. If Gates "will be pleased" to send Hamilton orders to that effect "I will have them immediately forwarded."[12]

Gates was thrown into one of his typical confusions between aggression and lack of resolution, a desire to dominate and a fear of being slapped down. He *did* want to take the top rank from Washington, *but—*

Before Hamilton had arrived, Gates had found the courage to justify, in a letter to Washington, his not informing the Commander in Chief of the victory. Congress, he explained, had requested him to communicate directly with them, and he had assumed that they would hand on the news.[13] However, the rebuke from Washington which Hamilton had brought so bothered the ambitious general that, after a considerable period of worry (and after Hamilton had departed) he sent to Congress a further defense of his behavior. He had notified Congress rather than Washington on the assumption that by using this means of communication "I should always be certain" that Washington, who moved around the countryside, would be informed.

Gates now drafted an angry letter for Hamilton to carry to Washington—and then scratched out the most fiery parts. He wrote (but omitted from the copy actually sent): Although "explicit obedience" should be paid during battle to verbal orders communicated by aides, "yet I believe it is never practiced to extend that dictatorial power to one aide de camp sent to an army 300 miles distant." He also wrote but did not send: "I told the Colonel that whatever orders were given in Your Excellency's name in writing would be obeyed, but in my opinion . . ."

The tone of the letter actually entrusted to Hamilton was less angry than condescending. Gates had thought that he had already sent enough "succor" to what he called not the main or the Continental Army but "the southern army." He then lectured Washington on the importance of keeping a strong force in Albany. However, he had, against his better judgment, given in to Hamilton. He had ordered away Glover's brigade as well as Patterson's.[14]

After Gates had been, as Hamilton stated to Washington, "prevailed upon" to relinquish the second brigade, he left it to Washington's insistent and pesky aide to get the troops in motion. Hamilton scurried around to procure river shipping that would carry Glover's as well as Patterson's men. Failing in this, he questioned inhabitants to find out on which side of the river the roads could be most quickly traversed. Having ordered Glover to take the east bank, he waited (lest Gates change his mind?) to see both brigades actually in motion. Then he mounted his own horse.[15] Galloping with Gibbs beside him, he reached Putnam's encampment while both brigades were still upriver. What he found there drove him into a "temper" that approached hysteria.

He found that Poor's and Learned's brigades, which Putnam had promised to send to Washington, had not marched. As for the militia regiments, they were downriver with Putnam himself preparing for the attack on New York, which Hamilton sarcastically described to Washington as the old general's "hobby horse."[16]

To Putnam, who was a much less dangerous adversary than Gates, the young aide dispatched a stinging rebuke. "I am astonished and alarmed beyond measure" at the delays by "which the cause of America is put to the utmost conceivable hazard." He had so fully explained Washington's situation "that I could not entertain a doubt you would make it the first object of your attention to reinforce him." Yet the major general had put objects "insignificant" in comparison "uppermost. I speak freely, emphatically, because I tremble at the consequences."

The force Howe had called for from New York "will give him a decisive superiority over our army. What may be the issue of such a state of things I leave to the feelings of every friend to his country capable of foreseeing consequences." Having put down what might well be interpreted as a sneer at Putnam's capabilities, Hamilton did not scratch out the passage but continued, "My expressions may, perhaps, have more warmth than is altogether proper, but they proceed from the overflowing of my heart in a matter where I conceive this continent essentially interested."

How Putnam's noncompliance with orders given in Washington's name "can be answered to General Washington," Hamilton continued, "you can best determine." In any case, Hamilton now gave the major general an "explicit" and "positive" order that all the Continental troops under his command be immediately hastened to Washington.[17]

Hamilton got in touch with Governor George Clinton and, having secured Clinton's approval, wrote Putnam, without any authority from Washington whatsoever, a definition of how Washington envisioned Putnam's command. Putnam's function did "not extend farther than covering the country from any little eruptions of small parties, and carrying on the works [fortifications] necessary for the security of the river. As to attacking New York, that he thinks ought to be out of the question at present."[18]

It developed that Poor's and Learned's brigades had refused to march because of lack of pay and necessary supplies. There had been a "high mutiny" in Poor's, during which a captain had killed a man and was shot in retaliation. Hamilton blamed Putnam for refusing cooperation with Governor Clinton's efforts to remove difficulties. Then he got to work with frenzied energy. He reported to Washington that Clinton had borrowed "for me" five or six thousand dollars which should keep

Learned's brigade "in good humor till they join you. . . . I shall as soon as possible see General Poor and do everything in my power to get him along."

"If your Excellency agrees with me in opinion," Hamilton continued, "it will be well to send instant directions to General Putnam, . . . for I doubt whether he will attend to anything I shall say, notwithstanding it comes in the shape of a positive order." Hamilton wished Putnam could be replaced by Clinton: "The blunders and caprices of the former are endless."

Concerning himself, Hamilton wrote: "Believe me, sir, nobody can be more impressed with the importance of forwarding the reinforcements coming to you with all speed, nor could anybody have endeavored more to promote it. . . . I am very unwell, but I shall not spare myself to get things immediately in a proper train."[19]

For the next two days, Hamilton was immobilized at Governor Clinton's house in New Windsor "by a fever and violent rheumatic pains throughout my body." This, he wrote Washington, prevented him from doing anything in person, "but I have taken every other method in my power, in which Governor Clinton has obligingly given me all the aid he could." General Poor's brigade was "under an operation for the itch [scabies], which made it impossible for them to proceed till the effects of it were over." Furthermore, the officers and men "have unfortunately imbibed an idea that they have done their part" for the present campaign "and are now entitled to repose. This and the want of pay make them averse to a long march at this advanced season."

Putnam was still riding his hobby horse of attacking New York. No one knew exactly where he was. He had not paid the least attention to Hamilton's letters. His conduct gave "general disgust."[20]

Word came that Sir Henry Clinton's detachment had now actually sailed from New York on their trip to join Howe. In his passion to leave no stone unturned, Hamilton wrote to Gates that Clinton's departure made it obvious there would be no action up the Hudson against Albany, and equally obvious that Washington needed further reinforcement. To Washington, Hamilton confided his hope that this letter would "*extort*" more men from Gates.

This hope, he went on to admit, was dim. Hamilton had heard and inferred things concerning Gates which he dared not put on paper. "I shall be under a necessity of speaking plainly to Your Excellency when I have the pleasure of seeing you. I shall not hesitate to say, I doubt whether you would have had a man from the Northern Army if the whole could have been kept at Albany with any decency."

The young lieutenant colonel who had done his best to push around major generals was worried, as he tossed on his sickbed, lest he had not been aggressive enough, lest Washington "think me blameable in not having exercised the powers you gave me, and given a positive order. Perhaps I have been so; but, deliberately weighing all circumstances, I did not and do not think it advisable to do it."[21]

Though still far from recovered, Hamilton crossed the river to hurry on Glover's brigade, which he expected to find below Fishkill. In his eagerness to "fall in" with them, he continued downriver to Peekskill, where he was forced to halt. He was incapable of riding any further. He was put to bed in the large, barnlike house of Dennis Kennedy, and he was soon believed to be mortally ill.[22]

All Hamilton's efforts proved to have been in vain: no substantial reinforcement left the Hudson Valley.

This fact may have been kept from the sufferer, but he was undoubtedly shown a letter that arrived from Washington, the first he had received since leaving the headquarters: "I approve entirely of all the steps you have taken, and have only to wish that the exertions of those you have had to deal with had kept pace with your zeal and good intentions. I hope your health will before this have permitted you to push on the rear of the whole reinforcement beyond New Windsor."

Washington reported that Sir Henry's force was beginning to arrive on the lower Delaware.[23] This information was soon followed with the news that the reinforced British army had smashed the obstructions which had kept their navy from navigating the Delaware to Philadelphia. The former American capital was now a safe and solid British haven.

Washington's headquarters was informed that Hamilton lay at Peekskill "dangerously ill." From the young man's bedside, Governor Clinton rushed off a messenger requesting the attendance of the distinguished doctor John Jones. Jones replied that "my regard for the public service as well as a high sense of Colonel Hamilton's public merit would be the highest inducement"—but he himself was sick. Perhaps he could send his brother.

On the evening of November 25, so Captain Gibbs wrote Governor Clinton, Hamilton "seemed to have all the appearance of drawing nigh his last, being seized with a coldness in his extremities, and remained so for a space of two hours, then survived. He remained calm, and the fever not so high on the 26th. On the 27th, in the morning, the coldness came on again and increased. He was then cold as high as the knees in so much so the doctor thought he could not survive. He remained in this situation for near four hours, after which the fever abated very much, and from that time he has been getting much better."[24]

When Hamilton had been sick in the same bed with his dying mother, "a chicken for Elicks" was one of the purchases for which his mother's estate was later billed. During early December, 1777, Hamilton was fed, at the expense of the United States, "twelve fowl." He was induced to drink "shrub" concocted from rum and orange juice. Eggs and potatoes were not spared. He ate three quarters of mutton, a pheasant, and a partridge.[25]

Gates's partisans were unsympathetic. On December 19, Colonel Hugh Hughes wrote Gates, "Colonel Hamilton, who has been very ill of a nervous disorder at Peekskill, is out of danger, unless it be from his own sweet temper."[26]

Hamilton was mourning his "slow recovery" and expressing "my impatience to get home." Home was where Washington's Family was. On December 22, he informed Clinton that he would start out for Valley Forge the next day.[27]

The governor responded with a warning that if Hamilton rose too soon, the result "in all probability would prove fatal." But Hamilton was already on the move. He spent Christmas at Pompton, near Morristown. Then he collapsed. On January 5, Gibbs took him back to Peekskill in a hired coach.[28]

Three days later, the two officers set out again. The trip through the Jersey mountains to the banks of the Schuylkill, which had taken them a day and a half on their way to see Gates, now took them fourteen days. It was January 20, 1778, when Hamilton embraced his "brothers" at Valley Forge.[29]

22

Valley Forge

[JANUARY–JUNE, 1778   AGE 21]

HAMILTON discovered that a congressional committee on reorganization of the army was expected at Valley Forge, and that Washington had asked the various generals for suggestions to be made to the committee. Hamilton instantly dashed down his own ideas. "There are," he began, "still existing in the army so many abuses absolutely contrary to the military constitution that, without a speedy stop is put to them, it will be impossible even to establish any order or discipline among the troops." He "submitted" to Washington to decide which of the regulations he proposed could be directly ordered, and which would "require the sanction and authority of the committee of Congress." Hamilton's extensive paper dealt on a practical basis with many details involved in meshing together an efficient military force.[1]

But this document was only the beginning of Hamilton's immediate labors. Within nine days of his arrival at headquarters, the recovered invalid had pruned and correlated, under Washington's supervision, the suggestions that had reached headquarters. The resulting official report to the congressional committee fills forty-six pages in Washington's collected works.[2]

Hamilton had rejoined the Continental Army at so dark a time that it has gone down in American history and legend as the epitome of physical hardship. Unwilling to do what any regular commander would do, quarter his troops on civilians, Washington had induced his men to build their own city of log cabins on a series of frozen hillsides overlooking Valley Forge. But his act of ingenuity and generosity had only been the start of the ordeal. The civilian authorities failed to feed or clothe the troops. The most telling expression of those first winter months in Valley Forge is a great passage of amateur prose by the physician-diarist Albigence Waldo: "Poor food—hard lodging—cold weather—fatigue—nasty clothes—nasty cookery—vomit half my time—smoked out of my senses—the devil's in it—I can't endure it. . . . A pox on my bad luck. There comes a bowl of beef soup—full of burnt leaves and dirt, sickish enough to make a Hector spew—away with it boys—I'll live like the chameleon upon air! . . .

"There comes a soldier, his bare feet are seen through his worn-out shoes, his legs nearly naked from the tattered remains of an only pair of stockings, his breeches not sufficient to cover his nakedness, his shirt hanging in strings; his hair disheveled; his face meager. . . . He comes, and cries with an air of wretchedness and despair, 'I am sick, my feet lame, my legs are sore, my body covered with this tormenting itch . . . and all the reward I shall get will be—"Poor Will is dead!" ' "[3]

After he had been at Valley Forge for a little more than a month, Hamilton, in writing to Governor Clinton, blamed the plight of the army on "the folly, caprice, a want of foresight, comprehension, and dignity" that characterized the Continental Congress.

"False and contracted views of economy" had prevented Congress from making enough provision for the officers "to interest them in the service, which has produced such carelessness and indifference . . . as is subversive to every officer-like quality." Furthermore, Congress had "disgusted the army by repeated instances of the most whimsical favoritism in their promotions." Foreigners boasted that they needed only "to assume a high tone and assert their own merit with confidence and perseverance" to get any rank they pleased. "These things wound my feelings as a republican more than I can express; and in some degree make me contemptible in my own eyes.

"By injudicious changes and arrangements in the commissary's department, in the middle of a campaign, they have exposed the army frequently to temporary want, and to the danger of a dissolution, from absolute famine. At this very day there are complaints from the whole line, of having been three or four days without provisions; desertions have been immense, and strong features of mutiny begin to show themselves. It is indeed to be wondered at, that the soldiery have manifested so unparalleled a degree of patience, as they have. If effectual measures are not speedily adopted, I know not how we shall keep the army together or make another campaign.

"I omit saying any thing of the want of clothing for the army. It may be disputed whether more could have been done than has been done.

"If you look into their conduct in the civil line, you will equally discover a deficiency of energy, dignity and extensiveness of views; but of this you can better judge than myself, and it is unnecessary to particularize."

The difficulty was a shocking degeneration in the quality of the members of Congress. "America once had a representation that would do honor to any age or nation." What, he asked, was the cause of the falling off? "The great men who composed our first council, are they dead, have they deserted the cause, or what has become of them?" Hamilton answered that "local attachment, falsely operating," has made many leaders more concerned with "the particular interests of the states to which they belonged than for the common interests of the confederacy."

Inspired by the terrible situation at Valley Forge, Hamilton then launched into his first known advocacy of the superiority of the federal system of government:

"However important it is to give form and efficiency to your interior constitutions and police, it is infinitely more important to have a wise general council. Otherwise a failure of the measures of the union will overturn all your labors for the advancement of your particular good and ruin the common cause. You should not beggar the councils of the United States to enrich the administration of the several members. Realize to yourself the consequences of having a Congress despised at home and abroad. How can the common force be exerted if the power of collecting it be put in weak, foolish, and unsteady hands? How can we hope for success in our European negotiations if the nations of Europe have no confidence in the wisdom and vigor of the great Continental Government? This is the object on which their eyes are fixed, hence it is America will derive its importance or insignificance in their estimation."[4]

As far back as the history of British America ran, the various colonies, although severally linked to the Crown, had been mutually independent. Like all neighboring nations, they had been economic rivals, jealous of each other's power. It was the Revolution which had brought them into alliance, and as an alliance not a union their connection was still, by most politicians, viewed. Washington, like Hamilton, complained that once the initial excitement had passed, many leaders had turned their energies from the federal to the state governments.

In the army camps, the movement of thought flowed oppositely. However much the states insisted that the regiments of each be organized separately from the others, the army had to function as a unit. If a South Carolina brigade gave way in battle or advanced, it could mean death or life for the neighboring Massachusetts brigade. And, as the situation at Valley Forge so dramatically exemplified, the supply and pay of the army depended on the efficiency and practical capabilities of the central Continental Congress.

Washington's Family was made up of men from various states. However, all but Hamilton had grown up, as had most of their forebears, in colonial America. They realized that local sentiment was so powerful that the issue of state versus federal power could not be effectively confronted head on. To get done what had to be done you had to infiltrate around the edges. Furthermore, they had in their own blood local loyalties that gave them some understanding and sympathy of the divisionist point of view. Although Washington was now completely convinced of the importance of union, he had only a few years before referred to Virginia as "my country." The recent immigrant Hamilton shared no such memories, yet he had been warned at headquarters concerning discretion.

He continued to Clinton: "The sentiments I have advanced are not fit for the vulgar ear; and, circumstanced as I am, I should with caution utter them except to those in whom I place entire confidence." Remembering that his own political base was in New York, he stated that he had no idea of criticizing that state. New York was well represented in Congress, despite (so he could not resist adding) the absence of Jay, Robert R. Livingston, and Clinton himself. Indeed he had only written Clinton so that the governor could use his influence to warn "other states" of their delinquencies.[5]

As a matter of fact, Hamilton had not chosen his correspondent well: Clinton was to oppose Hamilton's federalism down the long years. Now he did not go beyond conceding in his reply that many of the measures of the Continental Congress were unwise. On the substantive issue, he wrote only, "I wish Jay or Livingston or both in Congress, though they could be illy spared from here, but this can't be at present."[6]

While in New York, on his way back from his confrontation with Gates, Hamilton had been unable to convince Governor Clinton of "the existence of a certain faction" that was scheming to give Gates Washington's command. After his arrival at headquarters, he wrote

Clinton that he had "discovered such convincing traits of the monster that I cannot doubt its reality in the most extensive sense."[7]

Hamilton had been brought up to date by Washington and the Family on what has gone down in history as the Conway Cabal. Thomas Conway, after whom the cabal was to be named, was the most conspicuous and the most objectionable of the generals from the French service who had been foisted on the Continental Army. By birth and upbringing an Irishman, he spoke English, which made him less dependent than the other foreigners on Hamilton's ministrations. It also enabled him to enunciate clearly the foreigners' common disdain for the American command as a whole and for George Washington in particular. Conway persuaded those political leaders who were most anti-Washington that his own presence was essential to counteract the army's amateur leadership. But, so he made clear, an officer of his skill could not be expected to stay on if he were not given his due by being raised from brigadier to major general.

Hamilton characterized Conway as "one of the vermin bred in the entrails of this chimera dire. . . . There does not exist a more villainous calumniator or incendiary."[8] Washington, condescended to by Conway at Councils of War, came to hate the Franco-Irishman as perhaps he never had hated any other man. In his rage, the Commander in Chief gave his own enemies a handle by implying that he would resign if the army were disrupted by the unmerited promotion of Conway over the heads of so many worthy American officers.

"In the indulgence of his dislike for Washington," Troup remembered, "and in the hope of profiting by General Gates's favor, General Conway opened a correspondence with General Gates, in which General Washington's conduct as commander in chief was made the subject of free discussion and injurious remarks. To this correspondence General Gates lent a willing ear; and accordingly his answers to General Conway's letters were very much the echoes of the sentiments those letters contained."[9]

While Hamilton was up north, arguing with Gates and renewing his friendship with Troup, another one of Gates's aides, James Wilkinson, was riding south with the official news of Burgoyne's surrender. Wilkinson got drunk at the house of one of Washington's partisans and babbled. His indiscretions resulted in Washington's writing Conway:

Sir:

A letter I received last night contained the following paragraph:

"In a letter from General Conway to General Gates he says, 'Heaven has been determined to save your country, or a weak general and bad councillors would have ruined it.'"

I am, sir, your humble servant,

George Washington[10]

Conway showed this letter to another leading opponent of Washington, Major General Thomas Mifflin, a Pennsylvanian politician who had secured high rank by vote of Congress but could not persuade Washington, who considered him as hysterical as he was oratorical, to give him any important command. Mifflin assumed that Washington had got hold of an actual letter from Conway to Gates. He rushed off to Gates a warning that his files were being rifled. Gates replied that he was "infinitely distressed." He could not imagine who was "the villain who has played me this cursed trick." But Gates soon reached what seemed the obvious conclusion.[11]

On Wilkinson's return, Gates said to him, "I have had a spy in my camp." Washington's creature Hamilton had been "left alone an hour in this room, during which time he took Conway's letter out of that closet and copied it, and the copy has been furnished to Washington."[12]

Wilkinson, who did not yet realize that his own indiscretion was to blame, expressed doubt to Gates that Hamilton had sneaked into his files. Since Troup and Hamilton were such friends, it was more probable that Troup had "innocently communicated the import of General Conway's letter."

Troup registered a stout denial, but Gates preferred to believe the more serious charge. He was enchanted to conclude that he could discredit Washington for conniving in the dishonorable act of the aide whose influence with the Commander in Chief was (as Troup put it) a source of "jealousy" to Washington's opponents. Gates boasted to his family that he had "adopted a plan which would *compel* General Washington to give him [Hamilton] up, and that the receiver and the thief would alike be disgraced."[13]

In a letter of which he sent copies both to Congress and his fellow conspirator Mifflin, Gates informed Washington that his private files had been "stealingly copied." Surely, so Gates continued, Washington would unmask "the author of the infidelity which put extracts of General Conway's letters in your hands." Gates then lectured Washington

211

Washington's headquarters at Valley Forge. General and Mrs. Washington, with all the aides-de-camp, slept in this small house, where all the headquarters business and also the General's entertaining were conducted. Photograph, taken in 1906. Courtesy New-York Historical Society

on how "crimes of this magnitude" endangered "the safety of these states."[14]

Washington did not miss the chance of making a fool out of his opponent by publicly revealing that his source had been the drunken blabbering of Gates's own messenger, Wilkinson. And Hamilton thereafter considered Gates his enemy because of "unjust and unprovoked attacks on my character."[15]

The dispatches Hamilton had sent down from Albany had included no mention of Conway. However, his warnings that Gates was intransigent and had the power to make trouble had strengthened fears ripe at headquarters. Gates had already shown himself insubordinate; and what was to be more expected than a movement to replace a defeated general with a victorious one? Extenuating circumstances were not likely to be considered. Had Washington's role been purely military, he would probably have been toppled.

The correspondence of the time makes clear that many leading patriots had twinges of worry concerning the military abilities of the commander who had been defeated in every battle with the main British army. But few could visualize going on without him. In every crisis Congress heaped more civil powers on Washington's shoulders than he desired. Their very action showed that in effect the Commander in Chief was also the chief executive. Since he had labored to mobilize behind the revolt the broadest possible range of opinion, opposition to him could not find any unified base of support. The so-called Conway Cabal was a loose coming together of men motivated by a variety of reasons, often personal. Mifflin, who was the ablest politician among them, realized that Congress would never fire the Commander in Chief. It would be necessary to create, by inconspicuous movements behind the scenes, a situation that would force Washington to resign.

Congress's uneasiness about the record of the Continental Army enabled Mifflin to have set up a Board of War with supervisory powers over Washington. He saw to it that Gates was made president of the Board and that the other members, among whom he included himself, were anti-Washington. But the master stroke—or so it seemed —was to send to Valley Forge, promoted to major general and to the new office of inspector general, the man Washington most hated. Conway was to keep his eye on everything Washington did and report back to the Board.

Conway had arrived at Valley Forge while Hamilton was convalescing at Peekskill. On a technicality, Washington refused to acknowledge his power. Conway thereupon wrote Washington two letters mocking the American commander as an amateur soldier: "I do not pretend, sir, to be a consulate general, but . . . an old sailor knows more of ships than admirals who have never been to sea." That such sentiments, while insulting the national hero, claimed superiority for all foreigners over the native officers, did not make the letters more palatable when Washington allowed them to become public.[16]

Hamilton had reached Valley Forge when the cabal was at its most malignant and about to come into the open. Gossip was flowing from crossroads to crossroads, warnings were pouring into headquarters, and a ground swell of anger was rising at reports of a plot to humiliate Washington until he resigned.

Washington himself was deeply hurt. That he confided to his young aide more than he wished to have known outside the Family was revealed when Hamilton drafted a letter to William Livingston, his own old Elizabethtown patron.

The draft expressed for Washington "sensible pleasure" that a plot to assassinate Livingston had been detected in time. "It is a tax, however severe, which all those must pay who are called to eminent stations of trust, not only to be held up as conspicuous marks to the enmity of the public adversaries of their country, but to the malice of secret traitors and the *envious intrigues* of false friends and factions."

This much Washington was willing to have said, but what Hamilton then wrote cut so deep that Washington scratched it out: Calumny by enemies of the cause was easy to bear, "yet I confess I cannot help feeling the most painful sensations whenever I have reason to believe I am the object of persecution to men who are embarked in the same general interest, and whose friendship my heart does not reproach me with ever having done anything to forfeit. But with many, it is a sufficient cause to hate and wish the ruin of a man because he has been happy enough to be the object of *his country's* favor."[17]

By early February, Hamilton believed, as he wrote Clinton, that the cabal had "unmasked its batteries too soon and begins to hide its head." However, he feared that it would continue to operate secretly, changing, as he put it in a military metaphor, "the storm to a sap. All the true and sensible friends to their country, and of course to a certain great man, ought to be upon the watch to counterplot the secret machinations of his enemies."[18]

Enmity against Washington did go on, but popular outrage rose to such heights that the loose grouping of Washington's enemies broke apart, each man seeking his own hiding place. The foreigner Conway was sacrificed, driven from the army and severely wounded by one of Washington's supporters in a duel.

In the eighteenth century, it was the humane custom to return prisoners of war by exchange. Washington had suggested to Howe in July, 1776, that periodic exchanges be made "officer for officer of equal rank, soldier for soldier, and citizen for citizen,"[19] but the plan, although acceded to, had proved so badly worked out in detail that it had not functioned. Now the British, probably to secure the release of Burgoyne's surrendered army, had urged a negotiation that would activate the exchanges. This would be to the British advantage, since the soldiers returned to them would be professionals who could otherwise only be replaced expensively and tediously from overseas, while the American prisoners were amateurs who could be replaced from the local population. To Hamilton's expressed outrage, Congress was hesitating on how to proceed.

It was, he admitted, "bad policy to go into an exchange, but . . . it is much worse policy to commit such frequent breaches of faith and ruin our national character. Whatever refined politicians may think, it is of great consequence to preserve a national character. . . . The general notions of justice and humanity are implanted in almost every human breast, and ought not to be too freely shocked."

Negotiations with foreign powers would unquestionably be damaged if the United States got the reputation of violating its faith whenever that was convenient. At home, the government would be brought "into contempt." Furthermore, "in the present case, the passions of the country and the army are on the side of an exchange, and a studied attempt to avoid it will disgust both, and serve to make the service odious," discouraging drafting, recruiting, and militia activity. "The prospect of hopeless captivity cannot but be very disagreeable to men constantly exposed to the chance of it." And those actually caught in the eternal net "will have little scruple to get rid of it by joining the enemy. . . .

"For my own part, I have so much of the milk of humanity in me that I abhor such *Neronian* maxims; and I look upon the old proverb that *honesty is the best policy* to be so generally true that I can never expect any good from a systematical deviation from it, and I can never adopt the reasonings of some *American* politicians deductible from their practice, that no regard is to be paid to national character or rules of good faith."

For all its moral tone, its claim to "the milk of humanity," Hamilton's statement was equivocal. Hamilton did not denounce dishonesty itself but dishonesty as a "systematical deviation." National character should not be violated "whenever it is convenient"; justice and humanity should not be shocked "too freely."[20]

Hamilton was almost instantly to put his principles in practice on the very issue he had discussed: a prisoner exchange.

On March 28, 1778, Washington appointed Colonel William Grayson, Lieutenant Colonels Harrison and Hamilton, and Hamilton's old Elizabethtown patron Elias Boudinot to meet with representatives of General Howe.[21] According to Boudinot, Congress wished the negotiation to be a sham "for the purpose of satisfying the army" and throwing the blame on the British for failure to achieve an accord. But the commissioners, including Hamilton, insisted that "we would not be made the instruments of so dishonest a measure." Washington agreed, stating that "his troops looked upon him as their protector, and that he would not suffer an opportunity being lost of liberating every soldier who was then in captivity, let the consequence be what it might." In a major delegation of power, he commanded his commissioners "to make the best treaty in our power, and he would ratify it and take the risk upon himself."[22]

The commissioners rode to the rendezvous at Germantown with a guard of cavalry selected from among the ragged American troops to "make the best possible appearance."[23] After their trumpeter had sounded his tune, the British received them with the "great ceremony" at which professional armies were so expert. Then the head of the British delegation, Colonel Charles O'Hara, invited them to dinner.

"We had previously," wrote Boudinot, "obtained the characters of our opponents and were convinced that they depended much on out-drinking us." In this contest, Hamilton was not considered an accomplished enough champion. However, "we knew that Colonel Grayson was a match for any of them, and therefore left all that part of the business to him." The Britons, Boudinot boasted, soon "found themselves foiled."[24]

At the start of the actual negotiations, it became clear that the powers given by Howe to the British commissioners were by no means commensurate with those given by Washington to the Americans. Here was an issue on which the conference could at any moment be scuttled. But the Americans agreed to negotiate while the Britons sought further powers.

On the evening of the third day, the Englishmen returned to Philadelphia to attend a "great ball." They reappeared somewhat sheep-ishly. Howe had told them that Germantown was too close to Phila-delphia to be considered neutral ground: the American commissioners would have to spend every night in their own camp, seventeen miles away. Hamilton and his colleagues, considering that Howe had broken his agreement with Washington and insulted their personal honor, "gathered up their papers and announced the negotiations were at an end." An effort of the Britons to embarrass the American departure was frustrated by Grayson, who heroically got the opposition so drunk "they could scarcely sit upright."[25]

Making a conspicuous concession, Washington agreed that the con-ference reconvene in American-controlled territory. At Newtown, Pennsylvania, the delegates labored to establish permanent rules for periodic exchanges: once every two months was suggested. A basic issue was how, when the two sides did not have the same numbers of prisoners in each rank, the exchange could be made equal. Hamilton drafted a table: Washington, as commander in chief, would be worth 192 of the lowest officers (ensigns); Hamilton, as a lieutenant colonel, would be worth five.[26]

But the basic dilemma remained. Washington had received from Congress full powers, which he had delegated to Hamilton and his other negotiators. Howe did not specify any powers beyond his per-sonal word as commander in chief.

The British commissioners "intimated," so Hamilton and his col-leagues reported to Washington, "an impropriety in treating with us on a national ground in a contest of such a nature as the present, which might imply an acknowledgment inconsistent with their claims." Translated into clear English, the British wished to avoid any implica-tion that they acknowledged Congress as the governing body of an independent nation. Hamilton and his colleagues replied that, in their eagerness to remove "every impediment" to a prisoner exchange, they would agree that "no expression" in their cartel "should be construed to affect the political claims of either country in anything not directly necessary to the due and faithful observance of the treaty."[27]

This concession seemed more helpful than it actually was. For Howe to go beyond his own personal word, he would have to get powers from a Parliament that was months of sailing away. He could not bind his successor, and there was reason to believe that he was about to be replaced by his second-in-command, Sir Henry Clinton. The situation was ironclad: there was no way that the British could escape onus for the failure of the cartel. Finally acknowledging this, O'Hara made the practical suggestion: "Let us continue till our stores are exhausted, and then separate."[28]

Hamilton had hardly returned to Valley Forge when there came an explosion of continent-shaking news. The French had in effect declared war on England by recognizing the United States as an independent nation. Clinton had replaced Howe as commander in chief. Presumably because the new international situation required that a part of their army in America be sent elsewhere, the British were going to evacuate Philadelphia and concentrate their remaining forces in New York.

Clinton offered for exchange the 790 American prisoners "at present in the city of Philadelphia." Having failed in an effort to summon Boudinot, Washington put the negotiation in the hands of Hamilton, writing officially, "I hearby assure you that your proceedings in this instance will be ratified by me." The aide had no difficulty carrying out his limited assignment with success.[29]

During February, 1781, Hamilton wrote concerning Washington: "For more than three years past I have felt no friendship for him and have professed none." Then he sharpened his recollection and scratched out "more than." Three years placed the change in his feelings within a month or two of his own arrival at Valley Forge.[30]

Interpretation of his brief avowal is made more difficult by his statement in the same letter that from the very start of their relationship he had repelled any "advances" by Washington towards adding "private attachment" to "military confidence." Furthermore, careful scrutiny cannot find in the many documents concerning Hamilton's services to Washington before and after the Valley Forge period any consistent difference of tone: the aide remained a perfect subordinate. Yet one change became visible: Hamilton was soon to begin his efforts to escape from headquarters by persuading His Excellency that he should be permanently assigned to important military duties elsewhere.

When Hamilton came to specify his resentment against Washington, he stressed His Excellency's ill-humor.[31] Never did this trait show itself more than at Valley Forge. The General's proclivity for rage, usually kept by willpower under control, had been incited to break all bonds by what he considered the injustice of the attacks made on him by the Conway Cabal. To hide weaknesses in the cause, he had, down the years, borne silently much criticism for situations beyond his control—but this was too much! He expressed hatred for his opponents; hinted (as he never did at any other time) that he might resign; encouraged, despite his often-expressed disapproval of dueling, his young supporters to challenge his enemies.[32] When a man who has long suppressed angry emotions allows them to fly free, they are likely to land where not primarily intended. He surely scattered spare vitriol on his Family, including the aide whose pride was most vulnerable.

Although Hamilton found Washington's character not impulsive enough, this kind of impulsiveness was not to the young man's taste. Hamilton's own excesses were not disorderly. They were the flight of a controlled instrument when the controls are awry, of an arrow shot straight from a warped bow. But Washington's rages resembled volcanic explosions: extreme if temporary examples of such a breakdown of control as Hamilton felt menaced him and his sanity. Everyone found Washington's rages unbearable, and there was nothing to do except wait for them to blow themselves out.

In Washington's service on the mission to Gates and Putnam, Hamilton had so exerted himself that he finally collapsed into an illness feared mortal. Washington had sent him a short, hurried letter while he was assumed to be still active, expressing approval but more devoted to urging further services. As Hamilton lay ill, the busy commander had not written him at all. And after Hamilton had finally come home, he shrank to becoming again one, even if the most prominent, of the little group of aides.

The youth who had wrestled as an equal with the second-in-command of the entire army; who had, with the approval of the governor of New York, ordered around Major General Israel Putnam, was back at his old "drugery" (as he called it) of expressing his chief's ideas by drafting innumerable letters. "I have," he complained to Boudinot, "no passion for scribbling."[33]

Hamilton's labors were, it is true, varied by assignments in relation to prisoner exchange which other young men would have regarded as great honors. But such responsibilities were minor compared to his mission to Gates. And he may have recognized that no other equivalent opportunity might open to him as long as he remained Washington's aide.

To Governor Clinton, Hamilton complained of "my insignificance." His efforts at influencing events were limited to giving hints to men of greater importance "who are pleased to favor me with their confidence."[34] Here surely was the principal rub! For an artillery captain to join the Commander in Chief's staff had been a step up. Becoming in effect chief of staff was another. But that was as high as it was possible to mount in Washington's Family. He would have to find some way of shifting, without any intermediate descent, onto some other ladder, one that extended higher, and would open to his ambition either true personal power or personal renown in battle.

23

A Frenzy of Valor

A T the very end of May, 1778, the British fleet sailed, loaded with the army's baggage, from Philadelphia to New York. The army was clearly going to march across the New Jersey lowlands. Out from behind their fortifications, they would be vulnerable to attack—but on a terrain where Washington had always avoided battle because it was so suited to conventional military skills. The Continental Army had been learning these skills. The question whether they had acquired enough to justify a fight in open country tormented headquarters.[1]

The hardships for which Valley Forge was infamous had been mitigated at about the time the Conway Cabal faded: during mid-February. The cabins the men had built for themselves were by then chinked against the weather and the chimneys had been taught to draw. "Poor Will" was no longer sick and dying. Enough food and clothing were dribbling in to change destitution into adventure, particularly as all the participants were men "whose tempers, attachments and circumstances disposed them," so Washington wrote, to physical exploits and long military service. There were no militiamen staggering around to strike an amateurish note.[2]

Into this congenial situation there rode a bogus German baron who had seen much military service with the French army and was an expert drillmaster. "Baron" von Steuben spoke no English, which made him rely on Hamilton's services as an interpreter, and although almost twice Hamilton's age, he established a dependence on the younger man that was to continue long after the war ended.

"The Baron," as he was commonly called, was like an overgrown child, and it was his childishness along with his competence that enabled him to win the affection of the army he trained. The soldiers, who had been inclined from ignorance to proceed in single file, were taught how to move in ranks without falling over each other: this enabled them to exert much more power in attack. They were shown how to use bayonets for more than roasting meat over campfires. To celebrate the French alliance, they had staged a review that seemed miraculous to those used to their previous straggling. But would their recently acquired discipline hold up on the battlefield?

On June 18, 1778, the British army finally crossed onto the Jersey plains that led to New York. Washington had led no triumphal parade into Boston after that city had been won from the British; he led none now into repossessed Philadelphia. Instead of riding behind his commander down cheering streets, Hamilton accompanied him on a quick river crossing north of the British retreat. Hamilton knew that this speed did not indicate any specific intention to attack. Washington intended to keep pace with the enemy "and avail ourselves of any favorable circumstances that may offer." If none offered, the Continental Army would reach the Hudson above New York City at about the same time the British arrived in the city below. In the meanwhile, American guerrillas would skirmish on the British flanks and rear.[3]

For whatever reason—some said the enemy waited at each bridge the patriots had destroyed until their professional engineers had rebuilt it in style; others believed the enemy were trying to lure Washington into battle—the British advanced across the Jersey lowlands with amazing slowness. Moving ahead equally slowly, Washington established his headquarters each night in a different farmhouse. His aides concerned themselves with the farmers' daughters, as a journal kept by Colonel James McHenry reveals:

For June 20th he noted, "A rainy evening. Let me see what company we have indoors. A pretty, full-faced, youthful, playful lass, and a family of Quakers, meek and unsuspicious. Hamilton, thou shalt not tread this ground! I mark it for myself.

"The pretty girl gives me some excellent milk and sits by me and chats with me 'till bedtime. She was no subject for gallantry, and I too innocent to attempt sudden mischief. So I kissed her hand, telling her we should all be gone before she got up, but not to forget that one man is often more dangerous to a woman than a whole army."

Concerning headquarters on the 23rd, McHenry noted gleefully, "Here are some charming girls, but one of the drums of the guard [is] more a favorite than Hamilton."[4]

On June 24, Washington summoned a Council of War. Hamilton kept the minutes which began: "His Excellency informs the Council." According to the best estimate, the British numbered nine to ten thousand. The American army "on this ground" numbered 10,684. In addition, about twenty-four hundred Continentals and militia were hovering "in the neighborhood of the enemy. . . . Considering the present situation of our national affairs and the probable prospects of the enemy, the General requests the sentiments of the council on the following questions": Should the army hazard "of choice" a general action? Should they initiate or invite a partial action? Otherwise, "what measures can be taken, with safety to this army, to annoy the enemy on the march? As Hamilton fidgeted with increasing rage, the subsequent discussion was dominated by General Charles Lee.[5]

At the outbreak of the Revolution, Lee had been considered the ablest soldier on the American side, and might well have been elected commander in chief in place of Washington had he been American-born and not so eccentric. He had been commissioned in the British regular army as a boy; in America during the French and Indian War and in Spain thereafter he had had much battle experience. Seeking more fighting when England was at peace, he had adventured to Poland where he became a major general and accompanied a Russian army against the Turks. On his return to England he had written radical pamphlets and insulted George III to his face. In 1773, he had settled in Virginia, where Washington had listened raptly to his lectures on strategy.

Hamilton had first seen Lee at the same moment when he first saw Washington: as the two generals passed through New York on their way to the army in Cambridge. Second in command under Washington, Lee was captured during the retreat across New Jersey. Hamilton had been ordered to achieve his exchange, which had been consummated exactly a month before the Council of War Lee was now dominating. The returned prodigal was the kind of disorderly, uncontrolled, irrational man that filled Hamilton with disgust. Physically dirty, he was foulmouthed by unthinking habit. He was endlessly ebullient and self-confident. That he did not hide his scorn of everything Washington and Steuben and Hamilton had achieved in training the army during his captivity only made the obvious brilliance he radiated more annoying.

General Charles Lee, the brilliant and eccentric British-born American officer whose equivocal behavior at the Battle of Monmouth led to a court-martial and a duel in which Hamilton was a second. Courtesy, New York Public Library

Lee's repudiation of the possibility that the Americans might be able to face the British on any other basis than guerrilla warfare lay at the base of his oration to the Council of War. The British army, he stated, had never been better trained than at this very place and moment. For the American amateurs to interfere with them would be, particularly when the French were on the way to America's aid, more than foolhardy: it would be insane. Lafayette's answering effusion that honor required an attack did not help much.

In the minutes to the Council, Hamilton noted laconically the decision to avoid a major battle but send an additional fifteen hundred men to annoy the enemy's left flank and rear. Privately, Hamilton commented that Lee had been the primum mobile of a "sage plan" that would "have done honor to the most honorable society of midwives, and to them only."[6]

The outrage in which Hamilton played his part found expression in letters from Generals Greene and Wayne to Washington. Greene urged that since the enemy's line of march stretched for miles—the baggage train itself was twelve miles long—light troops could make a "serious impression" on their flank and rear without "suffering them to bring us into a general action." However, the main army should be close, and if a general action should ensue, Greene believed, "the chance is greatly in our favor."[7]

Washington seems to have hoped that the Council of War would help him make up his mind to attack. He now found the determination to override the Council's decision. He added a thousand men to the force hovering close to the British and ordered an attack on the enemy's rear if "a fair opportunity offered."[8]

The enlarged command was proffered, as protocol required, to the ranking major general, Charles Lee. Hamilton could only have been delighted when Lee, saying that he disapproved of the whole operation, declined. Who would then get the command? Would Washington pass over General Stirling, who was next in rank but more proficient with the bottle than the sword, and give the opportunity to the young major general who was Hamilton's daily companion? Washington did call on Lafayette. But even as the Marquis, who was "in raptures with his Command and burning to distinguish himself," was being congratulated, Lee reappeared to say that his own refusal was being criticized and he would accept after all. Renewed questioning having brought out his continuing doubts, Lee refused again, but now Stirling was protesting. Washington somehow silenced Stirling, only to have Lee appear a third time. He became, Hamilton remembered, "very importunate." But Washington "grew tired of such fickle behavior, and ordered the Marquis to proceed." Hamilton secured permission to serve as principal aide to the aristocrat, who was slightly his junior.[9]

The two youths rode out together. Their first task was to locate the considerable part of their command that was skirmishing in detachments at different locations near the British column, whose position was also not clear. There were so many directions in which to look that Hamilton and Lafayette soon separated. After receiving a dispatch from Hamilton, Lafayette reported to Washington that the enemy were further down the road than he had supposed. "We want to be very well furnished with spirits as a long, quick march may be necessary, and if General Scott's detachment is not provided, it should also be furnished with liquor." The troops needed food, too.[10]

The next day, Hamilton reported directly to Washington. Although still separated from Lafayette, he sent the Commander in Chief Lafayette's compliments as if the Marquis were present. He wrote as if theirs were a joint command, and insisted, in a way the aristocrat himself would have done, that "our personal honor" was involved in their attempting "whatever the disposition of our men will second and prudence authorize."

Hamilton expressed chagrin that an opportunity which had existed early that morning had been missed for lack of information. After riding all night he had, at Robin's Tavern six miles from Allentown, come up with Wayne's brigade. To his indignation (which he surely expressed to Brigadier General Wayne as he was now doing to the Commander in Chief) he found that "every precaution was neglected. No horse was near the enemy." He personally ordered an adequate reconnoiter only to discover that the enemy, who had been in reach, were now "in full march." Wayne's troops were unable to follow because they were "almost starving."[11]

After further reports had come in, Hamilton started to write a second letter to Washington: The British had so strengthened their rear that to attack them "without being supported by the whole army would be folly in the extreme." The aide was advising his commander to embarrass the enemy by moving near to their left flank, when Lafayette appeared at the head of a considerable column. Lafayette had a pocketful of letters from Washington, all written that day. The first warned Lafayette not to "distress your men by an overhasty march. The weather is extremely warm and by too great an exertion in pushing the troops, many of them will fall sick." Shortly thereafter Washington had written that his own troops could not advance to support

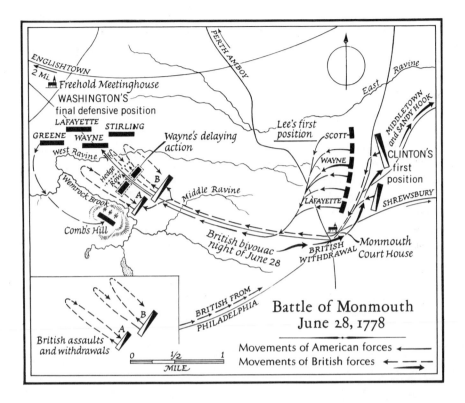

ENGLISHTOWN
2 Mi.

Freehold Meetinghouse
WASHINGTON'S
final defensive position
LAFAYETTE
STIRLING
GREENE WAYNE

West Ravine

Wayne's delaying
action

Hedge Row

B

A

Middle Ravine

Wentock Brook

Comb's Hill

British bivouac
night of June 28

PERTH AMBOY

Lee's first
position SCOTT

WAYNE

LAFAYETTE

East Ravine

MIDDLETOWN
and SANDY HOOK

CLINTON'S
first
position

SHREWSBURY

BRITISH
WITHDRAWAL

Monmouth
Court House

British assaults
and withdrawals

B

A

BRITISH FROM
PHILADELPHIA

Battle of Monmouth
June 28, 1778

0   ½   1

MILE

Movements of American forces
Movements of British forces

an attack for want of provisions and that in any case they were stopped "by the severe rain now falling." A third letter ordered Lafayette to withdraw some miles to Englishtown.

But it was a fourth letter that was particularly disturbing. It stated that, General Lee's "uneasiness" at having refused so important a command "rather increasing than abating," Washington had decided to relieve the veteran's "distress of mind" by sending him on, with further reinforcements, to take from Lafayette the leadership of the advance force.[12]

Hamilton and Lafayette's personal adventure was over. Lafayette stayed with his troops and Hamilton returned to headquarters.

On the night of April 27, the head of the main American army was encamped some nine miles from the British rear at Monmouth Court House. Lee's select command of from five to six thousand was three miles closer to the enemy. In Washington's opinion, the last chance for decisive action was at hand. The British were within a day's march of strong country where they could with difficulty be attacked. They would probably start across the intervening space that night or early the next morning.

Washington's encampment was silent—armies like farmers get up with dawn and quiet down with sunset—when Washington summoned Hamilton after midnight to prepare a dispatch to Lee. Although this was to be an order of first importance (a major court-martial was to hinge much upon it), Washington allowed Hamilton to sign the paper as aide-de-camp.

According to Hamilton's later testimony, the paper ordered Lee to detach a party of six or eight hundred men "to lie very near the enemy" and "report instantly should they begin to move off." The detachment was then "to skirmish with them so as to produce some delay," giving the rest of Lee's troops time to come up. "This," Hamilton continued, "I understood from General Washington, was in pursuance of his intention to have the enemy attacked . . . conformable to the spirit of previous orders he had given General Lee for that purpose. This letter was sent off by a light horseman."[13]

At 5 A.M., Washington learned that the British had indeed begun to march. Sending other aides to urge Lee to attack, Washington ordered Hamilton "to reconnoitre the immediate country between him and the advanced corps."

Hamilton, of course, could not resist riding to the very front. This involved traversing a field that stretched for several miles and was cut by three ravines with brooks running in them. He reached Lee's army just as they were coming close enough to see the enemy's rear. Seeing "the enemy drawn up" a mile or two beyond Monmouth Court House, Hamilton concluded "there were not more than a thousand men." He was told that the head of the British line was more than ten miles away.[14]

(Modern scholars calculate the force that Hamilton saw as fifteen hundred to two thousand. None of the Americans realized that Clinton was nearby with more than four thousand of what the historian John R. Alden describes as "some of the best soldiers in the world.")[15]

Hamilton viewed the American advance with disapproval. The two or three columns that were emerging onto the field from a wood on the left of the Court House were, in his opinion, staying so close to the flank of the wood and so close to each other that they could not spread out into an effective line. As they came within cannon shot of the enemy's right, Hamilton could see no cannon.* Speaking to Lee, he got

---

* General Knox, who was riding with Hamilton, remembered artillery fire from both sides.[16]

the impression that there were more troops in the wood. They did not emerge.

Hamilton continued to ride ahead until he was in the very front of the American advance. Some cavalry appeared from the enemy's left and seemed to be preparing for an attack on the American right. Spurring his horse back to where General Lee had stationed himself, Hamilton reported concerning the horsemen "and submitted to him whether it would be proper to send some troops to counteract that manoeuvre of theirs and turn their left flank." Lee not only "approved the suggestion" but empowered Hamilton to give the order. The youth galloped eagerly to the commander on the right, who was his friend Lafayette. He told the Marquis "to wheel by his right and attack the enemy's left."

Hamilton now considered the situation well suited to an American victory. "The ground in front of the columns as far as the enemy seemed plain and open. That which was more immediately occupied by General Lee's troops was something lower than that which was occupied by the enemy, but the difference in my apprehension was not so material as to be any considerable impediment to an attack." Indeed, to go ahead was essential "since the distance between the enemy and the advanced corps was such" that a retreat in the face of the enemy "appeared to be extremely dangerous."

Although he hated to leave a battle, Hamilton felt he could no longer postpone reporting "to General Washington what I had done." The day, now that the sun was well up, had become unbearably hot. Even under the overhanging foliage of forest roads, the atmosphere almost stifled the young man who had been on horseback almost continuously for four or five days.[17]

Knowing that Washington had intended to set out with the Continental Army shortly after he himself had departed, Hamilton expected to meet them, as he did, after he had ridden a few miles. He told Washington, so Colonel Fitzgerald remembered, that "he had imagined, from the situation he had left our van and the enemy's rear in, they would soon engage." Suspecting that more danger hovered on the American right than the enemy horse which he had urged Lafayette to counteract (it was, indeed, there that Clinton's four thousand men were advancing), Hamilton advised Washington not to limit his advance to supporting Lee from the rear. A considerable detachment should take a wood road that branched off to the right. "He gave his reasons for this disposition, which were thought good."[18]

This discussion was being conducted in eerie silence. From the direction where Hamilton had believed a battle was developing, the heavy, clammy air brought no sound of firing.

Tilghman remembered: "While the order was given to make the disposition [that Hamilton had suggested], a countryman rode up." He was asked, "What news?" He had said he had "heard our people were retreating." In reply to impetuous questioning concerning the source of this information, he pointed to a man bearing the insignia of a fifer who came limping down the road.

The General, so that other aide, Harrison, remembered, "asked him whether he was a soldier belonging to the army, and the cause of his returning that way. He answered that he was a soldier, and that the Continental troops that had been advanced were retreating. On this answer, the General seemed to be exceedingly surprised, and rather more exasperated, appearing to discredit the account, and threatened the man, if he mentioned a thing of the sort, he would have him whipped. We then moved a few paces forward (perhaps about fifty yards) when we met two or three persons more on that road; one was, I think in the habit of a soldier." In reply to questioning, they all stated that all of Lee's detachment were retreating.

This was inconceivable since Lee could not have been defeated without a battle and no battle had sounded. Washington sent ahead, "to bring him a true account of the situation of matters," his aides Harrison and Fitzgerald. He himself, whether or not accompanied by Hamilton, remained at the head of the army as it advanced at a walking pace.[19]

Again and again Washington and the officers around him met retreating regiments, some proceeding in good order, some raggedly, all exhausted from the heat and the marching, none having fought that day. Their commanding officers proved unable to give any explanation other than that they had been ordered to withdraw.[20]

Hamilton was not present during the confrontation, so famous in American history, when Washington, his whole herculean temper alive, upbraided Lee for what he considered an unjustified retreat. But, wherever he was, Hamilton received the shocking news that the retiring army had not successfully disengaged. The enemy was on the march after them, "pressing hard," and were to be expected in a quarter of an hour.

No one could fail to recognize a terrifying crisis. If pounced on when in such disarray by an organized force of expert regulars, the American soldiers would be unable to defend themselves. Hamilton galloped to find Washington engaged in a second colloquy with Lee. "I heard General Washington say to General Lee that it would be necessary for him (General Washington) to leave the ground and form the main body of the army, while I understood he recommended to General Lee to remain there and take measures for checking the advance of the enemy. General Lee said he should obey his orders and would not be the first man to leave the field."[21]

Hamilton now burst into speech. According to Lee's aide, Major John Mercer, Hamilton had ridden up "in great heat." He now shouted to Lee, "I will stay here with you, my dear General, and die with you! Let us all die rather than retreat!"

Lee also remembered the conversation. He testified that after he had told Washington that he would be "one of the last to leave the field, Colonel Hamilton, flourishing his sword, immediately exclaimed, 'That's right, my dear General, and I will stay and we will all die here on the spot.'" Lee, who felt that the spot was not a good one to defend, to the death or otherwise, was much "surprised" by Hamilton's exclamation, which he attributed to the young man's being "much flustered and in a sort of frenzy of valor." Hamilton had, indeed, now reached a mental state so far isolated from the normal activities of his consciousness that what was said, although of such crucial drama that it should have been engraved deep on his memory, failed to leave the least impression there.

As the confrontation went on, Lee, who had just been so dressed down by Washington, asked Hamilton "to observe me well and tell me if I did not appear tranquil and master of my faculties." What Washington's influential aide had replied became of great interest to the court that attempted, after the battle, to assess Lee's behavior. Lee insisted that Hamilton had said, "He must own that I was entirely possessed of myself."[22]

Hamilton had to admit to the court-martial—it was less than three months later—that he "now forgot" what he had replied about Lee's behavior. Back in his lodgings, he endeavored, as he wrote the president of the court, "to recollect more particularly." His memory still refused "to serve me . . . in so clear a manner as I could wish; but I have been able to form some distinct ideas."

They were far from distinct. His mind remained completely blank concerning that part of the interview in which, so others testified, he had shouted dramatically that he would die there on the spot. To Lee's question, so he continued, "I may have replied in terms of less reserve and caution than I should have done at a moment of greater tranquillity and cooler reflection." But he did remember what his attitude was: He believed that Lee had shown no cowardice and could not be said to be out of his senses, but that Lee lacked the self-possession for making necessary decisions with promptitude.[23]

Concerning what had happened after his colloquy with Lee, Hamilton's memory returned. He testified that for "some little time" he remained near the general but did not hear him direct any measures.

"I understood that a body of our troops . . . had been previously thrown into a wood on the left . . . which I was afterwards told had been done by direction of General Washington. On the right, I saw some pieces of artillery pretty advantageously posted." They were on a hillside, "destitute of covering and support." Hamilton galloped over to Colonel Henry Beekman Livingston, "who was at the head of a detachment of troops." He "advised" Livingston "to march to the succour of the artillery." Not pleased to be told what to do by an inferior officer (the Commander in Chief's aide was acting on his own), Livingston refused to order the march. "This," Hamilton noted, elicited "some conversation between us."[24]

Having failed to achieve anything on his own authority, Hamilton rode to Lee and joined other officers who were urging the general to protect the artillery. Lee listened to the clamor of voices for a while, and then ordered that the artillery be withdrawn. This would force the whole defense to move backward towards where Washington was trying to prepare a stronger stand. Hamilton decided to gallop towards the rear and help Washington. He saw over his shoulder that Colonel Livingston was at last marching towards the artillery.

After Hamilton had got a little way back, "I found Colonel Olney retreating with a part of General Varnum's brigade." Seeing that this regiment was in excellent array, Hamilton, so Olney remembered, "ordered us to form with all possible dispatch or he feared the artillery in front would be lost." He pointed out a live fence (i.e. thick, impervious hedge) behind which Olney's men lined up.

Livingston had not moved fast enough to hold down the artillery. Just as an enemy column appeared, retreating gunners got between Oney's regiment and the British. There was a moment of confusion before the artillery had passed into the rear. Then, so Hamilton wrote, "a smart conflict" ensued.

It was not long before Olney's outnumbered troops were forced to abandon their stand. But, during the brief engagement, so Hamilton testified, "my horse received a wound which occasioned me a fall, by which I was considerably hurt. This and previous fatigue obliged me to retire, and prevented my knowing what became of the detachments of the advanced corps after that circumstance."[25]

One may well wonder why, when his injury was by itself enough of an explanation, Hamilton added in his public testimony that he had also succumbed to "fatigue." He had, it is true, done more riding around in the previous few days than most of the other officers, yet to admit lack of stamina was not to the advantage of a soldier.

The fact remained that Hamilton had distinguished himself. Lee admitted that he had demonstrated "valor," although the general added, "It is not that sort of valor, unless by practice and philosophy he can correct, [that] will ever be of any great use to the community." Tilghman wrote to Boudinot: "I am happy to have it in my power to mention the merit of your young friend Hammy. He was incessant in his endeavors during the whole day in reconnoitering the enemy and rallying and charging." He exhibited "singular proofs of bravery." He seemed, indeed, "to court death under our doubtful circumstances, and triumphed over it."[26]

Although the British were not halted in their march to New York nor was the party that engaged the Americans severely damaged, the Battle of Monmouth must be considered an American victory because in the end the enemy were forced to retreat, leaving the field to the Americans. Hamilton remained too indisposed to join the Family in examining the conquered terrain, but he heard the battle endlessly discussed.

Lee, convinced that the Continentals could not stand up to European regulars, had retreated as soon as he realized that he was faced not with an obviously vulnerable rear guard but a powerful British force. Washington (with Hamilton's assistance) had so rallied the retreating battalions that they fell back slowly, delaying the British advance until he had time to organize the fresh troops to make a stand and then drive the regulars into the defensive position from which they subsequently sneaked off at night.

Hamilton was moved into eulogies of Washington: "I never saw the General to so much advantage. His coolness and firmness were admirable. . . . The sequel is, we beat the enemy and killed or wounded at least a thousand of their best troops. America owes a great deal to General Washington for this day's work: a general rout, dismay and disgrace would have attended the whole army in any other hands but his. By his own good sense and fortitude he turned the fate of the day. Other officers have great merit in performing their parts well, but he directed the whole with the skill of a master workman."[27]

It was the contention of headquarters that the way the army had conducted themselves, when given the opportunity, had discredited Lee's cautions: "Our troops, after the first impulse of mismanagement, behaved with more spirit and moved with greater order than the British troops. You know," Hamilton continued to Boudinot, "my way of thinking about our army, and that I am not apt to flatter it. I assure you I never was pleased with them before this day."

Hamilton boasted of the exploits of Washington's Family, three of whom, including himself, had been slightly wounded. "If the rest escaped, it is only to be ascribed to better fortune, not more prudence in keeping out of the way." Then he made a comment which referred to the custom whereby generals delegated staff officers to report victories so that the staff officers would be rewarded. (To the irritation of everyone around General Washington, Congress had breveted Wilkinson a brigadier after he had reported the victory at Saratoga.) "That Congress is not troubled with any messenger-aides to give swords and other pretty toys to, let them ascribe to the good sense of the Commander in Chief and to a certain turn of thinking in those about him which put them above such shifts."

The success to be reported was "far inferior to what we, in all probability should have had, had not the finest opportunity America ever possessed been fooled away by a man in whom she placed a large share of the most ill-judged confidence . . . I mean General Lee. This man is either a driveler in the business of soldiership or something worse. . . . Whatever a court-martial may decide, I shall continue to believe and say—his conduct was monstrous and unpardonable."[28]

24

Grapeshot

HAMILTON had not completely recovered from the bruises and fatigues he had suffered at Monmouth before Washington sent him galloping to Black Point, New Jersey, at the base of Sandy Hook. His party consisted of servants and five pilots familiar with New York Harbor and Narragansett Bay. Offshore, he saw a large fleet anchored.

The arrival in American waters of a French naval force under the command of Vice Admiral Count d'Estaing had given the American side, for the first time in the war, naval superiority in local waters. But the superiority would not last for long. A strong British fleet, under "Foul Weather Jack" Byron (the poet's grandfather), was dashing, hell for topsail, across the Atlantic. If the momentary opportunity were not immediately grasped, it would be lost.[1]

Hamilton and his pilots were ferried aboard d'Estaing's flagship. Washington hoped that his French-speaking aide could persuade the admiral to do what Washington had assumed the British would do when the Americans were trying to hold New York City. The French should sail before a strong wind up the bay. They should sink the British fleet at its anchorage, and then attack the city. Washington's army would cooperate by coming in from New Jersey.

D'Estaing told Hamilton that the major French warships drew twenty-seven feet to the British twenty. The admiral "had sounded the river and found that he cannot enter." But he agreed to the contingent plan. Some six thousand enemy troops, mostly Hessians, were en-

235

camped on Rhode Island, offshore in Narragansett Bay. D'Estaing would join an American force under General Sullivan in attacking these.

Hamilton assured Washington that "all the ideas interchanged between the Count and myself were such as were familiar before I left headquarters." His mission had required no personal initiative. He felt no overwhelming drive to get back "home" to the General and his Family: "I hope your Excellency will indulge me if [I] do not make all the dispatch back which a case of emergency would require, though I do not mean to delay more than a moderate attention to my frail constitution may make not improper."[2]

On his arrival at headquarters, Hamilton found General von Steuben "in a temper." Although a staff officer, he was determined that Congress should give him a command in the fighting line, and he threatened to resign if refused. Obeying Washington's orders, Hamilton drafted a letter to Congress for the General's signature which stated that Steuben, although "extremely useful," could not be inserted in the line over the heads of officers "whose rank and merits give them every claim to attention," without producing "much dissatisfaction and extensive evil-consequences." If necessary, Steuben's resignation would have to be accepted.[3]

Hamilton wrote out Washington's sentiments with an aching heart, since they would prevent him—he was like Steuben a staff officer with no rank in the line—from exchanging his "personal dependence" as an aide to the kind of command his martial ambitions desired. Furthermore, Steuben was appealing to him, as a friend, piteously and angrily for help.

"Far be it from me," Hamilton wrote Boudinot, who was now President of Congress, "to wish to contravene his [Washington's] views. . . . But if anything could be done consistent with them to satisfy the Baron, it would be extremely desirable." One remedy would be to raise Steuben's staff position as inspector general to "a more important employment." (This Congress did.) A second remedy would be to pass a resolution "giving the Baron a right to be employed on detachments": that is, troops separated from the main body for a special mission. Such a step, Hamilton wrote hopefully, "might not be disagreeable to the officers." But Congress eschewed this step, one that would have opened possibilities to Hamilton as well.[4]

The Rhode Island campaign Hamilton had been instrumental in getting under way developed in a manner that endangered the nascent

D'Estaing's fleet off Sandy Hook in July, 1788. The arrival of Admiral d'Estaing inaugurated active French cooperation in American campaigns. Hamilton was deputized by Washington to go on the flagship and work out with the
admiral methods and objectives. Watercolor. Courtesy, Library of Congress

Franco-American alliance. After d'Estaing had encouraged General Sullivan, as part of a joint expedition, to land his American troops near Newport on the island in Narragansett Bay, the Frenchman had recalled his marines and taken his fleet off into the Atlantic. His departure was motivated by the fear that Admiral Byron's stronger force had actually arrived to make the British naval force superior. Although Byron had not come, d'Estaing decided he would be safer in Boston Harbor. The deserted Americans were stranded face to face with a superior force of Hessians: nothing but their skill at running away saved them. Hotheaded and ever indiscreet, Sullivan published in his general orders sentiments insulting to the French.

Lafayette, who had been assigned to Sullivan as a liaison with d'Estaing, wrote Hamilton two long letters in which he spluttered in rage. Interestingly, he regarded Hamilton as also being not really American. He denounced "a number of our *adopted compatriots*" as "unjust, ingrates, egoists, lacking not only regard to politeness but all the most common impulses of honesty."[5]

Hamilton moaned in a letter to Boudinot that the Frenchmen in America and in all probability the court of France expected Congress to reprobate Sullivan for attempting to "stain" French honor, but the American people might make "common cause" with Sullivan, all the more because of his "happy and well-conducted retreat." Here was "a question of great delicacy and difficulty which I find myself unable to solve."[6]

In a minor matter, Hamilton had not shown himself as eager to help things along. D'Estaing's representative at headquarters, Major André Michel Victor, Marquis de Chouin, was dissatisfied with the Family's way of life, which failed to remind him of Versailles.[7] To please him as far as possible was doubly important, since he was a near relative of the French minister of marine. Yet his perpetual superiorities and complaints were irritating. Hamilton wrote an unidentified correspondent: "Mr. Chouin, the French gentleman who lives at headquarters, informs me he has heard you had a bear skin which you would part with and requests me to inquire if it is so. I told him I thought it very improbable you should have any but what you wanted for your own use, but for his satisfaction would enquire how the matter stands."[8]

Whether or not Chouin got the bearskin, the Franco-American crisis was resolved in a way that Hamilton never understood or would approve of: not by planning but by letting things take care of themselves. After French sailors had been attacked by mobs in the Boston streets, it became evident to all that the French alliance was in danger. To save what was considered advantageous to both nations, everyone with any authority cooperated to heal the breach.

Having learned a new respect for the Continental Army at Monmouth, and greatly weakened by the troops that had been called away to other theaters of war, the British stayed behind their fortifications during the rest of 1778. There was some minor skirmishing, and wherever he was, Washington kept himself and those around him perpetually tensed in preparation for the worst. Hamilton slaved away daily at a desk, escaping from headquarters only once: a quick trip to Sharon, Connecticut, to straighten out a militia confusion.

On September 21, McHenry, who had studied medicine, wrote out a regimen aimed at assisting Hamilton "to get rid of your present accumulations" and enable his stomach to recover "its natural powers." McHenry preferred "brown sugar to loaf because it is more laxative." Milk was forbidden; water was to be Hamilton's table drink. "When you indulge in wine, let [it] be sparingly—never go beyond three glasses—but by no means every day." Lean meat, preferably beef, and bread were to be his main sustenance, with vegetables only sparely eaten. If Hamilton abided by his diet, he should soon recover "that degree of health which is compatible with the nature of your constitution." Since this was a serious document, with no evidence of high spirits or teasing, an addition of McHenry's seems significant: what he recommended "will have a tendency also to correct your wit."

The diagnosis is clear: Hamilton was suffering from nervous tension that affected his digestive tract.[9]

For the first recorded time since he had become a soldier, Hamilton wrote polemics for the press. Had his three letters signed "Publius," which were published during October and November, 1778,[10] come to the attention of Jefferson some fifteen years later, when the two men were warring in Washington's cabinet, Jefferson would have been unable to believe his eyes. For Hamilton was employing his pen in an effort to root out what he called "practices as pernicious as base,"[11] the very practices Secretary of State Jefferson believed that Secretary of the Treasury Hamilton was trying to plant deep in the American government.

The butt of Hamilton's attack was Congressman Samuel Chase of Maryland, who was accused of using knowledge gained in his official capacity to engross flour to be bought for the French fleet, thus doubling the price the government had to pay. Hamilton's prose was modeled on the elaborate—even elegant—style of insult that had made notorious the anonymous *Letters of Junius* published in London between 1769 and 1772.

Here is Hamilton's sonorous greeting to his victim: "Sir: The honor of being the hero of a public panegyric is what you could hardly have aspired to, either from your talents or from your good qualities. The partiality of your friends has never given you credit for more than mediocrity in the former, and experience has proved that you are indebted for all your consequence to the reverse of the latter. Had you not struck out a new line of prostitution for yourself, you might still have remained unnoticed and contemptible—your name scarcely known beyond the little circle of your electors and clients, and recorded only in the journals of C——ss. But you have now forced yourself into view in a light too singular and conspicuous to be overlooked, and have acquired an indisputable title to be immortalized in infamy."[12]

Hamilton blamed "that tribe who, taking advantage of the times, have carried the spirit of monopoly and extortion to an excess" for the mounting depreciation of the Continental currency, and commented, "When avarice takes the lead in a state, it is commonly the forerunner of its fall."

In what could be considered a pitiful comment on the humiliating expedients that had been forced on his father, Hamilton stated that the artifices of the poor, aimed at raising themselves above "indigence," were to be expected and could "only incite contempt." When those with moderate wealth engaged in dishonesty, "our contempt is mixed with indignation. . . . But when," so Hamilton continued, stating the aristocratic doctrine of noblesse oblige, "a man appointed to be a guardian of the state and the depository of the happiness and the morals of the people, forgetful of the solemn relation in which he stands, descends to the dishonest artifices of a mercantile projector, and sacrifices his conscience and his trust to pecuniary motives, there is no strain of abhorrence of which the human mind is capable, nor punishment the vengeance of the people can inflict which may not be applied to him with justice. . . . The station of a member of C——ss is the most illustrious and important of any I am able to conceive. He is to be regarded not only as a legislator but as the founder of an empire. A man of virtue and ability, dignified with so precious a trust, would rejoice that fortune had given him birth at a time, and placed him in circumstances so favorable for promoting public happiness. . . . To form useful alliances abroad, to establish wise government at home, to improve the internal resources and finances of the nation, would be the generous objects of his care." He would not "confound in the same person the representative of the commonwealth and the little member of a trading company."[13]

That Hamilton was not just striking a public posture is revealed by a private letter he soon wrote to the man who had become his closest friend, Colonel John Laurens. He stated that in the controversy which was going on between two former American representatives to France, Silas Deane and Arthur Lee, it was necessary to support Deane because Lee was distrusted by the French court: "Their friendship is the pillar of our security . . . our *unum necessarium*." He regretted this necessary choice because Deane was a merchant: "I hate money-making men."[14]

In the court-martial of General Lee, the fundamental issue was a matter of judgment. Had Lee been justified in trying to protect the army by retreat or had he, as Washington claimed, by cowardice or bad judgment robbed America of a great victory? Those officers and politicians who were opposed to Washington, many of them former adherents to the Conway Cabal, rushed to Lee's defense. The result was a long and complicated controversy, which Washington and his family found infuriating. Finally, the court found Lee guilty but gave him a ridiculously light sentence. Congress, which had to approve the verdict, postponed any vote until Hamilton expressed fear that Lee had so strong a party there that the sentence would be annulled.[15]

Early in December, 1778, Lee published his *Vindication to the Public*, in which he attacked Washington as a military incompetent who, out of jealousy, tried to wreck any general with skill: first Conway, now Lee. Washington believed that he could make no move to defend himself because that would involve interference in an undecided judicial process, but he was worried lest his silence be taken to demonstrate that he could not answer Lee's charges. Laurens, who was also an aide to Washington, urged Hamilton to take up again "the pen of Junius" in Washington's defense.[16] But this Hamilton did not do. The circle around Washington decided to defend His Excellency's honor not with the pen but with swords and pistols.

Steuben, taking the offense upon himself, challenged Lee on the grounds that the *Vindication* impugned his own bravery. Lee dodged the challenge by replying that he had not meant to impugn Steuben. Hamilton wrote Steuben: "I have read your letter to Lee with pleasure. . . . Considering the pointedness and severity of your expressions, his answer . . . proved that he had not a violent appetite for so close a *tête-à-tête* as you seemed disposed to insist upon."[17]

Laurens now challenged Lee for casting aspersions on Washington's character. This challenge Lee accepted. It was as Laurens's second that Hamilton attended his first duel. Unable to foresee what this event presaged for the termination of his own life, he wrote, in his "Narrative of an Affair of Honor," a highly enthusiastic account of what had taken place.

At the dueling ground, designated as "Point no Point Road," the preparations were carried out with military ceremony. After each of the principals had been provided with a pair of pistols, they were "asked in what manner they were to proceed. General Lee proposed to advance upon one another, and each fire at what time and distance he thought proper." Laurens politely "expressed his preference for this mode."

The two duelists started some distance apart and, as Hamilton watched passionately, moved slowly closer together, stance dignified and eyes intent. When separated by about four or five paces, they fired simultaneously. Both seemed to have missed. But, as Laurens lifted his second pistol, "General Lee declared himself wounded. Colonel Laurens [so continues Hamilton's report], as if apprehending the wound to be more serious than it proved, advanced towards the general to offer his support." Hamilton and also Lee's second, Major Evan Edwards, hurried forward.

Blood was beginning to soak one side of Lee's uniform but he announced that his wound "was less than he had imagined at the first stroke of the ball [the ball had grazed his side, carrying away some flesh] and proposed to fire a second time. This was warmly opposed both by Colonel Hamilton and Major Edwards, who declared it to be their opinion that the affair should terminate as it then stood. But General Lee repeated his desire that there should be a second discharge and Colonel Laurens agreed to the proposal."

Hamilton then observed that unless Lee was "influenced by motives of personal enmity," the affair should not be continued, yet, since Lee seemed determined, "he was too tender of his friend's honor to persist in opposing it." The combat was about to be renewed when Major Edwards declared his agreement with Hamilton. "General Lee then expressed his confidence in the honor of the gentlemen concerned as seconds, and said he should be willing to comply with whatever they should coolly and deliberately determine. Colonel Laurens consented to the same." Edwards and Hamilton withdrew and, after conversing for a while on the subject, still agreed "that the affair should terminate."

Lee and Laurens were conversing at the same time. Laurens, so Hamilton was later informed, told Lee that he was motivated by no personal enmity. His deep friendship and respect for Washington's character had bound him to resent what he had heard on good authority, namely, "that General Lee had spoken of General Washington in the grossest and most opprobrious terms of personal abuse." Lee replied that he had, it was true, given his "opinion against Washington's military character to his particular friends and might perhaps do it again." But he had never spoken unfavorably of Washington's personal character. He had always esteemed General Washington as a man. Furthermore, "such abuse would be incompatible with the character he would ever wish to sustain as a Gentleman."

When the seconds brought their conclusion to the principals they found Lee and Laurens ready to agree. All "immediately returned to town, General Lee slightly wounded in the right side."

"Upon the whole," Hamilton exulted, "we think it a piece of justice to the two gentlemen to declare that after they met, their conduct was strongly marked with all the politeness, generosity, coolness, and firmness that ought to characterize a transaction of this nature."[18]

Hamilton may well have envied Laurens his starring role. In any case, he was soon busily issuing challenges of his own.

By the time of the Lee–Laurens duel, the Family, including Hamilton, were with their general in Philadelphia. Having put the army into winter quarters, they arrived late in December to stay until early February. Their mission was to consult with Congress and its committees concerning the next campaign. What they saw around them induced Washington to write that he would never "be again surprised at anything." Philadelphia was a scene of the wildest and most expensive gaiety, engaged in by the money-making men, while inflation was so great that the fighting men could not be clothed or supplied. Washington fulminated in rage.[19] Not a single personal letter written by Hamilton during his Philadelphia stay remains, but an account of something he was reputed to have said in a Philadelphia coffeehouse was to appear a few months later to infuriate him and endanger his career.

25

A Deadly Rumor

[JULY, 1779–MAY, 1780   AGES 22–23]

ON July 4, 1779, Lieutenant Colonel John Brooks wrote Hamilton of something that had taken place at an informal gathering of Revolutionary leaders in Philadelphia. Congressman Francis Dana of Massachusetts had said "that many persons in the army were acting, under a cloak of defending their country, from principles totally incompatible with its safety." Urged to be more specific, "he fixed at length on Colonel Hamilton, who he asserted had declared in a public coffeehouse in Philadelphia that it was high time for the people to rise, join General Washington, and turn Congress out of doors. . . . He further observed that Mr. Hamilton could be in no ways interested in the defense of this country, and therefore was most likely to pursue such a line of conduct as his great ambition dictated."

This disclosure was made more unpleasant to Hamilton because of his informant's attitude. Brooks was an impressive fighter. He had been one of the first Americans to fire at a Briton (at Concord) and had subsequently taken part in as many battles as could be reached by one man. He knew Hamilton well, having served as a top assistant at Valley Forge to Steuben. Flatteringly, he wrote that Hamilton occupied "so highly dignified a station." But he went on to say that Hamilton's prominence increased the seriousness of the charge. His object was "to place the matter in a more just point of light than it stands in at present among the circle of officers who have been made acquainted with it."

Brooks wanted to know whether Dana's statement concerning what Hamilton had said was correct? If it was correct, that "would be a sad proof of the fallacy of appearances and the impropriety of making either words or actions the criterion of forming a judgment of characters." Yet Brooks did not exclude the possibility that Hamilton might have been guilty of such "an instance of a want of that honor and regard to truth so eminently necessary in the patriot and statesman."[1]

Hamilton thereupon wrote Dana, who was one of the leading members of Congress. The Massachusetts delegate had known Hamilton well, having spent five months at Valley Forge as chairman of the congressional committee that had met with the high command to work out a reorganization of the army. Hamilton informed Dana that "the whole affair" was "absolutely false and groundless." If Dana had actually enunciated the statements attributed to him, their "personal and illiberal complexion . . . will oblige me to make them the subject of a very different kind of discussion from the present." To underline his meaning, he sent the letter not directly to Dana, but for delivery by Colonel David Henley, a soldier well suited to serve as the second in a duel. As for Dana, he was a thirty-six-year-old lawyer with no military experience whatsoever.[2]

Dana's reply, although carefully phrased to avoid giving cause for a duel, was far from conciliatory. He admitted that he had repeated the charge against Hamilton—but only as something he had heard. He had said, "How true it is I know not." But he had, he informed Hamilton, also said that any officer who had in fact thus expressed himself "ought to be broke [discharged] whatever his particular services may have been."[3] Not altogether denying that he had stated that Hamilton, as a foreigner, could have no patriotism to block his ambition, Dana wrote that the remark might easily have been made by some other member of the conversing group. The congressman added the information that his authority for quoting Hamilton had been the Reverend Dr. Gordon.

Hamilton sent Dana's letter to Brooks. In his reply, Brooks brushed aside Dana's disclaimers, and gave further details that darkened the situation. Dana had warned his hearers that there were "dangerous designing men" in the army against whom they should "watch and guard." The schemes proposed by men like Hamilton "would be fatal to the liberties of this country," and pleasing to the Tories, who would be glad to join any such movement as Hamilton had proposed. "The words *desperate fortune* . . ." so Brooks continued, "were more than once applied to you."

Brooks had consulted two Massachusetts colonels, James Wesson and Thomas Marshall. They had been present and agreed with what Brooks remembered.[4]

Hamilton sent Dana a copy of Brooks's letter. He stated that only a positive denial of the charges would prevent him from acting on a presumption of their reality. Having thus threatened the civilian congressman, Hamilton sent a similar threat to a fifty-one-year-old Congregational minister.[5]

The Reverend William Gordon was collecting archives in preparation for writing a history of the war. Since he had not been in Philadelphia when Hamilton was there, he must have repeated to Dana what someone had reported to him. In a letter to Gordon, Hamilton demanded that the minister disclose his informant or, as was clearly implied, fight Hamilton.[6]

Dana's next letter further demonstrated that the matter moved on high levels. General Artemus Ward, who at the start of the war had been Washington's second-in-command, had been present at the conversation. He testified that Dana had made no direct charge against Hamilton, merely mentioning suppositions and possibilities. In an effort to show that Brooks might have confused several conversations, Dana referred to a deep uneasiness that made what Hamilton was reputed to have said seem a very serious matter indeed:

"Perhaps it may occur to Colonel Brooks, upon recollection, that we had some conversation respecting the army and some characters in it, on our passage over [the] Charles River from Boston to Charlestown, which was occasioned by a report that two regiments in Glover's brigade, at Rhode Island, had thrown down their arms and disbanded themselves, and somebody's saying 'that the army would, by and by, turn their arms upon the country and do themselves justice.' "[7]

Distrust of the military was ingrained in America and particularly in New England. Even a cursory reading of history demonstrated that armies, once conjured up, were, like the devil, hard to lay again. And the American army had veritable grievances. The troops were outraged by the inflation that wiped out their pay; indignant that the profiteers were wallowing in luxuries and farmers sitting well fed and snug by their fires while the soldiers who were protecting them were starving and freezing. Furthermore, the officers were demanding what was traditional in European armies but which Congress was unwilling to grant: half pay for life on retirement when the war was over. There was every reason to fear and, if possible, root out influential soldiers with such ideas as were ascribed to Hamilton.

246

The Reverend Gordon's answer treated Washington's aide as if he were an untrained puppy. When the youth was "more conversant with the world and read *mankind* more," he would realize that "a gentleman" was under no necessity to identify the sources of confidential information. Gordon assumed that Hamilton had spoken as charged but had forgotten what he had said. His having forgotten was, so the minister continued with maddening condescension, a good sign since it showed that the indiscretion was "an effect of a sudden *transport* and not of a depraved judgment." Gordon then reached out to larger implications by connecting Hamilton's "transport" with Silas Deane's attack on Congress, which had alarmed "weak but good minds."

The minister then expressed concern lest such "oversights" by important officers encourage prejudice against the army and damage Washington by giving the idea "that such sentiments were dropped in his presence without meeting with a proper check." For his part, Gordon was magnanimous enough to believe that "notwithstanding the natural tendency of martial manners, there are as good citizens *in* the military line as *out* of it."

Having stated that he would reveal the name of his informant if Hamilton completely relinquished the idea of a duel, the minister favored Hamilton with a lecture on the evils of dueling. He added the stipulation that, if the matter were to be carried any further, it be "examined into by Congress or individuals of the first character."[8]

Hamilton's reply dwelt on Gordon's insistence that he abjure recourse to a duel, a condition "which you knew as a gentleman I should be obliged to reject." Hamilton's further comments on dueling were as confused as his thoughts on the subject were to remain until his last, suicidal decision. He admitted that "we do not now live in the days of chivalry." He admitted that "to prove your own innocence or the malice of an accuser, the worst method you can take is to run him through the body or shoot him through the head." Why should the minister assume that Hamilton did not share his religious scruples against dueling? But still Hamilton would not promise. "Whatever may be my final determination on this point ought to be [to Gordon] a matter of indifference. 'Tis a good old maxim . . . that we ought to do our duty and leave the rest to the care of heaven." Gordon's duty was to give Hamilton the information that would enable him to prove his innocence.

In writing his friend Laurens about Gordon's condition concerning dueling, Hamilton explained: "Pleasant terms enough! I am first to be calumniated and then, if my calumniator takes it into his head, I am to bear a cudgeling from him with Christian patience and forebearance.

. . . I have ridiculed the proposal," and insisted on *"unconditional surrender."* Hamilton attributed the whole matter to "the cabal" (undoubtedly those who had supported Conway and Gates and subsequently Lee), and stated that he was making fun of these "miserable detractors . . . running the rogues pretty hard." But his protestations to Gordon struck a hysterical note:

He "abhorred" the notion of military intervention with Congress. "It never could have had a momentary place in my mind, consequently could never have dishonored my lips. The supposition is absurd that I could have used the expression, when I cannot recognize the remotest trace of an idea at any period that could possibly have led to them. In this consciousness, I again appeal to you, and demand, by all the ties of truth, justice and honor, that you immediately give up your author. I stake my life and reputation upon the issue."[9]

For Hamilton to claim that the idea had "never had a momentary place in his mind" was on the face of it ridiculous. Rumors and fears (and even anticipations) of military intervention were part of everyday discussion.

The controversy went on and on: it was still throwing up angry letters a year and a half after the purported indiscretion.[10] Gordon was never convinced of Hamilton's innocence, nor did any of the patriot leaders associated with spreading the rumor ever deny that they believed it. They merely phrased their intransigence carefully to give no cause for a duel. Hamilton may well have been reminded of occasions in his childhood, when, hooted at on West Indian streets, he had turned on his tormentors, only to have them mock his rage and ignore his challenges to fight.

It was never determined who started the rumor, but it was only too clear that many influential patriots were glad to repeat it. Yet writers on Hamilton have regarded the controversy as of little significance. They have either not mentioned it at all, or, like Mitchell, regarded it as a ploy engaged in by critics of Washington.[11] Since Gordon was in fact a supporter and personal friend of Washington's, the darts could not actually have been aimed over Hamilton's shoulder. He was the direct target.

Rumor is discounted, or believed and spread, according to the preconceptions of the hearers. Why was Hamilton, when still only twenty-two, already subjected to such charges of desiring to subvert the popular government as were later so copiously hurled upon him?

26

Frustrations

URING the stay in Philadelphia when he made or did not make the much-bruited indiscreet remark, Hamilton was deep enough in the central councils to help to plan the 1779 campaign. Washington agreed with the legislators that the greatest hazards to the cause were not military but economic. To keep from being sunk beneath a tidal wave of worthless paper money, it was necessary to establish a pause during which the financial situation could somehow be strengthened. The army should, without expensive reinforcements, initiate nothing beyond sending a few thousand men to the northern frontier to chastise the Iroquois who had been falling on the frontier settlements in New York and Pennsylvania. More extensive action, which would call for a sudden incursion of militia, would only be undertaken if the British marched out of New York City, an adventure they were considered too weak to risk; or if d'Estaing reappeared with his reinforcing fleet and marines, a possibility concerning which no dispatches had been received. Hamilton could look ahead to routine tasks undertaken in defensive positions.

Early in February, the Family was back in Middlebrook, New Jersey, Since Washington's force was small enough to be supplied, hardships were not overwhelming, and they ameliorated as the weather abated. The men were all veterans who had survived the prevalent diseases; the encampment was healthy. Few British detachments appeared to be skirmished with. Preparations for the Indian expedition hardly taxed the resources of headquarters.

Hamilton was undoubtedly glad of the diversion supplied by a letter from Susanna Livingston, whom he had known since his school days in Middlebrook, although she had been too old—some nine years his senior—for him to flirt with. Three of her female cousins, who were with the British in New York, wished to be given a pass through the American lines to see their relations. Her father, William Livingston, was the governor of New Jersey, but Susanna had preferred not to appeal to him, since his policy was to prevent communication "with our bad neighbors," and he would surely "from a motive of delicacy," deal most rigidly with his own family. She wished Hamilton to wheedle the permission from Washington. "I might urge many reasons to induce you to do this, but your own humanity will tell you that the anxious solicitude of sisters to see their brothers . . . who have passed through various perils in our service, is of itself a sufficient one."[1]

Hamilton's reply to this friendly but not flirtatious letter reveals that he was unwilling to assume with a desirable woman anything but a flirtatious tone: "I can hardly forgive an application to my *humanity* to induce me to exert my influence in an affair in which ladies are concerned; and especially when you are of the party. Had you appealed to my friendship or to my gallantry, it would have been irresistible. I should have thought myself bound to have set prudence and policy at defiance, and even to have attacked *windmills* in your Ladyship's service. I am not sure, but my imagination would have gone so far as to have fancied New York an *enchanted castle*—the three ladies, so many fair damsels, ravished from their friends and held in captivity, by the *spells* of some wicked magician—General Clinton a huge giant placed as keeper of the gates, and myself a valorous knight, destined to be their champion and deliverer.

"But when instead of availing yourself of so much better titles, you appealed to the cold general principle of humanity; I confess, I felt myself mortified, and determined, by way of revenge, to mortify you in turn. I resolved to show you, that all the eloquence of your fine pen could not tempt our Fabius [Washington] to do wrong; and avoiding any representations of my own, I put your letter into his hands and let it speak for itself." Agreeing with Governor Livingston's policy, Washington had said no.[2]

The doldrums were suddenly broken in early June when the British reversed precedent by getting into motion while the Continental Army was still bedded down in winter quarters. They sailed up the Hudson in power and easily overran the two small fortifications at Stony Point and Verplanck's Point which, from opposite shores, guarded the crossing at King's Ferry. This was a serious loss since, as Hamilton wrote, it will entirely interrupt "our best communication between the eastern and southern states, and tend greatly to distress and disaffect the country."[3] Yet headquarters feared worse to come. The Americans were building further upriver, at West Point, major fortifications aimed at permanently blocking the river. These were incomplete and vulnerable. The British seemed to be advancing upon them.

Hamilton drafted for Washington a dispatch to the garrison at West Point: "I am determined at the utmost hazard to support the fort and . . . I expect it to hold out to the last extremity." Headquarters was in a scramble trying to get the army ready to move. Hamilton was personally distressed to leave behind "my mare and her colt." He begged Colonel Clement Biddle, the commissary in charge of forage, to send for her "as soon as convenient. I hardly think her safe here."[4]

Washington hurried the army from its New Jersey encampment to the Clove, that mountainous pass through the Highlands to the west bank of the Hudson. However, the British, contenting themselves with consolidating their hold on King's Ferry, made no effort to reach West Point. They began rebuilding the patriots' small redoubts into professional fortifications. Accepting the loss of the river crossing, Washington encamped his army at New Windsor, on the west bank north of the enemy.

Irritating reports soon came in that the British were raising a great to-do about the capture of Stony and Verplanck's points, trying to make out that two major castles had bowed to His Majesty's might. Washington, conscious that a patriot victory was needed "to satisfy the expectations of the people and reconcile them to the defensive plan we are obliged to pursue," decided to imitate the enemy. The main British army had returned to New York City, and the captured forts were not too strongly garrisoned. The more noise the enemy made about their triumph, the more effective reversing the triumph would be. Furthermore, it would be valuable to have King's Ferry back again.

The strengthened fortifications called not for a direct assault but for a surprise attack. Washington decided to take them one at a time, starting at Stony Point. Hamilton helped draft the orders to General Wayne, but he was prevented by the need for secrecy—British spies had to see the General and his Family sitting quietly at headquarters—from going along when, on a dark night, Wayne led his detachment of picked light infantry downriver. The next morning, July 16, headquarters received a short dispatch stating that Stony Point had been taken "with but very inconsiderable loss."[5]

Washington and his aides were now released from the need to look relaxed. They galloped downriver, eager to extend the victory across the Hudson to the fort at Verplanck's Point (which would surely be in confusion). Both posts would then be held against British counter-attack.

But, however passionately Hamilton and the other aides galloped around to straighten things out, the force intended for Verplanck's Point remained in confusion because of missent orders and accidental delays. And when the headquarters staff rode up to Stony Point, they met a great disappointment. In strengthening the fortifications, the British had done nothing to protect the side towards the river, where they were supreme and whence the most powerful counterattack would now surely come.

There was nothing for the Americans to do except try to smash the fortifications, at the same time carrying away everything useful that could be picked up or pried loose. Hamilton helped to mobilize wagons to receive the lighter objects, boats to carry the heavier. Washington was so busy and became so fatigued that he secured no information concerning Wayne's action or the number of prisoners taken. We can assume that Hamilton was no less active. They continued their salvage operations for more than twenty-four hours, only desisting when British warships hove in sight. The last patriot boats moved away under enemy fire.[6]

The hope of the summer was that d'Estaing would sail up from West Indian waters, making it possible to set the smoldering war aflame. For as long as was feasible, Washington kept on the leash the intended attack on the Indians—it was entrusted to General Sullivan—so that the main army would not be weakened if the French admiral appeared. It was May 31 before the expedition was ordered to march. During August, reports came in that d'Estaing had early in July defeated a British fleet near the island of Grenada. In mid-September, Hamilton informed his correspondent Duane of rumors brought to New England ports by three different ships' captains that the admiral was coming north with twenty-five ships of the line and transports containing six thousand troops. His first objective was to capture the British garrison in Savannah, Georgia. He would then join Washington. "These concurrent accounts," Hamilton commented warily, "are not entirely unworthy of attention, though I am not disposed to give them entire credit." Washington did not dare to spend money and raise expectations by calling out militia until the news was more certain.[7]

Whether because of expense, or the overall shortage of horses, or discouragement, Hamilton had allowed himself to become, as he put it, "dismounted." Unable to ride from camp, he was more than ever tied to the succession of tables on which he drafted letters from Washington. Preparing for the press an account of Sullivan's eventual victory over Tories and Indians, Hamilton made the triumph seem more impressive "with a few of the usual embellishments."[8]

The incident of the crab apple showed Hamilton in a playful mood tinged with exasperation. While vacationing on the Hudson, Duane found in the woods a peculiar apple. "I have never," he wrote Hamilton, "seen Hughes' crab, from which the fine Virginia cider is produced, but from [the] description I believe this to be the same fruit. Be so good as to show it to His Excellency, and enquire from him."

Hamilton replied that he had "with my usual *distraction* suffered your apple to pass out of my hands and to be lost before it could be seen by the General. But Tilghman and Meade, who saw it and pretend to be connoisseurs in matters of this kind, laughed at me for my inquiries and insisted that it was nothing more than the common crab apple. . . . It was in vain that I pleaded that Mr. Duane was a virtuoso as well as themselves . . . and that I was not obliged to be acquainted with the natural productions of this country. They were unmerciful upon the occasion and baited me so hard that I almost thought the loss of the apple a happy riddance. . . . But notwithstanding the rating I have undergone, I will muster fortitude enough to endure a repetition of the storm if you will take the trouble to send me another apple. I promise to take care that it shall not be lost before it is seen by the General."[9]

On October 1, an explosion of hope: d'Estaing was actually off Georgia. The supposition was that, in cooperation with patriot land forces, he would quickly overwhelm the British garrison. Then the fleet would hurry north. American pilots had worked out a deepwater channel by which the French sixty-fours could traverse New York Harbor, and Washington hoped that the fleet would make use of it before the British knew they were in American waters. Hamilton was too conspicuous a member of Washington's staff to be sent, a second time, to await d'Estaing at Sandy Hook. That would tip the enemy off. Undoubtedly chafing at the inaction, Hamilton drew up orders for Major Henry Lee. The cavalryman was to pretend he was seeking forage for his horses.[10]

But then British movements revealed that they had been warned. They called to New York their garrison on Rhode Island, abandoned the forts at King's Ferry, sank hulks in the harbor channels, and began to build fortifications on Manhattan Island above the city. There was no more reason to keep Hamilton under wraps. Since the reports were that d'Estaing would sail for the Delaware Capes, Hamilton galloped there with the French engineer in the Continental service, Brigadier General Louis Le Bèque du Portail.

The engineer outranked Hamilton, but his role was as an expert on the enemy fortifications. Hamilton represented headquarters and this time he could not be, as during his previous mission to d'Estaing, merely a channel for carrying prefabricated orders. Now no one knew what the situation would be when the admiral arrived.

Hamilton received almost daily dispatches from Washington containing news of American developments, reports of British acts and intentions. His task was to be prepared in his mind from moment to moment for the exciting and exacting moment when Gallic sails came in view. Then he would advise d'Estaing how best to proceed.

Hamilton seemed to be mounted again on the winged horse of his genius. The whole future of the war, perhaps the victory that would drive the enemy from the United States, lay in his hands. Or would lie in his hands when the French fleet appeared. But none of the dispatch riders who came pounding in brought news of the French fleet. Day after day, Hamilton sent small boats out into the ocean. He stared through his spyglass. Every dawn lightened to a disappointed hope of sails—hundreds of sails—in the offing. Finally, too nervous to stay in one place any longer, Hamilton and du Portail speculated that maybe d'Estaing would (or had) bypassed the Delaware Capes. They mounted their horses and charged to Egg Harbor, New Jersey, where the staring and the waiting were repeated. Hamilton's hopes sank slowly and then precipitously. After seven weeks, he gave up and returned to Morristown, where the army, after its summer idleness, was bedding down for winter.[11]

27

A Romantic Friendship

[SEPTEMBER, 1777–JANUARY, 1780   AGES 20–23]

AS the military frustrations of 1779 had loomed all too foreseeably ahead, Hamilton had found himself overwhelmed by passionate emotions for his fellow aide, Lieutenant Colonel John Laurens. It was probably no coincidence that the full force did not strike him until an element of safety had been added by Laurens's departure for another theater of war.

Many men suffering from a sense of insecurity greatly resent rivals more successful and perhaps more able than they. Hamilton did not suffer from this weakness. His feelings for Laurens, who was only two years his senior, included hero worship.

Where Hamilton was intellectual, Laurens was physical. His was not a frail body that had to be whipped into strenuous action by overtight nerves. Laurens's body responded by sending to his brain thrills of power and joy. Despite Hamilton's explosions of irrational behavior, he wished to light with logic the path on which he wished to go. Laurens felt no such need. He struck as his instincts prompted him—and he struck hard. He was both more idealistic than Hamilton and more brutal.

In worldly endowments—inherited possessions, hereditary influence, formal education—Laurens incomparably outranked his friend. No family carried more weight than his in South Carolina. His father had personally taken him to Europe to organize his education, deciding that Geneva was the world's greatest intellectual and moral center.

Lieutenant Colonel John Laurens, the brilliant, aggressive soldier to whom Hamilton wrote passionate letters. Miniature by Charles Willson Peale. Courtesy, Independence National Historical Park Collection

John's course of study there included "Latin, Greek, Italian, belle-lettres, physics, history, geography, mathematics, experimental philosophy, fencing, riding, and civil law." In his spare time, Laurens moved in Geneva's highest social circles, acquiring elegant accomplishments and exterior polish. His father was assured that John would become "the Voltaire of South Carolina."

As soon as the Revolution broke out, Laurens yearned to fight, but his father sent him to London to study law. John found alternate excitement with a genteel but willing young woman. Fearing that marriage would further block his departure for the war, he preferred what he described as "a clandestine celebration." When her pregnancy could no longer be concealed, he told the girl's father he would make an honest woman of her provided that no effort were made to stop his going by himself to America. To his own family, in whose company his wife might have to spend much of her life, Laurens summarized the situation: "Pity obliged me to marry."[1]

Shortly after Brandywine, Laurens joined Washington's Family as a volunteer. Hamilton met a husky young man, whose large oval head was almost overcrowded with strongly sculptured features. Laurens's eyes were blue, his expression dissatisfied, daring, self-confident, supercilious.[2] Instantaneously, he rivaled Hamilton's hitherto unassailed position as the ablest and most energetic of Washington's aides. Laurens even invaded Hamilton's exclusive preserve, for he also spoke fluent French. And his father was currently President of Congress.

It is indicative of the relationship between the two men that, when Washington's circle decided to call Major General Charles Lee to account for his slanders, it was Laurens who challenged and fought Lee, while Hamilton served as a second.

Early in 1779, Laurens launched on a project as audacious as it was philanthropic.

Unable to alter the stalemate around New York, the British were making use of their command of the ocean to move their operations to the weakest part of the United States, inhabited by the largest number of Tories: the South. In late 1778 and early 1779, Georgia was for all practical purposes captured, North Carolina overrun, and Laurens's home state of South Carolina seriously threatened.

Defense was crippled by the South Carolinians' fear of their slaves, by whom they were greatly outnumbered. They did not dare join the army lest, in their absence, the blacks kill their families and burn their plantations. Ever bold, Laurens devised a scheme to convert the danger into a strength, while at the same time taking a giant step towards a social good. He had been persuaded during his European education of the evils of slavery. South Carolina, he argued, should raise by draft from the owners several thousand black troops who would serve against the British under white officers—he willingly offered himself as commander—with the promise of emancipation at the end of the war. This would not only in itself augment the army but, by drawing off the most aggressive blacks from the plantations, enable white militiamen also to leave.[3]

During March, 1779, Laurens posted from headquarters at Morristown to secure from Congress in Philadelphia a vote urging the scheme on his native state. His father, Henry Laurens, had retired from the presidency of Congress, but had been succeeded by Hamilton's friend Jay. Hamilton wrote to persuade Jay that the project was "most rational." It was, indeed, difficult to see "how a sufficient force can be collected in that quarter without it. . . . I have not the least doubt that the Negroes will make very excellent soldiers with proper management," and Laurens "has all the zeal, intelligence, enterprise, and every other qualification requisite to succeed in such an undertaking.

"It is a maxim with some great military judges that, with sensible officers, soldiers can hardly be too stupid; and on this principle it is thought that the Russians would make the best troops in the world if they were under other officers than their own. . . . I mention this because I frequently hear it objected" that Negroes are "too stupid to make soldiers. This is so far from appearing to me a valid objection that I think their want of cultivation (for their natural faculties are probably as good as ours) joined to that habit of subordination which they acquire from a life of servitude, will make them sooner become soldiers than our white inhabitants. Let officers be men of sense and sentiment, and the nearer the soldiers approach to machines perhaps the better."[4]

To Laurens himself, Hamilton wrote, "Cold in my professions, warm in my friendships, I wish, my dear Laurens, it might be in my power by action rather than words, to convince you that I love you. I shall only tell you that, 'till you bade us adieu, I hardly knew the value you had taught my heart to set upon you. Indeed, my friend, it was not well done. You know the opinion I entertain of mankind, and how much it is my desire to preserve myself free from particular attachments, and to keep my happiness independent on the caprice of others. You should not have taken advantage of my sensibility to steal into my affections without my consent. But as you have done it and as we are generally indulgent to those we love, I shall not scruple to pardon the fraud you have committed, on condition that for my sake, if not for your own, you will always continue to merit the partiality which you have so artfully instilled into me."

The next paragraph in this letter dealt with Laurens's having finally, after again refusing, accepted a commission as lieutenant colonel in the line. Laurens seems to have written his friend for reassurance that his action had not violated "delicacy." Hamilton replied that, as Washington's aide, Laurens had as much right as any officer to be officially a lieutenant colonel, and as he intended to command his own black brigade, he was not invading any established military hierarchy. Revealing himself on this occasion an adherent of the rigid military protocol which was likely to stand in his own way, Hamilton wrote that had Laurens been given additional seniority by having his commission dated "posterior to your appointment as aide-de-camp, I should have considered it derogatory to your former rank, to mine, and to that of the whole corps." As it was, Laurens's second refusal had revealed "overscrupulous delicacy. In hesitating you have refined upon the refinements of generosity."

Hamilton went on to send news concerning Laurens's connections in England. The phraseology reveals that Hamilton had been left ill informed concerning his friend's marriage—so much so, indeed, that he did not know Laurens had a daughter—and also that he understood the relationship might be treated with levity. He was enclosing, Hamilton wrote, some letters that would permit Laurens to have "sweet converse with your dearer self." They had been brought by a Mrs. Moore, "soi-disant parente de Madame votre épouse. [Laurens's mother-in-law was called Manning.] She speaks of a daughter of yours, well when she left England, perhaps—" Here someone, in going over Hamilton's papers, felt that propriety required scratching out three words.

"And now, my dear, as we are upon the subject of wife, I empower and command you to get me one in Carolina. . . . Take her description— She must be young, handsome (I lay most stress upon a good shape), sensible (a little learning will do), well bred (but she must have an aversion to the word *ton*), chaste and tender (I am an enthusiast in my notions of fidelity and fondness), of some good nature, a great deal of generosity (she must neither love money nor scolding, for I dislike equally a termagant and an economist). In politics, I am indifferent what side she may be of; I think I have arguments that will easily convert her to mine. As to religion, a moderate stock will satisfy

259

me. She must believe in God and hate a saint. But as to fortune, the larger stock of that the better. You know my temper and circumstances and will therefore pay special attention to this article in the treaty. Though I run no risk of going to purgatory for my avarice, yet as money is an essential ingredient to happiness in this world—as I have not much of my own and as I am very little calculated to get more either by my address or industry—it must needs be that my wife, if I get one, bring at least a sufficiency to administer to her own extravagancies. NB. You will be pleased to recollect in your negotiations that I have no invincible antipathy to the *maidenly beauties* and that I am willing to take the *trouble* of them upon myself.

"If you should not readily meet with a lady that you think answers my description, you can only advertise in the public papers and doubtless you will hear of many competitors for most of the qualifications required, who will be glad to become candidates for such a prize as I am. To excite their emulation, it will be necessary for you to give an account of the lover—his *size*, make, quality of mind and *body*, achievements, expectations, fortune, etc. In drawing my picture you will no doubt be civil to your friend; mind you do justice to the length of my nose, and don't forget that I—" Here about five words have been obliterated. Fortunately their import can be guessed: it is an ancient joke to interrelate the size of a man's nose and the size of his penis.

Hamilton ended by wondering what "put it into my head to hazard this *jeu de folie*. Do I want a wife? No—I have plagues enough without desiring to add to the number that *greatest of all*."[5]

Laurens was in no hurry to answer Hamilton. When he finally wrote from Charleston some three months later, his only response to his friend's personal ardors was to say that the bearer of his letter "will relate to you how many violent struggles I have had between duty and inclination—how much my heart was with you while I appeared to be most actively employed here." He could not leave while there was the slightest hope of his succeeding with his plan for black levies.

Although Laurens had secured the endorsement he had sought from the Continental Congress, the South Carolinians, who commonly searched their slave quarters daily to discover and confiscate any weapons, were horrified by the recommendation that they themselves arm their blacks. Rather than do that, the inhabitants of Charleston, whose city was now under siege, offered a deal to Sir Henry Clinton: if the British would leave the state, South Carolina would withdraw from the war, leaving the question of her eventual allegiance to be settled by the final treaty of peace. Only British refusal to accept this partial surrender kept the defenders of Charleston—of whom Laurens was now one—on guard on the city's walls.

Laurens's comment to Hamilton ran, "Oh, that I were Demosthenes —the Athenians never deserved more bitter exprobation than my countrymen!" He ended his letter, "I entreat you, my dear friend, write me as frequently as circumstances will permit, and enlighten me upon what is going forward." He sent his love not directly to Hamilton but "to all our dear colleagues."[6]

The lukewarmness of Laurens's sentiments did not prevent Hamilton from replying in his previous high tone: "I acknowledge but one letter from you since you left us, of the 14th of July, which just arrived in time to appease a violent conflict between my friendship and my pride. I have written you five or six letters since you left Philadelphia and I should have written you more had you made proper return. But like a jealous lover, when I thought you slighted my caresses, my affection was alarmed and my vanity piqued. I had almost resolved to lavish no more of them upon you and to reject you as an inconstant and an ungrateful. But you have now disarmed my resentment and by a single mark of attention made up the quarrel. You must at least allow me a large stock of good nature."

Hamilton went on to postulate that Spain's entry into the war on the side of France would so overextend the resources of Great Britain that negotiation not conquest would become her object. It followed that she would seek to acquire two or three southern states to counterbalance the loss of her West Indian islands, and give her "credit in Europe." The British could be expected to come down harder on South Carolina.

Laurens's "black scheme" was obviously the state's "best resource." But, "even the animated and persuasive eloquence of my young Demosthenes will not be able to rouse his countrymen from the lethargy of voluptuous indolence or dissolve the fascinating character of self-interest." It was impossible to inspire Americans with "the natural enthusiasm of republicans." Experience would convince Laurens "that there is no virtue in America; the commerce which presided over the birth and education of these states has fitted their inhabitants for the chain, and that the only condition that they sincerely desire is that it may be a golden one."

It was in this letter that Hamilton described to Laurens how "the cabal" was trying to ruin him by misquoting what he insisted he had not said. He did not mention to his friend the charges that, being a foreigner, he was motivated only by personal ambition.[7]

Laurens used his family position to get himself elected to the South Carolina legislature, where he continued his vain arguments. The immediate crisis ameliorated. The British besiegers, deciding they were too weak to continue their siege of Charleston, returned to Georgia. D'Estaing then appeared with his fleet. The reason he kept Hamilton waiting disconsolately on the Delaware Capes and the New Jersey shore was that he had joined American troops (including Laurens) in trying to reduce the British strong point at Savannah, Georgia. An assault was undertaken and repulsed. D'Estaing sailed back to the Indies and Laurens posted north to Washington's headquarters, seeking reinforcements for next year's southern campaign.

Concerning the reunion of Laurens and Hamilton there is not a shred of information. From Philadelphia on his way back south, Laurens expressed to Hamilton no warmer sentiments than the following: "Present my respects and love to our excellent General and the Family. May you enjoy all the pleasure, moral and physical, which you promise yourself in winter quarters, and be as happy as you deserve."[8]

Hamilton read his next letter from Laurens with pulsating emotion. For some time, there had been pressure on the South Carolina prodigy to allow himself to be elected by Congress as secretary to the American minister in France. Laurens had refused, but had finally come to the conclusion that a citizen had no right to decline any office offered him by his countrymen unless he could recommend a suitable substitute. He had, so he now wrote Hamilton, notified the congressional representatives that he had found a person equally qualified with himself "in point of integrity—and much better in point of ability." Laurens greatly hoped that Congress would appoint Alexander Hamilton. However, "if unhappily they could not agree on Colonel Hamilton," and it was felt absolutely necessary that he himself should serve, "I should think it my duty to obey the orders of Congress."

Laurens went on to report that the legislature had nominated Hamilton and three others: "I am sorry that you are not better known to Congress. Great stress is laid upon the probity and patriotism of the person to be employed in this commission. I have given my testimony of you in this and other equally essential points."[9]

In his reply, Hamilton started out courteously—he hoped Laurens would serve after all—and then unmasked his passion for the post and his bitterness that he could not expect to receive it. What Laurens had written about the stress being laid on patriotism must have hurt, since Hamilton knew that the Philadelphia coffeehouse rumor was being used to impugn his patriotism in important congressional circles. Did Laurens's mention of the issue mean that he had heard the gossip?

"Not one of the four in nomination," Hamilton exclaimed, "but would stand a better chance than myself, and yet my vanity tells me they do not all merit a preference. But I am a stranger in the country. I have no property here, no connexions. If I have talents and integrity (as you say I have) these are justly deemed very spurious titles in these enlightened days, when unsupported by others more solid." He supposed that three quarters of the congressmen were "mortal enemies" to talents, and "three fourths of the other fourth have a laudable contempt" for integrity.

Hamilton then confided to Laurens that he had already made an effort to escape from Washington's headquarters by joining his friend in fighting to the southward. He had "candidly" explained to His Excellency "my feelings with respect to military reputation, and how much it was my object to act a conspicuous part in some enterprise that might perhaps raise my military character as a soldier above mediocrity." Washington, so Hamilton continued, could not refuse, "but arguments have been made to dissuade me from it which, however little weight they may have had in my judgment, gave law to my feelings.* I am chagrined and unhappy, but I submit.

"In short, Laurens, I am disgusted with everything in this world but yourself and *very* few more honest fellows."

Then the man who was years later to die in a spectacular duel wrote: "I have no other wish than as soon as possible to make a brilliant exit. 'Tis a weakness; but I feel I am not fit for this terrestrial country."[10]

* Hamilton was undoubtedly told that he could serve the cause best in his role as assistant to the Commander in Chief.

28

A Dim Prophetic Vision

[JANUARY, 1775–MARCH, 1780   AGES 18–23]

HAMILTON spent the winter of 1779–1780 with his general and the main army at Morristown, sharing what was in many ways a replay of the agonies at Valley Forge. But this time the hardships were less forgivable. Then the British lion had been rampant, holding the patriot capital of Philadelphia between her ensanguined paws. Now, although powerful cubs were prowling down south, the lion had changed to a house cat who hardly dared leave her snug cushion in New York. Yet the Continental soldiers were owed years of back pay, were balanced on the brink of starvation, were kept almost as naked as they had been at Valley Forge, although this winter was even more severe. Four to six feet of snow were kept perpetually locked on the ground by freezing weather.

The army cursed the civilians for (as General Greene put it) allowing, in "a country overflowing with plenty . . . an army employed for the defense of everything that is dear and valuable to perish for lack of food." Washington pointed out that the shortages were not the result, as before, of "accidental obstructions." They reflected a breakdown in the whole system of government.[1]

The states, considering the United States to be no more than an alliance between independent powers, had never given the Continental Congress the power to tax. Congress had supported the war by printing paper money, which theoretically would be redeemed by payments from the states into the common treasury. But since Congress had no

264

financial power beyond writing anguished pleas, it had never been able to collect from the states adequate funds. As the value of the Continental paper began to vanish altogether, an effort was made to put the expenditure where the taxing power was. Each state was called on to support its own regiments. This in effect replaced one commissary with thirteen; most of the states were far away; roads were blocked and wagons few; and those states not actual theaters of war found other expenditures more pressing than to supply distant men. Behind every reluctance lurked the attitude that, since France was now an ally, the war would be won without the American citizenry's pinching themselves too hard.

The systemic nature of the difficulties appealed to Hamilton's bent for dealing with large problems on an inclusive scale. He had never, it is true, particularly concerned himself with broad questions of finance, but having been bred a merchant, he had demonstrated a continuing interest in trade and practical economics. In his precocious political pamphlets he had, in an effort to prove that an American boycott would severely damage the economy of Great Britain, cited statistics gathered from, among other standard sources, Malachy Postlethwayt's two-volume *Universal Dictionary of Trade and Commerce* (1751).[2]

He went back to Postlethwayt for more detailed study some two years later. This is known because his notes were incorporated in his artillery Pay Book and were therefore preserved, while most records of his reading have disappeared. The labor was probably undertaken during the first months of 1777, when Hamilton lay sick in Philadelphia just before he was summoned to become Washington's aide. The Pay Book also contained notes on Plutarch which Hamilton admitted "are selected more for their singularity than use, though some important facts are comprehended." The young captain was particularly interested in sexual customs: "A worthy man, who was in love with a married woman on *account of her modesty* and the beauty of her children was at liberty to beg of her husband admission to her that thus, by planting in good soil, he might raise a generous progeny."[3]

In November, 1778, Hamilton had expressed, as part of a letter to General McDougall, what he recognized as being "rather peculiar ideas" concerning the flood of paper that was every day making the dollar sink in value. Printing money, he argued, "will continue to draw out the resources of the country a good while longer. . . . This will make our public expenditures infinitely less, and will allow the states to attend to the arrangement of their finances, as well as [give] the country tranquillity to cultivate its resources."[4]

Now, early in 1780, Hamilton drafted a letter on finance to an un-named member of Congress. Far from retracting his contention (with which many modern economists would agree) that the unsupported printing of dollars had been a necessary expedient, he presented figures to show that since the American economy in its dominant agri-cultural aspects was so largely based on barter, there had been no better choice for finding the fluid assets necessary in wartime. But the inflation had now gone past usefulness to become a menace. Various shortages darkened the situation. He presented no plan by which the states could be drawn to the rescue of the Continental economy. In a manner he would later consider irresponsible, he argued that the first step in reversing the inflation should be securing another foreign loan.

"These reasonings," he admitted, "may appear useless, as the neces-sity of a foreign loan is now acknowledged and measures are taking to produce it. But they are intended to establish good principles."

The problem was how to use the foreign loan once it was secured. The two most obvious directions—to reestablish the currency by buy-ing in the paper money or to use the specie directly to buy goods—he ruled out on the grounds that either would be frustrated by "a few artful individuals." As soon as they knew that the paper money was to go up in value, speculators would engross it, making the government pay more and more to get their old bills out of circulation. If purchases were attempted, "the arts of the monopolizers" would take over, raising prices in a way that would eat up the foreign loan.

Without in any way taking back the disapproval of speculators he had expressed in his "Publius" letters—he referred now to them as "designing men" inspired by "avarice"—the twenty-two-year-old Hamilton made a statement endlessly explanatory of his future career: "The only plan that can preserve the currency is one that will make it to the *immediate* interest of the monied men to cooperate with the government in its support. . . . No plan could succeed which does not unite the interest and credit of rich individuals with that of the state."

Already he visualized the farmers (who, of course, made up the majority of the population) not as allies to be courted but as a prob-lem to be handled. "The farmers have the game in their own hands and will make it very difficult to lower the prices of their commodities. . . . If they do not like the price," they do not have to sell because "they have almost every necessity within themselves." They should be made to contribute through heavy taxation. Since they had little cash, produce should be collected instead of money. "This ought instantly to begin throughout the states."

But the real solution would be for Congress to authorize "The Bank of the United States." The foreign loan would be thrown into the bank to help attract an equal amount from private investors—they should supply two million pounds sterling, a sum completely unrealistic for an America devoid of authentic capitalists. The government would guarantee the investors a return of at least one twentieth of what they had risked. All taxes would go into the bank. The institution would be run by its own directors under government supervision. It would lend both to the government and private commerce. It would go into business in its own right, perhaps supplying the army.

The bank would also receive inflated paper currency, paying the reduced price which had been denounced in Congress but was soon actually to be adopted there: forty to one. In return, the bank would issue its own bills. He then demonstrated his belief (which was to continue) that the Americans, although the fight for independence was against Great Britain, would be reassured if they associated their financial institutions with British economic stability: the currency issued by the bank should be called not dollars but pounds. "It will," he explained, "produce a useful illusion. Mankind are much led by sounds and appearances, and the currency having changed its name will seem to have changed its nature."

The existence of sound capital funds should, by inspiring confidence, make the bank so stable that it could expand the circulating medium by issuing currency far beyond its capital. That the bills would pay two percent interest would further reduce the possibility of a hysterical run on the bank.

The government would hold one half of the stock and receive one half of the profits. "The share which the state has in the profits will induce it to grant more ample privileges, without which the trade of the company might often be under restrictions injurious to its success." But the bank should not, like various European prototypes, be given any monopoly that would destroy "the spirit of enterprise and competition on which the prosperity of commerce depends."

His plan, Hamilton explained, "is the product of some reading . . . and of occasional reflections on our particular situation, but want of leisure has prevented its being examined in so many lights and being digested so maturely as its importance requires." For precedents, Hamilton referred in particular to the Bank of England and the Royal Chamber of Commerce in France.

Whether or not Hamilton had at first intended to sign his epistle and get credit for it, he wrote at the conclusion that if his correspondent wanted further explanation "or if the plan is approved . . . a letter directed to James Montague, Esq., lodged in the post office in Morris-town" would be "a safe channel" through which he could be reached. "Though the writer has reasons which make him unwilling to be known, if a personal conference with him should be thought material, he will endeavor to comply."

Then Hamilton had further thoughts and resolved not to mail his manuscript, which he placed among his papers with various blank spaces not yet filled in.[5]

With whom, if anyone, Hamilton had discussed his ideas we do not know. He did have friends, such as General Greene, who were good businessmen, but a year later he felt that he had to introduce himself to Robert Morris, the leader of America's most sophisticated and crea-tive financiers.[6] He still had only a nodding acquaintance with General Schuyler. That he had not talked to Washington was demonstrated early in 1781, when General Sullivan, then a member of Congress, asked the Commander in Chief whether Hamilton might be made director of finance. Washington replied that he did not know whether Hamilton "has turned his thoughts to that particular study . . . be-cause I never entered upon a discussion on this point with him."[7]

Hamilton showed insight when, realizing he had gone off half-cocked, he suppressed his letter. His ideas were chaotic and extremely impractical in view of America's current financial preconceptions and possibilities. Yet, all the more because the letter was thrown off by a very young man at a military camp in what time he could reserve from serving his general, it was an amazingly prescient first jump into the deep ocean of finance.

The hope that a bank might fight inflation was, it is true, in the air. The Bank of Philadelphia was to be founded a few months later—but that beginning was an altogether private enterprise operating on a small scale. Hamilton had raised his sights infinitely higher, not only in conventional admiration of the Bank of England, but also through an unconventional appreciation of the positive accomplishments of a man usually reviled: John Law. A Scottish adventurer who established the Bank of France, Law did much to stabilize the French economy until he overextended and crashed into one of the most extensive and cele-brated failures in financial history.[8]

Not until Hamilton himself proposed and fought for it when he was Secretary of the Treasury more than ten years later was there to be what he had envisioned in his unmailed letter: a "Bank of the United States" that was a great public institution privately managed.

29

Engaged to Be Married

D URING January, 1780, Hamilton drew up a bill for his pay as aide-de-camp from June through December, 1779: $60 a month, total $360. A few days later, he subscribed, as did Washington and most of the leading military figures at Morristown, to "a dancing assembly," which, it was hoped, would enliven their winter quarters. The subscription cost him $400.[1]

We have here a strong hint of why Hamilton had no horse to ride. In excoriating the inflation, Washington fulminated that even "a rat in the shape of a horse is not to be bought at this time for less than two hundred pounds."[2]

How did Hamilton get along at all? As an officer, he received daily rations for himself and his servants, who were paid as soldiers. He was, of course, housed by the army, and he did not have to buy the wine that circulated at the headquarters table. For the rest, he did have some money invested in Philadelphia. With other members of Washington's Family he was concerned in that most profitable of speculations, privateering.*

* In August, 1778, when d'Estaing was off Rhode Island, Lafayette cooperated with Hamilton in an effort to procure for another aide, Lieutenant Colonel John Fitzgerald, the title of French consul so that he could handle the legalities that would enable ships of the French navy to collect the value of the British merchantmen they captured. Lafayette also forwarded to Hamilton two thousand louis to be invested in some aspect of the project. Lafayette's letter makes clear that Washington knew and approved.[3]

269

The dancing assemblies were held in the commissary's storehouse, where scarcity of supplies left plenty of room for dancers. Washington attended in black velvet; the foreign officers resplendent in gold lace and medals; the Americans less gaudy but as neat as possible; Martha Washington in simple dresses made of the finest materials; the belles in stiff brocades with their hair powdered and worn high. *Rivington's Gazette* scoffed from British-held New York that "fifty females" had been "picked up" for these dances. The females were in fact recruited from the families of the officers or from among the more elegant local inhabitants. Among the latter were the "four or five" daughters of Abraham Lott, described by General Greene as being all "of delicate sentiments and polite education."

Hamilton was so attendant on eighteen-year-old Cornelia Lott, and so talkative about her at headquarters, that Colonel Samuel Blacherly Webb felt required to summon his muse:

To Colonel Hamilton

What, bend the stubborn knee at last,
Confess the days of wisdom past?
He that could bow to every shrine;
And swear the last the most divine;
Like Hudibrass all subjects bend,
Had Ovid at his finger's end;
Could whistle ev'ry tune of love,
(You'd think him Ovid's self or Jove)
Now feels the inexorable dart
And yields Cornelia all his heart!

Webb went on to chide Hamilton for expatiating on "the charms that plague you so"; on Cornelia's "air that even Stoics praise." All this was

Mere rant, th'effusion of a brain
Oppress'd with love's distempered train . . .
She's but—sweet sir, nay do not fret,
She's but—a beautiful brunette.

The poet warned Hamilton that "even he who laughs life's cares away" should not trifle with a force as dangerous as love.[4]

This was written in January. By early February, Hamilton was paying court to a girl called Polly, with such effect that, when he moved on again, Tilghman mourned that he himself was too old to repair Polly's broken heart.*5

On January 10, General Schuyler wrote General von Steuben from Albany, New York. He apologized for being unable "to procure the wolf skins I promised." They were not to be had because of the depth of the snows, but he hoped that some wolves would be shot later in the season. After discussing politics, Schuyler continued: "The lady who will deliver this is my daughter. I have advised her to recommend herself to your attention." He had told her that Steuben and "my friend Colonel Harrison are the two most gallant men about Morristown, but I fear that friend Tilghman, Mr. Henry, and Washington will strive to take her hand from you both. I mean at a dance."6

On February 2, Steuben's aide, Major Benjamin Walker, wrote his general that Elizabeth (Betsey) Schuyler had arrived. Walker would have received her in Steuben's stead had the decrepitude of his coat not limited him to associating only with other officers who were also half naked because of the inflation. Indeed, so Walker continued, his subordinate officers were responding to their hardships by threatening to resign. The major was using General von Steuben's rations to give "one or two of them every night a good supper." Two had nonetheless departed.7

The Hamilton archives soon blossomed with an undated note: "Colonel Hamilton's compliments to Miss Livingston and Miss Schuyler. He is sorry to inform them that his zeal for their service makes him forget that he is so bad a charioteer as hardly to dare to trust himself with so precious a charge; though, if he were only to consult his own wishes, like Phaeton he would assemble the chariot of the sun, if he were sure of experiencing the same fate. Colonel Tilghman offers himself a volunteer. Colonel Hamilton is unwilling to lose the pleasure of the party; but one or the other will have the honor to attend the ladies."8

So much for the overture. The curtain rises on the main action with a letter written before March 8, obviously with Betsey's knowledge, to one of her sisters whom Hamilton had never met: "I venture to tell you in confidence that by some odd contrivance or other your sister [Betsey] has found out the secret of interesting me in everything that

---

* It is of course possible, nicknames being erratic, that Cornelia and Polly were the same girl. Cornelia was not to marry until she was thirty-six and then espoused a widower of forty-nine, but it would surely be taking a tremendous leap to conclude that Hamilton had broken her heart.

concerns her." Partly as a result of seeing a portrait that Betsey had herself drawn of the sister he was writing, Hamilton had acquired a "partiality" for his correspondent's "person and mind." You "will no doubt admit it as a full proof of my frankness and good opinion of you, that I with so little ceremony introduce myself to your acquaintance and at the first step make you my confidante. But I hope I run no risk of its being thought an impeachment of my discretion. Phlegmatists may say I take too great a license at first setting out, and witlings may sneer and wonder how a man the least acquainted with the world should show so great facility in his confidences—to a lady."

Hamilton described Betsey as being "most unmercifully handsome and so perverse that she has none of those pretty affectations which are the prerogatives of beauty. Her good sense is destitute of that happy mixture of vanity and ostentation which would make it conspicuous to the whole tribe of fools and foplings as well as to men of understanding, so that as the matter now stands it is very little known beyond the circle of these. She has good nature, affability and vivacity unembellished with that charming frivolousness which is justly deemed one of the principal accomplishments of a *belle*. In short she is so strange a creature that she possesses all the beauties, virtues, and graces of her sex without any of those amiable defects, which from their general prevalence are esteemed by connoisseurs necessary shades in the character of a fine woman. The most determined adversaries of Hymen can find in her no pretext for their hostility, and there are several of my friends, philosophers who railed at love as a weakness, men of the world who laughed at it as a phantasie, whom she has presumptuously and daringly compelled to acknowledge its power and surrender at discretion. I can the better assert the truth of this, as I am myself of the number. She has had the address to overset all the wise resolutions I had been framing for more than four years past, and from a rational sort of being and a professed contemner of Cupid has in a trice metamorphosed me into the veriest inamorato you perhaps ever saw."

Reading this letter in the context of the situation in which it was written, Betsey (as subsequent events revealed) found it much to her taste. A more dispassionate reading raises bothersome overtones. There is here no hint of the convention, usually assumed whether or not accurate, that the man is the pursuer: it is Betsey who has "by some odd contrivance or another . . . found out the secret of interesting me." More disturbing, although put forward as playful and complimentary, are the passages about Betsey's lacking "the principal accomplishments of a *belle*," what "connoisseurs" consider the "necessary

General Philip Schuyler, Hamilton's father-in-law, by
John Trumbull. The wealthy New York patrician not
only welcomed his daughter's marriage to the propertyless, illegitimate immigrant but became almost a
disciple to his brilliant son-in-law. Courtesy, New-
York Historical Society

Alexander Hamilton, by Charles Willson Peale. Painted in 1791, this oil reveals the peculiarities of feature, particularly the low bridge of the nose between close-set eyes, that kept Hamilton, as he himself mourned, from being "handsome." Courtesy, Independence National Historical Park Collection

Elizabeth Schuyler Hamilton, by Ralph Earl. The only portrait of Hamilton's wife painted during his lifetime (1787). Courtesy, Museum of the City of New York

shades in the character of a fine woman." We shall not be surprised to find Hamilton admonishing her some months later, "You excel most of your sex in most of the amiable qualities; endeavor to excel them equally in the more splendid ones."[9]

Interesting in another way are Hamilton's references to "phlegmatists" and "witlings" and "philosophers who rail at love." They are among the few conspicuously adolescent touches to be found in the correspondence of the precocious young man.

Hamilton was soon sent off on another of those abortive prisoner-exchange missions with which he had become so familiar. There was, indeed, no hope of its succeeding since the Americans were instructed only to treat if the British commissioners had authority from "His British Majesty" to negotiate "upon the principles of perfect equality and upon a national ground," which would have meant accepting independence. But gestures had to be duly made. They kept Hamilton from Morristown during most of March.[10]

He wrote Betsey "a hasty letter" (now lost), and subsequently he received news of her from Colonel Webb. On March 17, Hamilton wrote again, expressing "happiness" at hearing that she had not forgotten him. Webb had reported that she planned to go to Philadelphia. Hamilton stated that he hoped she would "leave a line" for him stating when she would get back. She should not forget that "your best friend is where I am."

Hamilton continued his letter with agreeable inanities: The British officers with whom he was negotiating were "a compound of grimace and jargon," principally accomplished at drinking more wine than Hamilton could dream of drinking—and so forth.

He was still composing his letter when there was a knock on his door. He was presented with a communication from Betsey enclosed in one from her "guardian," probably her aunt, Mrs. John Cochran, with whom she was staying near Morristown.

Resuming his pen, Hamilton wrote, "My Betsey's soul speaks in every line and bids me be the happiest of mortals." He exulted that her heart is "entirely mine." She was at fault, he continued, in stating that she did "not deserve the preference I give you. . . . Your diffidence with so many charms is an unpardonable amiableness. I am pleased with it, however, on one account, which is that it will induce you to call your good qualities into full activity, and there is nothing I shall always delight in more than to assist you in unfolding them in their highest perfection. . . .

"I have spun this letter out much longer than I intended." He was already half an hour late for a meeting with the British commissioners. "Adieu, my charmer. Take care of yourself and love your Hamilton as well as he does you. God bless you!"[11]

No letter from Betsey Schuyler to her fiancé remains. In fact, although she cherished her husband's letters to her, we have almost no letters she wrote to him at any point in their relationship. This raises questions as interesting as they are insoluble. Did he fail to keep her letters? Were they lost by her descendants? Or did she herself destroy them during her long period of widowhood? If she did destroy them, why? There is clear evidence that after her husband's death she greatly revered his memory. Did she during that long period of idolatry decide that *her* letters were unworthy? Or was she motivated (as Martha Washington had been when she burned her entire correspondence with her husband) by a desire to keep some part of her relationship with a public man altogether private? Did she strike as a result of hidden resentment or sudden anger? Whatever the answer, posterity has been deprived of many intimate insights into her feelings.

We know that Betsey Schuyler was almost exactly Hamilton's age. Throughout her childhood she had lived alternately in two houses, one wild, one conventional. Her father's residence at Saratoga, in the middle of his extensive western acres, was deep enough in the frontier to be subject to Indian raids. Her father's mansion at Albany was part of an ancient settlement, New York's second city, where Dutch was still spoken and the polite society was of Dutch descent. The prosperity of the Schuylers and the other great families with which they had intermarried rested on huge land grants made to Hollanders before the fall of New Amsterdam.

Tilghman, when stationed in Albany, had met Betsey some five years before she met Hamilton. "I was prepossessed," he wrote in his journal, "in favor of this lady the moment I saw her. A brunette with the most good-natured, lively dark eyes that I ever saw which threw a beam of good temper and benevolence over her whole countenance. Mr. Livingston informed me that I was not mistaken in the conjecture that she was the finest-tempered girl in the world." Tilghman further commented, when they visited the falls of Cohoes, "I fancy Miss Schuyler had been used to ramble over and climb grounds of this sort, since she disdained all assistance and made herself merry at the distress of the other ladies."[12]

When Betsey was wooed by Hamilton at Morristown, Tilghman,

while expressing concern for the displaced Polly, added sentimentally that no one could be jealous of "the little saint." Betsey was admired by everyone as "a very pretty, good-tempered girl."[13]

By far the most accomplished portrait of Betsey was painted in 1787 by Ralph Earl.[14] It shows her face, even after seven years of marriage, as basically childish, the added years and experience having done no more than draw disconsolate lines on a still-youthful visage. Her face is heart-shaped; the large black eyes Hamilton particularly admired dominate; her expression is eager, innocent, weary.

A phenomenon of the Schuyler household was that of the four daughters, three eloped. Although one of these made exactly such a marriage as her parents wished, she would not have her parents at the ceremony. Betsey's father, so the biographer of her mother wrote, was a "stern" parent. "Aristocratic in feeling, and convinced of the propriety and the observance of dignities . . . he brought to the performance of his own duties an orderly mind and prompt execution. The same qualities he demanded of others."[15]

The patrician's intolerant, toplofty behavior, which had ended his army career by bringing him the hatred of the New England troops, was equally in force at home. His sons were commanded to appear at breakfast booted and spurred, ready to carry their father's commands around the huge Schuyler estate. The sons rebelled. Betsey was the acquiescent member of the family.

The Marquis de Chastellux was struck, when he visited the Schuyler mansion in December, 1780, by how "mild" was her "agreeable countenance."[16] Yet, as time was to show, she was subject to hysteria. She took to her bed in such nervous paroxysms that, when she was pregnant, miscarriage was feared and in one instance, it seems, actually produced.

If Hamilton and Betsey had ever met before, it could only have been a casual encounter at Elizabethtown, when she was visiting her Livingston cousins and he was a schoolboy. Now he carried her off as from a whirlwind. From her arrival at Morristown to her letter of acceptance was less than seven weeks. It is easy to visualize how the diffident and emotional girl would have been overwhelmed by the dashing soldier, a man of great power and true brilliance, who was admired by his male companions for being able "to whistle every tune of love." She seems, indeed, to have hardly been able to believe her good fortune. Her experience with her father had acclimated her to domination by men.

Concerning Hamilton's emotions, we have the most detailed information. We know, for instance, that when he wrote Laurens almost two weeks after Betsey had accepted his suit, he failed to mention his engagement. Another thirty days passed before he asked his friend: "Have you not heard that I am on the point of becoming a benedict? I confess my sins. I am guilty. Next fall completes my doom. I give up my liberty to Miss Schuyler. She is a good-hearted girl who I am sure will never play the termagant; though not a genius she has good sense enough to be agreeable, and though not a beauty, she has fine black eyes—is rather handsome and has every other requisite of the exterior to make a lover happy. And believe me, I am lover in earnest, though I do not speak of the perfections of my Mistress in the enthusiasm of Chivalry."[17]

On almost the same date, he wrote Betsey herself: "I love you more and more every hour. The sweet softness and delicacy of your mind and manners, the elevation of your sentiments, the real goodness of your heart, its tenderness to me, the beauties of your face and person, your unpretending good sense and that innocent simplicity and frankness which pervade your actions; all these appear to me with increasing amiableness and place you in my estimation above all the rest of your sex."[18]

Each of these statements was tailored for its recipient. And, however seemingly contradictory, each reflected accurately aspects of Hamilton's emotion.

Hamilton, who always sought to put up a display before the world, truly regretted that Miss Schuyler was not a great belle, yet Rachel's son surely found reassurance that, while liked by all, she flashed only for him. Although he was addicted to turbulent emotions and strong sexual passions, his memories gave him good reason to conclude that such drives would not underlie happiness. But this did not mean that he failed to seek, for his own delectation as well as his bride's, the vision and rhetoric of passion. He intended to be, as he wrote Laurens, "a lover in earnest."

Hamilton's biographers have consistently protested against the very clear implication that Betsey's greatest charm to her suitor was the worldly position she occupied and offered. Such protests ignore historical realities. Down the long history of man, in every type of society from the most primitive to the most sophisticated, property and family have, on the whole, exerted a greater matrimonial appeal than character or brains or bright eyes or a bosom shaped according to the prevailing fashion. Sexual desire itself responds to worldly considerations. For either men or women to marry "beneath them" has, traditionally, been considered to indicate a lack of self-respect and also a betrayal of obligations to family and indeed the structure of society.

During the eighteenth century, heads may well have been shaken at a man of Hamilton's background wooing a patrician's daughter before asking the consent of her father. Criticism could correctly have been directed at Betsey for falling in love with a familyless and propertyless upstart. But it was altogether natural that Hamilton should serve ambition through an agreeable marriage.

The marriage, if he could carry it off, would be his solidest achievement to date. His position in the army was unstable, not only because it would evaporate with peace, but because he had no commission in the line to which he could switch if he ceased, for any reason, including his own volition, to serve Washington as an aide. Married to Betsey, he would never again have to lament that he had "no property, no position in this country." The Schuylers' prosperity, being primarily in huge landed estates, was as stable as any American property could be. Since the family was on the extreme right of the Revolutionary effort and England would surely not completely uproot American society, the Schuyler power could be counted on to survive even an eventual loss of the war. And in dynastic New York, where Hamilton was laboring to build his political base, he was allying himself with a puissant team.

There is some evidence that Betsey played with the romantic idea of eloping as her elder sister had done. But Hamilton would have none of it. His union with the Schuyler family was to be carried out as correctly as could be.[19]

The timetable of events reveals that after Hamilton got back to headquarters from the prisoner-exchange mission, he instantly undertook the nervous task of securing the approval of Betsy's class-minded father. Schuyler happened to be in Morristown, as part of a congressional committee to the army. Hamilton delivered to him a letter (now lost) asking for his daughter's hand.[20] It may be assumed that face-to-face discussion followed.

Some ten months later, after the marriage had taken place, Schuyler wrote Hamilton: "You cannot, my dear sir, be more happy at the connection you have made with my family than I am. Until a child has made a judicious choice, the heart of a parent is continually in anxiety, but this anxiety vanished in the moment I discovered where you and she had placed your affections. I am pleased," Schuyler went on, "with every instance of delicacy in those that are so dear to me, and I think

I read your soul on the occasion you mention. I shall therefore only entreat you to consider me as one who wishes in every way to promote your happiness, and that I shall never give or loan but with a view to *such* great ends."[21]

Hamilton's biographers have interpreted "the occasion you mention" as referring to the first interview and the "delicacy" as indicating that Hamilton had communicated the fact of his illegitimate birth.[22] But the paragraph as a whole deals with Schuyler's making him a gift or loan. If the first interview is indeed meant, the "delicacy" may well have alluded to an admission by Hamilton that he was a poor man.

It is clear that Hamilton told Betsey enough about his beginnings for him to write her, after he heard during 1782 that his legitimate half brother, Peter Lavien, had died, "You know the circumstances that abate my distress.[23] But what he told Schuyler during that first interview remains a matter of speculation. We can be sure that he dwelt on his father's being a Scot of good breeding.

Despite his pleasure, Schuyler refused, at Hamilton's first request, instantaneous approval. He would have to secure the agreement of his wife, who was in Albany. He would write her there.

It was exactly three weeks after Hamilton had received Betsey's letter of surrender that Schuyler wrote from Philadelphia: Mrs. Schuyler "consents to comply with your and her daughter's wishes." But the speed at which everything had been going must now halt. The couple's desire for an immediate marriage there at the army camp would create "impropriety. . . . Mrs. Schuyler did not see her eldest daughter married. That also gave me pain and we wish not to experience it a second time." The wedding would have to wait until Hamilton could get away to Albany—that would be late autumn or early winter, when the campaign ended.[24]

In this, the first of his many, many letters to Hamilton, Schuyler's final approval of the marriage occupied only one short paragraph. The general-turned-congressman devoted the rest of a long communication to the conduct of the war and to politics.[25] Thus, at the very start Schuyler revealed that he regarded the marriage as more than the joining of a man and a maid.

Although General Schuyler's estates and his dynastic connections were as solid as the foundations of an old palace, the superstructure—the rooms in which he currently moved—was sagging badly. His military reputation, damaged by the earlier defeat in Canada when he had been in command, had been almost dragged to the ground by the fall of Ticonderoga and the subsequent desperate situation in the northern sector when he was again in command. Cry as he might that he had so prepared for Burgoyne's defeat that his successor, Gates, had merely to pick the fruit, no one except his most violent partisans believed. He had demanded a court-martial, but had not felt his acquittal an adequate recompense for the obloquy he had endured. Angrily he resigned from the army.

He had merely to ask and he was made one of New York's members of Congress. He had come to Morristown during Hamilton's courtship as a member of the committee which was to plan efforts of Congress to strengthen the army. However, his fellow congressmen quickly decided that he was too pro-military and that their committee would be better off without him. In that first letter to Hamilton he wrote, "The pride, the folly, and perhaps too the wickedness of some on a certain floor combine to frustrate every intention to promote the public weal."[26] He soon followed his resignation from the army with a resignation from Congress and returned to Albany. Although he was still only in his middle forties, his body was wracked with gout.

Schuyler's power in New York remained, but politics in that dynastic state was a matter of families, and his rebellious sons were not eager to walk in their father's footsteps. No young champion was growing up under his roof. Schuyler was to write that "long before I had the least intimation that you [Hamilton] intended that connection with my family which is so very pleasing to me," he had concluded that Hamilton alone in Washington's Family had "those qualifications so essentially necessary to the man who is to aid and council a commanding general." There were whisperings among Schuyler's enemies that he had sold his daughter in order to gain so valuable an ally.[27]

As Hamilton prepared to take his great step upward, he had no intention of admitting inferiority. He tried to summon up from his past what a lesser man would have been all the more anxious to keep hidden. His father was still obscure and in penury, wandering in the Indies. But, so Hamilton informed his intended bride, he had invited James Hamilton to come to New York and join their household. He was, he wrote Betsey, informing his father how much the attentions of "his black-eyed daughter . . . will make the blessing of his grey hairs."[28]

30

The Dark Confusions
of a Summer

[DECEMBER, 1779–JUNE, 1780   AGES 22–23]

L ATE in December, 1779, before Betsey had reached Morristown, Sir Henry Clinton, the British commander in chief, had
sailed out of New York Harbor with a large expeditionary
force. This movement developed into a full-scale siege of Charleston,
South Carolina. Only Hessians were left in the New York base, and
most of the fleet had gone. Two years before, such an opportunity
would have brought the Continental Army storming at the gates of the
British bastion. But the army was too weak to do more than stir in its
debility.

Laurens was now serving as aide to General Benjamin Lincoln, the
American commander at Charleston. Hamilton wrote him, "My fears
are very much up." He feared that the defenses of the city "will be
vulnerable on the water side." He wished he could advise that reinforcements be sent from the Continental Army, but "we are very
weak," and in any case "our distresses" would make it almost impossible to transport any troops south. "Adieu, my dear. . . . Take care of
yourself as you ought for the public's sake and for the sake of your
affectionate A. Hamilton."[1]

Washington did manage to send some troops south, which left the
Continental Army even more crippled.[2]

On May 6—Hamilton had been engaged to Betsey for a month now—
the dishes were cleared from the supper table and the candles lighted

283

when a bombshell exploded at headquarters. It was a note headed, "At the entrance to Boston harbor." Lafayette was back from a mission to France bringing, he promised, news "of the utmost importance."[3]

Four days later, Hamilton wrote Steuben: "We have heard from the Marquis. He will be here at dinner. Will you dine with us also? The General requests it."[4]

The dinner was swept by excitement as well as friendship and hilarity. Lafayette's news was that a French fleet was going to accompany to America a French expeditionary force: seven to ten thousand men. There would also be a plethora of supplies for the Continental Army. Away with two years of agonizing frustration! On to victory!

Confident that this possibility of ending the war with an immediate stroke would inspire the nation, Washington called on Congress for more troops than he had been given even at the optimistic opening of the conflict: twenty-five thousand Continentals and seventeen thousand militia.

Hamilton exhorted Congressman Duane: "The fate of America is perhaps suspended on the issue! If we are found unprepared, it must disgrace us in the eyes of all Europe, besides defeating the good intention of our allies, and losing the happiest opportunity we ever have had to save ourselves." He went on to state what Washington could not state. The Commander in Chief had asked that Congress expedite matters—the French might arrive in less than a month—by sending to headquarters a small committee empowered to act for their large, distant body. Now Hamilton urged that Washington should not be obliged to consult the committee "oftener than he thinks proper. . . . It is the essence of many military operations that they should be trusted to as few as possible."[5]

Hamilton's growing importance in the minds of his military colleagues was twice exemplified that May.

General Greene, who had been doubling as quartermaster general, was suffering under an attack—instigated by Mifflin, the former leader of the Conway Cabal—for permitting dishonesty among his subordinates. In the resulting controversy, Greene relied heavily on Hamilton's advice. Thus, after he had composed a violent letter to the Treasury Board, he sent it to Hamilton, requesting that his friend read it and consider "the manner you think I ought to answer, keeping in mind the charge and insult, and that too tame a submission will confirm them in the truth of the charges."

Hamilton replied that if Greene's "target" were "so many individu-

als," the asperity would be abundantly justified. But his foes consti-
tuted one of the most powerful public bodies; Greene should remember that he would probably have to get on with them in the future.
"The Board, from the necessity of our affairs, may sue for peace, but
they will hate you for the humiliation you bring upon them."[6]

This was good advice, but had Hamilton been in Greene's place, his
temperament would not have permitted him to follow it.

Lafayette was eager to have honors showered on the Viscount de la
Touche-Tréville, the captain of the frigate in which he had come to
America. The Marquis considered that it would be an honor if Hamilton would advise the Viscount concerning what part of the ocean he
should prowl for the best possibility of capturing British prizes.

Hamilton wrote, "I execute with the greatest pleasure a commission
which the Marquis de La Fayette has done me the honor to charge me
for you, influenced by the double motive of complying with his desire
and giving you a mark of the esteem with which the character I have
heard of you has inspired me." Having admitted that "I am a bad
judge in affairs of this kind," he ventured on some "hints to satisfy the
Marquis' desire and to prove to you how happy I should be to have it
in my power to be useful to you."[7]

Thus Hamilton did his best, although his rhetoric was much less
elaborate and convoluted than that used when aristocrats wrote letters
of politeness to each other. Concerning another request of Lafayette's,
he expressed to Duane irritation. The Marquis had asked Hamilton to
urge on Congress a vote "recommending" the Viscount to the French
court. A bourgeois rather than an aristocrat when it came to insisting
that military honors should be earned and not be made mere matters
of compliment, Hamilton dismissed the suggestion as one of Lafayette's "thousand little whims. . . . Congress must not commit themselves!"[8]

On May 31 the first blow came. There was always mysterious movement through the military lines and thus there appeared at headquarters a handbill which had been published in New York City. It announced that Charleston, with all its garrison—twenty-five hundred
Continentals and two thousand militia—had unconditionally surrendered. Hamilton was surely nervous concerning Laurens, who was so
given to courting danger. In more general terms Hamilton wrote that
the surrender was "a severe stroke but it is vain to repine. . . . It may
indeed be useful to us in the present juncture by keeping the enemy's

force divided and giving a new motive to the exertions of the states. But it must be confessed, if it is a blessing 'tis a blessing in a very strange disguise."[9]

Word soon came that Sir Henry Clinton, leaving Lord Cornwallis behind with a force considered adequate to push over the tottering South, had set sail for New York with most of his fleet and army. Washington assumed that the British general would do what he himself would do: take advantage of his sudden reappearance by speeding up the Hudson in an attempt to surprise the major American fortification that was building at West Point. Washington ordered that the fort be prepared, but was himself kept from marching to the rescue by a development he had not foreseen.[10]

Baron Wilhelm von Knyphausen, the Hessian general who in Sir William's absence commanded in New York, marched most of the garrison onto the plains under the high ground Washington occupied. Headquarters judged this to be a ruse to take attention away from the defense of the Hudson. It was a most humiliating ruse. Thus to deplete New York's defenders, at the same time risking a weak column in New Jersey, would have been idiocy had the Continental Army had any sting left.[11]

Hamilton wrote Laurens, whom he now knew had been captured, not killed: "Would you believe it— A German baron at the head of 5,000 men in the month of June insulted and defied the main American army, with the commander in chief at their head, with impunity, and made them tremble for the security of their magazines forty miles in the country."

Hamilton then reported to Laurens that, despite the "golden opportunity" offered by the expected French expeditionary force, the states were responding to Washington's calls for reinforcements "by halves, and if we attempt anything we must do it on the principle of despair. . . . My dear Laurens, our countrymen have all the folly of the ass and all the passiveness of the sheep in their compositions. They are determined not to be free and they can neither be frightened, discouraged, nor persuaded to change their resolution. If we are saved, France and Spain must save us. I have the most pigmy feelings at the idea, and I almost wish to hide my disgrace in universal ruin."

The British had taken Laurens's parole and released him on condition that he would stay in Pennsylvania and not fight. Finding such inaction almost unbearable, the officer who usually refused to accept favoritism begged Hamilton to help him procure, although he was one of the most recently captured, such an exchange as was considered the prerogative of those longest prisoners of war. Hamilton's reply showed that he could bend his opposition to military favoritism for a very dear friend: "I have talked to the General . . . but the rigid rules of impartiality oppose our wishes. I am the only one in the family who think you can be exchanged with any propriety on the score of your relation to the Commander in Chief. . . . I have more of the infirmities of human nature than the others, and suspect myself of being bypassed by my partiality for you." Perhaps the Board of War could be induced to give him preference as a compliment to Washington. "But, my friend, let me give you a caution. . . . You must not have the air of bearing captivity worse than another."[12]

Knyphausen did little more than taunt the Continental Army by parading below them. He had been informed by Tories, so Clinton's aide Major André wrote, that the American soldiers were "so dissatisfied that they would desert and crumble into our hands." Furthermore, he nourished the old hope that the citizenry would, if given the necessary protection, eagerly seek the sheltering wing of George III. However, both the Continentals and the local inhabitants "behaved," as Hamilton admitted, "with singular spirit."[13] Knyphausen was slow in accepting the situation. The Hessian had not yet withdrawn from New Jersey when Clinton arrived in New York. The plans he had indeed made for dashing up the Hudson were frustrated by the absence of the New York garrison.

There had been hope at American headquarters that the French would arrive during Clinton's absence and take New York City. But Clinton had come in first. The Count de Rochambeau, general of the French troops, and the Chevalier de Ternay, admiral of the French fleet, sailed for Newport Harbor, occupying the island recently evacuated by the enemy.

It soon became clear that what had arrived represented only a part of the assistance the French had promised. The arms and other supplies the American headquarters had counted on for the enlarged army they were summoning had been left behind. The French force was much weaker than had been expected. A second wave was said to be on the way across the ocean, but when would it arrive?[14]

The numerical superiority in American waters brought by Ternay's fleet lasted for only one day. Enter under Admiral Graves a British reinforcement strong enough to keep the French from venturing from their harbor. Graves probed out the French position at Newport and then the combined British might, including a large part of the army under Clinton himself, sailed off to wipe out the French. The Continental Army could not move overland fast enough to be of any aid, but Washington now had an enlarged force (although less than half of what he had asked for) and he advanced with them as if for an attack on New York City. As he had hoped, Clinton came popping back to protect his essential British base.[15]

The French expeditionary force was now absorbed into the prevailing torpor. Rochambeau was horrified by what he saw of his nation's ally. He wrote to his government: "Send us troops, ships, money but do not depend on these people or their means. They have neither money nor credit. Their means of resistance are only momentary and called forth when they are attacked in their own homes."[16] He decided to stay, until things changed, on his island. The additional troops Washington had succeeded in raising impinged primarily as so many more mouths for the creaking supply system to feed.

By becoming engaged to Betsey, Hamilton had opened a Pandora's box of memories. In earnest about making the marriage succeed, he was doing what he had for years dreaded: exposing his most delicate sensibilities to the mercies of another human being. After Betsey had followed the normal pattern for the wives, fianceés, and daughters of the soldiers by going home with the return of fighting weather, Hamilton expressed his tribulations in letters.

In the first of these, as indeed in every one, he expatiates on his love in perfervid terms. He then reminds his "charmer" that he had urged her to employ "all your leisure in reading." Using the gifts with which nature had endowed her, she could expand from an "amiable" woman to a "splendid" one. "You can do it if you please. . . . It will be a fund, too, to diversify our amusements and fill our moments to advantage." He adds that he hopes soon to have a rendezvous with Laurens on the boundary of Pennsylvania.[17]

Hamilton begins his next letter, "Here we are, my love, in a house of great hospitality," with "a buxom girl under the same roof . . . and everything to make a soldier happy who is not in love and absent from his mistress." It is his maxim "to enjoy the present good with the highest relish . . . but alas, my dear girl . . . my heart every now and then cries, 'you are separated from the lovely partner of your life.'"

Betsey, so wrote the man who had been all alone in the world for so long, was "perhaps suffering the keenest anxiety for the situation of her lover . . . exposed to a thousand imaginary dangers. But, my dearest, quiet your apprehensions . . . and let your thoughts run only upon those delights which our reunion will afford."[18]

The following letter, dated almost exactly two weeks later, unfolds a new aspect of the situation: Betsey has not written. Is she ill? "Sometimes my anxiety accuses you of negligence, but I chide myself whenever it does. . . . You know the tender, apprehensive, amiable nature of my love." To hear from Betsey is his "only pleasure. . . . I cannot suppose you can in so short an absence have abated your affection. . . . For God's sake, my dear Betsey, try to write oftener!" He wants her, by giving him "the picture of your heart in all its varieties of light and shade," to make clear "whether what seemed to be love was nothing more than a generous sympathy. The possibility of this frequently torments me." He ends up by stating that "a military life has now grown insupportable to me because it keeps me from all my soul holds dear. . . . Do not suffer any part of my treasure, your sweet love, to be lost or stolen from me."[19]

Eleven days later, a quick note hurried by business: he has received three letters, "the sweetest ever dictated by a fond heart." He never really suspected her "tenderness."[20]

Another week. He has just returned from taking "a solitary walk to be at leisure to think of you." She has "bewitched" him: "[you have] rendered me as restless and unsatisfied with all about me as if I was the inhabitant of another world and had nothing in common with this." He must break the spell, for he is loving her "more than I ought; more than is consistent with my peace. A new mistress is supposed to be the best cure for an excessive attachment to the old. If I was convinced of the success of the scheme, I would be tempted to try it. . . . But I am afraid I should only go in quest of disquiet that would make me return to you with redoubled tenderness."[21]

The reason for his "torment" was that there were again no letters. "When I come to Albany, I shall find means to take satisfaction for your neglect. You recollect the mode I threatened to punish you in for all your delinquencies."[22]

Late in August, Hamilton permitted himself to express a sexual vision. His Betsey's pen would, he hoped, "paint me her feelings without reserve—even those tender moments of pillowed retirement when her soul, abstracted from every other object, delivers itself up to Love and me—yet with all that delicacy which suits the purity of her mind."[23]

Betsey wrote him that she expected a visit from him "before the close of the campaign, and that you will think me unkind if I do not come. How will you," he asks, "have the presumption to think me unkind, you saucy little charmer? . . . If this campaign is to end my military service, 'tis an additional reason for a constant and punctual attendance."[24]

He had, in the ardors of his courtship, promised to resign from the army if she wished it—but, of course, he intended to control her wishes: "I will one day cure you of these refractory notions about the right of resistance . . . and teach you the great advantage and absolute necessity of implicit obedience." In any case, "I know that you have so much of the Portia in you that you will not be outdone in this line by any of your sex, and that if you saw me inclined to quit the service of your country, you would dissuade me from it. . . . It remains with you to show whether you are a *Roman* or an *American wife*." After peace had brought an end to his army service, Betsey would enjoy "more domestic happiness and less fame."

Thus thinking, as he puts it, of "times to come," Hamilton is overwhelmed by nightmare memories of his mother's resentments about his father's financial woes. The man who is marrying into one of America's very solidest fortunes, asks his bride: "Tell me, my pretty damsel, have you made up your mind upon the subject of housekeeping? Do you soberly relish the pleasure of being a poor man's wife? Have you learned to think a homespun preferable to a brocade and the rumbling of a wagon wheel to the musical rattling of a coach and six? Will you be able to see with perfect composure your old acquaintances flaunting it in gay life, tripping it along in elegance and splendor, while you hold a humble station and have no other enjoyments than the sober comforts of a good wife? Can you in short be an Aquileia* and cheerfully plant turnips with me, if fortune should so order it? If you cannot, my dear, we are playing a comedy of all in the wrong, and you should correct the mistake before we begin to act the tragedy of the unhappy couple.

"I have not concealed my circumstances from my Betsey. They are far from splendid. They may possibly be even worse than I expect, for every day brings me fresh proof of the knavery of those to whom my little affairs are entrusted. . . . An indifference to property enters into my character too much. . . . Your future life is a perfect lottery: you may move in an exalted, you may move in a very humble sphere. The last is most probable. Examine well your heart." She should not harbor the "pretty dreams" of bliss in a cottage, which are "very apt to enter into the heads of lovers when they think of a connection without the

* A member of a Roman family of great antiquity and distinction.

advantages of fortune. . . . You must apply your situation to real life."

Having written all this, he bursts out: "My heart overflows with everything for you that admiration, esteem, and love can inspire, *I would this moment give the world to be near you only to kiss your sweet hand.* . . . Let our hearts melt in prayer to be soon united, never to be separated. Adieu, loveliest of your sex."[25]

Hamilton's next letter reveals a turbulence of mind which carries him close to free association. He has received from his fiancée the text of a song which he decides to interpret as demonstrating that "by sympathy" she had anticipated his inquiries. Taking the opportunity to make fun of his "sober questions," he accepts the verses as a perfect answer.

"After all the proofs of your tenderness and readiness to share every kind of fortune with me, it is a presumptuous diffidence of your heart to propose the examination I did. . . . Be assured, my angel, it is not diffidence of my Betsey's heart, but of a *female* heart that dictated the questions. I am ready to believe everything in favor of yours; but am restrained by experience I have had of human nature, and of the softer part of it."

All but a few women were "full of weaknesses . . . 'a fair defect of nature.' . . . Though I am satisfied, whenever I trust my senses and my judgment, that you are one of the exceptions, I cannot forbear having moments when I feel a disposition to make a more perfect discovery of your temper and character. In one of those moments, I wrote the letter in question."

Having stated that, whatever he thought of women, he had a much worse opinion of his own sex, Hamilton goes on: "We have been most fortunate of late in quarters. I gave you a description of a fair one in those we had at Tappan. We have found another here: a pretty little Dutch girl of fifteen. Everybody makes love to her, and she receives everybody kindly. She grants everything that is asked, and has too much simplicity to refuse anything, but she has so much innocence to shield her, that the most determined rake would not dare take advantage." She possessed "beauty, innocence, youth, simplicity. If all her sex were like her, I would become a disciple of Mahomet. I am persuaded she has no soul; and, as I am squeamish enough to require a soul in a woman, I run no risk of being one of her captives."

Then, having—so it seems—for the moment exorcised fears which his intelligence told him were needless in relation to Betsey, he proceeds banteringly: "You see I give you an account of all the pretty females I meet with; you tell me nothing of the pretty fellows you see. . . . I suppose you will pretend there is none of them engages the least of your attention, but you know I have been told you were something of a coquette. When your sister returns home, I shall try to get her in my interest and make her tell me of all your flirtations. . . .

"Adieu, my love."[26]

The second French division never came with its military and naval reinforcements and the promised supplies for the American army. Although Washington was easing demand by leaking away again the men he had gathered to cooperate with the French, he warned in a circular letter to the states (drafted by Hamilton) that if they did not take steps to requisition food that would carry the army through the winter, "either the army must disband or, if possible worse, subsist upon the plunder of the people."[27]

At the start of September, terrible news came up from the South. General Gates, who had, after the fall of Charleston, been sent to command in South Carolina, had met at Camden a smaller but more efficient force under Cornwallis. A letter to Hamilton from a colonel in the Sixth Maryland Regiment described not only the rout of Gates's army and the flight of that general, which carried him 180 miles from the battlefield, but—even more serious—how the inhabitants had fallen on the defeated troops, stealing their possessions and even firing on the wounded. "The Tories are now assembling in different parts of the country and there is actually a sort of partisan war waged between them and the Whigs."[28]

Under the shock of the news, Hamilton wrote Betsey a letter so amorous (as can be judged from the context) that someone obliterated fourteen lines. Having stated that almost everyone was extremely upset by the "very disagreeable piece of intelligence just come from the southward," he turned to Betsey's and his own plight.

"If America were lost, we should be happy on some clime more favorable to human rights. What think you of Geneva as a retreat? 'Tis a charming place where nature and society are in their greatest perfection. I once determined to let my existence and American liberty end together. My Betsey has given me a motive to outlive my pride, I almost said my honor. But America must not be a witness to my disgrace."

Then to his fiancée he struck a more cheerful note: "As it is always well to be prepared for the worst, I talk to you in this strain, not that I think it probable we shall fail in the contest, for, notwithstanding our perplexities, I think the chances are without comparison in our favor, and that my Aquileia and I will plant our turnips in our native land."[29]

Hamilton's communication to Laurens contained no such upbeat. "I gave you in a former letter my ideas of the situation of your country and the proper remedies to her disorders. You told me, my remedies were good, but you were afraid would not go down at this time. I tell you necessity must force them down; and that if they are not speedily taken the patient will die. She is in a galloping consumption, and her case will soon become desperate. Indeed, my dear friend, to drop allegory, you can hardly conceive in how dreadful a situation we are. The army, in the course of the present month, has received only four or five days rations of meal, and we really know not of any adequate relief in future. This distress at such a stage of the campaign sours the soldiery. 'Tis in vain you make apologies to them. The officers are out of humor, and the *worst* of evils seems to be coming upon us—*a loss of our virtue*. 'Tis in vain you attempt to appease; you are almost detested as an accomplice with the administration. I am losing character, my friend, because I am not overcomplaisant to the spirit of clamor, so that I am in a fair way to be out with everybody. With one set, I am considered as a friend to military pretensions however exorbitant; with another as a man who, secured by my situation from sharing the distress of the army, am inclined to treat it lightly. The truth is I am an unlucky honest man, that speak my sentiments to all and with emphasis. I say this to you because you know it and will not charge me with vanity. I hate Congress—I hate the army—I hate the world—I hate myself. The whole is a mass of fools and knaves; I could almost except you and Meade."*[30]

Hamilton's suggestion to Betsey that they might flee to Geneva (concerning which he had undoubtedly heard much from Laurens, who had studied there) helps explain his previous letter, in which he had warned that, although a Schuyler, she might have to face poverty if she persevered in marrying him. Any doubts that in the late summer of 1780 Hamilton was actually thinking of moving on are dispelled by what was undoubtedly an involuntary use of words. In writing Laurens on June 30, he denounced the supineness of "our countrymen"; but on September 12, he denounced "your country." He wrote Betsey that he and his American Aquileia might still be able to plant "our" turnips in "her" native land.[31]

* It may be noted that he does not here mention his fiancée or her father.

293

Equally significant is his statement to Betsey that he had "once" determined "to let my existence and American liberty end together." Not so long ago he had had no firm roots in his adopted country except within the army and the cause. So complete had been his identification that promotions of officers he considered unworthy wounded "my feelings . . . more than I can express and in some degree make me contemptible in my own eyes." Weaknesses in the cause seemed to diminish his own stature, giving him "a pigmy feeling." But Hamilton's engagement had greatly expanded his base. As he put it: "My Betsey has given me a motive to outlive my pride. I almost said my honor."[32]

Was it only his own pride and his own honor that he was called on to consider when he faced the possibility of American defeat? What of the men beside whom he had fought, whose fate could not be disentangled, as the immigrant's could be, from the land where they had been nurtured and all their hopes and property lay? What of the cause, which they would consider still noble in defeat and which might rise again from the ashes? What of the battered commonwealth, which had taken Hamilton in, fostering his explosion from obscurity to distinction? Disgusted with his adopted compatriots, willing to believe that Geneva was "more favorable to human liberty," he was thinking altogether of his own feelings. When tens of thousands of citizens would also suffer from an American defeat, he felt that eyes would be particularly on him. He could not bear to have America be "a witness to my disgrace."

Was Hamilton harking back to the time when his world had been his family and its disgrace had so conspicuously been also his own disgrace?

31

The Reveries of a Projector

HOWEVER much Hamilton may have meditated on moving to Geneva or some other clime that in his bitterness he considered "more favorable to human rights," America was undoubtedly offering opportunities he could not possibly find elsewhere. His childhood catastrophes had taught him that chaos cries for the establishment of order; that failure knocks down old structures, demanding the new. Hamilton had started to structure his mother's business affairs before she died. At Cruger's warehouse, he had thrown himself into the joys of system.

Were the American cause rolling along successfully, no more would be asked of Hamilton than that he ride on the triumphant juggernaut. How greatly to his advantage that there was no such juggernaut! The United States was an infant colossus tearing away old traditions as it lumbered clumsily to its feet. The United States had everything needed to become one of the world's great powers, but in casting away the old, no firm and well-organized new structure had been created.

A builder's paradise is ground unencumbered with anything that will interfere with the purity of his vision. However much Geneva might be the home of human rights, an immigrant like Hamilton could do no more than climb up existing stairs and, near the roof, alter details. But in America!

Himself starting anew, Hamilton envisioned the American scene as more blank and more ductile than it actually was. Had he been born among the people who had already found the common identity which had made British interference seem so alien, he would have realized that much of the current confusion was less due to emptiness than to lack of opportunity to recast, in the middle of crisis, old beliefs into a new form. Yet the fact remained that nowhere else in the civilized world could Hamilton have found such a fiscal tabula rasa.

Food was not in the huge, fertile country basically in short supply, nor, where spinning wheels turned in every farmhouse, was there a lack of clothing. The problems that were sinking the war effort were problems of organization. This was not generally realized because, among the ancestral microcosms in which most Americans lived, there had never been much need for organization. Farming communities were almost completely self-sufficient. And as long as no military activity smashed into their neighborhoods from the outside, most Americans could live comfortably whether the war ended tomorrow or in ten years. It was the army that was shivering and starving, not they.

Government services of every day were best supplied locally. You did not want someone to come in from outside to tell you how to plant your fields, regulate your schools and meetinghouses. What larger problems there were had been administered time out of mind by the colonial (now state) capitals and, presiding over the capitals, the Crown. The Crown having been banished, the states were the political units to which tradition turned.

The states had set up the Continental Congress as farmers would gather together to put out a barn fire. The blaze extinguished, the farmers would go home. Admittedly, the Revolutionary fire still smoldered, but it was generally believed that, since Great Britain was now entangled globally with France and Spain, the embers would die by themselves. It was of course prudent to have an army hanging around to deal with flare-ups, but the need to support the military moved easily into the backs of minds engaged with the fall plowing.

At the time of the Declaration of Independence, Congress had drawn up an agreement, the Articles of Confederation, which would define the interrelationships of the states. Now, more than three years later, the articles had not been ratified. Indeed, the powers of Congress had been consistently shrinking.

A vast continent; settlements up and down a thousand miles of seacoast; a nation capable of being mightier than all Europe; a government to be designed; and an ambitious genius, still in the flower of youth, who was in his basic aptitudes a builder!

Hamilton's son John was to contend that long before 1780 his father was "advancing alone and unsupported towards the chief object of his life": federal union.[1] This contention has been reiterated so often and so positively by the Hamiltonians that it is enshrined in innumerable textbooks. Many Americans have been taught that Hamilton was the political father of a unified United States.

As a matter of fact, Hamilton was far from being the pioneer in trying to solve the problems of a continental nation. He was not among the first to be deeply concerned. His experiences had not permitted him to play such a role. After his arrival in America as a teen-aged youth reared in a very different environment, he had moved rapidly from schoolboy to half-cocked propagandist, to artilleryman, to aide in an endlessly busy headquarters where the need was much more to cope with dislocations than to think out the fundamental causes.

When, early in 1780, he had for the first time (as far as the records reveal) made an effort to find large and coherent solutions, he made no claim to the deep thought and long preparation which his disciples attribute to him. In his letter intended for an unidentified congressman he had explained that his ideas were based on reading and personal reflections forced to be "occasional" by "want of leisure." On second thought, he decided he was not ready and did not mail the letter.

In the fall of 1780, he was still as busy at headquarters, but a new force had come intimately into Hamilton's life: General Schuyler.

While the West Indian boy had glimpsed aristocratic ideas as a dreamlike emanation from the broken figure of his father, Schuyler had been born into as much purple as ever flourished in America. He expressed himself in such aristocratic terms that the British were never able to believe he was not secretly their partisan, a judgment with which the New England egalitarians vociferously agreed. Although a farmer, he grew on his vast estates a large surplus for export, and he had always been fascinated with the business side of enterprises. As a soldier in the French and Indian War, he had been most conspicuous as a commissary officer. Again in the Revolution, he had allowed other men to command on the front line, while he attended to what he knew and really cared about—supply. Although his approach was that of a merchant rather than that of a financier, Schuyler was "a Hamiltonian" long before Hamilton.

As we have seen, Schuyler's first letter to Hamilton passed rapidly over family acceptance of him as a son-in-law to discuss at much greater length political matters. Hamilton's correspondence with Betsey makes it clear that (even when they were separated lovers before marriage) the packets also included letters to her father that dealt with the state of the cause: Betsey might read them if she wished to know.* The two men had had much chance to talk when, in the summer of 1780, Schuyler had been at Morristown. To the conversations Hamilton brought the enthusiasm of youth, the daring of ignorance, and the fire of a much greater genius than his father-in-law possessed. Schuyler brought the results of long thinking and extensive experience, but in several ways he was a dubious mentor of a youth temperamentally given to extremes. Although no one was more of a birthright American, Schuyler had become embittered against his countrymen by personal failures which outraged his conviction that he had been born to lead. In addition, he was the most conservative leader in a state which, because of its immediate situation, gave countenance to more extreme ideas towards federal power than any other part of America.

New York had, since the beginning of 1776, been the region most directly damaged by war. Its harbor, its capital city, most of Long Island, were in enemy hands. And its northern counties were separately embattled, not only because of the forces coming down from Canada—these had ceased with Burgoyne's defeat—but by continuing Indian raids, which bloodily destroyed its settlements west of Albany. As Hamilton was to put it in 1782, the "rulers" of New York "are jealous of their own power; but yet, as this state is the immediate theater of the war their apprehensions of danger and an opinion that they are obliged to do more than their neighbors make them very willing to part with power in favor of the federal government."[2]

Hamilton was to leap into the arena without adequate warnings of the opposition that across the union he would face.

Schuyler had returned from Congress and the army camps to New York, where he was working in the state senate to further a stronger central government, when Hamilton wrote a letter that was to become famous in history. It was dated September 3, 1780, and addressed to the New York congressman Duane.

Hamilton was "agreeable to your request and my promise" to send "my ideas of the defects of our present system and the changes necessary to save us from ruin. They may, perhaps, be the reveries of a projector rather than the sober views of a politician. . . . Make what use you please of them."

Towards fighting inflation, Hamilton put forward much of what he had urged in the earlier letter that he had suppressed: a foreign loan;

---

* Many of these letters do not survive.

taxes pecuniary for businessmen and in kind for farmers; and a bank founded on both public and private credit. He criticized the bank recently founded in Philadelphia because the directors made direct use of their funds rather than using them to float notes. He urged that the loan be extorted from France by the threat that otherwise the United States would make peace with Britain. France would have to knuckle under since "her interest and honor are too deeply involved in our fate, and she can make no possible compromise."

"Without a speedy change," he wrote, "the army must dissolve. It is now a mob rather than an army, without clothing, without pay, without provision, without morals, without discipline. We begin to hate the country for its neglect of us; the country begins to hate us for our oppressions of them. Congress have long been jealous of us; we have now lost all confidence in them and give the worst construction to all they do. Held together by the slenderest ties, we are ripening for dissolution."

Hamilton denounced "the fluctuating constitution of our army," which was due to short terms of enlistment and the army's inadequate and unequally distributed supplies. Congress, he went on, should cease trying to administer through committees of their own members sometimes advised by boards. They should appoint individual executives. For the department of war, he urged the appointment of his future father-in-law; for the navy, his old friend General McDougall; for finance, Robert Morris. He wrote that having individual administrators acting under congressional direction would blend the advantages of a republic with those of "monarchy"—at the least an interesting use of that highly charged word.

But Hamilton defined as the keystone of the crisis the lack of power in Congress. In suggesting how this should be remedied, he moved not only into visionary but dangerous ground. Although the Articles of Confederaton were considered so extreme that they had not yet achieved acceptance, Hamilton denounced them as namby-pamby, "neither fit for war nor peace." The states should have no powers that extended beyond their borders and even these should be subject to national veto. Any government less completely centralized would "make our union feeble and precarious."

Hamilton's list of federal powers was a fascinating presage of his future career: "Congress should be provided with perpetual revenues" outside state control. It "should have complete sovereignty in all that relates to war, peace, trade, finance, and to the management of foreign affairs; the right of declaring war; of raising armies, officering, paying them, directing their motions in every respect; of equipping fleets and doing the same with them; of building fortifications arsenals, magazines &c. &c.; of making peace on such conditions as they think proper; of regulating trade, determining with what countries it shall be carried on, granting indulgencies; laying prohibitions on all the articles of export or import; imposing duties, granting bounties and premiums for raising, exporting, importing, and applying to their own use the product of these duties, only giving credit to the states on whom they are raised in the general account of revenues and expences; instituting Admiralty courts &c.; of coining money; establishing banks on such terms, and with such privileges as they think proper; appropriating funds and doing whatever else relates to the operations of finance; transacting everything with foreign nations; making alliances offensive and defensive, treaties of commerce, &c. &c."

Towards achieving the political revolution that would make the above possible, Hamilton envisioned two roads. One was that Congress itself should dare mightily, as it had at the beginning of the war, when it had declared independence, declared war, levied an army and a navy, printed money, made alliances with foreign powers, appointed a dictator (that is, given Washington at moments of crisis dictatorial powers), and so on.

Hamilton then harked back to a conception he had advanced in his first political pamphlet: Congress possessed tremendous latitude because its powers had never been defined. "Undefined powers are . . . limited only by the object for which they were given—in the present case, the independence and freedom of America." However, he admitted that claiming the powers now necessary would "be thought too bold an expedient by the generality of Congress."

It might thus be a better possibility to persuade Congress to "call immediately a convention of all the states" to create a new confederation. Congress would so convincingly explain "the impracticability of supporting our affairs on the present footing" that the delegates of the convention would arrive "possessed of the proper sentiments." Because of the speed with which the crisis needed to be solved, the convention would be given "plenipotentiary power" to bind the nation to whatever it decided. It would establish a "coercive union": that is, the central government could impose its decision on delinquent states by force.

Where was this force to come from? An aspect of the situation that bothered Hamilton was that "some of the lines in the army would obey their states in opposition to Congress. . . . If anything would hinder this, it would be the personal influence of the General: a melancholy and mortifying situation." Several times, as his argument evolved, Hamilton came back to the following sentiment: "It ought to be the policy of Congress to destroy all ideas of state attachments in the army and make it look up wholly to them."

A strong way to bind the allegiance of the officers was for the central government to take responsibility for paying, as they had asked, pensions on retirement of half pay for life. Hamilton pointed out that postwar costs would be reduced because many officers would stay on in the service. "We shall find it indispensable after the war to keep on foot a considerable body of troops. . . . For to me it is an axiom that in our constitution an army is essential to our union." Its presence would enable Congress "to maintain an air of authority (not domineering) in all their measures with the states."[3]

Great claims are made by the Hamiltonians for this letter, even to the extent of asserting that it was the very foundation on which the American government was erected.[4] It is, indeed, most impressive when taken in its context: the work of a very young man, done in his spare time when he was the chief of staff of an army, prophetic of many reforms he was later to espouse more powerfully, some of which he was actually to achieve. Yet it is easy to claim too much.

It is, for instance, stated that here was the first recommendation of a separate constitutional convention. Actually, the suggestion had been made, even before the Declaration of Independence, in the most widely read of all Revolutionary pamphlets, Thomas Paine's *Common Sense*. Since then, the idea had remained in currency, although its realization was considered impractical when even the Articles of Confederation could not be got through the states.

Denunciations of the fluctuating nature of the army had been coming out of headquarters since before Hamilton had found a place there. The need for executives to supplant the incompetent congressional committees had long been recognized, and no one who saw the army in day-by-day action could doubt the ill effects of its inadequate and unequal supplies. And the need to strengthen Congress was not only very much in the air but the subject of active agitation.

Six days before the date of Hamilton's communication to Duane, he had drafted for Washington a letter to the influential Bostonian James Bowdoin, expressing approval of the resolutions adopted by a convention of four New England states. These urged that the central government be established on a permanent basis, thereby making it "competent" to determine all matters of continental concern.

The report of this convention had been seized on with alacrity by the New York legislature. While Hamilton was composing his letter, Schuyler was arguing before that body the need for a "supreme and coercive" central power.[5]

Despite all its detail in other directions, Hamilton's letter to Duane does not concern itself with how the puissant government he recommended, strengthened with so many new powers, was to be structured. He gives no indication that his thinking had gone beyond the conception, which he had expressed years before in relation to the New York State constitution, that the best governing body would be a unicameral legislature which appointed and controlled its executive officers. There is here no glimmer of the checks and balances that were to be a feature of the eventual federal Constitution, none of the demand for a strong executive, which Hamilton was later to make his hallmark.

Nor did Hamilton have any viable ideas on how his revolutionary plans were to be made palatable to the public. He merely recommended that Congress announce the necessity, and that powerful pamphleteers—his hand surely itched for his pen—present the arguments. John C. Miller sees an admirable prophecy of *The Federalist*, but that publication was written many years later, when the times had moved far in the necessary direction, after the Constitutional Convention had met rather than in recommendation for such a convention, and in defense of a document, thrashed out by major leaders, which did not contain the most frightening features of his 1780 proposal.

Hamilton wished the states, and through the states the people, to agree that whatever his constitutional convention decided on would become, without further vote or consultation, the law of the land. The law was to mandate a restriction of states' rights even greater than exists today after two hundred years of drift towards centralization.

Hamilton had got into trouble with a rumor, which he had passionately denied, that he had urged military intervention in civil affairs by having the army drive Congress out of doors. Now he proposed as "a solid basis of [central] authority" a standing army purposefully separated from all attachments to the state governments, which most Americans regarded as the palladia of their liberty.

Hamilton duly sent the letter to Duane. The congressman replied that Hamilton's suggestions were utterly impractical.[6]

Duane, indeed, could not with safety have shown the documents to anyone except a very few extremists. Had Hamilton's letter by some mischance fallen into the hands of the British, who would have gleefully published it, that would have been a disaster for the American cause. Washington would, of course, have discharged Hamilton out of hand, but this required act would hardly have saved the situation. A conspicuous figure at headquarters, engaged to the daughter of a major conservative leader, an intimate aide of Washington's, had spelled out a plan for action that was an embodiment of the very worst nightmare of those who trembled lest any accretion of strength to the Congress or the army command might be used to subvert American liberties. Americans did not need to be familiar, as many were, with the histories of ancient tyrannies to smell a plot to extinguish the thirteen existing democratic governments under military rule. Hamilton had completely misunderstood the environment in which he found himself. Had his ideas become public, they would have had exactly the opposite effect to what he desired, encouraging a weakening of Congress and the army to the ultimate point commensurate with holding off an immediate return to British rule.

32

Extreme Emotions

[SEPTEMBER, 1780   AGE 23]

AMERICAN hopes had come to depend more and more on the French. Only the French could supply the naval superiority necessary for an effective attack on the British harbor and bastion of New York, or for an effective defense of the South, where the British could strike suddenly from ships anywhere along the coast. Furthermore, in the bankruptcy of the American economy, French supplies, French loans, were desperately required.

Hamilton drafted for Washington an abject appeal to the Count de Guichen, the French commander in the West Indies, painting France's American ally as being on the verge of defeat by France's enemy, and begging that enough ships be sent into North American waters to give an "unequivocal naval superiority." But on September 16, 1780, Hamilton wrote Laurens, "The stars fight against us, my friend." Instead of Guichen, the British admiral Rodney had sailed into the local waters.[1]

Since Rochambeau's arrival many months before, Washington had avoided a face-to-face meeting, perhaps because he did not wish to be cross-questioned on American strength. But he had, in the first excitement, sent word that he would soon have fourteen thousand Continental troops and six thousand militia, with, shortly after, four to six thousand more. When, in the fall of 1780, he wished finally to confer with his ally, this unachieved promise loomed darkly.

In a memorandum for his general, Hamilton dilated on the "great importance" of making out that it was not the Americans but the

French who had been unready to act. Should Washington fail "to keep out of sight disappointments . . . it will be argued either that we wished to deceive or that we did not understand our true resources. The former would be a reflection on our honesty, the latter upon our judgment." Partly by counting state troops serving in their own regions as if they had been regulars in the Continental Army, he raised that force to thirteen thousand, without including reinforcements who were too obviously militia. This was "as near truth as rigid good faith requires."[2]

Whether or not he accepted this expedient, Washington, accompanied by Hamilton and other aides, finally met in late September with the French command at Hartford, Connecticut. He was now willing to admit that he had no idea how many troops he would have in the next fighting season. But he did have a plan to sell. The fleet which had arrived with Rochambeau, being outclassed by the British fleet, had never weighed anchor from Newport Harbor. And Rochambeau had insisted that his army had to stay there to protect the fleet. Washington wished the fleet to sail to Boston Harbor, where it would be protected by strong Massachusetts forces. Then, Rochambeau would be free to march for the Hudson and encamp next to Washington. This would, by increasing the pressure on New York City, reduce the ability of the British to send more detachments south.

Rochambeau replied that he did not trust the people of Boston, whose customs were so different from the French, and that, in any case, he had been ordered by his king to keep his army, until actual battle portended, by themselves on an island. So much for Washington's titular command of the French forces![3]

On the way back from Hartford, Washington intended to inspect America's greatest fortification, West Point, that all-important defense of the Hudson River, upper New York, and the back door to New England. The commandant of West Point was Benedict Arnold, and Washington's whole party intended to spend the night with General Arnold and his much-younger wife.

Washington was looking forward keenly to the visit, since he had the greatest respect for Arnold, who had been, until he was seriously wounded, the greatest combat general on either side. Furthermore, the Commander in Chief enjoyed flirting, in a ritualistic manner, with the pretty Peggy Arnold, who was an expert at this diversion. To Hamilton, the visit could only have been a matter of indifference. He liked pretty women, but had been too busy on army chores, during his

Left: The traitoress: Peggy Shippen Arnold, who fooled everyone, including Washington, into believing she was innocent. Depicted at a happier time by John André. Courtesy, Yale University Art Gallery.

Below: The victim: Major John André. Although an adjutant general in the British army, he could not escape being hanged as a spy. Miniature by an unidentified hand. Courtesy, James André

season with Washington at Philadelphia, to have had any particular contact with Peggy's high-flying set. He was, of course, familiar with Arnold, who had often been at headquarters, but the fighter did not combine, as did Laurens, any intellectual qualities with his physical prowess. Instead of engaging in interesting argument, he shouted and pounded on the table. Hamilton was willing, in his hatred for Gates, to credit Arnold with the victory at Saratoga, but when Arnold's aide, Major David S. Franks, had wished to leave that general's rough service, Hamilton had tried to find him a place with his own friend, Steuben.[4]

When traveling, Washington rode for several hours before breakfast. On September 15, he inspected some redoubts on his way to the Arnolds'. Lafayette finally complained that Mrs. Arnold was holding the meal for them. "Ah," said Washington, "I know that you young men are all in love with Mrs. Arnold. . . . You may go and take your breakfast with her, and tell her not to wait for me."[5] Most of the party decided to stay with His Excellency, while Majors Shaw and McHenry rode ahead.

The bright autumn day was far advanced when Washington's little cavalcade rode up to the wooden mansion, on a bluff above the river, that was Arnold's headquarters. Hamilton was undoubtedly surprised to see standing in the door not Arnold but Franks. The young man was foppishly dressed as always, but seemed infused with embarrassment. He reported that his general had set out for West Point to prepare a reception for His Excellency, and Mrs. Arnold had not yet come down from her room.

The explanation concerning Arnold was satisfactory, but it seemed strange that Peggy should not have arisen to receive her guests. However, breakfast was soon on the table. The meal completed, most of the party embarked in small boats for West Point. Hamilton was left behind to handle any dispatches that might come in during Washington's absence.[6]

As the maples around the house flamed with autumn, all was somnolent until feminine shrieks sounded overhead. Arnold's two aides hurried upstairs; there was a sound of doors shutting, and then all was quiet again.[7] Hamilton's curiosity was certainly aroused. As dinner time—three in the afternoon—approached, he was told that Mrs. Arnold was too indisposed to leave her bed. A messenger rode in from close to the British lines with a dispatch addressed to Washington. Since the thickness of the package suggested routine returns,

Hamilton decided not to open it. He had started a letter to Betsey when he heard boats landing and voices speaking. Washington's party was back from West Point. Hamilton had expected to see Arnold among them, but he was not there. When informed that Peggy was still in her room, Washington expressed disappointment.

His Excellency's bedroom was on the ground floor. After he had gone there to freshen up for dinner, Hamilton handed him the packet that had arrived during his absence. A minute or two later, Hamilton came dashing out of the room. He burst into Lafayette's bedroom and cried that the Marquis should attend on His Excellency. The two men ran back. They found Washington standing in the middle of the floor, his hands trembling, tears in his eyes. "Arnold has betrayed us! . . . Whom can we trust now?"

Washington was too overwhelmed to do anything but stand there. Hamilton and Lafayette took possession of the dispatches and hurried through them to ascertain what had happened.[8]

A horseman had been stopped on his way to the British lines, and his captors had discovered in his shoes papers in Arnold's handwriting that revealed a treasonous attempt to deliver West Point to the enemy. Another document, which proved to be a carefully composed letter from the captive, revealed that he was an amazingly high British officer: Major John André, the adjutant general of the British army.

The aides who had gone ahead for breakfast were summoned. They reported that, as they sat with Arnold at the table, he had received a dispatch that visibly upset him. He had rushed upstairs, probably to talk to his wife; had come charging downstairs again; had shouted over his shoulder that he was on his way to West Point to prepare a suitable reception; had galloped to the river; and departed in his barge.[9]

Washington then swore everyone to secrecy. In his anguish, he concluded that his first duty was to capture Arnold. Perhaps the traitor had not really been alerted and was somewhere within the American lines! Hamilton and McHenry were ordered to secure the fastest available horses and gallop to the American fortifications at King's Ferry with orders that Arnold's barge should not be allowed through into British-controlled waters.

Hamilton, who was not as confused by emotion as Washington, must have realized that he had been sent on a fool's errand. The dispatch Arnold had received had clearly been a warning—and there had been plenty of time for him to make good his escape. But Hamilton nonetheless used his spurs to keep his horse at maximum speed; he felt engaged on a much more important errand than the one entrusted to him. Every time the road swung from the woods to the banks of the Hudson, the ripples on the water, the feel of the air on his face, revealed that the wind was blowing strongly upriver. It was the perfect wind to speed British warships to West Point. And there had been no time to investigate the extent of the plot. It seemed improbable that Arnold had acted as a solitary individual. Had various commanders at West Point also been corrupted? The officers on the American lines had all been placed there by Arnold. What was their loyalty? Would they oppose or even report British movements? And what reason was there to believe that the enemy officer who had been apprehended was the only messenger? Others might have got through the lines to report that the trap was set to be sprung.

Alerting the forts on both banks at King's Ferry would help, but they could not by themselves stop a determined British thrust. The main army, under the present command of Greene, was in New Jersey, and the quickest road to their encampment started at King's Ferry.

Hamilton and McHenry appeared at a rush alongside the redoubt on the eastern shore of the Ferry. They were informed that Arnold had passed by in his barge so long before that there had been time for him to send back from the British warship anchored downriver letters addressed to His Excellency and to Peggy.

Hamilton claimed a pen and paper and hurriedly wrote Greene: "There has just been unfolded at this place a scene of the blackest treason. Arnold has fled to the enemy. André the British Adjt. Genl. is in our possession as a spy. This capture unraveled the mystery. West Point was to have been the sacrifice. All the dispositions have been made for the purpose and 'tis possible, though not probable tonight may see the execution. The wind is fair. I came here in pursuit of Arnold but was too late. I advise your putting the army under marching orders, and detaching a brigade immediately this way."[10]

Hamilton decided himself to find the Sixth Connecticut Regiment, which he knew was somewhere near King's Ferry, and order them to reinforce West Point. In the meantime, he sent to Washington a packet in which he included Arnold's two letters and a report on what he had done: "I hope Your Excellency will approve these steps, as there may be no time to be lost."[11]

During the night, Hamilton returned to his commander. Peggy had come alive, dominating the house with passionate hysterics. The young aide became so emotionally involved with the plight of the beautiful young woman that, when he wrote his own fiancée, his feelings obliterated the distinction between what had taken place during his absence (such as Washington's confrontation with Peggy) and what he had himself experienced.

He had, he stated, hardly been able to regret that Arnold had escaped when "I saw an amiable woman frantic with distress for the loss of a husband she tenderly loved—a traitor to his country and to his fame, a disgrace to his connections. It was the most affecting scene I ever was witness to. She for a considerable time entirely lost her senses. The General went up to see her and she upbraided him with being in a plot to murder her child. One moment she raved; another she melted into tears; sometimes she pressed her infant to her bosom and lamented its fate occasioned by the imprudence of its father in a manner that would have pierced insensibility itself. All the sweetness of beauty, all the loveliness of innocence, all the tenderness of a wife and the fondness of a mother showed themselves in her appearance and conduct. We have every reason to believe she was entirely unacquainted with the plan and that her first knowledge of it was when Arnold went to tell her he must banish himself from his country and from her forever. She instantly fell into a convulsion and he left her in that situation.

"This morning she is more composed. I paid her a visit and endeavored to soothe her by every method in my power, though you may imagine she is not easily to be consoled. Added to her other distresses, she is very apprehensive the resentment of her country will fall upon her (who is only unfortunate) for the guilt of her husband. I have tried to persuade her, her apprehensions are ill founded; but she has too many proofs of the illiberality of the state to which she belongs [Pennsylvania] to be convinced. She received us in bed, with every circumstance that could interest our sympathy. Her sufferings were so eloquent that I wished myself her brother, to have a right to become her defender. As it is, I have entreated her to enable me to give her proofs of my friendship."

Hamilton went on, as he was wont to do when he exposed his fiancée to his admiration for other women, to attribute his susceptibility to his love for her, since it showed his admiration for the sex she so charmingly represented. It is interesting to note that his realization that Peggy consciously used her sexual charms—"she received us in bed," and so on—to incite male sympathy increased his admiration and sympathy for the imperiled charmer. It did not make him suspect what was the truth: Although she successfully bamboozled the

officers from Washington down, Peggy had been as deep in the treason as her husband.[12]

Having decided to write an account of the entire affair for the press,
Hamilton couched it (as with the hurricane letter and his father) as a
letter to Laurens. (Betsey received a copy.) His long narrative went
further, than anything he had yet written, to establish him in many
minds as what he had originally wished to be: a writer.[13]

Following the official propaganda line, Hamilton compared Arnold's
discouraging infamy with the heart-warming nobility of "the three
simple peasants" who, "leaning only on their virtue and honest sense of
duty," had staunchly refused bribes as they carried through the capture of André, thus frustrating the treason. "While Arnold," Hamilton
exclaimed, "is handed down with execration to future times, posterity
will repeat with reverence the names of Van Wart, Paulding, and
Williams!" The danger the cause had suffered should be forgotten in
gratitude for the "happy escape." Other propagandists attributed this
escape to the intervention of God on the side of America but Hamilton, who had left his religious phase behind him, preferred to credit
"the value of an honest man."[14]

Most interesting to students of Hamilton's character was what he
wrote about André. The British adjutant general, who was only seven
years older than Hamilton, had been brought to Washington's headquarters at Tappan, New York. There, although kept under guard in a
tavern, he held court for the American officers. Hamilton wrote: "To
an excellent understanding well improved by education and travel, he
united a peculiar elegance of mind and manners, and the advantage of
a pleasing person. 'Tis said he possessed a pretty taste for the fine arts,
and had himself attained some proficiency in poetry, music, and painting. His knowledge appeared without ostentation, and embellished by
a diffidence that rarely accompanies so many talents and accomplishments, which left you to suppose more than appeared. His sentiments
were elevated and inspired esteem. They had a softness that con-
ciliated affection. His elocution was handsome; his address easy, polite
and insinuating. By his merit he had acquired the unlimited confidence
of his general and was making a rapid progress in military rank and
reputation. But in the height of his career, flushed with new hope from
the execution of a project the most beneficial to his party, that could be
devised, he was at once precipitated from the summit of prosperity
and saw all the expectations of his ambition blasted and himself
ruined."[15]

André's predicament was made, for the admiring and mourning American officers, much more poignant because it was painfully beneath his social position and his military rank. Fine gentlemen and high officers did not serve as spies: that was left to desperate men of the lower orders.

According to André's own account of what had happened (which Hamilton devoutly believed), his plight was due to the deceit of the villain Arnold. In strict accordance with the rules of war, André had come ashore from a British warship, in uniform, to meet Arnold at a neutral place between the lines. But the dastardly Arnold had lured him without his agreement or even knowledge, behind the American lines.* He was thus forced to behave in the manner of a spy by substituting civilian clothes for his uniform and, in order to get back to his own lines, carrying a pass made out to an assumed name.

In telling this story to the court-martial Washington had appointed to determine his fate, André made no further defense, admitting all the facts presented by the various witnesses. But, since he had been captured using an alias, in disguise, and trying to carry through the lines treasonous documents, there was only one possible verdict—guilty—and one possible punishment—death. "The members of the court," Hamilton wrote in his semiofficial account, "were not more impressed with the candor and firmness mixed with a becoming sensibility which he displayed than he was penetrated with their liberality and politeness." (It was a lachrymose occasion.)

In describing André's behavior after he knew of his doom, Hamilton wrote, "In one of the visits I made to him (and I saw him several times during his confinement) he begged me" to get Washington's permission for his sending a letter to his own general, who was also his loving patron, Sir Henry Clinton. " 'I foresee my fate [said he] and though I pretend not to play the hero, or to be indifferent about my life, yet I am reconciled to whatever may happen, conscious that misfortune, not guilt, has brought it upon me. There is only one thing that disturbs my tranquillity—Sir Henry Clinton has been too good to me; he has been lavish of his kindness. I am bound to him by too many obligations and love him too well to bear the thought, that he should reproach himself, or that others should reproach him on the supposition of my having conceived myself obliged by his instructions to run the risk I did. I would not for the world leave a sting in his mind, that should embitter his future days.' He could scarce finish the sentence, bursting into

---

* This was not the case. André had from the first been ready, should that prove necessary for the accomplishment of his mission, to go behind the American lines.

tears, in spite of his efforts to suppress them; and with difficulty collected himself enough afterwards to add, 'I wish to be permitted to
assure him, I did not act under this impression, but submitted to a
necessity imposed upon me as contrary to my own inclination as to his
orders.' His request was readily complied with."[16]

Did Hamilton, as he continued his public account addressed to
Laurens, remember that once, in a private letter, he had written the
same friend that he had no other wish than to make from the world "as
soon as possible a brilliant exit"? André was, like Hamilton, remarkably young for the staff post and position of trust he held with his
general; he could be considered Hamilton's vis-à-vis in the British
army. And André, as he faced certain doom with a fortitude and
elegance that kept many American officers (including Washington)
close to tears, was about to make from the world an exit of astounding
brilliance. But there lay in his path one disgusting obstacle. By military
law, spies were hanged. But kicking from a rope until dead was an
ignominious road to death reserved for ordinary offenders. Gentlemen
were shot.

André wrote Washington: "Sympathy towards a soldier will surely
induce Your Excellency and the military tribunal to adapt the mode of
my death to the feelings of a man of honor. Let me hope, sir, that if
aught in my character impressed you with esteem towards me, if aught
in my misfortunes marks me as the victim of policy not resentment, I
shall experience the operation of these feelings in your breast by being
informed that I am not to die on the gibbet."[17]

Most reluctantly, Washington concluded that not to execute André
in the manner established for a spy would play into the hands of the
British propaganda machine, which was howling that he had never
behaved as a spy and was about to be unjustly murdered. Hamilton
argued angrily with his general and commented, after failing, "Some
people are only sensible to motives of policy, and sometimes, from a
narrow disposition, mistake it!"[18]

The conviction that, while André was noble, Arnold was despicable
engendered a wild hope that perhaps it could be Arnold who would be
hanged. Since Sir Henry Clinton deeply loved his adjutant general,
perhaps he would save his favorite by enabling the Americans to get
their hands on the traitor. If only André could be induced to strike his
patron's emotions by himself making the suggestion. "It was proposed
to me," Hamilton confided to Betsey, "to suggest to him the idea."
Hamilton indignantly refused. "As a man of honor he could not but
reject it." Hamilton would insult him by suggesting it and thus forfeit

his esteem. "I confess to you," Hamilton continued strangely, "I had the weakness to value the esteem of a *dying* man."[19]

But there were other ways to tempt Clinton. When an august delegation from New York came under a flag of truce to persuade the Americans of André's innocence, a British aide was conscious, as he walked to one side with Hamilton, that something was being slipped into his pocket. It proved to be a note, written in an obviously disguised hand and signed "A.B.," which stated there was "great reason to believe" that Arnold had mediated "a double treachery" and had sacrificed André in order to achieve his own safety. If Arnold were "delivered up," it would be possible for Washington to pardon André.[20]

Clinton believed that the missive had come from Washington's aide-de-camp Hamilton; and, indeed, the signature on the letter, "A.B.," was later to be used, although in a very different context, by Hamilton.[21] The British commander would have been ecstatic to comply, but could not give up Arnold without destroying the British effort to deplete the rebel cause by winning over waverers. No way was found to save André. To spare the victim's feelings, he was kept in ignorance of his mode of death. "In going to the place of execution," so Hamilton's formal account reported, "he bowed familiarly as he went along to all those with whom he had been acquainted in his confinement. A smile of complacency expressed the serene fortitude of his mind. Arrived at the fatal spot, he asked with some emotion, *Must* I then die in this manner? He was told it had been unavoidable. 'I am reconciled to my fate [said he] but not to the mode.' Soon, however, re-collecting himself, he added, 'It will be but a momentary pang,' and springing upon the cart performed the last offices to himself with a composure that excited the admiration and melted the hearts of the beholders. Upon being told the final moment was at hand, and asked if he had anything to say, he answered: 'Nothing, but to request you will witness to the world, that I die like a brave man.' Among the extraordinary circumstances that attended him, in the midst of his enemies, he died universally esteemed and universally regretted."[22]

On the day of the execution, Hamilton wrote Betsey: "I wished myself possessed of André's accomplishments for your sake. . . . I am mortified that I do not unite in myself every valuable and agreeable qualification. I do not, my love, affect modesty. I am conscious of the advantages I possess. I know I have talents and a good heart: but why am I not handsome? Why have I not every acquirement that can embellish human nature? Why have I not fortune that I might hereafter have more leisure than I shall have to cultivate those improvements for which I am not entirely unfit?"[23]

33

Dissatisfactions and Marriage

[OCTOBER–DECEMBER, 1780   AGE 23]

IN the middle of October, 1780, Hamilton wrote Betsey, "A few weeks more and you are mine." He had, he stated, a "restless propensity of my mind, which will not allow me to be happy when I am not doing something in which you are concerned. This may seem a very idle disposition in a philosopher and a soldier; but I can plead illustrious examples in my justification. Achilles had liked to have sacrificed Greece and his glory to his passion for a female captive; and Anthony lost the world for a woman." He went on in this vein for more than a page, and then noted, "I stopped to read over my letter. It is a motley mixture of fond extravagance and sprightly dullness. The truth is I am too much in love to be either reasonable or witty; . . . when I attempt to speak my feelings, I rave. I have remarked to you before that real tenderness has always a tincture of sadness, and when I affect the lively, my melting heart rebels. . . . Love is a sort of insanity and everything I write savors strongly of it."[1]

He felt he was on the very verge of marriage. But two weeks later headquarters business still held him—it was "one month more." From his exile in Pennsylvania, Laurens was urging him to hurry to the altar so that he would get over his obsession with "Schuyler's black eyes." Hamilton laughed that his was "a strange cure by the way, as if after matrimony I was to be less devoted than I am now!" He intended to restore the empire of Hymen with Cupid as prime minister, "but I have still a part for the public and another for you." He was teaching his Betsey to love Laurens.[2]

However, in Laurens's absence Lafayette had become Hamilton's closest companion. To Hamilton the Marquis wrote, "Before this campaign, I was your friend and very intimate friend agreeable to the ideas of the world." Since he had returned from his visit to France, "my sentiment has increased to such a point the world knows nothing about."[3]

This statement, when considered with Hamilton's passionate effusions to Laurens, raises questions concerning homosexuality. They cannot be categorically answered. Surely physical attraction or repulsion enters, under the most normal circumstances, into one man's reaction to another. Hamilton and his fellow aides routinely sent each other their love; indeed, they often sent their love wholesale to the entire headquarters Family. What considerations carry an emotional relationship between members of the same sex over the edge? If the answer is, as the twentieth century seems to assume, a purely physical one, it can only be said that the essential data are lacking in relation to Hamilton and Laurens and Lafayette. Certainly no one at the time sensed anything to whisper about, but then in the eighteenth century homosexuality had by no means become the active issue that it is today.

We do know that Hamilton poured into Lafayette's sympathetic ears his growing frustrations at being forever held to what he considered menial services as Washington's desk-bound aide. A year had passed since Washington had, when refusing to let him join Laurens in the southern fighting, promised Hamilton that in due course he would "be glad to furnish me with an occasion."[4] That was a year ago, and, so Hamilton complained bitterly, nothing had happened. Lafayette expressed eagerness to furnish Hamilton with an occasion.

Despite the efforts of Hamilton and other publicists to concentrate attention on the patriotism of André's captors, the defection of the great warrior Arnold had been a blow to public confidence. And the fighting season that was now coming to an end had presented patriots with nothing that signaled any progress in ending what seemed an interminable war. If only, before the snow fell, the Continental Army could achieve some effective stroke!

The British base in New York could not be seriously attacked without a cooperating fleet. However, two edges could be reached by rowboats: Staten Island was separated from New Jersey only by a narrow channel; and on the other extremity, the northern tip of Manhattan (Kingsbridge) was separated from the New York mainland only by the narrow Harlem River. Washington contemplated attacks on both points. Since Kingsbridge was much closer to the center of the British position, an operation there would be much the more dramatic, but the fortifications at Staten Island were less strong and easier for the Americans to get to.

When Washington decided to begin with a raid on Staten Island, he turned to the light infantry. This elite corps had been founded to move quickly, skirmish, and undertake special missions, when Washington had decided that the riflemen from the frontier were too insubordinate to be relied on. The commander of the light infantry was Major General Lafayette, who had so quickly learned from Washington that he was now a competent general. Since the troops were detachments from various regiments, the light infantry could be considered less subject than the state lines to rigid progressions of rank and seniority.[5]

The Marquis and Hamilton put their heads together. One of the light-infantry brigades lacked a brigadier general, and they decided that Hamilton could fill the gap. Surely giving this disproportionate command to a lieutenant colonel and also switching him from a staff post to the line could be justified on the grounds that it created no precedent: the opening was both temporary and "accidental"! But Washington would have to be convinced.[6]

Lafayette set off to persuade his close friend and patron. He returned with a dark face. The General had refused on two grounds. However temporary and accidental, giving such an opportunity for glory to an aide and a lieutenant colonel would create dissatisfaction among all the officers who served regularly in the line. And with his staff as depleted as it was, Washington could not afford to let Hamilton take personal risks.[7]

This was surely one of the occasions on which Hamilton blasted at Washington so vehemently that Lafayette felt called on to dilate concerning "the General's friendship and gratitude for you." They were "greater than you perhaps imagine. I am sure he needs only to be told that something will suit you, and when he thinks he can do it, he certainly will."[8]

Although debarred, Hamilton preserved his passionate concern with Lafayette's raid. When it had to be canceled because Quartermaster General Pickering failed to procure the necessary wagons, Hamilton sent a series of insulting orders to the man who, as Secretary of State under President Adams, was to be his most valuable sycophant.[9]

Far from being discouraged, Lafayette and Hamilton replanned the Staten Island expedition on a much larger scale: twelve hundred men and forty boats. However, the lieutenant colonel's role was to be reduced to make it more palatable to Washington. His command was to be only two hundred men, but Lafayette, we may be sure, promised to give them a conspicuous assignment. The two projectors decided that they should begin by getting Washington's approval of the entire operation. Then they would "carry," as Lafayette put it, "your private affair."

Since Lafayette would be away from headquarters, Hamilton would secure the major permission from Washington in conversation. That done, he would present his personal appeal in the form of a letter. "Show me your letter," Lafayette wrote, "before you give it."[10]

Hamilton's report was that Washington vetoed the whole scheme. His Excellency had decided to put his total resources behind an attack on Kingsbridge. Hamilton correspondingly shifted his own ground, writing Washington a plea for a command in the new expedition:

"Sometime last fall when I spoke to your Excellency about going to the southward, I explained to you candidly my feelings with respect to military reputation, and how much it is my object to act a conspicuous part in some enterprise that might perhaps raise my character as a soldier above mediocrity." Washington had promised to cooperate and "the project you have in contemplation affords an occasion." Supposing Hamilton were killed or wounded? Harrison was on his way back to headquarters, and there would soon be less business since the army would settle down in winter quarters. In any case, Hamilton would soon be gone to get married.

Now he asked for a command "proportioned to my rank": one hundred fifty to two hundred men. To avoid the complaints that would arise if his men came altogether from Lafayette's light infantry, they should be gathered from various corps.

"The primary idea may be to attempt with my detachment Byard's Hill,* should we arrive early enough to undertake it. I should prefer this to anything else, both for the brilliancy of the attempt in itself and the decisive consequence of which its success would be productive. If we arrive too late to make this eligible (as there is reason to apprehend) my corps may form the van of one of the other attacks; and Byard's Hill may be a pretext for my being employed in the affair, on a supposition of my knowing the ground, which is partly true. I flatter myself also that my military character stands so high as to reconcile the officers in general to the measure.

---

* Byard's Hill has not been identified. It clearly could not have been the same as Bayard's Hill, the fortification miles below Kingsbridge at the northern edge of the actual city, through which Hamilton had passed during his retreat from the Kip's Bay Affair.

"I take this method of making the request to avoid the embarrassment of a personal explanation; I shall only add that however much I have the matter at heart, I wish Your Excellency entirely to consult your own inclination." Hamilton urged his general to do nothing "that may be disagreeable to you. . . . It will nonetheless make me singularly happy if your wishes correspond with mine."[11]

This is one of those letters, characteristic of Hamilton, which seem rational on the surface, but if dug into reveal ideas far from rational.

Hamilton's request resembles those visions of glory that arise in the mind between sleep and waking, more closely linked to hallucination than reality. The method Hamilton suggests of gathering his troops from various regiments could remove his corps from attachment to any chain of command. As the rest of the letter implies, he wished to operate on his own, with no officer between him and the top commander of the expedition. This had been the original organization of his artillery company, but then he had been an inconspicuous part of a large and widely-spread-out whole. Now he sees himself operating as he pleases with a picked force of men around the very front of a major operation. "If circumstances permit," he will carry through the brilliant and conspicuous exploit of storming a hill, the capture of which would be decisive in the success of the entire venture. Should this not be "eligible," he will shift to the head of another command, where he will usurp the van and harvest for himself the laurels of leading the attack.

In the view of the aide who had not previously distinguished himself in combat, his "military character stands so high" that the Continental Army will be happy to watch him thus move like an ancient hero, Achilles or David, in front of them in the face of the enemy. If Washington fails to approve, it will merely be because of his personal "inclination," his reluctance to agree to what is "disagreeable to you."

Two days after Hamilton delivered this letter to Washington, the Kingsbridge expedition had to be called off for strategic reasons.[12] From a historical point of view, this can be taken as neutralizing the issues raised in Hamilton's impossible request. But not from the biographical. If Washington actually refused the request, it must have been face to face, since no letter remains in the file of either man. More probably His Excellency, who was not given to crossing bridges before he came to them, allowed the matter to lapse with the expedition itself. Hamilton, who saw Washington many times every day, was not given to patience, and for a man whose desires are all aflame, two days' wait is an age.

When a new opportunity arose, Hamilton was too dispirited to reach for it.

Because of the resignation of Colonel Alexander Scammell, the post of adjutant general had become vacant. The man selected to fill it would handle on a larger scale and much more on his own authority matters of army organization which Hamilton had often dealt with as Washington's deputy. The post was, with that of quartermaster general (who dealt with supplies) one of the two top staff commands. Washington discussed with Hamilton who should be appointed, and Hamilton suggested Brigadier General Edward Hand.[13]

When Lafayette intervened, offering to impress on Washington what he considered Hamilton's overpowering claims, the dissatisfied aide revealed passionate eagerness. However, although Lafayette wished to march right in and talk with Washington, Hamilton persuaded his friend to write a letter. The aide was clearing up matters at headquarters so that he could ride off to Albany to get married. Probably he did not wish to set out chewing the bitterness of another refusal.

Before Hamilton actually took to horse, Lafayette wrote him that he had sent a letter urging Washington to "cast your eye on a man who I think would suit better than any other in the world: Hamilton. Then I go on with the idea that, at equal advantages, you deserve from him the preference, that your advantages are the greatest . . . and conclude that on every public and private account I advise him to take you."[14]

Lafayette's letter to Washington (which, of course, Hamilton did not see) states that Hamilton's "knowledge of your opinions and intentions on military arrangements, his love of discipline"; the advantage his knowledge of French would give him "when both armies will operate together; and his uncommon abilities will render him perfectly agreeable to you." His usefulness would be increased "and on other points he would render the same services." An adjutant general ought always to be with the commander in chief. Hamilton would therefore "remain in your family, and his great industry for business" would enable him to do his old tasks as well as his new.[15]

General Greene, on his way to replacing Gates in the southern command, also wrote Washington. Before leaving the Continental Army, Greene had ascertained that Hamilton would receive the appointment "with great gratitude. . . . It is his wish." Significantly, Greene like Lafayette felt that Washington's desire not to lose Hamilton's usefulness to his own staff presented a major stumbling block. Greene assured His Excellency that Hamilton could still serve importantly "in your family business 'if he employs [in the adjutant general's office] an extraordinary deputy."[16]

Bearing hopes of escaping, as adjutant general, from his personal service to Washington, Hamilton set out at the very end of November, 1780, in a direction that was an integral part of the life of almost every officer but that had previously not existed for him. During his four and a half years in the army, his three and a half years with Washington, he had never gone off on leave—there was no place to go. Now he was riding towards something he had not known since he was a little boy: a domestic home. True, it was a home he had never seen, but it would be his by right in a few days. And a woman was awaiting him who was eager to dedicate her life to his. The son of a mother who had betrayed him had never known such a woman. Was it all a mirage, or did such a woman exist? He could only hope—or, if he dared, trust.

As he approached, he saw the Schuyler mansion standing on "a handsome piece of table land" above the Hudson River and the city of Albany. The basement that peeped up from the ground and the dormer windows that peeped from the mansard roof made it four stories high; there was an elegant railing all around the house where the roof started; the facade was broad—a full sixty feet. A wing extended from the northwest angle; there was a commodious barn "of excellent framework." Hamilton, who had no particular eye for architecture, was probably most impressed by the combination of elegance and solidity. We are told that "the walls of the mansion house are of the most substantial kind, the basement stone, and those of the superstructure of bricks." Had Hamilton paused to look as he spurred up to the door, he would have seen "a good prospect of part of the city and river—for eight or ten miles up and down—and the country on the opposite shore."

Hamilton's reception surely made clear that this was really his home. Betsey was in his arms; his future mother-in-law and as many of Betsey's brothers and sisters as were present were warm and welcoming. The interior of the house proved to be spacious and light—the seven windows across the front were unusually large. The second-floor hall, not being reduced like the one below by an ornamental staircase, was as large as a ballroom. It was probably there that the festivities associated with the marriage took place.[17]

Hamilton had, of course, no personal family to be invited to his wedding, but at least one member of the headquarters Family was present. McHenry produced an epithalamium with a moral.

View of Bryan Place by Hooker.

The Schuyler mansion at Albany, New York, where Hamilton, as a son-in-law, made his home. Watercolor drawn in 1818 by Philip Hooker on a real estate prospectus when the property was up for sale. One John Bryan owned it at the time. Courtesy, New-York Historical Society.

The poet imagines himself supplicating "the muse" who

> . . . *swayed her wand*
> *Then pointed to a rising stand*
> *From whence the fairy world was seen*
> *And you embosomed with your Queen.*
> *(As thus ye lay, the happiest pair,*
> *A rosy scent enriched the air,*
> *While to a music softly sounding,*
> *Breathing, panting, slow rebounding.)*

Having proceeded in this vein for a while, the poet warns:

> *And now would friendship's voice prevail*
> *To point the moral of the tale.*
> *Know then, dear Ham, a truth confessed*
> *Soon beauty fades and love's a guest . . .*
> *For borne beyond a certain goal,*
> *The sweetest joys disgust the soul.*

At this point, "Prudence" intervenes and points out that "wealth" is what really matters in a marriage.[18]

Hamilton thanked "dear Mac for your poetry and your confidence. The piece is a good one—your best. It has wit, which you know is a rare thing. . . . You know I have often told you you wrote prose well, but had not genius for poetry. I retract."[19]

Many authors have described the marriage in detail: what Hamilton wore, what the bride wore, and so on; but in fact we know nothing except that the reputation of the dashing groom had not traveled so far that the clerk of the Reformed Church at Albany knew his first name. The marriage was thus recorded on December 14: "Colonel Hamilton and Elizabeth Schuyler." "Alexander" was subsequently added in a different hand.[20]

The couple did not set out across the snow-choked countryside on a honeymoon. Ten days after the ceremony, the Marquis de Chastellux found them living routinely as part of the bride's family.[21]

34

Rumblings

L AFAYETTE'S communication, which probably reached Albany
when Hamilton was a few days married, began by stating that
he assumed the bridegroom wished "nothing to do with anybody's letters. But I will now become the bolder in interrupting your
amorous occupations as, exclusive of other motives, the importance of
the matters I have to mention may countenance you indulging your
dear self with some minutes' respite. You may therefore, my good
friend, catch this opportunity of taking breath with decency, which
will be attributed to the *strength* of your friendship for me."

Lafayette then reported on his efforts to secure for Hamilton the
appointment as adjutant general. His letter to Washington having
miscarried, Lafayette had, "regardless of your wishes . . . made verbal application in my own name and about the same terms that had
been settled between us." Washington's reply was that, having remembered Hamilton's advice, he had not only offered the post to
General Hand, but had sent the recommendation to Congress. Lafayette pointed out that a fast rider could still overtake and recall the
recommendation. "I confess I became warmer on the occasion than
you would perhaps have wished me to be." However, "I took care not
to compromise you in this affair . . . in a manner you would have
been satisfied with." Washington insisted that, although he had "a true
desire of obliging you," he felt himself committed to Hand.*

---

* In explaining to Greene, Washington gave more specific reasons than Lafayette repeated to Hamilton. It had not occurred to him that his aide "had an eye
to the office of adjutant general." Furthermore, discontents would be engendered
if a lieutenant colonel were placed in a position to command full colonels.[1]

Hamilton was reading with dismay when his eye came to this sentence: "Now for the voyage to France." Congress had resolved "in the way you wish" to make dramatically clear, by sending to France a special envoy, the desperate need of the American cause for financial help. "Next Monday, the gentleman will be elected. I have already spoken to many members. I know a number of voices will be for you. This day and that of tomorrow will be employed by me in paying visits. As soon as the business is fixed upon, I shall send you an express. I think," so Lafayette continued to the so-recent bridegroom, "you ought to hold yourself in readiness, and, in case you are called for, come with all possible speed." This would be necessary if France's help were to be secured in time for the next campaign.[2]

Writers have assumed that the plan, which Hamilton had clearly encouraged before he rode off to his marriage, included giving Betsey a splendid honeymoon. But wives were not taken along on missions that included the danger of being captured in transit by British raiders. (Even that most uxorious of envoys, John Adams, left Abigail at home.) Hamilton undoubtedly said nothing to Betsey and tried to keep from watching too obviously for messages from Philadelphia. The news that came was not heartening.

Hamilton had been duly nominated for the French mission by a soldier turned congressman, General Sullivan, but Laurens was unanimously elected. The successful candidate wrote Washington that, preferring to fight in South Carolina, he had hoped that Congress "would have availed themselves of the abilities of Colonel Hamilton. . . . But, unfortunately for America, Colonel Hamilton was not sufficiently well known in Congress."[3]

Four days after Hamilton had been turned down for France, Congress decided to send a minister to Russia. Hamilton was nominated by John Matthews, Laurens's fellow South Carolinian who had served with Schuyler on the congressional committee sent to headquarters in 1780. But Hamilton was again passed over. The identity of the man who was elected suggests that Hamilton was in fact too well known (if perhaps misunderstood) by some members of Congress. The new Minister to Russia was Francis Dana, who had been particularly insistent in spreading the rumor that Hamilton had recommended that the army should drive Congress out of doors.[4]

No dispatch reached Hamilton revealing any exterior opportunity that would save him from his duty to return to his tasks as Washington's aide. His disappointment was not made easier by the stiffness of a letter that came in from His Excellency: "Mrs. Washington most cordially joins me in compliments of congratulations to Mrs. Hamilton and yourself on the late happy event of your marriage, and in wishes to see you both at headquarters." Washington did sign himself "with much truth and great personal regard, I am, dear Hamilton, your affectionate friend and servant"—but it was obvious, as both Lafayette and Greene agreed, that Washington was treating his aide unfairly. Because of the high quality of Hamilton's services, the General was keeping him shackled to headquarters.[5]

Only recently, if Hamilton had walked from headquarters he would have stepped, as if off a cliff, into empty air. But now he had a powerful and enthralled father-in-law—Schuyler signed himself "very affectionately and very proudly"—a wife, a mansion house as a home, and money which, even if he felt "delicacy" about asking for it, would be supplied him.[6]

Hamilton decided to watch out for an opportunity to break with Washington. "I resolved, whenever it should happen, not to be in the wrong." He was furthermore "determined, if there should ever happen a breach between us, never to consent to an accommodation." Yet, as long as he served Washington, he would do so conscientiously.[7]

In early January, 1781, after a little less than a month of honeymoon, leaving his wife behind to proceed in a more leisurely manner, Hamilton set out downriver for a return to his duties. At Fishkill, on the far side of the Hudson from Washington's headquarters at New Windsor, he found his way blocked by British operations on the river. Signing himself fully and impressively as "aide de camp to the commander in chief," he wrote passionately to one of the inhabitants: "I am extremely anxious to get across to headquarters this night and it seems hardly possible to cross the river here, or not without great risk. I wish to hire a couple of horses one for myself and one for my servant to cross the river at West Point, with a guide to conduct us across the Mountain. I will pay him handsomely for his trouble."[8]

Hamilton may well have heard on the road that the continuing inability of the institutions in the United States to clothe, feed, or pay the soldiery had spawned what had long been dreaded: a mutiny. The Pennsylvania line had banished their officers and were, under the command of sergeants, marching towards Philadelphia to demand of Congress pay and bounties. At headquarters, Hamilton learned that Washington did not dare march out to put the mutiny down, since, the grievances being true and universal, the troops he would lead might join the protesters. It was only practical to send dispatches warning Congress not to flee—finding that body gone the mutineers might sack Philadelphia—and urging mediation.

Since the soldiers remained completely loyal to the cause, resisting British blandishments, and stopped short of Philadelphia and an actual confrontation with Congress, this more resembled a strike than a treasonous insurrection. But armies are armies and soldiers are armed, and several officers were killed. The soldiers were finally placated, but only through concessions that for the time being put the Pennsylvania line out of action.[9]

Headquarters was in anguish for fear that the other state lines would achieve the same result in the same way, thus abolishing, for the time being at least, the Continental Army. Fortunately, the next mutiny proved to be so small—only some two hundred New Jersey soldiers—that it could probably be put down by a combination of available force and authority. Washington had carefully fed and clothed some six hundred men at West Point into a condition where it was believed they could be relied upon. They were ordered to march. Washington, not wishing to put his ultimate prestige on the line, did not lead them, but he could not bear to wait supinely at headquarters. His own horses proved to be so unfed for lack of forage that they could hardly stand, but the quartermaster managed to procure two horses capable of pulling a sleigh. In this, Hamilton set out with Washington across the frozen landscape. They waited anxiously at some distance from the confrontation between the mutineers and the force from West Point. That force remained loyal and the mutineers were terrified into lining up without arms. Hamilton wrote Laurens, "Of course, we uncivilly compelled them to an unconditional surrender and hanged their most incendiary leaders." It was hoped that this example would stop the general drift towards mutiny, as it did.[10]

Betsey had by now joined her husband at New Windsor. Headquarters—where Washington and Hamilton were to have their famous falling-out—was a story-and-a-half dwelling of Dutch design, the high gable roof breaking at an angle near the top of the lower story to stretch out over the capacious porch, which seems to have run around all four sides of the house. From much of the porch there was to be enjoyed by those early romantics who liked "picturesque scenery" an extensive view of the Hudson River below the high bluff on which the house stood. Others, probably including Hamilton, considered, in the classical manner, so wild a location "disagreeable."

The kitchen with its huge chimney was on the back, probably extending the whole width of the house (which no longer stands). Washington's workroom was behind a dormer window on the second floor, as was undoubtedly the bedroom he shared with Martha. For the headquarters Family, who were always crowded several to a room, a married aide was an anomaly; and Sergeant Uzal Knapp described the house as, although comfortable in cold weather, "not large." The Hamiltons undoubtedly lodged in the village, a short walk downriver. Betsey helped Martha entertain, as is revealed by the diary of the French staff officer Baron von Closen, which noted that Mrs. Hamilton served him tea "with much grace."[11]

On July 21, Betsey wrote her sister Margarita a letter that began with social chitchat—although there had been only one ball it had been "genteel"—and then continued: "I am the happiest of women. My dear Hamilton is fonder of me every day. Get married, I charge you, and give the advice to your friend! There is no possible felicity but in that state."[12]

In modern times, when we regard marriage as the crowning and continuation of fully ripened love, Betsey's happy conclusion that her husband was becoming fonder of her every day seems strange. Certainly it fits illy with the extreme paroxysms of passionate avowal that Hamilton had penned in his letters to her when they were engaged. It seems that Betsey, unconvinced by what her fiancé had so glibly written, had harbored doubts natural to a girl who understood the prudential and dynastic considerations involved in her marriage.

Hamilton could not resist adding to this letter a postscript in which he again playfully raised the possibility that all his ardors were just acting: "Because your sister has the talent of growing more amiable every day, or because I am a fanatic in love, or both—or, if you prefer another interpretation, because I have address enough to be a good dissembler—she fancies herself the happiest woman in the world," and wants everyone else to get married. But Margarita should beware: most marriages were unhappy: " 'Tis a dog's life when two dissonant tempers meet, and it's ten to one this is [would be] the case." He added, "I must tell you in confidence that I think I have been very fortunate."[13]

All the more because they were so contradictory, obscure, and complex in implication, Hamilton's letters to Betsey are peppered with peepholes into his inner feelings. They are even more revealing than his letters to Laurens. He was, in effect, stripping himself of his armor before the very species that had hurt him so before—woman—and in relation to the identical situation—marriage.

By shattering his precautionary determination never to let anyone get close enough to him to open the old wounds, Hamilton was succumbing, in violation of a deep inner fear, to a deep inner need. What had happened was, in the true meaning of the word (which travels far beyond the merely sexual), seduction. It is natural to feel, along with other emotions, anger against the seducer, who, while giving release, has called forth what one's judgment wishes to suppress. In Hamilton's letters to Betsey, there is a definite streak of cruelty.

That there is genuine feeling behind his romantic passages it is impossible to doubt, yet he cannot luxuriate with the feeling or relax in its presence. He has to mock it with exaggeration, diminish it with his references to raving and to wit. He has to make out to his male friends that Betsey does not amount to much after all. He has to keep in his own mind, and also in Betsey's, that he can always escape from his thralldom into the arms of other women.

Yet he has moments of great worry lest Betsey will, even as his mother betrayed him and his father, betray the emotions which, although he fights against them, remain close to his inner core. He knows in his intellect that Betsey is not the type—no attractive woman could be less like his mother. So far, so good, but this reassurance has its reverse side. It would suit his ambitions, his image of himself, to have his sparkle enhanced by a wife who also sparkled. And, furthermore, as he revealed when he urged his fiancée to improve herself, he was afraid that, once they were married and living together, he would find the sweet and simple girl boring.

Hamilton was, after his marriage, to find much more interesting Betsey's worldly and outgoing sister Angelica Church. She was to taunt Betsey: "Embrace poor Hamilton for me. . . . I am really so proud of his merit and abilities that even you, Eliza, might *envy my feelings*." Angelica offered to "pass with you the remainder of my days, that is if you will be so obliging as to permit my *brother* to give me his society, for you know how much I love and admire him."

Betsey responded to such ballyragging with doglike devotion to her older and more scintillating sister. When Angelica sailed for France, Betsey took to her bed in distress. "Do, my dear brother," Angelica wrote Hamilton, "endeavor to soothe my poor Betsey. Comfort her with assurances that I will certainly return to take care of her soon."[14]

35

The Crackup

W HATEVER was the inner situation between Hamilton and
his Betsey, during the early winter of 1781 the outside
world impinged darkly. Absences from headquarters—the
"Old Secretary," Harrison, had, for instance, resigned because on a
visit home he had found his family in penury—kept Hamilton forever
tied to his desk. Greene, newly arrived at his command in South
Carolina, wrote Hamilton in heartrending detail concerning the virtual hopelessness of achieving anything against the British forces in
the South. And what historians regard as a major forward step on the
road to national union, the final approval by all the states of the Articles of Confederation, more disturbed than pleased Hamilton. He was
afraid that making thus official the alliance between the thirteen
United States would spread the idea that the matter was solved, when,
as a matter of fact, the powers given Congress were completely inadequate. The central government was not even entrusted with raising
its own revenue![1]

Hamilton drafted a plan for supplying the army and sent it to
Schuyler. His father-in-law replied that he had proposed the same
ideas to Congress the year before, but in vain. He was sure Congress
would still "not venture on it." In his efforts to encourage continental thinking, Schuyler was now trying to persuade New York to sit
down at a conference with New England—but the possibilities were
dubious.[2]

There was one bright light: at long last, Congress was moving towards establishing an executive made up of individual heads of departments. Ministers of foreign affairs, finance, war, and marine were to be elected. Congressman Sullivan wrote Washington, "I wish your Excellency would be so obliging . . . as to give me your opinion with respect to Colonel Hamilton as a financier." Washington replied: "How far Colonel Hamilton, of whom you ask my opinion as a financier, has turned his thoughts to that particular study I am unable to answer because I never entered upon a discussion on this point with him; but this I can venture to advance from a thorough knowledge of him, that there are few men to be found, of his age, who has a more general knowledge than he possesses, and none whose soul is more firmly engaged in the cause, or who exceeds him in probity and sterling virtue."[3]

Whether or not Hamilton knew of Sullivan's query and Washington's answer, within two weeks an explosion occurred.

It was February 16, 1781. Headquarters was as usual a-boil with business. Going downstairs, so he reported to Schuyler, Hamilton met Washington coming up. The General said that he wanted to speak to his aide on some business. "I answered that I would wait upon him immediately." He proceeded downstairs and delivered to Tilghman a letter to Commissary Blaine "containing an order of a pressing and interesting nature." The letter was not to get off for two days.

As he started to return to his general, Hamilton was stopped by Lafayette. They conversed for what Hamilton first wrote down as a half a minute and later as a full minute. They discussed "a matter of business." Lafayette could "testify how impatient I was to get back, and that I left him in a manner which but for our intimacy would have been more than abrupt."

As he mounted the stairs, Hamilton saw Washington pacing on the landing. "Accosting me in a very angry tone, 'Colonel Hamilton,' said he, 'you have kept me waiting at the head of the stairs these ten minutes. I must tell you, sir, you treat me with disrespect!' "

The attack was completely unexpected, but Hamilton's mind had long been prepared for his instantaneous answer. "I replied without petulancy but with decision, 'I am not conscious of it, sir, but, since you have thought it necessary to tell me so, we must part.' "

" 'Very well, sir,' said he, 'if it be your choice.' Or something to this effect. And we separated."

Hamilton stamped downstairs and poured his outrage into the ears of Lafayette. The Marquis was horrified. "From the very first moment," he was to write Washington, "I exerted every means in my power to prevent a separation which I knew was not agreeable to Your Excellency."

"In less than an hour after," so Hamilton continued in his report to Schuyler, "Tilghman came to me in the General's name, assuring me of his great confidence in my abilities, integrity, usefulness, etc., and of his desire in a candid conversation to heal a difference which could not have happened but in a moment of passion.

"I requested Mr. Tilghman to tell him that I had taken my resolution in a manner not to be revoked; that, as a conversation would serve no other purpose than to produce explanations mutually disagreeable— though I certainly would not refuse an interview if he desired it—yet I should be happy [if] he would permit me to decline it; that, however, I did not wish to distress him or the public business by quitting him before he could derive other assistance by the return of some of the gentlemen who were absent; that, though determined to leave the Family, the same principles which had kept me so long in it would continue to direct my conduct towards him when out of it; and that, in the meantime, it depended on him to let our behavior to each other be the same as if nothing had happened."[4]

Making no further effort to dissuade his aide, Washington accepted the offer that Hamilton stay on until he could be spared. It must have been an embarrassing moment when the two men met again. Undoubtedly to Hamilton's relief and also perhaps to his disappointment, Washington used his famous control to behave as if nothing had happened.

It was Washington's understanding that Hamilton had requested that their falling out and intended separation should be mentioned to absolutely nobody. With this "injunction" he "religiously complied." He was shocked when he later learned that Hamilton had been talking and writing.[5]

In a letter written to McHenry two days after the break, Hamilton stated: "The Great Man and I have come to an open rupture. Proposals of accommodation have been made on his part, but rejected. I pledge my honor to you that you will find me inflexible. He shall, for once at least, repent his ill-humor."[6]

Hamilton's most crucial letter was one to Schuyler, whose help and countenance he had now to rely on, but who was among Washington's most passionate admirers. Hamilton assured his father-in-law that he had not acted precipitously or been motivated by resentment. His

Where Washington and Hamilton had a falling out and Hamilton angrily resigned: Washington's headquarters at New Windsor, New York. The painting was executed in 1852, after the house was demolished, by a member of the owner's family, J. L. Morton. Courtesy, New York Office of Parks and Recreation. Dennis Dunleavy, photographer.

behavior "was the deliberate result of maxims I had long formed for the government of my own conduct.

"I always disliked the office of an aide-de-camp as having in it a kind of personal dependence. I refused to serve in this capacity with two major generals at an early period of the war. Infected, however, with the enthusiasm of the times, an idea of the General's character, which experience soon taught me to be unfounded . . . induced me to *accept his invitation* to enter into his family. It was not long before I discovered he was neither remarkable for delicacy nor good temper, which revived my former aversion to the station in which I was acting, and it has been increasing ever since.

"It has been often with great difficulty that I have prevailed upon myself not to renounce it [his connection with Washington]; but while, from motives of public utility, I was doing violence to my feelings, I was always determined, if there should ever happen a breach between us, never to consent to an accommodation. I was persuaded, that when once that nice barrier, which marked the boundaries of what we owed to each other, should be thrown down, it might be propped again, but could never be restored.

"I believe you know the place I held in the General's confidence and councils, of which will make it the more extraordinary to you to learn that for three years past I have felt no friendship for him and have professed none. The truth is, our own dispositions are the opposites of each other, and the pride of my temper would not suffer me to profess what I did not feel. Indeed, when advances of this kind have been made to me on his part, they were received in a manner that showed at least I had no inclination to court them, and that I wished to stand rather upon a footing of military confidence than of private attachment. You are too good a judge of human nature not to be sensible how this conduct in me must have operated on [here he scratched out "the self-love of"] a man to whom all the world is offering incense. With this key, you will easily unlock the present mystery. At the end of the war, I may say many things to you concerning which I shall impose upon myself 'till then an inviolable silence.

"The General is a very honest man;—his competitors have slender abilities, and less integrity. His popularity has often been essential to the safety of America, and is still of great importance to it. These considerations have influenced my past conduct respecting him, and will influence my future;—I think it is necessary he should be supported.

"His estimation in your mind, whatever may be its amounts, I am persuaded has been formed on principles which a circumstance like this cannot materially affect; but if I thought it could diminish your friendship for him, I should almost forgo the motives that urge me to justify myself to you. I wish what I have said to make no other impression, than to satisfy you I have not been in the wrong. It is also said in confidence, for as a public knowledge of the breach would, in many ways, have an ill effect. It will, probably, be the policy of both sides to conceal it, and cover the separation with some plausible pretext."

Hamilton's expressed concern that, should he tell Schuyler the truth about Washington, that great admirer would be turned against his idol could have some plausibility because of his particular relation with his father-in-law. But the aide's concern went further. Why did Hamilton think that "public knowledge of the breach" would have so ill an effect that it would be "policy" for Washington to "cover the separation with some plausible pretext"? An answer is given in his letter to McHenry, when he explains that he wished to limit that knowledge to "a very few friends" because he felt it expedient to support "a popularity that has been essential, is still useful."[7]

Never did the megalomania that haunted the uncontrolled part of Hamilton's mind present itself more conspicuously. Did the West Indian immigrant, still in his early twenties, whose celebrity, such as it was, had been altogether earned in Washington's shadow, really believe that the great human rock on which the Revolutionary effort had been to so great an extent grounded could be seriously shifted from its base by knowledge of his own personal disapproval and his explosion of anger?

Hamilton had informed Schuyler that, although "my resolution is unalterable," he was "importuned by all such friends as are privy to the affair to listen to a reconciliation." Schuyler's reaction was, if phrased with aching tact, the same. He found no "impropriety in your conduct . . . for of that I am persuaded you are incapable." But he believed that consequences would be "prejudicial to my country which I love." Hamilton had, alone in the General's Family, "those qualifications so essentially necessary to a man who is to aid and council a commanding general," one environed with great difficulties, whose correspondence was "frequently so delicate as to require much judgment and address."

The breach, Schuyler continued, could not be kept secret. He was not "especially" worried about American opinion, but he feared the effect "with the French officers, with the French Minister, and even with the French court; these already observe so many divisions between us; they know and acknowledge your abilities, and how necessary you are to the General. Indeed, how will the loss be replaced? He will, if you leave him, have not one gentleman left sufficiently versed in the French to convey his ideas."

Schuyler went on by urging Hamilton to "make the sacrifice. The greater it is, the more glorious to you. Your services are wanted. They are wanted in that particular station which you have already filled so beneficially to the public and with such extensive reputation."[8]

But emotionally Hamilton had no choice.

The major event of the queasy cooperation that now existed between Washington and Hamilton was a gallop to Newport for the purpose of persuading the French to take full advantage of the damage a storm had inflicted on the British fleet. For a short time—until the battered ships could be refitted—the French flotilla could dominate the local ocean. Clinton had given the traitor Benedict Arnold a British command, and Arnold was rampaging in Virginia. If the French sailed while the opportunity remained, perhaps Washington could get his hands on Arnold for hanging!

There was first an exhilarating dash (if one cared to be exhilarated) during which Washington's horse fell through a bridge into the Housatonic River (His Excellency jumped free). At Newport, more than twenty-four hours were devoted to ceremonies during which Washington was accorded honors usually reserved, as was explained again and again, for a Marshal of France or a Prince of the Blood. However, Washington's private reaction was frustration because he could not break through the ceremonies to get the ships to sail in time. He could hardly have been in a good mood. Nor could Hamilton have been edified to see so much drilling and bowing and firing of cannon in honor of the man he thought overadmired and with whom he had quarreled.[9]

The General and Hamilton must have lodged apart since His Excellency had to write his aide a query concerning a draft of a document. Hamilton brought his knowledge of French to Washington's conferences with the allied command. We know that he talked of his presumably secret break, which Schuyler felt should particularly be hidden from the French, to at least one French friend, the Marquis de Fleury. We know that, his mind on other things, he "quit Newport" without paying his hairdresser, an oversight that subsequently bothered him.[10]

Despite Washington's efforts to be conciliatory—he had signed himself to Hamilton "sincerely and affectionately yours"—the young man was finding demonstrated what he had postulated to Schuyler: "once that nice barrier which marked the boundaries of what we owed to each other, should be thrown down," it could never be restored. They parted at Newport. Washington returned to headquarters, while Hamilton rode to his father-in-law's house in Albany. He had been unable to keep his promise that he would make his departure wait on "Humphreys's return from the eastward." For two weeks Tilghman was the only aide at headquarters. His Excellency had to draft routine letters in his own hand.[11]

But Hamilton had not yet officially left Washington's Family, and he was always uneasy about not doing his duty. Furthermore, he was not free of the need of the Commander in Chief's countenance. "I cannot think of quitting the army during the war," he had written Schuyler. He believed that he could reenter the artillery, taking the place of Lieutenant Colonel Thomas Forrest, who wished to retire, although his resulting rank in the line would be, he felt, far below his rights and merits. What he really wished was what Washington had so far denied him: a specially created "handsome command for the campaign in the light infantry."[12]

After about a month in Albany, Hamilton was back in the headquarters at New Windsor. He seems now to have attended mostly to business that did not require close association with the Commander in Chief. He drafted very few letters. Was it altogether coincidence that among these few was one which, although addressed to Lafayette, had a disastrous implication for what Washington knew were Hamilton's hopes? Even a major general, even the Marquis himself, so Hamilton wrote at Washington's orders, could not be, without an unfortunate effect on morale, inserted into any command from outside the regular succession.[13]

Ten days after he had rejoined headquarters, on April 19, 1781, Hamilton wrote Greene that the future which lay before him was "to be anything that fortune may cast up."[14]

36

Old or New Directions

W HATEVER hopes Betsey may have harbored that her husband's break with Washington would inaugurate peaceful domestic life at Albany were, of course, unrealized, although Alexander did make some preparations for housekeeping. Having written his business agents in Philadelphia to raise cash for him, he ordered "a pound of green tea, and a dozen knives and forks." These he would himself pay for, but he expected the army quartermaster to supply him with a small table, four kegs, two small tubs with handles, and "a light boat which two people can manage." This was not to be a pleasure boat. The quarters he had rented for himself and his bride were directly across the river from Washington's encampment at New Windsor.[1]

Hamilton had hardly crossed the river before he fired off a letter to Washington: "It is become necessary to me to apply to Your Excellency to know in what manner you foresee you will be able to employ me in the ensuing campaign." A corps of light infantry, drawn from various regiments, which would march at the head of a column going southward, would supply a suitable command for a man who had sacrificed so much and won such reputation when selflessly serving the cause as Washington's aide.[2]

Washington replied with irritation that Hamilton's letter had "not a little embarrassed me." He pointed out to the son-in-law of New England's bête noire, Schuyler, that whatever advanced corps was organized would be made up of New England troops. Washington was "convinced that no officer can with justice dispute your merit and abilities," but qualifications were not the issue. Officers could not be deprived of troops they had trained at the very time when opportunities opened for their "distinguishing themselves. . . .

"My principal concern rises from an apprehension that you will impute my refusal of your request to other motives than these I have expressed, but I beg you to be assured I am only influenced by the reasons which I have mentioned." Yet Washington did not, as he had at Newport when he still hoped to keep Hamilton in his service, sign himself "affectionately." His conclusion, "I am Dr. Sir Yr. Obedt. Hble. Servt.," was completely formal.[3]

Hamilton replied that he was "extremely sorry to have embarrassed your Excellency." Since he had, on receiving Washington's letter, "renounced my expectations," he was only writing again to demonstrate that he had not "desired a thing inconsistent with the good of the service. . . . I am incapable of wishing to obtain any object by importunity."

He went on to claim that his early entrance into the army—he had "made the campaign of 1776, the most disagreeable of the war"—entitled him to a commission "more ancient in date than I now possess." His "important and laborious services" would surely have weight with other officers. In any case, Washington could be assured that any offended officers would not resign; they would be restrained by "habit, inclination, and interest, as well as by patriotism."[4]

There is no evidence that Washington answered this letter.

Hamilton sent Schuyler copies of his challenging letters to Washington. Schuyler acknowledged their receipt, but withheld all comment. However, his countenance was not withdrawn. "I believe," he wrote in the same letter, "you may prepare yourself to go to Philadelphia, as there is little doubt but you will be appointed." We know nothing of this hope for appointment except that it was not realized.[5]

Washington was about to ride to Connecticut for another conference with the French command. Hamilton's connections, who believed his presence necessary whenever the Americans dealt with the French, assumed that he would be drafted to go along.[6] When no such request came from Washington, Hamilton returned with his wife to Albany.

Although Hamilton yearned to win renown as a warrior, his intelligence convinced him that " 'tis by introducing order into our finances; by restoring public credit not by gaining battles, that we are finally to gain our object." He wrote to borrow "a tract written by [Richard] Price in which he estimates the specie and current cash of Great Britain." He had also desired David Hume's *Political Discourses;* Wyndham Beawes's *Lex Mercatoria, or the Merchant's Directory;* and his old friend Postlethwayt's *The Universal Dictionary of Trade and Commerce.*[7]

The Philadelphia merchant Robert Morris had been named superintendent of finance, and Hamilton could hardly wait to send him a plan for the economic health of the United States. It became very long—many, many thousands of words—and Betsey helped make a copy for his own files, which she embellished with many misspellings.

Indicating no more than a casual acquaintance with Washington's friend Morris, the aide listed his credentials: he had been "among the first who were convinced" that finances should be entrusted to a single man; he had recommended Morris for the post "in a letter of mine last summer to Mr. Duane"; his contacts at headquarters had given him a better idea "than most others" of French attitudes. But what would have been the best credential he did not list: "I pretend not to be an able financier. It is a part of administration which has been least in my way and, of course, has least occupied my inquiries and reflections. Neither have I had leisure or materials to make accurate calculations. . . . With all these disadvantages, my plan must necessarily be crude and defective, but it may be a basis for something more perfect." Hamilton's distaste for allowing matters to drift, finding their own solution, made him comment to Morris, "There is scarcely any plan so bad as not to have something good in it."[8]

Hamilton's objective was to urge the establishment of a national bank, and then to present a quite detailed plan of how the bank could be organized. There was no call in this presentation to urge the value of central power or a standing army. But he did put forward an idea that would have been equally unsatisfactory to America's agrarian majority, who, practicing an economy where cash was hard to come by, regarded debt as the road to ruin: "A national debt, if it is not excessive, will be to us a national blessing. It will be a powerful cement of our union. It will also create a necessity for keeping up taxation to a degree which, without being oppressive, will be a spur to industry." Inclined to "parsimony and indulgence, we labor less now than any civilized nation of Europe, and a habit of labor in the people is as essential to the health and vigor of their minds and bodies as it is conducive to the welfare of the state."

In the last paragraph of his almost endless screed, Hamilton conceeded, "To develop the whole connection of my ideas on the subject and place my plan in the clearest light, I have indulged myself in many observations which might have been omitted." He had pointed out to America's great financial expert such matters as that America was suffering from inflation. He had included information on European resources and economic theory which a veteran like Morris would obviously know and understand ten times as well. Morris did not need his advice on banking. Hamilton seems to have written as a student wishing to convey to an expert his industry and nascent abilities.[9]

Perhaps Morris had heard talk of making Hamilton superintendent of finance in his stead. He certainly knew that Hamilton was the son-in-law of a man whose cooperation was essential for the success of his endeavors. The financier was furthermore in need of coadjutors who would put their minds on finance and think as he did. But he was so vague about Hamilton's career that he addressed him as a colonel in the artillery.[10]

Morris thanked Hamilton for his "performance," for the "good intentions and pains you have taken." He was encouraged to find that Hamilton backed his "judgment" by being so often in agreement with his own beliefs. Hamilton would see that a bank had been established, although with a smaller capital than Hamilton envisioned. Morris thought it better to start with what was possible and hope it would grow, rather than fail by being too ambitious at the outset. Morris then read Hamilton a lesson which the younger man was to remember in a way that was eventually to help embattle him with the American farmers. Hamilton had wished to give bank certificates in return for the investment of land. Morris feared that "interweaving a land security with the capital of this bank," would "convey to the public mind an idea of paper being circulated on that credit and that the bank of consequence must fail in its payments in the case of any considerable run on it."

"My office," Morris wrote, "is new and I am young in the execution of it. Communications from men of genius and abilities will always be acceptable." Hamilton could always "command" Morris's attention.[11]

It was a good start.

When proposing to Duane that a firmly federal constitution be drafted, Hamilton had stated that "the people ought to be prepared . . . by sensible and popular writings."[12] Now he undertook the preparation of what grew into seven long newspaper pieces headed

"The Continentalist."[13] The first appeared in the *New-York Packet and General Advertiser* on July 12, 1781, over the signature "A.B."

Not for Hamilton the modern journalistic device of a lead which stated the propositions to be proved. Carefully building up his contentions from the foundations, Hamilton begged his readers not to make up their minds until they had finished the entire series.

He began by stating that the Americans had entered the Revolution "with very vague and confined notions of the practical business of government." The men who possessed experience were primarily Tories and had vanished. And the advice of the few competent men who remained was "too commonly borne down by the prevailing torrent of ignorance and prejudice."[14]

The great difficulty was the "extreme jealousy of power" that is "attendant on all popular revolutions." The cause was sinking because of "A WANT OF POWER IN CONGRESS." He then gave a group of historical examples to demonstrate the sad fates of nations that had federated without a strong central sovereign. Flying in the face of the current sentimental classicism, he wrote, "No friend to order or to rational liberty can read without pain and disgust the history of the commonwealth of Greece." Showing surprising ignorance of the New England town meeting, he praised America because "every power with us is exercised by representation, not in tumultuous assemblies of the collective body of the people." More historical precedents, these aimed at disassociating central power from tyranny, were presented in the second installment of "The Continentalist," and on into the third, which appeared almost a month after the first.[15]

Finally, Hamilton got down to cases: "Nothing but a GENERAL DISAFFECTION of the PEOPLE or MISMANAGEMENT in their RULERS can account . . . for the distresses and perplexities we experience" considering how weak was the British force in America. Having demonstrated that the fault was not with the people, who had been astonishingly loyal in periods of darkest adversity, Hamilton achieved the conclusion that the government needed revision. He excoriated the tendency confidently to relax because Holland had joined the forces fighting against Great Britain. The more global the war became, he warned, the more American interests were likely to be forgotten in the eventual peace. "We ought, without delay, to ENLARGE THE POWERS OF CONGRESS."

"The Continentalist, No. IV," published on August 30, at long last reached specific recommendations. To save the nation "nothing short of the following articles will suffice":

First. The power of regulating trade. Congress should be empowered to collect customs duties in the states. Denouncing free trade (which Washington supported), Hamilton insisted that, through selective customs duties, the central government should achieve a favorable balance of trade by encouraging some types of enterprise and squeezing out others. As he was to do (vainly) in his *Report on Manufactures* Hamilton urged awarding bounties and premiums to infant industries.

Second. A land tax, granted to the federal government in perpetuity, to be collected, if Congress so wished, in the states by its own employees.

Third. The federal collection of a moderate tax on every male above fifteen years of age. He exempted day laborers but made no concession to the southerners' contention that they would be bankrupted by a head tax on slaves.

These three articles were of "IMMEDIATE NECESSITY": three more would be of "great present but of much greater future utility":

Fourth. The disposal for federal profit of all unlocated land, even within the territory of a state.

Fifth. Granting the federal government a certain proportion of the products of all mines.

Sixth. The appointment, by Congress, of all land and naval officers, a provision that had only too visibly hidden within it Hamilton's desire to have the military forces altogether under the control of the federal government. Even what the states relied on to preserve their integrity, the militia, would be taken out of their control.[16]

Hamilton then argued at length the absolute necessity that Congress have its own funds with which to pay the federal debts and to establish credit on which to borrow.

The final essay ended with a burst of what his biographer, Henry Cabot Lodge, Sr., called "the eloquence of sound reason and clear logic combined with great power and lucidity of expression and backed by a strong and passionate nature":[17]

"There is," so ran Hamilton's peroration, "something noble and magnificent in the perspective of a great Federal Republic, closely linked in the pursuit of a common interest, tranquil and prosperous at home, respectable abroad; but there is something proportionably diminutive and contemptible in the prospect of a number of petty states, with the appearance only of union, jarring, jealous and perverse, without any determined direction, fluctuating and unhappy at home, weak and insignificant by their dissensions, in the eyes of other nations. Happy

America! if those, to whom thou hast intrusted the guardianship of thy infancy, know how to provide for thy future repose; but miserable and undone, if their negligence or ignorance permits the spirit of discord to erect her banners on the ruins of thy tranquillity!"[18]

"The Continentalist" was Hamilton's first extensive propaganda publication since his pamphlets in argument with the Reverend Samuel Seabury, published in 1774 and 1775, some six years earlier. There is an immense change both in style of composition and polemical approach. Hamilton had learned to be a much better writer: sentences are clear, graceful, and energetic, unerringly designed to cover, without deviation or frills, exactly the desired ground. Each gives a strong lead to the one that follows. And the haphazard organization of the earlier works, which often flopped in circles like a chicken on the run, has given place to a shrewdly premeditated logical structure.

Hamilton had, like Seabury, sought in his earlier works to cajole the reader. The text was kept amusing with jokes, homely considerations, and impertinent sallies. There was something for everyone: logic for those logically minded; emotion for those who wish to be moved; an effort to appeal specially to special prejudices. But the style Hamilton was now inaugurating eschews altogether such a vaudeville atmosphere. He makes no concessions to those not inclined to climb after him up his logical ladder. The effectiveness of his method depended, indeed, on his leading the reader step by step from an accepted conclusion to another that must therefore be accepted. He ignored the possibility that readers would leap into his flow of prose in the middle, happening utterly unprepared on passages that caught their special attention because they seemed particularly outrageous.

Believing that his readers had become as passionate devotees of a strong, paternalistic central government as he himself was, Hamilton felt only a limited need to be discreet in presenting his final conclusions. He was, it is true, cautious to the extent of not coming out directly for a new constitution, but the powers he recommended were far greater than the eventual Constitution did entrust to the federal government.

When Hamilton's biographer Broadus Mitchell praised "The Continentalist" for "the moderation and practicality of its recommendations,"[19] he was judging as if the essay had been written many years later, when the passage of time had made such ideas seem reasonable. To take one example: now we have a standing army of several million men altogether under federal control. The largest standing army Congress would approve at the end of the Revolution comprised 435 men. When Hamilton envisioned a powerful federal force always available for overawing the states he was urging what was to many of his contemporaries a nightmare. Perhaps most of the readers of "The Continentalist" were led to opposite conclusions from those Hamilton intended. They were induced not to desire the reforms he advocated but to fear them.

Shortly before he began writing "The Continentalist" series, Hamilton had confided to Greene, "I have not been much in the way of knowing sentiments outside the army." After he had unhesitatingly published four of his essays, his attention was diverted to the Yorktown campaign. More than six months were to pass before the appearance of the last two numbers. By then he had come to realize the impracticability of what he had written. But he forged ahead. He merely added an explanation: what he was now bringing out had been "written last fall, but accidentally got out of the hands of the writer. He has lately recovered them, and gives them to the public more to finish the development of his plan than from any hope that the temper of the times will adopt the ideas."[20]

37

Endangering the Cause

[JULY, 1781   AGE 24]

HAMILTON had been in Albany for about a month, chewing on his military disappointments and writing "The Continentalist," when electrifying news came upriver. The French army, which had been motionless at Newport since their arrival in the United States, had suddenly marched. They were encamping beside the Continental Army on the east shore of the Hudson. Sure that some major stroke was in the making, Hamilton mounted his horse.

On July 8, 1781, he was with the American army. But he avoided any conversation with Washington concerning what he desired. Instead, he questioned his friends who were still in the Family. They reported, so he wrote Betsey, that "nothing was said on the subject of [giving him] a command. I wrote the General a letter and enclosed my commission." He was resigning from the army.[1] That the letter was angry and unpleasant is indicated by its absence from the usually complete headquarters files. Washington must have destroyed it.

The General was placed in a quandary. He was entirely conscious of the brilliance of his former aide. He knew that his own close friends, men like Lafayette and Greene, believed that he had been unfair to Hamilton by keeping the ambitious youth chained to a desk. Washington, who had kept himself so tied that he had not taken one day of furlough during the entire war, could not blame himself for complete selfishness. He truly believed that Hamilton had been making a greater contribution to the cause than if he had become one of the combat

officers of whom the army possessed many much more tried and experienced than he. Washington, who was so brilliant a judge of men,
may well have realized that the major gifts of the "frail" and intellectual young man were not for physical combat. Yet the fact remained
that Hamilton had yearned to get away; that he deserved well of the
cause and Washington personally; and that by holding him to his
duties as an aide, Washington had served his own convenience by
making his own tasks lighter.

Washington would not have been human had he not resented the
way Hamilton had seized on a tiny incident to smash their relationship. And the General had by now found out that his former aide had
violated the understanding he himself had honored that neither would
say anything about their falling out. Hamilton had taken advantage by
telling the story his own way. Yet Washington wished always to be
fair, and in all fairness, Hamilton's contributions to the cause and to
him personally greatly outweighed the sum of his derelictions. Furthermore, the concession which the young man wished was, although
clumsy to achieve, not unachievable.

Washington, who was overwhelmingly busy and glad to procrasti-
nate whenever a matter could be postponed, had probably not made
up his mind concerning what in the long run he would do about
Hamilton. Now there was a pistol at his head. He could not without
hurting his own conscience, and incurring the disapproval of friends
like Greene and Lafayette, allow Hamilton to stamp away from military life, blaming ingratitude.

Tilghman was again sent to Hamilton as Washington's emissary. He
"pressed me to retain my commission, with an assurance that he will
endeavor by all means to give me a command nearly such as I could
have desired. . . . Though I know," so Hamilton continued to his
wife, "my Betsey would be happy to hear I had rejected this proposal,
it is a pleasure my reputation would not permit me to afford her. I
consented to retain my commission and accept my command."[2]

Probably to disprove Washington's formerly expressed fear that
Hamilton could not without causing dissatisfaction command New
England troops, he stayed at the headquarters of the ranking Massachusetts general, Benjamin Lincoln, although this was some distance
from the center of the camp.

"I experience," he wrote, "every mark of esteem from the officers of
both armies."[3] The close proximity of the French and American
soldiers naturally cast Hamilton as a social hero. Most of his fellow

American officers, their regimentals soiled and torn by marching and fighting, seemed bedraggled beside the Frenchmen spruce from garrison duty. But Hamilton, the ever dapper, had surely brought new togs down with him from Albany. And how much more he was at home! The officers of the two armies were busily entertaining each other, but the meetings were usually of strangers who could only communicate with smiles and gestures and by getting agreeably tipsy together. Hamilton was already familiar with many of the French officers, and he was fluent in both French and English. Although he considered himself an abstemious drinker, his moderation never affected his conviviality. He was indeed conspicuous for vitality and grace at social affairs, and how much greater were his opportunities when he alone of the company could speak to everyone, was drawn into every conversation as an interpreter.

Yet, he admitted, "My dissipations are a very imperfect suspension of my uneasiness." That he was no longer at headquarters was plain to all, and it would have been undignified if not worse to spread any explanation into common gossip. He could, of course, confide that he had been promised a command, but the fact was that he had no command. He was an unassigned lieutenant colonel hanging around the army. While other officers were attending to their duties, he was embarrassingly, shamefully idle. "With no object of sufficient importance to occupy my attention here," he continued to his wife, "I am left to feel all the weight of our separation." Then in his anguish, he turned nasty. Being "lost to all the public and splendid passions and absorbed in you," he was "entirely changed, changed for the worse."[4]

As one week and then another dragged by, Hamilton could not help ruminating ever more darkly that Washington's promise had included no date and no absolute assurance: the General had merely said he would do his best to find for Hamilton something that would "nearly" suit his desires. Hamilton, who suspected that he had wounded "the self-love of a man to whom all the world is offering incense," had encountered, since he had finally carried through his determination to leave the Family, no friendship on the part of the General.[5]

It was some relief, at least from the questions he saw in the eyes of his fellow officers, when on July 27 Washington appointed Hamilton to one of the routine military courts that periodically heard whatever charges might appear.[6] Four days later, Hamilton was officially given a command. The general orders that circulated from headquarters revealed that Washington had not been persuaded concerning Massachusetts troops: in the light companies attached to two New York regiments should, when they reached camp, join with two companies of New York levies "to form a battalion under the command of Lieutenant Colonel Hamilton." He had obviously been indulged in being allowed to select his second-in-command, who was none other than Major Nicholas Fish, Hamilton's college friend with whom he had drilled before either joined the army. So far so good, but the last line of the order denied Hamilton's wish to be given an independent corps for the prowess of which he would alone reap the glory. Hamilton's battalion was to be part of "the advanced corps under the orders of Colonel Scammell."[7]

Hamilton was warmed with no gratitude to Washington. The assignment, short of what he believed himself entitled to, had come nineteen months after his first request for a combat command. He had been driven to resigning from the Family and to threatening to resign from the army. The following year, he was to remind Washington angrily "of the difficulties I experienced." Now he found an excuse for tweaking Washington's nose.[8]

Until the seasoned companies arrived, Hamilton's command consisted of the recently mustered levies. He was disgusted to find them barefoot or almost so. He asked Tilghman for an order that they be shod. Tilghman replied that "on a general principle, it could not be granted."

Although no one knew better than Hamilton how outrageous it was that the Commander in Chief be bothered with supply problems on the company level, Hamilton wrote Washington a letter of protest in which he lectured his former chief on military usage: "Your Excellency is sensible that the service of an advance corps must in general be more active than of the line, and that in a country like this, the article of shoes is indispensable." Having gone on like this to some length, he suddenly inserted a backwardly worded plea to be indulged. "I will not add any personal consideration to those which affect the service, though it certainly cannot be a matter of indifference to me." He ended with no more warmth than "very respectfully."[9]

Washington granted the shoes, but his reply was short and cold, mostly devoted to warning his former aide, who had handled this kind of problem a thousand times, to make sure that the shoes were safely delivered and properly accounted for.[10]

However, insofar as Washington had hesitated for fear Hamilton's appointment would stir resentment, he was reassured. The former aide was proved right in his assumption that the officer corps would acknowledge that his merits justified an exception in his favor. Washington was emboldened to add New England troops to the New Yorker's command: two companies from the Connecticut line, each consisting of a captain, two subalterns, four sergeants, and fifty rank and file. "It is to be expected," the general orders from headquarters continued, "that the companies will be composed of good men either engaged for the war or three years."[11]

"However remote you may be from your former post of an aide de camp," Lafayette wrote Hamilton, ". . . I am sure you are nevertheless acquainted with every transaction at headquarters."[12] Lafayette assumed correctly. The members of Washington's Family did not break the confidential habit built up over the years.

Hamilton heard that at the Wethersfield Conference, to which he had not been asked to serve as interpreter, Rochambeau had expressed a hope that Admiral de Grasse would, during the summer, bring his major fleet up from the Indies. The French general had agreed to marching his army to the Hudson for presumed preparations for an amphibious attack on New York. There was also talk of moving the entire operation to Virginia.

Before Hamilton rejoined the army, word had been received from Laurens in Paris that de Grasse had definitely been ordered to North America. Laurens also reported that he had succeeded in securing from the French a loan of six million livres.[13] The personal side of this achievement must have thrilled Laurens's passionate friend. Becoming disgusted by the perfumed diplomatic runaround he was receiving from the current ministers, the colonel had, to the horror of the subtle Benjamin Franklin, smashed etiquette by marching up to Louis XVI at a reception and handing him the American petition. The King and his court were delighted by this bold behavior on the part of so stalwart and handsome an American soldier—and the red tape had been effectively cut.

On August 14, five days after Hamilton had secured from Washington a promise of shoes, the dramatic dispatch reached headquarters: de Grasse had already left Santo Domingo and was heading not for New York but the Chesapeake, where he expected to arrive on September 3. He would bring a fleet powerful enough to take control of the ocean from the British, and also thirty-two hundred land troops. But, since he could not stay for long, use of his appearance would have to be made at once and near the spot where he arrived. Gone was all hope of attacking New York or having the troops carried south by the French ships. Washington's and Rochambeau's armies would have to find their way inland over the 450 miles to the Chesapeake.

As good luck would have it, Cornwallis, who had been ravaging inland Virginia, where he would be immune to amphibious attack, had marched to the coast and was fortifying, with his own small fleet around him, the harbor city of Yorktown. If he stayed on the coast, the enemy's main southern army would be ripe for annihilation. However, the Americans had no way to keep Cornwallis pinned down if he concluded that he should evade the reach of sea power by marching again inland. The success of the allied attack thus depended on Cornwallis's getting no inkling that de Grasse was on his way up from the Indies. At no time of the war had complete secrecy been of such crucial importance. Should spies tip off the British in New York, the enemy would send tearing down the coast a dispatch boat that would reach the endangered general long before the armies of Washington and Rochambeau could arrive outside Yorktown to hem him in.

Geography presented a golden opportunity for getting the allied armies far on the road without the British in New York suspecting their destination. Since Staten Island lay off that part of the Jersey shore, two thirds of the march from the allied encampment to inland shipping on the Delaware River could be seen as an effort to enter the British stronghold through a back door. Washington made every effort to encourage this interpretation, leaking wrong information to British spies and conspicuously building ovens in New Jersey as if to supply bread for a Staten Island attack.

There was the serious problem of sending out essential information to American officials who would have to cooperate: even the most carefully guarded dispatch might go astray. On August 17, Washington wrote the superintendent of finance, but avoided the need for a second dispatch by asking him to inform the President of Congress. Letters to the top officials of New Hampshire, Massachusetts, Connecticut, and New Jersey were drafted on August 21, but they were not immediately dispatched: the one to New Hampshire went off on the 24th.[14] However, on the 22nd, a lieutenant colonel no longer attached to headquarters abandoned discretion and sent the news to his wife.

Hamilton wrote Betsey, "A part of the army, my dear girl, is going to Virginia, and I must of necessity be separated at a much greater distance from my beloved wife. . . . But let no idea other than of the distance we shall be asunder disquiet you. . . . It is ten to one that our views will be disappointed by Cornwallis retiring to South Carolina by land." Hamilton included no injunction to Betsey not to repeat the news.[15] Probably he felt that by the time the letter could move up the Hudson to Albany and come down again, the British in New York would already know.

It was ten days after Hamilton's revealing letter to his wife that Sir Henry Clinton finally informed Cornwallis: "It would seem that Mr. Washington is moving an army to the southward." Another four days passed before Clinton knew enough to send a more positive message: "I can have no doubt that Mr. Washington is moving with at least 6,000 French and rebel troops against you."[16] But even yet the British did not know that Cornwallis could (as Hamilton had stated) "disappoint" the patriot effort by retiring inland. Unconscious of the contemplated arrival of a major French fleet, assuming the British would keep control of the ocean, Clinton promised to send Cornwallis the necessary reinforcements. Confident that the ocean would remain under British control—if the reinforcements did not come from New York he could sail there in his own fleet—Cornwallis decided not to withdraw inland. He concluded that his best strategy was to stay behind the fortifications at Yorktown, which he strengthened against the arrival of the most he expected: the armies from the Hudson.

Had Hamilton's communication fallen into British hands, the history of the war and perhaps of the world would have been changed: peace and independence, had they arrived at all, would have been delayed. We cannot doubt that Hamilton used a means of conveyance he considered altogether safe, but dispatches were intercepted in many ways. As Hamilton well knew, it is an axiom of military secrecy to reduce to the absolute minimum the chances for a slip.

Hamilton's act, by which the future of the United States was endangered, has never before been noted. It is all the more difficult to explain because during the years when the aide had been an official custodian of secrets, he had been scrupulously discreet. His present indiscretion served no public end. Even in the private sphere it seemed uncalled for. The ever-apprehensive Betsey, who was three months pregnant with their first child,[17] would undoubtedly have been grateful to have had her period of anxiety reduced by later news. (Before the campaign was done, her father feared that her nervous distress would bring on a miscarriage.[18]) Did Hamilton crave for his own emotional reasons that she should be at once informed? Was he anxious to reveal to his wife and his father-in-law that, even if no longer at headquarters, he had access to the greatest secrets? Was his anger against Washington expressing itself? Or was he demonstrating, like a lover who endangers (but not too much) the life of his beloved, that the American cause was so much his own that he could risk it as he pleased?

352

38

The Road to the British Redoubt

[AUGUST–OCTOBER, 1781   AGE 24]

WHENEVER possible the allied armies took advantage, on their trip to Yorktown, of inland waterways. The first was to be, after the march across New Jersey, the Delaware, but Washington had delayed concentration of ships at Trenton lest the British suspect that Staten Island was not really the objective. Most of the army had to proceed on their feet, parading through Philadelphia. But the light infantry was an elite corps intended for the van. Hamilton floated down the Delaware to Christiana, whence it was a short march to the top of the Chesapeake.[1]

From the Head of Elk (Elkton), where the British had disembarked in 1777, Hamilton wrote Betsey. Extreme discretion had taken the place of wild indiscretion. Although the joyful news that de Grasse's fleet had actually arrived at the mouth of the Chesapeake was announced in general orders on the day he wrote, Hamilton stated only, "Circumstances that have just come to my knowledge assure me that our operations will be expeditious as well as our success certain." Then, at this triumphant moment, when it seemed that at long last he would share as a fighter in a great victory, he doubled on himself. "Every day confirms me in the intention of renouncing public life and devoting myself wholly to you. Let others waste their time and their tranquility in a vain pursuit of power and glory. Be it my object to be happy in a quiet retreat with my better angel."[2]

Despite Washington's anguished pleas to boatowners in Baltimore and Annapolis, there was a great shortage of shipping to take the troops down the Chesapeake. (De Grasse's boats required deeper water.) But again Hamilton's brigade was embarked. They had not gone very far before orders were spread along and over the Bay that all military vessels should retire into creeks and shallows where large ships could not reach them. A powerful British fleet had appeared on the ocean; de Grasse had raised his sails and gone off to meet the enemy. Everything was up for grabs again. At any moment, British warships might come scudding up the Chesapeake.

But in a naval skirmish which some historians consider the most determining engagement of the entire Revolution, de Grasse scared the British ships away. All the many chances that could have frustrated the Yorktown campaign had now fallen correctly. The trap was shut.[3]

Hamilton resumed the trip down the Chesapeake which was for the first (and the last) time to carry him into the American South. As he proceeded, the river spread out to become a small ocean. Captain James Duncan noted, "We hugged close to the western shore, but the many bays and mouths of rivers we had to cross rendered it extremely dangerous." Duncan's boat was almost sunk by "a furious wind" which arose as they were crossing the mouth of the Rappahannock, the river on whose banks Washington had passed his childhood.[4]

Eventually, Hamilton reached Williamsburg. He must have been amazed—and far from impressed—to see that the capital of the great state of Virginia was a village hardly larger than Christiansted. The town was alive with military. There were drinking parties and games of billiards and a dance. On September 24, Hamilton's battalion was attached to Brigadier General Moses Hazen's brigade, which was in turn assigned to the left wing, under the command of Hamilton's intimate, Lafayette.[5]

In the dark before dawn on September 28, the army began its advance of some fifteen miles from Williamsburg to the outskirts of Yorktown. "If," so read Washington's general order, "the enemy should be tempted to meet the army on its march, the General particularly enjoins the troops to place their principal reliance on the bayonet, that they may prove the vanity of the boast which the British make of their particular prowess in deciding battles with that weapon. . . . A generous emulation" of the French, "whose national weapon is that of close fight," was urged.[6]

As part of the light infantry, Hamilton's brigade led the march, and surely no officer in the whole American army was more eager than Hamilton to outdo the French in a close fight. He stared into the darkness, he stared as dawn gradually revealed a fertile but war-torn country, the fields running wild with weeds, even great manor houses dilapidated. But Hamilton had only minor attention for that: he was waiting for an enemy to pounce on. It must have been a disappointment to cover the fifteen miles as quietly as if on a Sunday stroll. But when at last the troops passed through a final thicket to view the enemy encampment there was a thrill. On the extensive, completely flat area before the fortified city, the British cavalry were displaying themselves: gleam of helmet and saber, the cantering in unison of purebred horses. For infantrymen to stand up to cavalry with the bayonet, there would be a feat! But the horsemen, on being fired at by French cannon, cantered gracefully back behind their walls.[7]

The small city of Yorktown—one main and several cross streets— which backed on the York River, was, except for the tops of a few church steeples, invisible behind high defensive walls of earth and masonry. In front stretched a huge plain, more than a mile deep in the center, that was bare of all vegetation higher than a few inches: everything had been removed that could impede the domination of the space by the many cannon that peered through loopholes in the enemy ramparts. Most of the empty earth appeared flat, no hillocks higher than a few feet; but there were places where the ground dropped into marshy gullies, which contained the elaborately branching courses of two streams. The larger creek intervened in front of most of the town, and to cooperate with this natural defense, the British had built, at some distance from their walls, several small redoubts.

Considerably beyond the range of the enemy cannon, Hamilton and his battalion spent their first night lying under the sky. Sleep was several times shattered by the cries of sentries, but the shadowy figures that appeared from the darkness presented no danger. They were deserters from the enemy. They were firmly interrogated, but proved to have "little or no intelligence that could be counted upon."[8]

The next morning, Hazen's brigade was ordered to reconnoiter the approaches to the fortress-city. After they had advanced to within a half mile of the enemy's left, they halted on the edges of a morass. What was Hamilton's disappointment not to have his battalion but Colonel Muhlenberg's Pennsylvania Germans ordered to wade across! They moved onto ground that was probably within enemy cannon range, but there was no firing. The Germans waded back, and the whole brigade returned to its quarters.[9]

When Hamilton awoke the following morning, he learned that during the darkness the enemy had evacuated their advanced redoubts. Cornwallis, whose army was greatly outnumbered by the combined

American-French force, had decided to rely altogether on his high walls and his cannon.

Any romantic visions Hamilton cherished of a *coup de main*—the Franco-American troops dramatically scaling the walls—were stilled by news from headquarters that the French engineers were giving the American command, from Washington down, lessons in siege warfare. The need was to get cannon within range of the British ramparts without at the same time exposing them to the enemy fire. This would be done by digging trenches—known as the first parallel—which, as they approached the walls, were so angled that they could not be enfiladed by cannonballs traveling, as they had to do, in a straight line from the fixed enemy positions.

After French and American cannon had been pulled into range through the trenches, an artillery duel would begin. Better protected in their holes than the enemy guns that bristled from perpendicular walls, and with greater firepower, the allied cannon would have an irrevocable advantage. After they had silenced the British long-range guns, a second parallel would be dug so close to the walls that mortar shells could be lobbed into the city. It was then just a question of how much carnage the enemy would accept before they surrendered.

This was all mechanical and long-range, but one opportunity for a bloody assault remained. Two small, freestanding British redoubts blocked the intended route of the second parallel. Although they would be, when the time came for the attack, indefensible (unless supported, as seemed improbable, by a sortie from behind Yorktown's walls) the honor of the British army would require that they be defended. To capture one would be a sensational feat, but would not require a larger force than could correctly be commanded by an officer of Hamilton's rank. And, as good fortune would have it, the redoubts were directly in front of Hamilton's command. The time was not yet—even the first parallel had not been started—but perhaps! Surely, Hamilton's star, which had led him so far and so high, still moved in the heavens.

Captain James Duncan, of Muhlenberg's battalion, served with and under Hamilton in Hazen's brigade. We learn from his diary that the troops helped dig the first parallel. Bending, while they worked, as low as they could in the trench, few were hit even after the operation had advanced into the range of the enemy cannon. However, one militiaman "stood constantly on the parapet and d—d his soul if he would dodge for the buggers." After he had made himself conspicuous by brandishing his spade, "a ball came and put an end to his capers."[10]

One section of the first parallel was dug by the Americans, another by the French. When time came for the American trench to be ceremoniously occupied, the honor was conferred on Hamilton's part of the light infantry. Drums beating and flags flying, the men marched into the far end of the ditch. As they disappeared into the ground, the enemy responded with a tremendous burst of cannon fire. The route had been roofed over to form "a covered way." The roof held. No blood gushed. But Hamilton was unhappily conscious that his advance was invisible to the thousands of watchers in all three armies. At the final parapet, flags were raised to show the troops were there, but still no human form could be seen.

Then Duncan heard Hamilton give an "extraordinary" order. The lieutenant colonel led the men who were under his command over the parapet onto the open ground where they were completely exposed to enemy cannonballs. He commanded the men to line up as on a parade ground. Standing tense and straight, he crisply put the ranks through the manual of arms. "Although the enemy had been firing a little before, they did not now give us a single shot. I suppose," Duncan continued, "their astonishment at our conduct must have prevented them, for I can assign no other reason. Colonel Hamilton gave these orders, and, although I esteem him one of the first officers in the American army, must beg in this instance to think he wantonly exposed the lives of his men."[11]

When the shivering men got back into the trench after their terrifying drill, Hamilton gave them further commands. They were to spend the night where they were and, if the enemy made an effort to capture the trench, "we were to give them one fire from the barquet, rush over the parapet, and meet them with the bayonet." After dark, Hamilton sent pickets out into the no-man's-land to give advance warning.

Towards dawn, musket shots sounded. Almost instantly shadows dashing in from the dark leaped over the parapet. They solidified into the bodies of the terrified pickets. They had been fired at—they assumed by a British reconnaissance party. One had been killed and the rest had taken to their heels. Hamilton angrily ordered them out again, but whatever force had fired—Duncan suspected it may have been another American party—had vanished.

With daylight, cannonballs were directed against the trench, wounding two of Hamilton's men. The corps was relieved about noon.[12]

By the afternoon of the next day, the trench in which Hamilton had spent the night had been enlarged into a gun emplacement, and a powerful battery dragged there: three twenty-four–pounders, three twelves, and a fourteen-inch mortar. Further emplacements were opened up on both the French and the American parallels. With a French ball flecking a piece of masonry off a British rampart, the artillery duel began on October 9. The battle was now as much in the air as on the ground. Shells sailed past each other, moving in opposite directions, each, as it curved up and then earthward, dragging a long train of fire. Hamilton often watched from the trenches when his battalion were taking their turn at guarding against enemy sorties. As the days passed, the British walls, which had seemed as solid as creation, began to take on, here and there, the appearance of lacework, and the voices of their cannon grew less numerous.

During the night of October 11, Hamilton may well have been treated with a stupendous sight. The small fleet assigned to Cornwallis's army was anchored in the York River so tightly behind the city that the ships were protected by its walls. But finally, French gunners achieved an angle that enabled them to ignite one of the vessels with red-hot shot. From the riverbank near his tent, Hamilton could have seen, if he was there at the time, the flames move from ship to ship, leap from the dry wood of the hulls up the masts high into the darkness while the reflecting water repeated the vision but now downward, as if the holocaust were originating in hell. There were periodic explosions, which seemed to rock the battlefield, as powder magazines took fire.[13]

The time had now come for the second parallel. As it angled ever closer to Yorktown, the enemy unmasked a battery of "royals" which they had been holding secretly in reserve. These large brass mortars could, at the new close range, lob twenty-pound shells into the trenches that were impervious to the horizontal thrust of cannonballs.

By the time Hamilton's battalion was ordered into the augmenting second parallel, "the enemy, by practice, were enabled to throw their shells with great certainty." Sentries were posted to yell out, "A shell!" at which the men would throw themselves flat on the ground. However, this was small protection against a real hit. Hamilton could probably have written with Duncan, "Were I to recount all the narrow escapes I made that night, it would be almost incredible."[14]

As the American and French trenches advanced despite mortar fire, the time soon came when the two small enemy redoubts that stood in the way would have to be taken by daring assaults over the walls. Since the little fortifications—each contained hardly more than a hundred men—were being held by the British as a matter of honor, it was equally a matter of honor that the inevitable capture should be achieved briskly and with conspicuous heroism. Here was, in the grand style of martial symbolism, such a ritual of blood and sacrifice as spoke deeply to Hamilton's heart.

Etiquette required that one redoubt be assigned to each ally. The American operation was to be under the top command of the light-infantry general, Lafayette. Lafayette was Hamilton's dear friend. But Lafayette had other dear friends. Among the French soldiers who had come with the Marquis to America was Jean-Joseph Sourbader de Gimat. Gimat had been the first to tend Lafayette when the Marquis had been wounded at Brandywine. He had served for years as Lafayette's personal aide. It had been Lafayette's insistence on moving Gimat into the fighting line which had created the dissatisfaction Washington had liked to cite to demonstrate that a similar commission could not be given to Hamilton.[15] Now Gimat commanded one battalion in Lafayette's light infantry, Hamilton another. The Marquis assigned to his fellow Frenchman the spectacular task of taking the redoubt.

Hamilton rushed into the tent of his old friend. This was preposterous! His commission, which was dated back to when he had become Washington's aide, was senior to Gimat's, and, as it happened, the date of the proposed attack was his turn to serve as officer of the day.

Lafayette could have pointed out, whether or not he did so, that Gimat possessed much combat experience as an infantryman and Hamilton had none. All we know for sure of what must have been a very stormy interview—how Hamilton railed at seeing the prize about to be snatched from him!—is what he later told Light-Horse Harry Lee. "Lafayette excused himself by saying that the arrangements made had been sanctioned by the commander in chief, and could not be changed." Hamilton "repelled this answer . . . announcing his determination to appeal to headquarters."[16]

And so Hamilton sat down at his camp desk to write another appeal to Washington, whom he had estranged and who had refused him so often.

39

The Longed-for Consummation

Wbox{W}ASHINGTON'S feelings when he read, in the handwriting he knew so well, what Lee called "a spirited and manly letter," can only be conjectured. He hated to change a decision, but there must have lingered in his breast friendship and a sense of obligation towards Hamilton. And then there was the matter of American prestige. The Yorktown campaign had been in essence a French affair. It had been forced on Washington by Rochambeau and made possible by French might. Since no American officer had been familiar with the sophisticated techniques of a siege, the strategy and tactics pursued had been from day to day explained to the Americans by the French. Furthermore, the French artillery, using brand-new cannon with shells that exactly fitted, had consistently outshot the American gunners.

One of the two enemy redoubts had been assigned to each ally. Was that entrusted to the Americans also to be taken by French officers— Gimat obeying Lafayette? Washington may well have been happy to discover that since Hamilton was to be the officer of that day, Gimat "had been called to command out of the tour of service."[1]

Fish remembered that Hamilton ran up to him shouting, "We have it! We have it!"[2]

The Frenchman who was assigned the attack on the other redoubt, the Count de Deux Ponts, remembered how his companions, while wishing him "success and glory," expressed "regrets at not being able to be with me." It was all "very sweet and elevating to the soul." Hamilton's fellow officers undoubtedly expressed a similar envy, which Hamilton, like Deux Ponts, found delightful.[3]

Rivalry instantly developed between the two services. The French officers remarked "in the most natural way" that, of course, the Americans lacked the training and ability to storm a professionally defended redoubt.[4] Such comments, made to Lafayette among others, must have come to Hamilton's ears.

Lafayette, perhaps in consultation with Hamilton, prepared for the possibility that the enemy would respond with a major sortie from the city. Since the entire light infantry would be deployed, Hamilton's corps would serve as a spearhead. He was assigned some "pioneers" with axes to chop at the works, and three infantry battalions. Hamilton having the command, Gimat's battalion would lead the frontal attack, followed by Hamilton's battalion directed by his former college mate Major Fish. The third battalion, under his dear friend Laurens, was "destined to take the enemy in reverse and intercept their retreat." Further back would be the first battalion of the supporting force, commanded by Hamilton's former Elizabethtown schoolmaster, Colonel Francis Barber.[5]

The night of October 14 came down clear but suitably dark. When visibility was extinguished, Hamilton's force gathered at the mouth of the American second parallel. The troops were already excited and uneasy—they saw officers attaching bayonets to staves—when, at Hamilton's command, the officers explained to the men their mission. All guns were to be unloaded, lest telltale shots give away the intended surprise. The men were to fight with bayonet only. And all hostilities were to cease the instant the enemy surrendered.*[6]

Washington came riding up, accompanied probably by Lafayette, an appearance which emphasized the importance of the operation. With what mixture of emotions did Hamilton salute the General who had, after so much unpleasantness and so long a delay, finally given him such a command as he desired? Washington, so Captain Stephen Olney remembered, "made a short harangue, admonishing us to act

---

* Benedict Arnold, now a British general, had led a raid on his own former community, New London, Connecticut. After the redcoats had with considerable loss captured an American redoubt, they had avenged their killed comrades by massacring the surrendered defenders. In anticipation of the fall of the British redoubt, many officers had argued, so Lafayette remembered, "that reprisals must be resorted to as the only means to stop such cruelties."[7]

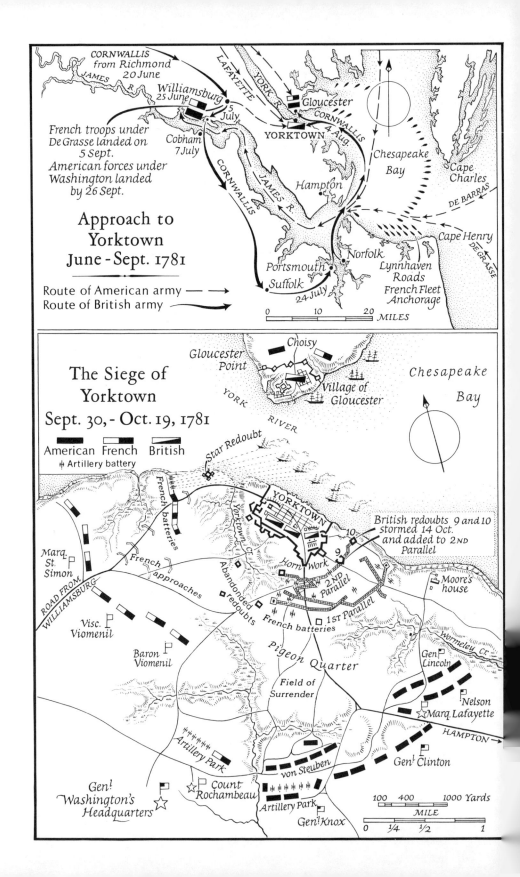

Approach to Yorktown June–Sept. 1781

CORNWALLIS from Richmond 20 June

JAMES R.

LAFAYETTE

YORK R.

Williamsburg 25 June

5 July

Gloucester

CORNWALLIS

YORKTOWN

4 Aug.

Cobham 7 July

CORNWALLIS

French troops under De Grasse landed on 5 Sept. American forces under Washington landed by 26 Sept.

JAMES R.

Hampton

Chesapeake Bay

Cape Charles

DE BARRAS

Cape Henry

DE GRASSE

Norfolk

Lynnhaven Roads French Fleet Anchorage

Portsmouth

Suffolk

24 July

Route of American army —→
Route of British army ⟶

0   10   20   MILES

The Siege of Yorktown Sept. 30, – Oct. 19, 1781

American French British
⚜ Artillery battery

Gloucester Point

Choisy

Village of Gloucester

YORK RIVER

Chesapeake Bay

Star Redoubt

French batteries

YORKTOWN

Yorktown Cr.

10

British redoubts 9 and 10 stormed 14 Oct. and added to 2ND Parallel

Marq. St. Simon

French approaches

Abandoned redoubts

Horn Work

9

2ND Parallel

Moore's house

ROAD FROM WILLIAMSBURG

French batteries

1ST Parallel

Visc. Viomenil

Baron Viomenil

Pigeon Quarter

Wormeley Cr.

Gen.l Lincoln

Field of Surrender

Nelson

Marq. Lafayette

HAMPTON →

Artillery Park

von Steuben

Gen.l Clinton

Gen.l Washington's Headquarters

Count Rochambeau

Artillery Park

Gen.l Knox

100   400   1000 Yards

MILE

0   ¼   ½   1

the part of firm and brave soldiers, showing the necessity of accomplishing the object, as the attack on both redoubts depended on our success."[8]

After Washington had ridden away, Hamilton led his corps into the ditch. Directly behind him were the pioneers, dangling their axes. Next came Gimat, advancing in a low babble of French since he had invited to take part in the honorific action a group of titled French volunteers. Then, although invisible to Hamilton, came the long snake of nervous men, the ranks cramped between the tightly packed dirt walls.

Hamilton knew that in another trench, close by on the left, the French detachment was similarly advancing. The two columns were to emerge at the same moment onto level ground that extended to the separate but closely placed enemy redoubts. The signal to take off would be a succession of five French shells rising into a tranquil section of the sky. Two brilliant planets, Jupiter and Venus, were in close conjunction there. When Hamilton caught sight of them, he had a momentary shock, thinking they were the signals. The men were all allowed to sit down. Surely Hamilton paced as best he could in the narrow space where the trench ended.[9]

At last, the signal! With the minimum of noise—only a rustling and an occasional clang of arms—the men emerged from underground onto the huge, flat, bare plain. To hushed orders they were rearranged into longer ranks, dim in a darkness deepened by bright flashes far to the left, where an artillery barrage was being mounted to distract the attention of the enemy.

Hamilton gave another whispered order that was in whispers disseminated among the soldiers: one man from each company should volunteer to lead the attack as part of what was known in military parlance as a "forlorn hope."[10] In a few moments, some twenty soldiers had moved to the front. Hamilton stepped ahead of them and took off at a run. The whole column, he assumed, would come pelting behind him.

At a distance of a quarter of a mile, the enemy redoubt was visible in the starlight, square and high. At every step Hamilton took, it became larger and more distinct. There was no nearby sound of firing, yet Hamilton saw some of his men topple and vanish as though transmuted into air. They were, he discovered, dropping into craters, hardly visible in the dark, which had been dug by exploding shells. Perhaps Hamilton fell into one himself. In any case, the advance moved so swiftly that Hamilton and the "forlorn hope" and perhaps some of

Gimat's battalion had reached the outside of the fort before the silence was shattered by musket fire sounding from the ramparts. The bangs and flashes, which indicated that the attack had been discovered, unlocked the throats of the American soldiers. A Hessian remembered, "They made such a terrible yell and loud cheering that one believed the whole wild hunt had broken out."*[11]

The fire from many muskets flared overhead, revealing the walls, the crenellations from which the flashes issued, and, directly in front of Hamilton, an abatis. This was the eighteenth-century equivalent of a barbed-wire entanglement. Tree trunks had been fastened to the ground with strong branches, shortened and sharpened, pointing outward to form an impenetrable thicket. Here the pioneers were to use their axes while the troops waited. Lead was pouring down from above. Men were falling around Hamilton. He may well have seen Gimat slump to the ground.

The infantrymen did not wait for the pioneers. The abatis having been made ragged by cannonballs, soldiers managed to squeeze between the sharpened branches to where the trunks were fastened to the ground. A tug and a heave-ho, and at least one trunk was unsettled. Into the resulting gap men crowded, those further back pushing, during deadly seconds, against the backs of those before them.[12]

Hamilton was surely one of the first through. With the others, he jumped into a ditch. He gave orders to bring up the saucissons—tightly tied bundles, four to six feet long, of small branches—which had been prepared to fill the ditch. But, "the ardor of the troops" (as Hamilton put it) would not permit them to wait. From the wall that rose from the ditch protruded a bristle of sharpened sticks. By swinging on these, the men broke the points off, changing a defense into a succession of footrests with which to climb the wall. Up they went to find, rising vertically from the top, a "palisade" of sharpened wood. But some of the palisade had been broken during the previous bombardment. Hamilton, who was determined always to be first, squeezed through to find footing on the parapet. He and the men around him were now face to face with the enemy.[13]

"Captain Olney," Hamilton was to write, "who commanded the first platoon of Gimat's battalion, is entitled to peculiar applause." Olney himself tells us that, when he reached the parapet, he had "not less than six or eight bayonets pushed at me. I parried as well as I could with my espontoon [a combination of spear and battle-axe carried by officers], but they broke off the blade part. . . . One bayonet pierced

* The wild hunt takes place at the winter solstice, when Odin, the god of the dead, summons a storm in which he leads his subjects howling across the sky.

my thigh and another stabbed me in the abdomen, just above the hip bone. One fellow fired at me, and I thought the ball took effect in my arm. By the light of his gun, I made a thrust with the remains of my espontoon, in order to injure the sight of his eyes, but, as it happened, I only made a hard stroke in his forehead. At this instant two of my men, John Strange and Benjamin Bennett, who had loaded their guns while they were in the ditch, came up and fired upon the enemy, who part ran away and some surrendered; so that we entered the redoubt without further opposition."[14]

When Gimat's battalion, which Hamilton wrote "came under my immediate observation," had reached the abatis, his own battalion under Major Fish "unlocked" themselves by moving to the left, "as had been directed," and "advanced with such celerity as to arrive in time to participate in the assault." Laurens's battalion came in from behind to capture the British commander. Even the pioneers had, although this was against orders, climbed over the rampart, menacing the enemy with their axes. As Hamilton put it, "there was a happy coincidence of movement," the redoubt being "in the same moment enveloped and carried in every part." The British and Hessian garrison of about sixty men surrendered. They had, so Hamilton wrote, "made an honorable defense." But "from the firing of the first shot by the enemy to their surrender was less than ten minutes."[15]

The French were still embroiled in their assault, partly because the redoubt they were attacking was somewhat stronger than Hamilton's, but more because the men, suffering the while heavy casualties, stood still, as they were trained to do, while the French equivalent of the pioneers correctly tore down the obstructions. Hearing battle sounds after Hamilton's redoubt had been silenced, Lafayette, remembering the slurs of the French regulars, sent Major Barber with an offer of American assistance. However, the delay was slight before this redoubt also surrendered.[16]

What Hamilton had captured, the little square of bloody soil surrounded with walls of sod and masonry and a broken palisade, teemed with men. As Major Campbell prepared to hand his sword to Hamilton, a captain from Vermont threatened to kill the enemy commander as a reprisal for New London, and was prevented, so camp gossip ran, by Hamilton. Hamilton was to report: "Incapable of imitating examples of barbarity and forgetting recent provocations, the soldiery spared every man who had ceased to resist." The twenty or so prisoners were gathered in a corner under guard.[17]

Barber's battalion came up over the wall to help the defense against possible counterattack, thus raising to six hundred the number of men in a space built to hold about sixty. Corpses—nine from Hamilton's corps and some eight from the enemy—were laid out in the ditch for future removal. The severely wounded—Hamilton had thirty-one in all—were being treated by doctors beside the dead.[18]

The British were now directing at the environs of the fort a tremendous cannonade. ("I never," wrote the exhilarated commander of the French assault, "saw a sight more beautiful and majestic.")[19] Yet fresh light infantry succeeded in passing through the barrage to relieve Hamilton and his men. As they withdrew across the dark no-man's-land that was weirdly lit by bursting shells, Hamilton could descry an advancing line of earth thrown up as if by a gargantuan mole. By dawn, the hundred American diggers had extended the second parallel to include the captured redoubt.

To varying degrees in varying personalities, exterior recognition is necessary to private satisfaction. Insofar as Hamilton's yearnings could be satisfied by a demonstration purely to himself, his triumphant achievement of what he had so passionately desired must have been deeply healing. But the appreciation of the world failed to reach the pitch he had anticipated and now considered his due.

Hamilton's dream in its entirety had been to stun the world with what would be recognized as an individual exploit. But his success had been only part of a larger whole, and military praise automatically mounts the ladder of rank. We know of General Patton, but not of the officers who commanded his tank spearheads. Even Hamilton's intimates McHenry and Lee gave the main credit to the commander of the entire light infantry operation, Lafayette.[20]

Furthermore, the nature of the assault Hamilton commanded militated against its being regarded as his personal achievement. He had, in a last-minute power play, taken away from Gimat an already organized operation. And once he had given the order to charge, his control vanished. On reaching the redoubt, the men did not listen for Hamilton's orders: they were off and Hamilton was hardly more than one of the crush. In his official report, he wrote, "As it would have been attended with delay and loss to wait for the removal of the abatis and palisades, the ardor of the troops was indulged in passing over them."[21] Indulged? There was no way Hamilton could have stopped them!

The attack was so quickly successful because of the unstructured aspects of American society which Hamilton came so to deplore. Since every man had thought and operated for himself, the credit for the victory did not focus naturally on the official commander. In their accounts of the battle, none of our diarists, not Duncan nor Olney nor Martin, even mention Hamilton.[22]

Hamilton wrote his pregnant wife: "Two nights ago, my Eliza, my duty and my honor obliged me to take a step in which your happiness was too much risked. I commanded an attack upon one of the enemy's redoubts; we carried it in an instant, and with little loss. . . . There will be, certainly, nothing more of this kind; all the rest will be by approach; and if there should be another occasion, it will not fall to my turn to execute it.

"You will see the particulars in the Philadelphia newspapers."[23]

There having been in those days no newspaper correspondents with the army, the account of the assault, which traveled slowly across the land as one paper printed from another, consisted of the complete publication of three official reports: first, Washington's to the President of Congress; next, Lafayette's to Washington; and then Hamilton's to Lafayette.

Washington lumped together the attack made by "the American light infantry under the command of the Marquis of Lafayette" and the French attack. "I have the pleasure to inform your Excellency that we succeeded in both. Nothing could exceed the firmness and bravery of the troops." Hamilton was only mentioned as the author of a report that followed.[24]

Lafayette's letter, while describing the operation on a larger scale, specifies that Hamilton "commanded the whole advanced corps." His "well-known talents and gallantry were on this occasion most conspicuous and serviceable."[25]

Hamilton's report to Lafayette showed him at his most controlled best. He began, "I have the honor to render you an account of the corps under my command in your attack." This, and his signature at the end, were the only overt assertions of his leadership. For the rest, he gave a brisk and enthusiastic account of what had taken place, mentioning favorably by name thirteen officers, and praising, in general, every soldier engaged. "I sensibly felt at a critical period the loss of the assistance of Lt. Col. Gimat who received a musket ball in his foot, which obliged him to retire from the field." If the implication throughout was that Hamilton and the other officers had more control of the battle than they actually did, this was the least that could be expected.[26]

Although Washington might have praised his former aide by name, it had been suitable within the realms of military protocol that Lieutenant Colonel Hamilton be shown as in a subordinate position. Concerning this—and its reflection in the newspapers—Hamilton did not, as far as his writings show, complain. But he was infuriated that no notice of his achievement was taken by Congress. He was allowed, he wrote, "no reason to believe that my services have appeared of particular value to Congress as they declined giving them any marks of their notice on an occasion which appeared to my friends to entitle me to it, as well by the common practice of sovereigns as by particular practice in this country in repeated instances."[27]

Congress had signalized the capture of Stony Point by having a gold medal struck for General Wayne. For just bringing the news of Cornwallis's surrender, Tilghman was voted "a horse properly caparisoned and an elegant sword." Hamilton anticipated (as it turned out correctly) that the King of France would honor the Count de Deux Ponts for his capture of the other redoubt. But in relation to Hamilton, Congress did nothing.[28]

Although this was the most conspicuous occasion, it was far from being the first time that Congress had slighted the young genius, a phenomenon difficult to explain did we not know that Hamilton, who was throughout his career to be so trusted and distrusted, had already inspired the distrust of influential civilian leaders.

40

Enter the Law

URING the rest of the Yorktown campaign nothing happened
to endanger the on-rushing victory. The night after the capture of the redoubts, the British did make a gesture to save
their honor: Cornwallis sent out into the second parallel some 350
troops. But, after inflicting and receiving a sufficient number of casualties, the survivors dashed back into the citadel. Uninterrupted, the
second parallel advanced so close to the walls that mortar shells could
be lobbed into the British encampment at will. In a last twitch, Cornwallis made a gesture towards fleeing across the York River, but he
lacked boats and horses and allowed himself to be turned back by a
thunderstorm. The next morning an officer with a white flag appeared,
bearing Cornwallis's offer to surrender.[1]

Once the fighting had ended, Hamilton abandoned his battalion,
leaving the command to Major Fish. Concerning his trip home to
Albany, Schuyler wrote, "He thought of nothing but reaching [home]
the soonest possible, and, indeed, he tired his horse to accomplish it,
and was obliged to hire others at Red Hook."[2]

Home again, he was "very sick." Two months later, he was still
"alternately in and out of bed."[3] This was, of course, the routine reaction of his "frail constitution" to the withdrawal of extreme strain, but
how different in its surroundings was this illness from the others!
Then, he had suffered in some hired lodging, attended, if at all, by
fellow officers. Now he lay luxuriously in the only solid and prosperous

Hamilton at Yorktown. Detail of *The Surrender of Cornwallis* by John Trumbull. Standing at the extreme right are Hamilton, Laurens, Colonel Walter Stewart, and Major Nicholas Fish. Their portraits were all painted from life. Copyright, Yale University Art Gallery, 1975

home he had ever experienced. The rich master of the house loved and admired him. And Hamilton had a wife who adored him. On January 22, 1782, she bore him a son whom they named Philip in honor of the patriarch.[4]

After being reproached for not writing enough "about our little stranger," Hamilton replied, "When I wrote last, I was not sufficiently acquainted with him to give you his character. I may now assure you that . . . he is truly a very fine young gentleman, the most agreeable in his conversation and manners of any I ever knew. . . . His features are good, his eye is not only sprightly and expressive, but it is full of benignity. His attitude in sitting is by connoisseurs esteemed graceful and he has a method of waving his hand that announces the future orator. He stands, however, rather awkwardly and his legs have not all the delicate slimness of his father's. It is feared he may never excel as much in dancing, which is probably the only accomplishment in which he will not be a model. If he has any fault in manners, he laughs too much. He has now passed his seventh month."[5]

When out in the world, Hamilton had again and again reiterated to Betsey that he longed to give up ambition and live only in the light of her shining black eyes. Every overtense individual has dreams of happiness achieved not by struggle but in relaxation. Yet relaxation is a gift men like Hamilton do not possess. His correspondence breathes no contentment. To Major Fish, he complained querulously that a bundle of goods, which had been his share of the booty taken at Yorktown, had been so incompetently sent as to be plundered on the road. He had received only some scraps of clothing, among them "one silk stocking, two odd gloves, and a parcel of thread." Fish should think twice about breaking off his engagement to an unnamed lady: "The girls have got it among them that this is not your first infidelity."[6]

As for Laurens, he received from Hamilton a letter which he considered "as masterly a piece of cynicism as was ever penned."[7]

How could Hamilton put his mind, as he admitted he should do, on preparing to make his living after the war was over, when he was chewing the cud of wrath at having been deprived of his just reputation as a warrior and slighted by Congress? And what of the upcoming campaign?

Despite Yorktown, the war was going on. Cornwallis's surrender had involved only about a fourth of the enemy force in North America, and the British lion, although embroiled in many parts of the world, was quite capable of sending, if she pleased, reinforcements to her former colonies. It was hard for Hamilton to believe that Washington, who was in Philadelphia conferring with Congress about the coming campaign, would not call for his services. General Lincoln, the Secretary of War, had kept the possibility open through making a great exception when ordered to save scarce funds by discharging officers not on active duty. Lincoln had kept on only five such: four Frenchmen, who had important connections abroad, and Hamilton, who, so Lincoln explained to Congress, possessed "superior abilities and knowledge of his profession."[8]

In late February, having heard nothing from Washington, Hamilton posted for Philadelphia, where the Commander in Chief was still conferring. His questions to members of the Family elicited the old frustrating answer: nothing was planned for him. On October 1, he dispatched to Washington two letters: one specifically for His Excellency, the other to be forwarded, he hoped, to Congress. Their combined intention was an amazing one: although Congress had been unwilling to reward Hamilton, Hamilton was trying, while demonstrating himself to be altogether high-minded, to threaten Washington with possible congressional disapproval if he were not employed.

Should Congress "hereafter learn that though retained on the list of officers, I am not in execution of the duties of my station," he did not wish to have that attributed to a lack of zeal. Although "the difficulties I experienced last campaign in obtaining a command will not suffer me to make any further application [to Washington] on that head," he wished Congress to be apprised "upon what footing my future continuance in the army is placed that they may judge how far it is expedient to permit it." Congress should know that he would obey "the call of the public in any capacity civil or military (consistent with what I owe to myself)."

Demonstrating an aristocratic disdain for money, he made a renunciation which his heirs were to petition later Congresses to counteract. Lest the legislators should conclude that, having no post, he was taking money for nothing, he renounced all present salary and (to complete the grand gesture) all rights he would have to half pay after the peace. But he would not resign altogether. The present prosperous appearances might decline, and the cause need again "the services of persons whose zeal, in worse times, was found not altogether useless."[9]

If Hamilton had hoped to elicit from Washington an assignment, he was disappointed. Receiving absolutely no answer to his letter, he became "in such a hurry to get home that I could think of nothing else."[10]

For almost exactly a year, there was no further direct communication between Hamilton and Washington. When during June the former aide, now in Albany, felt a need to advise His Excellency, he wrote Knox, asking him to use in this crisis "your influence with the General."

The situation had been caused by the growing propensity of loyalists in the British service to hang random patriot prisoners in retaliation for the killing of loyalists behind the American lines. After Captain Joseph Huddy had been thus executed, Washington decided that, to prevent a mounting succession of murders on both sides, strong measures were required. With the approval of Congress, he announced that, unless the British command brought the killers of Huddy to justice, he would hang a British military prisoner chosen by lot. Hamilton wished Knox to point out to Washington that "so solemn and deliberate a sacrifice of the innocent for the guilty must be condemned on the present received notions of humanity," and would encourage in Europe "an opinion that we were in a certain degree in a state of barbarism." Then, as was usual when he questioned a policy on moral grounds, Hamilton pointed out a way by which, should expediency so require, the policy could nonetheless be carried through with the least damage to the state. It was not necessary to risk the reputation of the Commander in Chief, who was "considered" America's "first and most respectable character. . . . Let us . . . appoint some obscure agents to perform the ceremony and bear the odium which must always attend even justice itself when directed by extreme severity."[11]

As it turned out, the British command acted in a manner that made it feasible to spare the hostage.

"You cannot imagine," Hamilton wrote, "how entirely domestic I am growing. I lose all taste for the pursuits of ambition; I sigh for nothing but the comforts of my wife and baby. The ties of duty alone—or imagined duty—keep me from renouncing public life altogether. It is probable, I may not any longer be actively engaged in it." Yet ambition would not doze and be silent.

France had entered the war not because of any real sympathy with the American revolutionaries, but because she wished to lighten the weight Britain could exert on the balance of power. Since all the nations of Europe were weighed in that balance, readjustments presented to every ruler a chance to gain or lose power. From almost the moment of France's entry into the war, various European courts had sought, by serving as mediators, to help establish a new stability satisfactory to themselves. Only after Spain's "good offices" were spurned by the British did Spain become a belligerent.

By 1782, all the belligerents were sick of the conflict. For England, 1781 had been in particular a disastrous year, not only at Yorktown, but in the West Indies, the Mediterranean, and the Near East. Peace feelers were emerging from Whitehall like the tentacles of an octopus.

It was ever more clear that the future destiny of the United States would now depend much less on battlefields than on the council chambers of Europe—Paris seemed to be the chosen spot—where American representatives would try to keep American interests from disappearing under the towering breakers of European politics. Since December, 1779, when Hamilton had been nominated secretary to Franklin at Versailles, he and his friends had made efforts to shift him to the international scene. His possibilities had been considerably dampened when, in June, 1781, Congress had appointed five peace commissioners: Franklin, John Adams, John Jay, John Laurens's father Henry, and Jefferson. But this conclave had not yet been assembled because there was yet no call for their meeting. Only Franklin was in Paris. Laurens, who had been captured, was imprisoned in the Tower of London; Jay was in Spain; Adams was in Holland; and Jefferson, recovering at Monticello from his tribulations as wartime governor of Virginia, had actually resigned. Before Lafayette had sailed back to France, he had established with Hamilton a code through which he could send him secret diplomatic information. During June, Lafayette wrote encouragingly from Paris: "Jefferson does not come. Mr. Laurens, I am told, intends to return home." Adams considered his presence necessary in Holland. "You have a good chance, and I believe you have time."[12]

Thus arose Hamilton's first concern with Jefferson. If the Virginian stuck to his resignation, Hamilton might slip into the breach. But Congress reelected Jefferson and the Virginian (although he never got to Paris on time) agreed to serve. None of the other commissioners withdrew. Hamilton's chances shredded to nothing.

On resigning from Washington's Family, Hamilton had expressed a determination to pursue "studies relative to my future career in life."[13] Since then more than a year had elapsed, but he had not even indicated, in any document that survives, what that career was to be. The break came in April, 1782: he petitioned the Supreme Court of New York to suspend in his case the imminent lapse of a provision that would exempt men who had been studying law when they entered the army from a required three years' service as a lawyer's clerk before being admitted to practice. In granting Hamilton a stay until October, the court noted that he had declared he had "previous to the war directed his studies to the profession of law."[14]

This was an exaggeration. Writing in 1797 to an uncle in Scotland, Hamilton stated the situation more accurately: "Having always had a strong propensity to literary pursuits . . . I was able, by the age of nineteen, to qualify myself for the degree of Bachelor of Arts in the College of New-York, and to lay the foundation for preparatory study for the future profession of the law."[15]

This foundation had been in the reading he had undertaken as part of his pamphlet battle with the Reverend Seabury. In *The Farmer Refuted,* he revealed that he had read Locke, Montesquieu, Pufendorf, and others, whose works on the law of nature and nations were considered prerequisite to the study of English law. He had read Blackstone, Coke's *Reports,* Beawes's *Lex Mercatoria,* and some source on the principles of feudal tenure. Further to aid him in his arguments, he had examined both English statutes and acts of American legislatures.[16]

We know exactly when Hamilton started on his new career. It was May 2, 1782, when his and Schuyler's friend, the lawyer James Duane, wrote him, "I am much pleased to find that you have set yourself seriously to the study of the law."[17] Why had Hamilton put off for so long committing himself to the obvious profession for a magnetic and logically minded young man whose emotions turned so naturally to adversary proceedings?

During November, Hamilton wrote Lafayette that he was "studying the art of fleecing my neighbors."[18] This was his only characterization, during those early months, of his new profession.

Hamilton had written Laurens succinctly, "I hate money-making men." There can be no doubt that he would have been more comfortable had he possessed an independent income that made unnecessary the earning of money. That he imbibed this attitude from his father is obvious.

Hamilton enjoyed squandering money like a lord. He had spent his only equivalent of patrimony on uniforms to make resplendent his artillery company, and in acts of generosity to his soldiers. He had just renounced, like an earl throwing away a bauble, his claims to half his military pay for life. Such gestures were more agreeable to him than making a living, but make a living he must.

It was, of course, true that he had married money. In the Old World, it would have been the most natural thing for him to live off the Schuylers while he collaborated with them on ruling the state. Yet this was the New World. Hamilton's aristocratic leanings were not a natural growth of any environment he had ever himself experienced. And Schuyler would have seemed a freak in London high society: he lived on the edge of a wilderness and, far from relying on men of lower class, he was his own estate manager and business agent.

Financial relations between Hamilton and his father-in-law, although cordial and affectionate, were never relaxed. When subsidy came naturally, as when Betsey and the baby and Hamilton himself were living at Albany, there seems to have been no problem. But when Betsey set out to join her husband away from home, Alexander scrambled to raise cash for her expenses. If he needed to borrow from Schuyler, both men were embarrassed, and the father-in-law, while complying graciously, made it clear that Hamilton held no automatic entrée to his strongbox.

Hamilton, who had resented the dependence of serving Washington as aide, had, in fact, no desire to depend on his father-in-law. Nor did he wish to settle under his wife's dynastic roof. He intended, as soon as the British evacuated New York City, to establish his own home there. The Schuyler prosperity had enabled him to dawdle, but the time had come when he needed to "make a more solid establishment."

After he had been in actual practice for more than a year, Hamilton wrote, "Legislative folly has afforded so plentiful a harvest to us lawyers that we have scarcely a moment to spare from the substantial business of reaping."[19] In those days, before courts had found the power to establish law except on the most minor scale; when there was, indeed, no court with jurisdiction beyond state lines, Hamilton saw the practice of law primarily as a scratching for private advantage. Ordinary litigations, in which each attorney sought not to present the totality of the law but only those aspects that would best serve his client's ends, tended more to pull order apart than to put it together—and Hamilton's passion was for order. It was in emending governmental folly that the true contribution—and the satisfaction—lay. Partly, perhaps, because of the strength of his private obsessions, Hamilton was always more at ease operating in the public rather than the private sector. Throughout his career, he was always ready to abandon his lawyer's office for any public call that was "consistent with what I owe to myself."[20] And he defined what he owed himself only very secondarily in terms of money.

The young genius scorned the normal procedure of studying law under a preceptor. He had available for consultation John Lansing, Jr., the custodian of Duane's law library, which Hamilton used. Lansing

The scene of Hamilton's temporary retirement: a street in Albany revealing the essentially Dutch character of the old town. From the *Columbian Magazine*, December, 1789. Courtesy, Library of Congress

had, after serving as Schuyler's military secretary, returned during 1777 to an already started legal practice in Albany. Hamilton described the lawyer, who was only slightly his senior, as "accurate and active in business," with a "just view of public affairs," which meant that he favored a strong federal government and reformed administration in New York State. Closer at hand, staying indeed on the Schuyler estate so that they could study side by side, was Hamilton's old friend Troup, who had been in and out of the study of the law since before the Revolution, but was only a little further along than Hamilton.[21]

Ever since he had found surcease from a dreadful past in keeping Cruger's books, Hamilton got pleasure from mastering details. And his refusal to work under a preceptor presented him with delightfully complicated problems.

The legal manuals used in America were all imported from England, but American practice down the years had evolved in its own directions. The new usages were, furthermore, different from state to state. (One reason that Troup, despite his long studies, was hardly more than level with Hamilton was that he had become conversant with New Jersey rather than New York law.) A major function of a preceptor was to communicate to his students the local usages that were general knowledge but had never been written down.

Seeking to master such information, which he had acquired from diverse sources, Hamilton began an extensive compendium headed by a subsequent copyist "Practice Proceedings in the Supreme Court of the State of New York." When finally printed in 1964, the manuscript ran to over 150 pages. It is characterized by Julius Goebel, Jr., the editor of Hamilton's law papers, as bearing "all the earmarks of a student work. . . . Indeed, the cursory fashion in which Hamilton deals with some of the thirty-eight topics into which the work is divided bears a striking resemblance to the sort of synthesis which a law student might devise today if interested in the procedural aspects of the law for a particular examination." Hamilton frankly admitted when he did not understand, and was not sparing of such comments as "the court . . . lately acquired . . . some faint idea that the end of suits in law is to investigate the merits of the case and not to entangle in nets of technical terms." He writes of "the absurdities in which law abounds."[22]

The document Hamilton produces is the first known effort to summarize in writing the law as particularly practiced in one of the American states. Troup tells us that it "served as an instructive grammar for future students, and has been the groundwork of subsequent practical treatises by others on a larger scale." There exist, in fact, in hands not Hamilton's, one complete copy and a partial one.[23]

Less than three months after he had started seriously on studies that under a preceptor were supposed to take three years, Hamilton was formally accepted as an attorney qualified to practice before the Supreme Court of the State of New York. In another three months, the minutes of the court read: "Alexander Hamilton, Esquire, having on examination been found of sufficient ability and competent learning to practice as council [the equivalent of an English barrister] in this court, ordered that he be admitted accordingly." The speed with which he had proceeded would have been sensational under any circumstances, yet his preparations had occupied only part of his time. His principal attention had turned to other things.[24]

41

Tax Collector

WHEN Hamilton had been in Philadelphia, he surely took advantage of Robert Morris's suggestion that they keep in touch. He was impressed into writing, "Our financier has hitherto conducted himself with great ability, has acquired an entire personal confidence, revived in some measure the public credit, and is conciliating fast the support of moneyed men."[1] However, he had given Morris to understand that his own ambitions were still military.

But it became obvious that, even if at long last he were somehow to secure a command, there would be no honor to gain. The British, quiescent at Charleston, Savannah, and New York, were not disturbing the patriots elsewhere. Word came in that Parliament had voted against the continuation of the war, thus forcing the resignation of the North ministry. True, North's successor, Lord Shelburne, was opposed to independence, but he would pursue his ends at the conference table. And the Americans could not, as Hamilton noted, attack the British in any of their fortified bases without the military assistance of France. However, Rochambeau's army had sailed home, and de Grasse had suffered a defeat in the Indies that removed the French fleet, at least for the time being, from the board. The Americans needed an army only to keep the British from being tempted to change their intentions.[2]

After Hamilton had stuck exclusively to his lawbooks for about a month and a half, a mutual acquaintance informed Morris that he was "disposed to quit the military line" and "would accept the office of receiver of the continental taxes for the state of New York." Morris offered Hamilton the office. His salary would be "four percent on the monies you receive."[3]

Hamilton replied, "My military situation has indeed become so negative that I have no motive to continue in it, and if my services could be of importance to the public in any civil line I should cheerfully obey its command." But he could not "relinquish" his studies of the law unless he was given "a sufficient inducement." He feared that, because taxes were so hard to collect, his percentage would not total more than a hundred pounds annually. "You will perceive, sir, that an engagement of this kind does not correspond with my views."[4]

When Morris offered to pay Hamilton a percentage on the whole quota of the state, whether it was collected or not, Hamilton's eagerness was such that he was disappointed at not catching the return mail. The answer was yes. However, he was worried because the system of taxation in New York was so "vicious" that his service might not be "an equivalent of the compensation." The best hope was that "by personal discussions" he could persuade the legislators to emend the system. The legislature would meet early in July. Would Morris empower him to act as the treasury's representative? He was not making this request "to augment the importance of [the] office but to advance the public interest."[5]

Morris replied that one of the principal objects of his appointment was to take advantage of Hamilton's former position in the army, "your connections in the state, your perfect knowledge of men and measures, and the abilities which heaven has blessed you with." Hamilton could certainly forward the public service by convincing the legislature that the army must be copiously supplied. "What remains of the war," he should point out, is "only a war of finance."[6]

The brand-new position Hamilton now held represented a halfway step towards the idea, which Hamilton had supported, of having congressional appointees collect taxes in the states. He was empowered only to demand and receive taxes which would be collected for continental use by state appointees. A second function was to collect information for Morris.

The financier had been ordered to balance the accounts of the states with the continental government, but the federal books had been so badly kept that Morris had to ferret out where the balances lay. Hamilton was to discover what money, goods, transportation, and so on,

New York had supplied. Morris also wanted to know the tax laws of the state, how they were enforced, the amount and nature of the paper currency still in circulation, and what sums were in or were expected in the state treasury.[7]

When Hamilton sought information, no man was ever more assiduous in collecting it. He set fervently to work, cross-questioning by letter and in person every official who should know. He received an impressive lack of cooperation. Governor Clinton pleaded being busy and also a lack of authority. He passed the buck to lesser officials, who delayed or did not answer or sent fragmentary information Hamilton often did not believe. The "studied backwardness," Hamilton wrote Morris, seemed an effort to hide disorderly records or derelictions even worse.[8]

Hamilton's efforts were not helped by the resentment of the Clinton faction that a Schuyler man should have been appointed receiver of taxes instead of their candidate, Robert Yates. At a presumably conciliatory meeting between Hamilton and Yates, Hamilton argued, with all his fire and prolixity, the importance of strengthening federal authority. Yates, becoming as he admitted "a little hot under the collar," answered that in his opinion Congress already had too much power. To Morris, Hamilton characterized his rival as "a man whose ignorance and perverseness are only surpassed by his pertinacity and conceit. He hates all high-flyers, which is the appellation he gives to men of genius."[9]

When in mid-July Hamilton journeyed to Poughkeepsie for the meeting of the state legislature, he was far from "sanguine." Although the legislature would probably do "something," nothing effective could be achieved without an entire change in the system of taxation. "To effect this, mountains of prejudice and particular interest are to be leveled." He intended to point out that, despite the seeming calm, the situation was "critical." French military help had evaporated, and the universal reluctance of the American states to do their duty would encourage the British to abandon their own "blunder, perverseness, and dissension." Unless Congress received funds to carry on the war and reform the economy, independence could still be extinguished.[10]

The legislature passed a resolution deploring the lack of power permitted Congress, particularly in relation to the raising of funds, and urging a convention of the states expressly authorized to revise and amend the Articles of Confederation. This preshadowing of the Constitutional Convention is, of course, attributed to Hamilton, who is said to have drafted the document. There are three good reasons to doubt this: Hamilton was not a member of the legislature; the literary style is too clumsy to be his; in a letter to Morris reporting what he had done, Hamilton mentions the resolution without claiming any specific part in it. But Schuyler, the leader of the Federalist faction, was undoubtedly involved, and Hamilton was, of course, in cahoots with Schuyler.[11]

Hamilton explained to the financier that at his request a committee of both houses had been appointed to confer with him. He had expounded to them the defects of their tax system. They all agreed that something was wrong, "but few were willing to recognize the mischief when defined and consent to a proper remedy." In the end the legislature voted to raise £18,000 in hard money appropriated—"at present," Hamilton commented—to the federal treasury. Hamilton doubted that Morris would see much. A more promising achievement was the appointment "at my instance" of another committee "to devise in the recess a more effectual system of taxation and to communicate with me on this subject."[12]

When the legislature elected their delegates to the Continental Congress for the next year, Hamilton was among the choices for the assembly, Schuyler for the senate. Schuyler withdrew in favor of his son-in-law. This family arrangement was not mentioned by Hamilton when he wrote to various friends that he had been "pretty unanimously" elected to Congress. Since the session to which he was accredited would not begin until late October, Hamilton had time till then to work for the financier.[13]

After three months of investigation, Hamilton sent Morris his "full view of the situation and temper of this state."[14]

New York had been the main theater of the war. The capital and its environs were perpetually occupied by the British, and the northern frontier was periodically devastated by Indian raids. The state had, in effect, been reduced to "little more than four counties." When military calamities had threatened, the population had been subjected to "extraordinary" calls for assistance, which "distressed and disgusted the people." Apprehension of further dangers and the opinion that the state had been obliged to contribute more than its neighbors, had made "the rulers [sic] . . . very willing to part with power in favor of the federal government."[15]

"As to the people," almost half had in the early periods of the war been pro-British. "The state by different means has been purged of a large part of its malcontents; but there still remains, I dare say, a third whose secret wishes are on the side of the enemy; the remainder sigh for peace, murmur at taxes, clamor at their rulers, change one incapable man for another more incapable." Too many would, if left to themselves, accept peace at any price, not from a disinclination to independence, "but from mere supineness and avarice."[16]

The internal government suffered "from the general disease which infects all our constitutions: an excess of popularity. There is no *order* that has a will of its own. The inquiry constantly is what will *please* not what will *benefit* the people." The result: "temporary expedient, fickleness and folly."

Taxes were supposed to be collected according to "*circumstances and abilities.* . . . The ostensible reason for adopting this vague basis was a desire of equality. . . . The true reason was a desire to discriminate between the Whigs and Tories." Assessments were based on the likes and dislikes of the assessors. On a higher level, the legislature established quotas for the various counties. This produced "cabal and intrigue" to shift the burden. Indeed, no one down the line wished to assume the onus of collecting taxes, and the pay for collecting was so small that there was "no sufficient incentive. . . . Notwithstanding there is a pretty general discontent . . . , ancient habits, ignorance, the spirit of the times" and the opportunities offered to profit from favoritism "have hitherto proved an overmatch for common sense and common justice, as well as the manifest advantage of the state and of the United States."[17]

From all this, Hamilton concluded that Morris could expect little money from New York.

In describing the political situation with which he and Morris had to cope, Hamilton made clear that the groupings were much less based on issues than the personal alliances of certain powerful individuals. The man with literary ambitions then gleefully launched on thumbnail sketches of these individuals. Not surprisingly, whether his judgments were favorable or unfavorable turned on how far his subjects shared his concern and Schuyler's with federal power.

"There is no man in the government who has a decided influence in it." Governor Clinton was the most powerful, Schuyler next. Clinton could be firm when necessary, and "passes with his particular friends for a statesman," but his ambition, and also the fact that "the preservation of his place is an object to his private fortune," made him temporize, particularly as an election approached. The implication was clear that, because wealthy, Schuyler was more to be trusted. Hamilton wrote that Schuyler had more weight than Clinton with the legislature,

Above: Gouverneur Morris and Robert Morris, by Charles Willson Peale. The two co-operating Revolutionary financiers (they were not related) were both associated with Hamilton. Courtesy, Pennsylvania Academy of the Fine Arts

Left: James Madison, by Charles Willson Peale. Looking amazingly youthful for his thirty-two years, the constitutional genius was thus depicted when, at the end of the Revolutionary War, he was collaborating with Hamilton in the Continental Congress. Courtesy, Library of Congress

but he was nonetheless "exposed to the mortification of seeing important measures patronized [sic] by him frequently miscarry."

Hamilton enjoyed dipping his pen in vitriol. John Morin Scott, to
whose regiment his artillery company had been linked for purposes of
supply, "has his little objects and his little party. Nature gave him
genius, but *habit* has impaired it. He never had judgment; he now has
scarcely plausibility. His influence is just extensive enough to embarrass measures he does not like; and his only aim seems to be by violent
professions of popular principles to acquire a popularity which has
hitherto coyly eluded his pursuit."[18]

Cornelius Humphreys "has his admirers because he is pretty remarkable for *blunder* and vociferation. He said the last session in the
assembly that it was very inconvenient for the country members to be
detained at that season, that for his own part no motive would induce
him to stay but to *sacrifice* the interest of his country."[19]

It was fun to write those pen portraits, but did they really help the
financier carry out his duties? Hamilton seems to have sent them off
without any concern that they would get into wrong hands, a misfortune that might well have brought his political career in New York
to an end. However, when a month had passed without Morris's acknowledging receipt of his letter, he expressed "anxiety to learn the
safe arrival."[20] The letter had arrived safely.

On September 9, 1782, Congress resolved no longer to use its best
source of income, loans from France, to pay interest on the internal
debt of the United States. This pinched the financiers who had lent the
government money and also the speculators who had bought up, for a
few pennies on the dollar, certificates given for goods and services that
had been issued to poorer men who could not await eventual payment.

Led by the creditors in Philadelphia, an effort was made to organize,
on a national basis, the possessors of federal obligations that were
being defaulted on. Partly in response to this call, a group of moneymen from the Albany area met there on September 25 under Schuyler's
chairmanship. They issued a call for a statewide meeting of creditors
(it never met). The explanatory statement, which demanded sound
financial institutions and insisted that the "purity of faith" of the American people required financial probity, has again been attributed to
Hamilton. From the style in which the statement was written, the
attribution is not impossible, yet in mentioning the document to
Morris, Hamilton made no claim to authorship. Discretion, it is true,
required that a federal employee should not be known as the author,
but Hamilton was never discreet with Morris.[21]

In October, Hamilton met with the committee the legislature had appointed to confer on the general question of taxation. Under his dynamic influence, they agreed to taxes on land at its actual value, on all personal property, on carriages, clocks, watches, and other articles of luxury. But even the eloquence of the abstemious Hamilton could not make them agree to an excise on all distilled liquors. Worse still, when adjournment approached, the committee outraged their young mentor by refusing to put anything in writing. Although Hamilton insisted that this would "leave everything afloat to be governed by the impressions of the moment when the legislature meet," they would not go beyond promising a verbal report.[22]

At raising actual money to send on to the financier, Hamilton was no more successful than he had foreseen. His explanations did not impress Morris, who was used to having every state plead poverty: "I believe your state is exhausted, but perhaps even you consider it as being more so than it is." Finally the financier, beleaguered at every side by bills he could not pay, snapped out at his New York collector:

Sir,

I have received your favor dated at Albany on the 19th instant with the enclosures. What you say of your prospect with respect to the receipt of money for taxes is as you may easily suppose very unpleasing. I hope it will soon assume a different appearance. Unless something more be done by the states, many very dangerous as well as disagreeable consequences are to be apprehended.

With sincere esteem I am, sir,
your most obedient servant

Robert Morris[23]

This put on Hamilton blame for what he himself deplored. As he wrote Lafayette, "I make no apology for the inertness of this country; I detest it."[24] But he took no offense with Morris. His role as receiver of taxes, with any servility that it might imply, was almost at an end. Soon he would be off to Congress, where he would be as much a free agent as any elected official can be.

In his effort to raise taxes, Hamilton had seen nothing to alter his conviction of "the worthlessness of the human race,"[25] but he had begun what could be a most fruitful collaboration. He had established cordial relations with a financier much more skillful and resourceful than his previous mentor, Schuyler. A professional moneyman, who did not divide his attention with soldiering or farming or dynastic politics, Morris combined solid financial skills and a speculator's audacity. Sometimes he seemed able to pick funds out of the air.

Although, for "many reasons" that he did not specify, he did not appoint the man Hamilton recommended to be the next tax collector, Morris wrote the departing aide, "The justness of your sentiments on public affairs induce my warm wish that you may find a place in Congress so agreeable as that you will be induced to continue in it."[26] Hamilton was soon to find himself collaborating, from a position no longer subordinate, with "the financier of the American Revolution."

42

Temptation

" I AM going to throw away a few more months in public life," the
new congressman wrote the Marquis de Lafayette, "and then I
retire a simple citizen and good paterfamilias. . . . You see the
disposition I am in. You are condemned to run the race of ambition all
your life. I am already tired of the career and dare to leave it."[1] Most
men would regard the entry into public life as daring, not the leaving
of it.

To Meade, Hamilton wrote confusedly: "No man looks forward to a
peace with more pleasure than I do, though no man would sacrifice
less to it than myself, if I were not convinced the people sigh for
peace."[2] What sacrifice would Hamilton be unwilling to make for the
peace that he so desired? Was it personal? Or did he mean that he
would go on with the war rather than accept a peace treaty not altogether advantageous to the United States?

In reporting to Meade his election to Congress, Hamilton commented, "I do not hope to reform the state, although I shall endeavor
to do all the good I can." To Laurens, he looked forward with more
resolution and enthusiasm: "Peace made, my dear friend, a new scene
opens. The object then will be to make our independence a blessing.
To do this, we must secure our *union* on solid foundations, a herculean
task, and to effect which mountains of prejudice must be leveled! It
requires all the virtue and all the abilities of the country. Quit your
sword, my friend, put on the *toga*, come to Congress. We know each

other's sentiments; our views are the same; we have fought side by side to make America free. Let us hand in hand struggle to make her happy."[3]

Hamilton's letter probably never reached his friend. What Washington called Laurens's "intrepidity bordering on rashness" made him break the doldrums in South Carolina by taking the lead of a skirmishing party, an exercise "unworthy," as Greene put it, "of his rank." He was killed.[4]

Thus was banished from the world a spirit whose continuing presence would have undoubtedly altered Hamilton's career. The two extraordinarily able young soldiers, both audacious, both possessing the gift of commanding loyalty and attention, would surely have continued to interact. Mitchell, assuming that Laurens would have been to his hero a faithful satellite, sees the loss as a detriment to Hamilton.[5] Yet, while Laurens lived, he had always been the more successful, throwing away opportunities that Hamilton vainly yearned for. Would the roles have been reversed, making Hamilton the leader? More probably, the two men whose temperaments and ideas only partially overlapped, would have broken apart, adding to Hamilton's opponents in his own age group—Madison, Monroe, Burr, and others—a very potent force. Laurens was profoundly oriented towards the South, where Hamilton's greatest opposition was to grow, and he was passionately concerned with an issue that Hamilton regarded as a digression dangerous to more important considerations: emancipation.

Hamilton wrote Greene: "I feel the deepest affliction at the news we have just received of the loss of our dear and inestimable friend Laurens. His career of virtue is at an end. How strangely are human affairs conducted that so many excellent qualities could not ensure a more happy fate? The world will feel the loss of a man who has left few like him behind, and America of a citizen whose heart realized that patriotism of which others only talk. I feel the loss of a friend I truly and most tenderly loved, and one of a very small number."[6]

Money was so scarce and subsistence in Philadelphia so expensive that the New York legislature, although they correctly elected five congressmen, expected only two to serve. The perpetual workhorse was William Floyd, who had signed the Declaration of Independence and was excellent at committee work. Hamilton was to replace the flashing member, James Duane. Ruling Hamilton "eminently qualified," Duane was eager to be relieved so that he could get back to his law practice in New York, but his complaints and Hamilton's own passion for continental government did not make Hamilton violate the habit, which was one of Congress's many impediments, of drifting in whenever it was convenient. Due on November 4, he did not arrive until the 26th.[7]

Betsey had stayed behind in Albany. On December 18, he wrote to her to come by sleigh over the first snow. "I do not know whom you will get to travel with you. I am loath that you should make so long a journey alone. For God's sake take care of my child on the journey."[8]

Three weeks later he complained that he had received no news. "I am inexpressibly anxious to learn you have begun your journey. I write this for fear of the worst, but I should be miserable if I thought it would find you at Albany. . . . I have borne your absence with patience till about a week since, but the period we fixed for our re-union being come, I can no longer reconcile myself to it. Every hour in the day I feel a severe pang . . . and half my nights are sleepless. Come, my charmer, and relieve me. Bring my* darling boy to my bosom!"[9]

By mid-February Betsey was with her husband. But she was back in Albany during July.[10]

Hamilton had dealt with legislative committees but had never before sat in any legislative body. He may well, since there were then no galleries for the public, have never before attended a legislative debate. Although he entered Congress as a man well known, he was not universally trusted or admired. It is a testament to his competence, his magnetism, his gift for leadership, that he quickly became an influential member and was, before the year was out, to pull the Congress after him in one of his most obsessive adventures.

Importantly for his future career, he found himself in close collaboration with a man physically smaller than himself, who had a large head, eyes dimly blue and inward-looking, a scholar's body, and spindly legs. Six years Hamilton's senior, James Madison possessed a theoretical mind which had, at the outbreak of the troubles with Great Britain, moved from theology to terrestrial government. Through years of experience, he had become a seasoned legislator. He often hung onto Hamilton's coattails, trying to curb the firebrand's intolerance and indiscretion.

Not that Hamilton always needed to be held back. He revealed the prescient statesmanship that characterized him at his most intellectual

* Hamilton referred, in writing his wife, to "my child" or "my son," not to "our child" or "our son."

and controlled when dealing with the issues raised by the region now called Vermont. He was saddled with them because of his official role as a representative of New York.

Both New York and New Hampshire had long claimed the territory, and each state had granted to different people titles to the same land. The New York titles, usually for large areas, had been given to prosperous political leaders, including Schuyler. The New Hampshire grants went to poor men who actually settled the land. New York sheriffs who tried to drive off the settlers were met with gunfire. Some of the gunfire almost certainly came from the Green Mountain Boys, the settlers' private army that had played an important part in early patriot victories. But when it became clear that the inhabitants' claims would not be accepted either by New York or Congress, they established an independent nation, which they called Vermont. They petitioned to enter the union as a state, and at the same time, in part to scare Congress, they negotiated to join Britain as an extension of Canada.[11]

Being New York's official spokesman, Hamilton steered through Congress a resolution threatening Vermont with violence. However, in warning Governor Clinton not to count on "the coercive part," he urged negotiation and conciliation. The Continental Army would be far from enthusiastic at being sent on such an errand, all the more because many officers had procured land grants from "the usurped government of Vermont."[12]

There had never, in fact, been a less propitious moment for demanding of the army so divisive an errand.

The financial crises that had long bothered the United States were tremendously accelerated by the arrival in December of European dispatches which made it appear that peace was at hand, independence won. The existing scene seemed about to close as a new one opened. Everything became less significant for its immediate impact than for its long-range effect.

The hopes that Congress would be enabled to meet its debts to the soldiers and private creditors, that it would secure the money to carry on the war, were all centered on the acceptance, by the unanimous vote of the states called for in the Articles of Confederation, of the proposal that the federal government should be given its own source of income by being empowered to collect customs revenues. By December, the states had slowly, one after another, all agreed—all except tiny Rhode Island. Fearing perpetual interference with its sovereignty,

Rhode Island now voted no. If the smallest state could not be made to change its decision, federal solvency was scuttled.

Hamilton secured a congressional vote for a deputation to be sent to Rhode Island. Collaborating now with Madison, he prepared for the deputies an argument to take along that was much milder and more conciliatory than any Hamilton would have written by himself. The statement could only frighten those who were already in a state of mind to be frightened.

It was not true, so the argument ran, that a federal impost would bear hardest on the commercial states. These states would pass on their costs to consumers everywhere, thus receiving, in fact, an additional profit from their markup on the increased price. The result would be throughout the nation the most equitable of taxes. Imported goods being primarily bought by the well-to-do, the tax would be apportioned according to people's ability to pay.

To Rhode Island's contention that the impost would, by enabling Congress to be financially independent, permanently endanger the liberty of the states, Hamilton and Madison responded with arguments that presaged their defense of the eventual national Constitution in *The Federalist*. The security of general liberty lay not in clipping the wings of the central authority, but in frequent elections and rotation of offices that would keep the central power representative of all interests. The statement that the impost "if not within the letter is within the spirit of the Confederation" contained the soul of the doctrine of "implied powers," which was to be established eight years later with the chartering of Hamilton's Bank of the United States. As in Hamilton's other expositions, he insisted that the honor of the United States was deeply committed to paying just debts to civilian creditors.[13]

Madison's and Hamilton's draft was unanimously endorsed by Congress; even the Rhode Island delegation voted for it.[14] But before the congressional delegates could reach the delinquent state, word came in that the Virginia legislature had rescinded their approval of the impost. The measure, on which federal solvency depended, lay dead on the floor. And at that moment representatives of the army came storming in.

In its necessary efforts to save money, Congress had, during the previous August, voted to reduce the size of the army, but there had been no money to pay what was owed the officers who were being retired. Washington wrote Secretary of War Lincoln: "I cannot help fearing the result . . . when I see such a number of men, goaded by a thousand stings of reflection on the past and of anticipation on the future, about to be turned into the world, soured by penury and what they call the ingratitude of the public, involved in debts, without one farthing of money to carry them home, after having spent the flower of their days, and many of them their patrimonies, in establishing the freedom and independence of their country, and suffered everything human nature is capable of enduring on this side of death. I repeat it: these irritable circumstances, without one thing to soothe their feelings or frighten the gloomy prospects—I cannot avoid apprehending that a train of evils will follow of a very serious and distressing nature. . . .

"You may rely upon it, the patience and long sufferance of this army are almost exhausted, and that there never was so great a spirit of discontent as at this instant. While in the field, I think it may be kept from breaking out into acts of outrage, but when we retire into winter quarters (unless the storm is previously dissipated) I cannot be at ease respecting the consequences."

The army was now wintering on the hills behind Newburgh, New York, where they had nothing to do in the dreary weather but think. During previous periods of depression, the officers had, sometimes "at the hazards of their lives," labored to quell mutinies, but now they were threatening to resign in a body, leaving, on the very verge of triumph, the United States defenseless. They felt that once the peace came and they were disbanded, they would be forgotten.[15]

By laboring hard, Washington had channeled the protest into a respectfully worded address to Congress. But the officer corps had added an unspoken threat: a three-man delegation would carry the address to Philadelphia, wait there to find whether the soldiers would be accorded justice, and then report back.[16]

Reaching Philadelphia on December 29, the delegation began by conferring with individual congressmen. Since the chairman was Hamilton's first military sponsor, General McDougall, and another member was his friend Colonel John Brooks, he was surely among those informed of the dangerous situation at Newburgh and given a preview of the address:

"To the United States in congress assembled: We, the officers of the army of the United States, in behalf of ourselves and our brethren the soldiers, beg leave freely to state to the supreme power, our head and sovereign, the distress under which we labor. Our embarrassments thicken so fast that many of us are unable to go further. Shadows have been offered to us, while the substance has been gleaned by others. The citizens murmur at the greatness of their taxes, and no part reaches the army. We have borne all that men can bear. Our property is expended; our private resources are at an end. We therefore beg that a supply of money may be forwarded to the army as soon as possible.

"The uneasiness of the soldiers for want of pay is great and dangerous; further experiments on their patience may have fatal effects. There is a balance due upon the account for retained rations, forage, and arrearages on the score of clothing. Whenever there has been a want of means, defect in system, or neglect in execution, we have invariably been the sufferers by hunger and nakedness and languishing in a hospital. We beg leave to urge an immediate adjustment of all dues.

"We see with chagrin the odious point of view in which too many of the states endeavor to place the men entitled to a pension of half-pay. For the honor of human nature we hope that there are none so hardened in the sin of ingratitude as to deny the justice of the reward."

For the officers, the pension was the most important issue. During 1781, when the mutiny of the Pennsylvania line was sending shock waves across the land, Congress had enacted what was an established right in the British army: the officers who served until the end of the war should be rewarded with half pay for life. This had caused a storm of protest in the states. Many civilians, particularly those in New England, automatically distrusted soldiers. Were soldiers to be perpetuated through peacetime as a privileged class, supported in idleness by the sweat of honest workers' brows? Conscious of an opposition too great to be overcome, and also eager for more available funds, the officers suggested, as part of their petition, "commutation." Instead of half pay for life, they would receive full pay for a number of years, calculated as half the average life expectancy after the peace. This at least the officers were determined to have.[17]

On January 6, the petition was laid before Congress. To show how seriously they took the matter, Congress made its most impressive gesture: it appointed a "Grand Committee" made up of a representative of each state. Hamilton and Madison were members.

Phenomena which seem inexplicable have a way of being omitted from historical writings as making no sense. Thus, an important aspect of the various financial plans and arguments Hamilton had fathered after he was no longer active as a soldier has been overlooked. In his statements that the United States should not sully her virtue, honor, and reliability by repudiating debts, Hamilton referred primarily to civilians, whose contribution to the war effort had been property. The distresses of the soldiers, who had suffered physical hardship, expended blood, and put their lives, the years of their youth, into the balance—or of the widows and orphans of soldiers who had died in the cause—were added only as makeweights.

This may have made sense for Hamilton's allies. Madison, with his spindly legs and scholar's stoop, had no congeniality with fighting men. Schuyler's military career had been frustrated, leaving him hurt and angry, partly because, as a wealthy patrician, he had tended to despise the cannon fodder he commanded. Hamilton, too, carried a chip on his shoulder concerning the military, but his rise in prominence had been as a soldier, and from his first preserved letter to his death on the dueling field, he visualized himself as a warrior.

When Hamilton passionately sought an objective, he moved like a missile that pulls all air currents into patterns that will serve its flight. His objective now was to establish national financial credit as a firm foundation on which a strong nation could be built. Dribbling out money to soldiers and widows and orphans would not do this. Like water poured on sand, the money would disappear in small purchases.

Hamilton had, as a gesture of magnanimity and anger, renounced for himself all that the soldiers had a right to and were crying for. He had been able to do this because of his marriage and his confidence in his own abilities. He was a young man who had, despite his slight frame, not been physically weakened by the war. What about the innumerable other officers whose position was much less fortunate? Hamilton, who could be marvelously solicitous of and generous to his friends and dependents, was never interested in the welfare of groups, except insofar as their well-being contributed to his conception of a strong, well-organized nation.

There had been many small civilian creditors—farmers, for instance, whose hay had been requisitioned and paid for with a certificate—who would, like the soldiers, dribble away in small purchases any sums they might receive. But as good luck (at least from Hamilton's point of view) would have it, most had been too financially strapped to hold on to their paper. Sold for a fraction of presumed value, the certificates had moved into the strongboxes of the men who also held larger government liabilities. Thus, the payment of federal obligations would concentrate large sums in deep pools from which money could be drawn to turn the wheels of progress. That this would foster a class of capitalists Hamilton welcomed. The financially powerful class would owe its prosperity to national institutions, and therefore be cemented to the union.

At first glance, Hamilton's intentions seemed to clash with his often-expressed disdain for money men, but within his total philosophy these seeming irreconcilables came into easy accord. Since he had a low opinion of the human race and did not believe, as did Jefferson, that much could be achieved by appealing to disinterested virtue, Hamilton concluded that men were best led through their vices. To lead them thus for ends that served the public good was admirable as long as the projector kept himself pure. Hamilton intended to remain personally immune to financial lures. As time went on, his Jeffersonian enemies became desperately frustrated that they could not catch him taking advantage of the dubious expedients he was opening to others. As it turned out, the financial planner who opened such wealth to others died bankrupt.

That Hamilton felt, when his system was finally in train, an agreeable superiority to those who guzzled in the trough, and that his followers admired his abstemiousness to the point of making him a secular saint, cannot be denied. However, it is doubtful that at this early date he foresaw what was going to take place. He did not realize that he would draw to himself a band of devoted followers. He did not foresee that he was creating a pressure group for special interests, a political party, what Jefferson vituperatively called "a corrupt squadron." In 1781, Hamilton saw only powerful individuals being lured to support Congress.

There remains in Hamilton's attitude a contradiction hard to explain. His vision of a strong government involved support for a powerful standing army. Why then did he now give a secondary position to paying debts to the soldiers? Perhaps he felt that human gratitude was as evanescent as any money the soldiers might receive when they went home to their families. When a peacetime army was established and paid, its allegiance would be secured. Or perhaps he was off too strongly on one tangent to worry about another.

Although the references to the "dissatisfactions" of the soldiery had been put by Hamilton into the arguments for federal funding largely as a bogeyman to scare the public, the army had, without invitation, come roaring in. The first reaction of Congress and even of Morris had been disapproval: the military was stepping out of its rightful place by petitioning civil authorities and sending observers to report back the result. But the military delegates proved to see eye to eye with the two Morrises and with Hamilton concerning continental power and continental funding.*

* Because of its makeup and experience, the army was, of course, a continental body. Furthermore, the Massachusetts line had already appealed to their state legislature, which had been happy to pass the problem—although without any money with which to solve it—to the Continental Congress.[18]

On January 12, Hamilton wrote Governor Clinton: "We have now here a deputation from the army, and feel a mortification of a total disability to comply with their just expectations. If, however, the matter is taken up in a proper manner, I think their application may be turned to good account."[19] It could be used to strengthen Congress and secure permanent funds with which to fund the continental debt.

The way the cards were now falling had been foreseen and dreaded since the Revolution had started. History taught the lesson. Civil conflicts create chaos, which can be returned to order most efficiently by force. And it is the army that has the guns. A movement that is started to create governmental reforms usually ends up in tyranny.

The possibility had been viewed by all responsible American leaders with dismay. Hamilton had envisioned an army as the muscle of strong government, but no more wished that government to be in itself military than did such financial leaders as Robert Morris and Gouverneur Morris. Furthermore, the Continental Army was a band not of mercenaries but of idealists who themselves dreaded tyranny. None of them had created the crisis out of a desire to seize power.

Yet the situation did exist. It lay like a sharpened sword before beleaguered men. If the sword were picked up, what would happen? Would a mere brandishing in the air suffice to dispel injustice and create order? Or would it be necessary to strike? If force were actually used, could that force be limited? Could the sword, after immediate objectives had been achieved, be laid down again? And suppose it were picked up, how should it be manipulated to achieve the desired result? Might not the movement get out of hand? Might not opposing swords be drawn? Might not the resulting conflict tear apart the nation Hamilton and his allies wished to pull more tightly together? The sword could be plunged into the breasts of those who had first unsheathed it.

Such quandaries disturbed all thinking men, and Hamilton was a thinking man. But he was bolder than most, more reckless, more prone to extremes.

43

The Edge of the Precipice

[JANUARY–MARCH, 1783   AGE 26]

H AMILTON'S position, as a congressman in Philadelphia, was in the very nexus of the approaching storm. Although as a planner his main concern was with the interests of the moneymen, he was personally closer to General McDougall, who headed the army delegation, than with Morris, the financier. And in Congress he was regarded, because of his military service, as an army spokesman.

Morris admitted that the army's demands were just. He added that he had no money with which to pay these just demands because of the refusal of the states to permit Congress to levy its own funds. On January 9, McDougall reported to General Knox, his contact in the Newburgh camp, that "a great majority" of Congress were anxious to help and many were more pleased than otherwise "at the army's address coming on." However, because of the behavior of the states, Congress was helpless. "What," asked McDougall, "if it should be proposed to unite the influence of Congress with that of the army and the public creditors to obtain funds for the United States?"[1]

On January 13, the Grand Committee of Congress (Hamilton present) "gave audience" to the army delegation, and were threatened. Colonel Ogden announced that "he wished not to return to the army if he was to be a messenger of disappointment to them." McDougall stated that the army "were verging on that state which we are told will make a wise man mad." Colonel Brooks added that "the temper of the army was such that they did not reason or deliberate coolly on consequences, and therefore a disappointment might throw them blindly into extremities."[2]

As a member, with Madison and Rutledge, of a subcommittee, Hamilton drew up the report.

Concerning the debts accumulated from the past Hamilton argued that the troops, *"in common with all creditors,"* had the right to expect that Congress would make every effort to obtain "substantial funds adequate to the object of funding the *whole* debt of the United States."* Funding meant that Congress would not operate from hand to mouth, but would establish and sequester a pool of money for the specific purpose of meeting eventual capital payments, and, in the meantime, paying interest.

Each officer, so the report continued, should be allowed to determine whether he would receive, after the peace, half pay for life or full pay for a number of years. If not paid in cash (which was, of course, at the time, impossible), the obligation should be met with notes bearing interest and grounded on good funded security. Here were laid out in embryo some of the major measures that Hamilton was, when Secretary of the Treasury, to achieve.[3]

Hamilton's recommendation, in the committee report, that Congress give immediate consideration "to the most likely mode of raising permanent funds" initiated a long debate during which Hamilton was often on his feet. He dismayed Madison by repeating, in a manner "imprudent and injurious to the cause," what he had already argued in "The Continentalist": having federal tax collectors in the states would in itself extend the power of Congress by "pervading and uniting the states." Madison commented, "All the members of Congress who concurred in any degree with the states in this jealousy [suspicion of the impost] smiled at this disclosure." Hamilton, they said, "had let out the secret."[4]

As the debate continued, Hamilton opposed, as tending to weaken federal power, every concession that might make a federal impost more palatable to the states. Having thrashed around in other directions vainly, Congress finally resolved to try to make work the method of taxation specified for them in the Articles of Confederation: a tax on land and buildings collected for Congress by the states according to valuations locally established. Hamilton passionately pointed out pitfalls. The states would vie with each other in undervaluing their land.

* Italics added.

The states would not raise anything substantial because their collectors, being "chosen by the people," were "more subservient to their popularity than to the public revenue." When Congress finally decided they had no choice but accept the tax to which they had an obvious legal right, Hamilton expressed pleasure that "its impracticality and futility" would now become manifest.[5]

The army delegation was looking on hungrily, but the tax system adopted could not, even if it worked, bring in any revenue until the following year. Morris took this moment to hurl a thunderbolt by offering his resignation on the grounds that all hope of raising funds to meet the federal debt was at an end. Although he was persuaded to wait a while before making his resignation public, the secret, known to Congress, could not be prevented from reaching McDougall's ears.[6]

It had become known that a British representative had been empowered by his government to treat with "the thirteen United States," which was, in diplomatic parlance, an acknowledgment of independence. Although no further news concerning the peace talks had come across the winter ocean, this was enough to reveal that, unless steps were taken soon—very soon—the states could comfortably shelve their continental alliance and the debts that had, as a result, been incurred.

On February 8, McDougall made his official report to Knox. Concerning present pay, nothing could be obtained beyond a promise of what was owed for one month, and even that to be met not in specie but in paper. The Grand Committee (of which Hamilton was a member), had calculated the life expectancy of officers at twelve years,* and had recommended commutation to full pay for six years. Congress, considering this too generous, had appointed a new, smaller committee. In the end, the whole half-pay issue might be voted down.

McDougall stated that he was trying to frighten the proponents of federal power with the possibility that the army would turn to the states for justice, but "some of our best friends" (surely including Hamilton) had responded with the threat that Congress would pass a resolution opposing, until every possibility of securing federal funds was extinguished, any payments by the states. The states would, of course, not object to being let off the hook.[7]

On February 12, the noose was pulled tighter by the appearance from the stormy Atlantic of a ship bearing what was purported to be a

---

* This is a startling revelation of how much briefer life was in the eighteenth century.

speech by George III in which he told Parliament that he would declare American independence and sign a preliminary peace treaty, already completed, between England and the United States. On the day this news arrived, McDougall took advantage of an arrangement he had made by which he could communicate indiscreetly with Knox over the signature "Brutus."

Brutus wrote: "The sentiment is daily gaining ground that the army will not or ought not to disband until justice is done them. . . . The army ought not to lose a moment in preparing for . . . the worst that may happen to them."[8]

One day after Brutus had thus recommended that the army prepare to mutiny against any command from Congress that they go home with the peace, Hamilton broke the silence that had existed between him and Washington for more than a year. His own statement on what he intended to achieve was recorded in Madison's account of a gathering of congressmen at the home of a Philadelphia member. Hamilton and Richard Peters, who had formerly been secretary of the Board of War, were regarded as the experts on "the temper, transactions, and views of the army." They stated that "it was certain that the army had secretly determined not to lay down their arms" until their pay was assured them. There was reason to expect that a public announcement would soon be made. "Plans had been agitated, if not formed, for subsisting themselves after such declaration."

Hamilton put forward as a proof of the army's earnestness that Washington "was already become extremely unpopular among almost all ranks from his known dislike to any unlawful proceeding; that this unpopularity was daily increasing and was industriously promoted by many leading characters; that his choice of unfit and indiscreet persons into his family [Hamilton's successors] was the pretext and with some real motive; but the substantial one a desire to displace him from the respect and confidence of the army in order to substitute General [name later obliterated] as the conductor of their efforts to obtain justice.

"Mr. Hamilton said that he knew General Washington intimately and perfectly; that his extreme reserve, mixed sometimes with a degree of asperity of temper, both of which were said to have increased of late, had contributed to the decline of his popularity; but that his virtue, his patriotism and his firmness would, it might be depended upon, never yield to any dishonorable or disloyal plans into which he might be called; that he would sooner suffer himself to be cut into pieces; that he (Mr. Hamilton), knowing this to be his true character, wished him to be the conductor of the army in their plans for redress, in order that they might be moderated and directed to proper objects, and exclude some other leader who might foment and misguide their councils; that with this view he had taken the liberty to write to the General on this subject and to recommend such a policy to him."⁹

To Washington, Hamilton wrote that he flattered himself "that your knowledge of me will induce you to receive the observations I make as dictated by a regard to the public good." He did not need to comment on "how far the temper and situation of the army" gave the current situation "delicacy and importance. . . . The state of our finances was perhaps never more critical." Since Congress was unfortunately "not governed by reason or foresight but by circumstances, it is probable we shall not take the proper measures. . . . If the war continues, it would seem that the army must in June subsist itself *to defend the* country; if peace should take place, it *will* subsist itself to *procure justice to itself.*"

Hamilton, who had not been with the troops for some eleven months, informed Washington that it was the general opinion in the army "that if they once lay down their arms they will part with the means of obtaining justice. It is to be lamented that appearances afford too much ground for their distrust."

What then was "the true line of policy? The claims of the army, urged with moderation but with firmness, may operate on those weak minds which are influenced by their apprehensions more than their judgments, so as to produce a concurrence in the measures which the exigencies of affairs demand. They may add weight to the applications of Congress to the several states. . . . But the difficulty will be to keep a *complaining* and *suffering army* within the bounds of moderation. This Your Excellency's influence must effect."

Hamilton urged Washington not to discourage the efforts of the army to procure relief but "*take the direction of them.* This, however, must not appear," since it was of "moment to the public tranquillity that Your Excellency should preserve the confidence of the army without losing that of the people." Knowing that Washington was not much of an intriguer, Hamilton stated the need for "address."

"I will not conceal from Your Excellency a truth which it is necessary you should know. An idea is propagated in the army that delicacy carried to an extreme prevents your espousing its interests with sufficient warmth. The falsehood of this opinion no one can be better acquainted with than myself, but it is not the less mischievous for being false." It tended to impair his ability, "should any commotions unhappily ensue, to moderate the pretensions of the army and make their conduct correspond with their duty.

"The great *desideratum* at present is the establishment of general funds, which alone can do justice to the creditors of the United States, of whom [so Hamilton stated to Washington] the army forms the most meritorious class; restore public credit; and supply the future wants of government. This is the object of all men of sense. In this the influence of the army, properly directed, may cooperate."

Hamilton added a postscript which showed that he knew of McDougall's correspondence and felt himself closer in this matter than Washington himself was to one of Washington's intimates: "General Knox has the confidence of the army and is a man of sense. I think he may safely be made use of. Situated as I am, Your Excellency will feel the confidential nature of these observations."[10]

The day after he sent this appeal to Washington, Hamilton moved towards establishing a haven, a smaller nation where, should the United States go up in flames, he could still build such governmental institutions as he wished to build. He wrote Governor Clinton: "It is to be suspected the army will not disband till solid arrangements are made for doing it justice, and I fear these arrangements will not be made. In this position of things it will be wise in the state of New York to consider what conduct will be most consistent with its safety and interest. I wish the legislature would set apart a tract of territory, and make a liberal allowance to every officer and soldier of the army at large who will become a citizen of the state. . . . It is the first wish of my heart that the union may last; but feeble as the links are, what prudent man would rely upon it? Should a disunion take place, any person who will cast his eye upon the map will see how essential it is to our state to provide for its own security. I believe a large part of the army would incline to sit down among us, and then all we shall have to do will be to govern well."[11]

As Hamilton awaited an answer from Washington, a letter for McDougall came in from Knox. The agitators' correspondent was revealed in a state of utter confusion. He mourned that the efforts to procure redress had only demonstrated that there was no effective governmental body to whom the soldiers could appeal—and the army's muscle could only be brought to bear at one point. Knox hoped "in God" that the military power would "never be directed except against the enemies of America. . . . But still it is particularly hard that the army principally should be the immediate sufferer. . . . I consider the reputation of the American army one of the most immaculate things on earth. But there is a point beyond which there is no sufferance." While assuming that the defects of government could only be righted if a special convention were called for that purpose, Knox hoped that matters would somehow improve in Philadelphia. In the meanwhile, he had not "taken the pulse of the army" or even "called any considerable number of officers together."[12]

Brutus returned to the attack, warning Knox that there was a movement in Congress "to split the army into detachments to prevent their being formidable." Should this be done, the soldiers and the civilian creditors, deprived of the ability to "compel" payment, would receive the shortest shrift. Brutus suggested that the army should "supplicate Congress and the people to keep them together and supplied even into peacetime." Congress would probably agree. If they did not? Brutus could give no advice, not knowing "the present temper" of the army.[13]

As Congress tried desperately to slug out something that might ameliorate the situation, both Morris and Hamilton were leery about accepting palliatives that would hide the need for fundamental and revolutionary financial decisions. Morris publicly announced that unless sound and immediate federal funds were provided, he would resign. This was interpreted as an overt effort to arouse insurrection, and Hamilton (who may or may not have advised him against it) was later to admit to Washington that it had been a mistake. For his own part, Hamilton took advantage of his ability to speak out without determining policy. He explained to Clinton that, while having "a just deference for the expectations of the states," he had made it a "leading rule" of his conduct never to "amuse" the states "by accepting measures based on false principles." He had therefore been part of "a small minority" that had voted against the state-collected land tax on which Congress had finally decided. But he admitted that this tax was the most that public opinion would accept. He hoped that the states would cooperate. Otherwise, "there is an end to the union."[14]

Washington proved in no hurry to answer Hamilton's letter. Some three weeks after it had been dispatched, the reply came in. His Excellency began by complaining that he was not being kept well enough informed; he had not conceived that the financial situation was so dark as Hamilton had pictured. He then expressed dismay that the former aide, who had seen "the unhappy spirit of licentiousness" which had been encouraged in the army during the few instances when they had been forced to be their own providers, should not be more upset by "the fatal tendency of such a measure. But I shall give it as my opinion that it would at this day be productive of civil commotions and end in blood. Unhappy situation this! God forbid we should be involved in it."

Washington agreed that unless Congress were given "powers competent to all *general* purposes . . . the distresses we have encountered, the expenses we have incurred, and the blood we have spilt in the course of an eight years' war will avail us nothing." But "it would be impolitic to introduce the army on the tapis, lest it should excite jealousy." Perhaps Congress should adjourn for a few months, the delegates going home to convince the states. Making no mention of the financiers, Washington hoped that the just claims of the army would have weight with every local legislature.

"The predicament in which I stand as citizen and soldier," Washington continued, "is as critical and delicate as can well be conceived. It has been the subject of many contemplative hours. The sufferings of a complaining army on one hand and the inability of Congress and tardiness of the states on the other, are the forebodings of evil." But he had no intention of leading any such military power play as Hamilton had suggested. "I shall pursue the same steady line of conduct which has governed me hitherto, fully convinced that the sensible and discerning part of the army cannot be unacquainted (although I never took pains to inform them) of the services I have rendered it on more occasions than one." He was under "no *great* apprehension" that the officers would exceed "the bounds of reason and moderation, notwithstanding the prevailing sentiment in the army is that the present prospect of compensation for past services will terminate with the war."

Yet, so Washington admitted, "I may be mistaken if those ideas which you have informed me are propagated in the army should be extensive; the source of which may be easily traced as the old leaven— *it is said,* for I have no proof of it—is again begining to work under the mask of the most perfect dissimulation and apparent cordiality."[15]

The old leaven! Hamilton could not doubt what that meant.

Hamilton had seen in Washington a chance for safe leadership if His Excellency would do what he recommended: lead the army in its refusal to separate or lay down its weapons until national funds were established for three interrelated purposes: pay the federal obligations to the army, pay the civilian creditors, and put the federal government in its own right, apart from the support of the states, on a sound financial base. But, despite his boasted "intimate and perfect" knowledge of his former general, he had clearly failed to persuade Washington. And so Hamilton had to face the quandary that faced all the agitators: if Washington could not be persuaded, who would lead the mutiny?

Knox could not be expected to oppose Washington. Knox had been trained as a soldier by His Excellency; so had all the senior officers still in the service—all except one. What opposition there remained in high military circles was "the old leaven," which had, in the Conway Cabal, supported against Washington the hero of Saratoga, Horatio Gates.

Since then, Gates had been the loser at Camden, but he was now second-in-command of the army at the Newburgh encampment. He was considered a populist and was beloved of the New England democrats, yet he had close ties to the Philadelphia financiers, as is shown by the fact that he had succeeded in borrowing considerable sums from Robert Morris.[16] Various proponents in Philadelphia of military intransigence looked beyond Washington to Gates, whose headquarters was, indeed, soon to unmask itself in Newburgh as the center of agitation.

But Hamilton had many reasons for disliking and distrusting Gates. Gates had intrigued against Schuyler and (according to the family version) stolen from him the victory at Saratoga. Gates had accused Hamilton of dishonorably rifling his papers. Hamilton's other experiences with the then-northern commander had shown him as dishonest, intriguing, and lacking in strength of character. What he would do at the head of a revolting army could not be foreseen. He might be superseded by some firmer, more determined leader. That at present unidentifiable character might well prove an enemy of the moneymen, who were regarded by many soldiers as profiteers responsible for their hardships.

It must be assumed that Hamilton argued against Gates—but he had no one else to suggest. During the sensational denouement of the "Newburgh Conspiracy,"[17] he undoubtedly suffered from the excitement, confusion, and frustration of a man whose hopes and fears are tugging at him from several directions.

Some eight days after the first letter arrived, Hamilton received a second letter from Washington: "When I wrote you last, we were in a state of tranquillity, but . . . a storm very suddenly arose," which Washington had "diverted," although he could not see the end.

In his own letter to Washington, Hamilton had expressed what he claimed was the general opinion of the army. Now Washington wrote Hamilton: "There is something very mysterious in this business. It appears reports have been propagated in Philadelphia that dangerous combinations were forming in the army; and this at a time when there was not a syllable of the kind in agitation in camp." But on the arrival from Philadelphia of Colonel Walter Stewart, a former aide to Gates, it was "immediately circulated that it was universally expected the army would not disband until they had obtained justice; that the public creditors, looked up to them for redress of their own grievances, would afford them every aid and even join them in the field if necessary; that some members of Congress wished the measure might take effect, in order to compel the public, particularly the delinquent states, to do justice." Was there accusation in Washington's report of a suspicion—he was withholding his own judgment for further evidence—that "the scheme was not only planned but also digested and matured in Philadelphia"?[18]

Hamilton undoubtedly heard in detail from other sources what had happened. Two anonymous addresses (they had been written at Gates's headquarters by Gates's aide Major John Armstrong) had been circulated in the Newburgh encampment. The ingratitude of the country was described in the most lurid terms, and the plight of the soldiers, if they went home without pay, in the most pathetic. The author asked the officers, as they huddled together in the frozen countryside: "Can you consent to wade through the vile mire of despondency and owe the miserable remnant of that life to charity which has hitherto been spent in honor? If you can—GO—and carry with you the jest of the Tories and scorn of Whigs—the ridicule and, what is worse, the pity of the world. Go starve and be forgotten."

Otherwise, the officers should "suspect the man who would advise more moderation and further forbearance." They should gather at a mass meeting (which was in effect mutinous since not officially ordered) and draw up an address stating that "the slightest mark of indignity from Congress must now operate like a grave and part you forever; that in any political event, the army has its alternative. If peace, nothing will separate them from your arms but death. If war, that, courting the auspices and inviting the direction of your illustrious leader, you will retire to some unsettled country, smile in your turn, and 'mock when the fear cometh on.' "[19]

Washington read these eloquent words with "inexpressible concern."[20] He had no such equivocal reactions as Hamilton's to employing against the civilian governments military force or threats. He felt obliged, so he wrote his former aide, "to arrest on the spot the foot that stood wavering on a tremendous precipice; to prevent the officers from being taken by surprise while the passions were all inflamed; and to rescue them from plunging themselves into a gulf of civil horror from which there might be no receding." This was done upon the principle that "it is easier to divert from a wrong and point to a right path than to recall the hasty and fatal steps which have already been taken."

The Commander in Chief had denounced the anonymous summons, which was abandoned when he called a later meeting of his own. To Hamilton he explained: "Now they will have leisure to view the matter more calmly. . . . It is to be hoped they will be induced to adopt more rational measures and wait a while longer for a settlement of their accounts."[21]

The officers were to gather at the Temple, a combined meetinghouse and dance hall, on March 15. Whether Washington would face them there personally was not announced, but on the result depended whether or not the army would pass out of bounds and out of Washington's control into the boundless reaches of mutiny and interference with the elected governments. In his concern for order, for due process, Hamilton's rational mind could only hope that Washington would appear and prevail.

44

Financial Collapse

O N March 17, before word had reached Philadelphia of what had happened in Newburgh,[1] Hamilton wrote Washington a letter that showed he had his emotions under complete control except for one slip, which he scratched out. He chose to disregard Washington's refusal to lead any mutinous protest, and to regard His Excellency's call for an official mass meeting as a demonstration that "you coincide in opinion with me on the conduct proper to be observed by yourself."

Hamilton then put forward reasons why, because of the complications of European politics, peace was not absolutely assured. "Some use perhaps may be made of these ideas to induce moderation in the army." However, "I cannot forebear adding that, if no excesses take place, I shall not be sorry that ill-humors have appeared. I shall not regret importunity, if temperate, from the army."

Hamilton stated it was partly true that the conception of an alliance between the army and the other public creditors had been formed in Philadelphia. However, the conception, which he had supported, was merely that the conjunction of all might form "a mass of influence in each state in favor of the measures of Congress. . . . As to any combination of *force*, it would only be productive of the horrors of a civil war, might end in the ruin of the country, and would certainly end in the ruin of the army."

The slip came when he stated that necessity alone could counteract the "dangerous prejudices" against "those measures which alone can give stability and prosperity to the union." He wrote and scratched out "but how is this necessity to be produced?" In the dispatched letter, prudently skirting the possibility of manipulation, Hamilton merely asked how the necessity could be applied and kept "within salutary bounds."[2]

It soon became known that, at the mass meeting at Newburgh, Washington had risked his command by firm opposition to aggressive action. At the beginning it seemed as if his words of caution would be angrily overwhelmed, but his personal magnetism and the love felt for him by his troops combined to draw from the wells of the officers' being their patriotism and their love of freedom. They agreed to do no more than send Congress another petition requesting that they be not discharged or separated until obligations were met.

Washington wrote Congress that if the army were not granted their requests, now scaled down to the utter minimum, "then shall I have learned what ingratitude is; then shall I have realized a tale that will embitter every moment of my future life. But I am under no such apprehensions: a country rescued by their arms from impending ruin, will never leave unpaid the debt of gratitude."[3]

The need was to ascertain the amount owed to each officer and give him a certificate for future payment; to provide for the promised half pay for life or commutation to full pay on half of what was considered the normal life expectancy; and to give some cash to carry home. The solution to the first two necessities required, if it were to be more than empty hum, the establishment of federal funds; the third meant somehow conjuring cash—about $750,000—out of the air. Hamilton was put on the committee to deal with the army's demands. As the hopelessness of doing so remained clear, his confused yearnings for military intervention revived.

On March 25, Hamilton sent Washington two letters: one official, one private. The best Hamilton could officially recommend to Washington was that he assure the army that "the Congress are doing, and will continue to do, everything in their power."[4]

In his private letter, Hamilton mourned that "ingratitude" was so deep in the human heart and so well implanted in Congress. Although he urged the army to moderation and advised Washington to "endeavor to confine them within the bounds of duty, I cannot as an honest man conceal from you that I am afraid their distrusts have too much foundation. Republican jealousy has in it a principle of hostility

to an army. . . . But . . . what can the army do? . . . To seek redress by its arms would end in its ruin. The army would molder by its
own weight and for want of the means of keeping together. The soldiery would abandon their officers [to Hamilton a most frightening
possibility]. There would be no chance of success without having
recourse to means that would reverse our revolution.

"I often feel," Hamilton confided, "a mortification, which it would be
impolitic to express, that sets my passions at variance with my reason."
He confessed that, "could force avail, I should almost wish to see it
employed. I have an indifferent opinion of the honesty of this country,
and ill-forebodings as to its future system."[5]

Washington replied that he had read Hamilton's private letter "with
pain, and contemplated the picture it had drawn with astonishment
and horror—but I will yet hope for the best." Although Hamilton's
imagination had clearly been at work, Washington wrote: "The idea of
redress by force is too chimerical to have had a place in the imagination of any serious mind in this army. But there is no telling what
unhappy disturbances may result from distress and distrust of justice."
He warned Hamilton against trying to separate the army until the
accounts were settled, even if not actually paid.

Suspicions were beginning to be entertained by important officers, so
Washington continued, "that Congress, or some members of it," were,
despite the fact that the army had "contributed more than any other
class to the establishment of independency," trying to make the soldiers "mere puppets to establish Continental funds, and that rather
than not succeed in this measure or weaken their ground, they would
make a sacrifice of the army and all its interests." Washington did not
accuse Hamilton—he mentioned only Morris—but he warned his
former aide: "The army . . . is a dangerous instrument to play with."[6]

Hamilton, who had in Congress "vehemently" (the adverb is Madison's) opposed an effort to lay taxes for the specific purpose of paying
the army, wrote Washington that he "would not be surprised to hear
that I have been pointed out as one of the persons concerned in
playing in the game [you] describe[d]." He explained that it was
necessary to blend the interests of the army with those of the other
creditors, since otherwise the other creditors, who were men of influence, would sabotage in the states any efforts to raise money for the
army. "It is vain to tell men who have parted with a large part of their
property on the public faith that the services of the army were entitled
to a preference. . . . It is essential to our cause that vigorous efforts

should be made to restore public credit," and the "discontents of the army presented themselves as a powerful engine."

As for Morris, he "certainly deserves a great deal from his country." No other man "could have kept the money machine going." Indeed, "the men against whom the suspicions you mention must be directed are in general the most sensible, the most liberal, the most independent, and most respectable characters in our body, as well as the most unequivocal friends to the army. In a word, they are the men who think continentally."[7]

His Excellency replied that the army considered that Hamilton had been zealous in their support. Stating that his own conduct had "been one continuous evidence" of his opposition to "state funds and local prejudice," he went on to warn Hamilton that, should the army believe that Congress was blocking their rights, the soldiers would, irrespective of the long-range political consequences, turn to the states. This would leave the civilian creditors out in the cold, and "might," Washington stated with sarcastic underemphasis, "*tend* to defeat the end they themselves had in view by endeavoring to involve the army."[8]

As it turned out, the menace of the army was dispelled, without serving any of the continentalists' aims, by the very developments which had, in their early stages, heightened the menace. The army had feared being disbanded without satisfaction when no longer needed by war, but as more and more demonstrations of victory came in, as the skies of independence cleared, the individual soldiers felt an increasing need to escape, to go home. The problem changed from getting rid of a possibly mutinous army to how the government could keep in service the token force required until the final documents had been signed and the British had removed their last troops from New York. The soldiers were willing to accept the shadow for the substance.

Congress voted to determine the debts owed each soldier, but the records had been so badly kept that this was impossible. Stingily, the legislators reduced the assumed life expectancy of the officers from twelve to ten years. Full pay for one half of this time should be paid—but not in money. The officers were to receive certificates on which six percent interest was supposed to be paid (if the money were ever available).

In the end, Congress proved unable to give the officers any cash to take home, or even the certificates, since it could not afford the paper on which the documents would have been printed.[9] Although the officers were so angry that they canceled a final dinner at which Washington was to be the guest of honor, a large majority of them did go home.[10] Washington wished he could follow them, but felt it his duty to preside over the remaining rump of the army until peace was official and one hundred percent certain.

As everyone waited for the definitive peace to carry them into a new landscape, Hamilton continued to serve in a Congress that was often hobbled by the absence of enough delegations to pass important legislation (representation from at least nine states was required). In one moment of adequate representation, a bill asking the states to enable Congress to fund the public debt was finally passed. But Hamilton, although he urged New York to cooperate, made his own personal statement by voting no. His "principal objections" were that the length of time specified was only twenty-five years (this would not serve to liquidate Congress's obligations), and more particularly that the funds asked for did not go beyond customs duties and these were to be collected not by federal employees but by officials appointed by the states.[11]

All the more because of the sparse representation Hamilton, often in collaboration with "Maddison"—he could not learn to spell the name— became concerned in almost all the problems that appeared before Congress. Very vexatious was the fact that the American delegates at Paris had evaded their instructions by not informing the French, whom they suspected of wishing to subordinate American interests to theirs, of their negotiations with the British, which had eventuated in the preliminary peace treaty. They had also included a clause which, after the rest of the treaty was disclosed, the French had not been allowed to see. The debate on how Congress should react and whether they should show the secret clause to the French minister, raised issues concerning America's relative confidence in Britain and France, issues that were to appear in a much more virulent form during the wars of the French Revolution, when Hamilton was in Washington's cabinet.

In the 1790s, when the French torch of extreme revolution was igniting much of Europe and might, Hamilton feared, spread its radical fire to the United States, he wanted, even at the risk of war with France, to assist to the utmost brink of possible neutrality the efforts of the British to extinguish by force of arms the French conflagration. Jefferson, of course, opposed Hamilton, wishing similarly to risk war with England. Washington was in the middle, supporting the point of view which in 1783, when France was still a monarchy, Hamilton stated as his own: "We have, I fear, men among us, and men in trust, who have a hankering after British connection. We have others whose confidence in France savors of credulity. The intrigues of the former and the incautiousness of the latter . . . may make it difficult for prudent men to steer a proper course." Then Hamilton went on to express exactly the opposite preference from the one he was to harbor later: If a choice were necessary, one should contrast the comparatively mild French intrigues with Great Britain's "past cruelty and present duplicity; . . . behold her . . . trying every project for dissolving the honorable ties which bind the United States to their ally, and then say on which side our resentments and jealousies ought to lie!"[12]

Hamilton became one of five committeemen assigned to what seems on paper the most impressive of tasks: to provide, in preparation for peace, "a system for foreign affairs, for Indian affairs, for military and naval peace establishments, and also to carry into execution the regulation of weights and measures and other articles of the Confederation not attended to during the war." Hamilton wrote that the committee was "chiefly desirous of establishing good principles, that will have a permanently salutary operation." However, they found themselves making limited reports on immediate and temporary measures, reports on which Congress, in its impotence, usually took no action.[13]

Naturally Hamilton was much concerned with planning a peacetime military establishment. As a member of the committee asking Washington for advice, Hamilton wrote, "I will just hint to Your Excellency that our prejudice will make us wish to keep as few troops as possible." This hint was not necessary since Washington did not share Hamilton's preference for a standing army as a muscle of government. His Excellency recommended, primarily to man West Point and various western forts, a federal force of 2,631 men. The main reliance in case of war would be on state-controlled militias organized, in a consistent manner, under federal advice.[14]

The report of Hamilton's committee, which enlarged the federal force by only 403 men, accepted Washington's basic reliance on militia. Hamilton did slip into a preamble that the militia "ought in all respects to be under the authority of the United States as well for military as for political reasons," but this idea was not taken up again in the detailed plan that followed.[15]

The congressional committee had to face a problem outside Washington's military province: in giving Congress military powers for wartime, the Articles of Confederation made no mention of peace. Pointing out that an army could not be conjured up overnight, and that the forts protected territory beyond the states where they happened to be, Hamilton invoked "implied powers." Since a peacetime army was preparation for wartime, it was, he argued, included in Congress's wartime powers.[16]

In pursuing this theme, Hamilton quietly "surpressed" a resolution sent him for presentation to Congress by the state legislature he represented. The most important forts—West Point, Ticonderoga, Oswego, Niagara—were in New York. Placing his concern for the union over his sometimes despairing wish that New York be able to defend herself, Hamilton explained to Governor Clinton that having the posts supported federally would not only be logical but would save New York the expense of protecting her neighbors.[17]

Hamilton could not have been surprised when the plan for a peacetime army he had drafted vanished, like everything else he was trying to achieve, into what he considered the incompetence and irresolution of Congress.

As April, 1783, shifted to May, Mrs. Hamilton returned to Albany. On May 14, Hamilton wrote Governor Clinton, asking to be relieved by some other representative from New York. "It would be very injurious to me to remain much longer here. Having no future view in public life, I owe it to myself without delay to enter upon the care of my private concerns in earnest." On June 1, he importuned the governor not to let New York become one of the delinquent states that was unrepresented. On June 11, he warned Clinton that he would only stay another ten days. Eight of those days had passed when a crisis struck that would have been better, in light of Hamilton's future career, for him to have missed.[18]

45

Leading Congress on a Wild Path

[JUNE–DECEMBER, 1783   AGE 26]

THE soldiers from the Newburgh encampment were, however resentfully, on their way home when anger over the unpaid debts to the army raised a menacing head on Hamilton's very doorstep.

The Supreme Executive Council of Pennsylvania and the Continental Congress both met in the State House in Philadelphia. On June 19, 1783, the Council communicated to the Congress that they had received warnings that eighty frontiersmen, enlisted in the Continental Army, had escaped from their officers at Lancaster and were marching on Philadelphia to demand pay and other rights. This was doubly disturbing since the troops already in the Philadelphia barracks, "emboldened," as Madison noted, "by the arrival of a furloughed regiment returning [from Washington's army] to Maryland," had sent to Congress two days before a remonstrance that was considered "very mutinous." It had been drawn without the approval of the officers and had, in demanding justice, stated that if an answer were not given that very afternoon, the soldiers would take such measures as seemed right to themselves. Congress had not deigned to reply and the protesters had abandoned their threats. But now there was to be this new infusion of angry soldiers.[1]

Congress appointed Hamilton to a committee of three to handle the situation. One of the other members, being a Pennsylvania representative, soon withdrew. The other, Oliver Ellsworth of Connecticut, was swept along. The young firebrand from New York ran away with the issue, dragging the whole Congress after him.[2]

The first move was to command Major William Jackson, the Assistant Secretary of War, to induce, by using all the persuasion in his power (he had nothing else in his power), the approaching mutineers to go back to Lancaster. Unheeding, the mutineers, commanded by their noncommissioned officers, entered Philadelphia "in a very orderly manner," and joined the other troops in the barracks. The five hundred or so men now there controlled what was also there: the state powder house, which contained all the government-owned ammunition. There were also several small cannon.[3]

The next morning—June 19, 1783—all the soldiers in the barracks repudiated the authority of their officers, an act which seemed to presage "a troublesome evening." It was Saturday, when Congress did not ordinarily meet, but the President, Hamilton's friend Boudinot, called a special session for the early afternoon. The congressmen had hardly gathered when four or five hundred mutineers "very unexpectedly appeared."[4] To Hamilton's excitement and outrage, they surrounded the State House, waving muskets glittering with bayonets.

The fifteen or so men with whom Hamilton was meeting in the building where the Declaration of Independence had been signed were, although the successors of the signers, impotent: fewer states were represented than the quorum needed for any action. Overheard, in session, the Supreme Executive Council of Pennsylvania was also gathered. The report was that the mutineers, only too visible outside the windows, were "inflamed by misrepresentation and intoxicated with liquor." A congressman rose to advise his fellow members "to think of eternity, for he confidently believed that in the space of an hour not an individual of their body would be left alive." How Hamilton and the others longed to call soldiers to their aid! However, the only federal forces available were the mutineers themselves. Congress did have a general. St. Clair appeared, and was ordered to go out and reason with the dissidents. He did go out, but the heads, often hatless, the angry faces, and the menacing bayonets continued to move outside the windows.[5]

Surely the state of Pennsylvania would call out its militia! No militiamen appeared. "To my mortification," Boudinot remembered, no citizen made any effort to help.

Hamilton had undoubtedly cocked his pistols and was keeping a belligerent eye on door and windows. No assault developed, not even

ARCH STREET, with the Second Presbyterian CHURCH.

PHILADELPHIA.

Philadelphia as Hamilton knew it. Drawn and engraved by W. Birch and Son, 1799. Courtesy, I. N. Phelps Stokes Collection, New York Public Library

a threatening gesture. The congressmen were left in isolation while sounds indicated movement in the room where the Pennsylvania Council was meeting. Although it seemed intolerable to remain uninformed, the Congress would not lower its national prestige by sending upstairs to the state body for information.

Finally a knock on the door. If Hamilton raised his pistols, he could lower them again. The newcomer was John Dickinson, the president of Pennsylvania. He reported that the mutineers had demanded of the State Council the authority to replace the officers they had repudiated with officers of their own choice who would see to it that their grievances were righted. Of course, since the mutineers were federal troops, only Congress could legally grant their request. If Hamilton or some other congressman pointed this out, Dickinson may well have asked, with a wry smile, who wanted the responsibility? The representatives of the mutineers had threatened that, if the Council did not agree, "we shall instantly let these injured soldiers in upon you." When the Council had stated that they wouldn't knuckle under to threats, the mutineers had announced that they would give the Pennsylvanian government a little time to meditate. Then the delegates had returned to their men.[6]

His report concluded, Dickinson departed. The congressmen stared at each other: they could not believe that, since they were the rightful power, they were not also menaced by the mutineers' threat. Any minute the door might be stormed! But nothing happened.

Eventually, there was another knock. Dickinson reappeared to say that the period of grace the mutineers had given the Pennsylvania Council had lapsed and there had been no hostile action. The Council had therefore concluded that, if they reached a decision they would no longer be doing so under a threat. They had decided to agree that the mutineers might select officers to present their grievances, and they wished Congress's approval. The approval given, Dickinson was off again.

The Congress now assumed that the unruly troops would withdraw from around the State House. But not so: the heads and the raised bayonets went on passing the windows. None of the congressmen could guess why the mutiny was continuing, and no one took the trouble to inform them. The watches in their pockets, and perhaps a big clock on the wall, ticked and ticked. After being slighted and then ignored for all of three hours, the congressmen decided they could put up with the situation no longer. They would adjourn and walk out, bravely baring their breasts to the protesting soldiery.[7]

Hamilton paced out in a dignified manner with the others, his pistols cocked; he would unflinchingly meet his fate. But the mutineers expressed no hostility. Neither did they express respect. They simply paid no attention. Some, it is true, recognized Boudinot and began to argue, but they were quickly shushed by a sergeant. Hamilton found himself ignored in a crisis that he considered clearly the responsibility of a congressman of the United States![8]

The Pennsylvania Council was still besieged in the State House. If Hamilton, in his chagrin and his wish for some incitation that would demand strong congressional action, visualized a cutting of Pennsylvanian throats, he was disappointed. Shortly after the congressmen departed, the mutineers returned to the barracks, where they continued to occupy federal property and control the powder magazine.[9]

The slighting of Congress had been too intolerable to be acknowledged. Hamilton was to insist that mutinous soldiers had been permitted "to surround and in fact imprison Congress." Boudinot claimed that Congress had been "in a manner" kept prisoner. He implored Washington to send "some of your best troops." At any moment the members of Congress might be seized and held as hostages![10]

That evening, Congress met again, this time less conspicuously in Carpenter's Hall. Hamilton presented a resolution that began: "The authority of the United States has this day been grossly insulted." He wished that his committee be instructed to inform the Supreme Executive Council of Pennsylvania that effectual measures to stop the mutiny had to be taken. If the committee (which meant in effect Hamilton) determined that "there is no satisfactory ground for expectation of adequate and prompt exertions of this state for supporting the dignity of the federal government," they were to recommend to Boudinot that Congress take an extremely grave step. Congress should move out of Philadelphia, which had, except when enemy action intervened, been the national capital since the Revolution started. If Boudinot agreed with Hamilton's committee, he should, without further consultation, rule that the capital be reestablished in New Jersey, either in Trenton or Princeton.[11]

Hamilton's motion was passed.

On the following (Sunday) morning, Hamilton, accompanied by Ellsworth, met with the Pennsylvania Council. He insisted that "the militia of the state be immediately called forth in sufficient force to reduce the soldiers to obedience, disarm, and put them in the power of

Congress." To the Council's objection that negotiations were in progress that might end the whole matter peaceably, Hamilton replied that "palliatives" were "improper." The Council then expressed concern lest the militia prove more sympathetic to the mutineers than to Congress. Furthermore, since "the state magazine was in the hands of the soldiery," there was hardly any ammunition. Hamilton announced dramatically that he could personally collect from private sources in fifteen minutes "any quantity of musket and cannon cartridges." The meeting ended with the Council's stating that they would consult their militia commanders and report the next day.[12]

The meeting over, Hamilton and Ellsworth decided on a novel move to enhance the wounded prestige of Congress. Although there was no precedent for this, they demanded an answer in writing. According to governmental protocol, the "supreme" executive body of a state would thus be equated with a committee—no more than a subdivision—of Congress.

The next morning, Hamilton and Ellsworth waited on the Council. The Pennsylvanians refused to give an answer in writing on the grounds that this "might appear an innovation." Hamilton was outraged. As he stated later, the refusal "struck me either as uncandid reserve or an unbecoming stateliness, and in either supposition a disrespect to the body of which the committee were members. Though nothing enters less into my temper than an inclination to fetter business with punctilio, after the Council had discovered such overweening nicety, I should have thought it a degradation of my official character to have consented to the proposal."[13]

Nor was Hamilton pleased with the Council's verbal answers. Their consultations with militia officers, they stated, had revealed that calling out the militia might endanger rather than protect Congress, since the citizenry, noting that the protesters had manifested throughout "a pacific disposition," believed that, under sympathetic negotiation, they would accept what was "just and reasonable."

As Hamilton put it angrily, "the Council did not believe any exertions were to be looked for . . . except in case of further outrage and actual violence to person and property. That in such case a respectable body of citizens would arm from the security of their property and of the public peace, but it was to be doubted what measure of outrage would produce this effect." Hamilton went on to quote the Council as making a statement that Dickinson subsequently denied: intervention "was not to be expected from a repetition of the insult which had happened." Whether or not this was actually said, it was clear that the Pennsylvania authorities were unsympathetic to avenging what Hamilton considered Congress's outraged honor. Nor would they agree that "the excesses of the mutineers had passed those bounds within which a spirit of compromise might consist with the dignity and even the safety of government."[14]

Dickinson wrote, "In this unhappy affair we found ourselves extremely distressed." The citizenry would not condone shedding the blood of noble veterans to avenge congressional dignity, which had been "accidentally and undesignedly offended." He added that no explanation had been given why Congress, which normally did not meet on Saturdays, had thus inserted themselves into the situation. However, the Council wished to preserve Philadelphia as the national capital. They expressed "reverence" for Congress and pleaded for understanding of their plight.[15]

Hamilton was unimpressed. It had, he later stated, become his duty to make the negative report that would inspire a move to New Jersey—but he saw dangers. The admission that a minor mutiny could dislodge Congress would be damaging internationally and could give the impression internally that the federal government was too weak to be relied upon. Particularly if the crisis were to be solved without bloodshed, Congress could be accused of "levity, timidity, and rashness." He decided to stretch his authority by agreeing to postpone action for another day.[16]

The next morning, the Council had another meeting with their militia officers. As Hamilton was awaiting their verdict in his lodgings, the man who had given assurances concerning the instant availability of ammunition dropped in. "In conversation," he admitted that there were in fact nothing more than two hundred musket cartridges. Hamilton had no choice but to lower his dignity and that of Congress by bursting in on the Pennsylvania meeting to tell Dickinson "of a great mistake that had been committed." Dickinson took the opportunity to plead with Hamilton for understanding and further delay, but when Hamilton learned that the militia officers had again insisted that they could do nothing, he could only conclude that "the conduct of the executive of this state is to the last degree weak and disgusting. In short, they pretended it was out of their power to bring out the militia without making the experiment."[17]

Hamilton so reported to Boudinot, and Boudinot proclaimed that the capital had been moved to Princeton.[18]

Congress had hardly opened its doors in Princeton before the mutiny evaporated. Rumors that the bank was about to be robbed had brought out armed citizens; the Council finally issued a determined proclamation; reports came in that Washington had ordered a large force under General Robert Howe to march from West Point; the mutineers squabbled with the officers they had chosen to represent them, and all became frightened. The soldiers marched back to Lancaster and the officers went underground, two fleeing to England. Hamilton's contention that Congress's departure had frightened the mutineers into submission was greeted with mirth. Major John Armstrong wrote Gates, "The grand Sanhedrin of the nation, with all their solemnity and emptiness, have removed to Princeton and left a state where their wisdom has long been questioned, their virtue suspected, and their dignity a jest."[19]

Although Congress was no longer on the scene and the crisis had solved itself, Hamilton did not intend that the federal government should vanish into inaction. He presented two belligerent resolutions. They skirted around the authority of Washington, who, he may well have suspected, would not approve. Congress should give direct orders to General Howe not to halt his march on Philadelphia despite the return of quiet. Howe was to search out and arrest the soldiers who were ringleaders of the mutiny. A further provision that the army arrest suspected civilians for later civil trial was scratched out, it is assumed by Boudinot; but in any case, Hamilton's fellow congressmen did not have his intransigent spirit. The resolutions were not passed.[20]

Hamilton, whose dominant role in the proceedings was recognized by all, soon found himself under violent attack. Most Philadelphians were outraged by having their city's long-held position as the national capital taken from them. They insisted that Congress, although responsible for the soldiers' plight, had not been threatened. (Dr. Benjamin Rush stated that Congress would have been wiser to have kept quiet: "Physicians should talk sparingly at the funerals of their patients.") The Pennsylvania Council had taken the brunt and faced the music while Congress fled. Hamilton, it was charged, had been plotting to get the capital away from Philadelphia so that it could be settled in New York. (It is, indeed, a fact that Hamilton urged the New York legislature to prepare an acceptable invitation to Congress, but the whole drift of thoughts and events makes it clear that such was not his guiding motive.)[21]

To soothe his connections in Philadelphia, Hamilton made a trip there. Being angrily received, he importuned Madison to testify (which Madison was glad to do) that he had slowed down rather than hurried the departure from Philadelphia, which he insisted the Pennsylvania Council had forced. Back in Congress he tried to build political bridges by drafting and seconding a resolution (which he correctly suspected would not pass) that Congress return to Philadelphia.[22]

While with Congress at Princeton, Hamilton began to write for the press a defense of his behavior and that of the body he led. The first necessity, he decided, was to demonstrate that the honor of Congress was worth preserving. This led him to state that, since the Congress was a rotating body, the present members were not responsible for past errors. In his eagerness to promote reform, he then wrote that should the present Congress enter into further debts "without effectual provision at their disposal, they will merit the indignation of honest men."

Hamilton must have realized that he was getting himself into a mare's nest. If Congress was not regarded as an entity that absorbed the rotation of its members, it clearly had no dignity to be upheld. And the present body, lacking effectual provision, had to incur debts. Hamilton filed away the unfinished manuscript and abandoned, for the time being, the effort to defend the move from Philadelphia.[23]

However, the issue was too close to the Pennsylvanian interests to be allowed to drop. During September, 1783, the Supreme Executive Council published in the *Pennsylvania Gazette* its report to the Pennsylvania Assembly. It was very damaging to the position Hamilton had taken.[24]

Although he had by this time retired from Congress and (so he stated) public life, Hamilton could not resist "indulging my feelings" in a most voluminous reply.[25] Perhaps because he wished to feel free to express some sentiments which even he knew would outrage public opinion, he couched his essay as a private letter to Dickinson: "I decline any attempt to set public opinion right upon this subject because, after all that can be said, the judgments of men will eventually be determined by personal and party prepossessions."[26]

Realizing the necessity to refute the charge that Congress had "discovered a prudish nicety and irritability about their dignity," he pointed out that some of the same soldiers had previously made what he considered an indecent protest directly to Congress. Even if the mutineers had been (as he doubted) well enough informed to know that Congress did not ordinarily meet on Saturdays, when they arrived and found that Congress was surprisingly in session, they should have shown their respect by returning immediately to their barracks.[27]

In answering the charge that the Congress had been cowardly to flee the State House while the Pennsylvania authorities braved the mutineers, Hamilton wrote that while congressmen "might have a right to expose their own persons to insult and outrage, they had no right to expose the character of representative, or the dignity of the states they represent or the union."[28]

To Madison, Hamilton admitted concisely, "My idea was clearly this: that the mutiny ought not to be terminated by negotiation."[29]

To Dickinson, he skirted around his belief that the dignity of the Congress and the future health of the union depended on the use of force, even if blood were to flow in the streets when the crisis could have been otherwise resolved. He did, however, denounce to Dickinson "the propensity of the human mind to lean to the speciousness of professed humanity rather than to the necessary harshness of authority —the vague and imperfect notions of what is due to public authority in an infant popular government. . . ."[30]

"This was not to be considered as the disorderly riot of an unarmed mob but as the deliberate mutiny of incensed soldiery carried to the utmost point of outrage short of assassination. The licentiousness of an army is to be dreaded in every government; but in a republic it is more particularly to be restrained, and, when directed against the civil authority, to be checked with energy and punished with severity."[31]

Hamilton could have claimed that he was following the example of Washington. In 1781, the whole Pennsylvania line had marched towards Philadelphia and, in the subsequent settlement, had been almost disbanded. Washington, fearing that further mutinies would destroy the entire army, had determined to stop the trend by putting down a minor mutiny of New Jersey troops in a way that permitted the exemplary execution of ringleaders. But that had been in the middle of the war and the issue was an undeniably lethal danger to the whole cause.[32]

Dickinson may not have been well enough informed to wonder how Hamilton's denunciation of mutinies could be made to accord with Hamilton's recent effort to have Washington lead a military protest that would frighten civilian governments. In a different part of his long letter, Hamilton gave his answer. Had the Philadelphia insurgents been "an army with their officers at their head, demanding justice of their country . . . caution and concession" on the part of the civil authorities might have been "respectable." But since the insurgents were disobeying their officers, they "equally violated the laws of discipline as the rights of public authority."[33]

Hamilton expressed his preference for an organized military uprising despite his contention that it would be much harder for the civil au-

426

thorities to resist. He had, so he remembered, told the Pennsylvania Council that "a small body of disciplined troops headed and led by their officers with a plan of conduct, could have effected a great deal in similar circumstances." However, the existing insurgents could be easily put down because "nothing can be more contemptible than a body of men used to be commanded and to obey when deprived of their officers. They are infinitely less to be dreaded than an equal number of men who have never been broken to command nor exchanged their natural courage for that artificial kind which is the effect of discipline and habit. . . . In the present case," he continued to Dickinson, ". . . the appearance of opposition would instantly bring the mutineers to a sense of their insignificance and to submission."[34]

Thus Hamilton equated the American soldiery with the Hessian semi-serfs and the British paupers who were made into automatons easily managed by officers representing ruling castes. His myopia was all the more remarkable because the Philadelphia mutineers had been mostly new recruits, and as frontiersmen from western Pennsylvania, they had belonged to the most self-reliant group of all self-reliant Americans.

Larger risks were, of course, involved. Dr. Benjamin Rush had asked rhetorically, "Supposing the militia had been called out and so forth?" Might they not have joined their fellow Pennsylvanians? Might not even troops sent in from the Continental Army have preferred the mutineers? Could one be sure that the soldiers from Washington's encampment "with arms in their hands, and who are now straggling through the country, would not have rallied to the sound of pay and repaired to their standard?" And what about "the half-informed, despairing public creditors? . . . Are you sure we have no desperado among us, no man of ruined prospects and character who would not have increased this flame, fed the hopes of the distressed and injured" in the hope of raising "himself into power and consequences?"[35]

Although Hamilton stated them in less emphatic terms, he had recognized these dangers. They had only made him believe more firmly that the government was called on for instantaneous violence. You extinguish a fire at once so that it will not spread. Despite the favorable outcome, the wishy-washiness of the Pennsylvania Council had endangered the nation.

This had not, of course, been the first time Hamilton had impelled Congress to depart from Philadelphia. But on the previous occasion, he had only briefly anticipated the necessary flight from the British army, and the government had returned when the British left. Now the justification was much less clear and the act threw ahead a long shadow. Philadelphia was not to become the capital again until 1790, and then its eminence was defined as only temporary, until a new city could be built in the District of Columbia. Had Philadelphia been, except for breaks caused by military necessity, the capital from the very start, since 1774, it might never have lost that position, all the more because one argument for creating a federally controlled district was based on what had happened in 1783. The departure Hamilton had inspired was said to prove that the government could not surely be dependent for protection on any one state.

It is amazing to consider that the District of Columbia might never have been established, the city of Washington never built, had it not been for tiny scenes enacted years before on the faraway streets of the Leeward Islands. Hamilton, in whose mature body the wounded child still lived, had reacted according to an old pattern.

Long undervalued and deprived of power, the Continental Congress had received another insult, to Hamilton unbearable. He had demanded that Congress's honor be bloodily avenged. When Congress's impotence had been further demonstrated by the refusal of the Pennsylvanians to back his demands, he had promoted flight. Following him, the governing body of the continental United States had stalked indignantly away, shouting as it departed in rage and chagrin. What a demonstration of Hamilton's gifts for leadership!

46

Retreat to Domesticity

[MARCH–DECEMBER, 1783   AGE 26]

I
N March, 1783, after the signing of the provisional peace treaty
had been definitely confirmed, Hamilton had written Washington, "I congratulate Your Excellency on this happy conclusion
of your labors. It now only remains to make solid establishments
within to perpetuate our union to prevent our being a ball in the hands
of European powers bandied against each other at their pleasure—in
fine, to make independence truly a blessing. This, it is to be lamented,
will be an arduous work, for . . . the seeds of disunion [are] much
more numerous than those of union. I will add that Your Excellency's
exertions are as essential to accomplish this end as they have been to
establish independence. I will upon a future occasion open myself
upon this subject."[1]

Washington replied that no man could be more deeply impressed
than he with the need to reform the Confederation. He blamed on its
defects and the "want of powers in Congress . . . more than half the
perplexities I have experienced in the course of my command and
almost the whole of the difficulties and distress of the army. . . . All
my private letters have teemed with these sentiments, and whenever
this topic has been the subject of conversation, I have endeavored to
diffuse and enforce them." He had acted thus as a private citizen. But
should a soldier make a public political statement? Whether so doing
"might be productive of the wished-for end or appear to arrogate more
than belongs to me depends so much upon popular opinion, and the
temper and disposition of people, that it is not easy to decide. I shall

be obliged to you, however, for the thoughts which you have promised me on this subject, and as soon as you can make it convenient."[2]

Hamilton was not quick to reply. Washington's worry about military interference with civilian concerns did not bother Hamilton. And the action he intended to recommend to His Excellency was to be part of a scheme that would take time to mature. He intended to shock the nation, perhaps as effectively as if the military protest of the organized army had not been aborted.

After Hamilton had left the Congress, James McHenry, a fellow member of Washington's Family who had also been Hamilton's fellow congressman, wrote to him: "The homilies you delivered in Congress are still recollected with pleasure. The impressions they made are in favor of your integrity and no one but believes you a man of honor and republican principles. Were you ten years older and twenty thousand pounds richer, there is no doubt but that you might obtain the suffrages of Congress for the highest office in their gift. You are supposed to possess various knowledge, useful—substantial—and ornamental. Your very grave and your cautious—your men who measure others by the standard of their own creeping politics—think you sometimes intemperate, but seldom visionary, and that were you to pursue your object with as much cold perseverance as you do with ardor and argument you would become irresistible. In a word, if you could submit to spend a whole life in depicting a fly, you would be in their opinion one of the greatest men in the world. Bold designs—measures calculated for their rapid execution—a wisdom that would convince from its own weight—a project that would surprise the people in greater happiness, without giving them an opportunity to view it and reject it, are not adapted to a council composed of discordant elements, or a people who have thirteen heads, each of which pays superstitious adoration to inferior divinities."[3]

Hamilton's plan for surprising the people into greater happiness was that, as soon as the definite peace treaty arrived, the entire Continental Congress and also Washington should resign. In a "full and forcible" parting resolution, Congress would "inform their constituents of the imperfections of the present system and of the impossibility of conducting public affairs with honor to themselves and advantage to the community with powers so disproportioned to their responsibility." Washington would "in a solemn manner" express his "opinion of the present government and of the absolute necessity of a change."[4]

But Washington did not wait to receive the advice he had asked of his former aide. On June 8, a few days before the mutineers appeared in Philadelphia, His Excellency distributed to the states a circular letter which, before anyone had dreamed of a presidential "farewell address," achieved great currency as "Washington's Testament." He justified interfering in governmental affairs by stating that this would be the last public paper he would ever issue, since, as soon as the peace would permit him to retire, he would never (as he fondly believed) return to public life.

In his private correspondence Washington had urged "a convention of the people" to establish "a federal constitution," but he did not confuse his public appeal with what he knew was not practically obtainable. He urged in general terms that the Articles of Confederation be interpreted and extended to give the federal government power adequate to its needs.[5]

Hamilton was not too impressed with Washington's Testament. "I trust," he later wrote the General, "it will not be without effect though I am persuaded that it would have had more combined" with what Hamilton had intended.[6]

That Washington had gone ahead without waiting for Hamilton scuttled the plan of staging a simultaneous resignation of the Commander in Chief and the congressmen: Hamilton espoused a lesser scheme. He drafted, for presentation to the Congress still in session at Princeton, a resolution that pointed out the weaknesses in the Articles of Confederation, and urged the states to appoint a convention to meet at a specific place and time with full powers to propose alterations in the Articles, which would then have to be ratified by the states. In allowing the initiative to the states, in limiting the convention to revising the Articles rather than drafting a new constitution, and in conceding to the states a subsequent right to ratify, Hamilton had undoubtedly allowed himself to be toned down by the more practical Madison. He surely felt that it would be impossible to be more conciliatory, yet "lack of support" prevented him from even proposing the resolution to Congress.[7]

As early as June, 1783, when he had served in Congress some seven months, Hamilton wrote General Greene that he saw "so little disposition . . . to give solidity to our national system that there is no motive to a man to lose his time in the public service, who has no other view than to promote its welfare." He intended, as soon as the British evacuated New York City, to "set down there seriously on the business of making my fortune."[8]

431

Had the British chosen to anticipate the definitive treaty, as he had foreseen,[9] by moving out that spring, would Hamilton have deserted Congress to make sure that other lawyers did not get a head start? There is no indication that he contemplated doing so. There is no indication that he looked forward to practicing the law and making his fortune. There can be absolutely no doubt that had he succeeded in achieving what as a member of Congress he hoped to achieve he would have allowed the support of his family to devolve on Schuyler, who would certainly have cheered him on. Had there been a possibility of building a strong and financially sound federal government, Hamilton would rather have cut off his right hand than not be there to build.

He had continued, indeed, long after common sense would have told him that his effort was vain. His fight with Pennsylvania over the handling of the mutiny had been a desperate effort to use an almost irrelevant happening to prove what could not be proved. And he had drawn up and tried out his resolution for a convention to recast the government when there was absolutely no chance that it would be passed by Congress. With the determination of a fanatic, a prophet, or a martyr, he banged his head again and again against solid walls.

When he stopped, it was not to seek some subtle way around the walls, but rather to nurse his bruises and go elsewhere. When he finally left Congress during the first days of August, 1783, it was with the intention of putting politics and government and national planning utterly to one side. He had his fortune to make and he would concentrate on making his fortune.[10]

There was a pause of more than three months: the British did not leave New York until late November. In that time, Hamilton got started in a minor but preparatory way on his legal practice,[11] and produced two documents concerned with the past. One was his interminable letter to Dickinson defending his behavior in relocating Congress; the other was a letter to Washington, an almost pitiful cry, now that he had been frustrated as a congressman, for belated recognition of his military successes.

He asked that he not be retired along with all the other officers who had served in the Continental Army, except for the very few who would continue in active service as part of the "peace establishment" (that is, the peacetime army). Hamilton wished to be a conspicuous and probably unique exception. He wanted to retain his rank, "without emoluments and unattached to any corps, as an honorary reward for the time I have devoted to the public. As I may hereafter travel, I may find it an agreeable circumstance to appear in the character I have supported in the Revolution.

"I rest my claim solely on the sacrifice I have made, because I have no reason to believe that my services have appeared of any value to Congress." He expressed his bitterness at not having received a conspicuous reward for the capture of the redoubt at Yorktown. "The only thing I ask of your Excellency is that my application may come into view in the course of the consultations on the peace establishment."[12]

From Rocky Hill, New Jersey, where he was trying to persuade Congress to keep an adequate force in service, Washington wrote that Congress had "unexpectedly and surprisingly to me" adjourned, without bringing the peace establishment or any of the many other pressing matters to a decision. He had then shown Hamilton's letter "to some of your particular friends and consulted them on the propriety of making your wishes known, with my testimonial of your services, to Congress, but they advised me to decline it" on the grounds that no "discrimination" could be made "as every other officer, from the highest to the lowest grades (not in actual command) was retiring without retention of rank." Washington, although he no longer signed himself "affectionately," tried to soften the blow by procuring for Hamilton all that was in his power: a brevet commission that raised him, for the last few days of the Continental Army, from lieutenant colonel to colonel.[13]

This action might have seemed to call for a letter of thanks, which might well have opened up between Hamilton and Washington such a friendly correspondence, containing invitations to Mount Vernon, as Washington after his retirement conducted with many of his fellow veterans, including various of the young men who had served with Hamilton in his Family. Hamilton wrote no such letter.

The Definitive Treaty having arrived and the British having finally sailed away from New York, Hamilton moved late in November with his wife and infant son to 57 Wall Street, and entered seriously into his legal practice. The probability is strong that Hamilton was in New York (or could have been there if he wished) when Washington said farewell to his officers on December 4 at Fraunces Tavern. However, there is no record, not even a claim from any of the biographers who consider him Washington's most intimate companion, that Hamilton was one of the officers who took part in that highly charged, tearful scene.

Hamilton was soon immersed in the practice of the law, an occupation which suited his intellectual bent and filled his pocketbook, even if it gave little scope to his urge towards nation building and brought him no glory.[14]

In addition to being discouraged and angry, Hamilton was puzzled. He had never reconciled his lack of faith in the people with his conceptions of government. He had, it is true, as part of the resolution that Congress had refused to pass, stated that "the most approved and well founded maxims of free government . . . require that the legislative, executive and judicial authorities should be deposited in distinct and separate hands."[15] But this seems to have been an addition made by Madison, since Hamilton, who went into considerable length about matters that particularly concerned him, passed quickly over this weighty conception. His own thinking had not yet really gone beyond a unicameral legislature, such as the Congress whose hands he had so tried to strengthen, which appointed and controlled executive officers and assigned to each a limited duty. His ideas on the importance of the judiciary were still rudimentary. The vision of checks and balances, which would both accept and control popular voices, had not come to him.

He had hoped that when men became congressmen they would take on a new entity. He had hoped they would become resolute enough to fly in the faces of the state legislators that had chosen them, would become leaders capable of dominating the people for their own good. His experience had convinced him that these were false hopes.

Where and how were the strong men with whom he wished to surround himself to be found? He understood enough of the American spirit to know that monarchy was not an open option. As the speech that was to be his major effort at the Constitutional Convention was to reveal, he finally evolved a system for an elective monarchy.[16] But there is every reason to believe that in the years immediately after the Revolution he was confused as to how government could be organized to achieve what he considered the necessary ends. And confusion was a state of mind which the man who wished to create order found psychologically painful. He had to absorb himself in other things.

On December 27, 1783, having seen in a newspaper that he had been nominated for the New York Assembly, Hamilton informed the press that he declined to run. When a new election came up in April, 1785, he wrote to Robert R. Livingston, with whom he was transacting legal business, "It may appear to you, sir, a little extraordinary that I should take occasion in this professional letter to mention politics, but the situation of the state at this time is so critical that it is become a serious object of attention to those who are concerned for the *security of property,* of the prosperity of government, to endeavor to put men in the legislature whose principles are not of the *leveling kind.*" Livingston should use his "power" to influence the election. Hamilton wrote William Duer, "Abilities like yours ought always to be employed for the public good." But Hamilton again wrote to the editor of the *New-York Packet* that he himself would not run.[17]

Hamilton continued to use his pen to support the idea of a strong federal government. Engaging in law cases the winning of which involved strengthening national rather than local ends, he mocked himself, writing, "Legislative folly has afforded so plentiful a harvest to us lawyers that we have scarcely a moment to spare from the substantial business of reaping."[18] He was far from content, but he was incapable of the tacking, the compromise that was needed to edge the ship of state through countercurrents to a desired end. The first significant shifts towards a strong federal union emerged not in New York but in Virginia, under the leadership not of Hamilton but of Madison and Washington. Their moves led to the Annapolis Convention of 1786, at which Hamilton, appearing as a delegate from New York, stepped back on the active national scene.

Hamilton had not shared, during the governmental confusion that (as he had prophesied) came on with peace and independence, the optimism expressed by the Virginians. Washington wrote of the American people, "Like heirs come a little prematurely perhaps to a large inheritance, it is more than probable they will riot for a while." But this would "work its own cure, because there is virtue at the bottom."[19]

But Hamilton, who did not believe there was virtue at the bottom, doubted that he would live long enough to see a happy ending. In 1784 he wrote Gouverneur Morris from New York: "I ought . . . to give you an account of what we are doing here, but I will in the lump tell you that we are doing those things which we ought not to do, and leaving undone those things which we ought to do. Instead of wholesome regulations for the improvement of our polity and commerce, we are laboring to contrive methods to mortify and punish Tories and to explain away treaties. Let us both erect a temple to time, only regretting that we shall not command a longer portion of it to see what will be the event of the American drama."[20]

47

Trajectory's End

[1784–1804   AGES 27–47]

H AMILTON did as much as any man—with the possible
exception of Washington—to complete the Revolution by
bringing the states together into a unified nation. But this
often-accepted assessment covers only half the situation. The other half
is that while Hamilton's genius built national unity, his psychic wounds
sowed disunion that was also absorbed into the continuing structure
of the United States.

Hamilton's lack of balance was such that his greatest contributions
were realized only when he was working side by side with another
statesman, also brilliant but more stable. He had two major collabo-
rators: James Madison and George Washington.

At the Annapolis Convention of 1786, Madison changed into what
was almost a new document the overaggressive and overvisionary call
Hamilton had drafted, which was successfully to summon up the Constitutional Convention. And Madison was a collaborator on the *Federalist* papers, in which Hamilton supported and explicated, with such
lasting effect, a constitution which he had opposed as too mild and in
which he was never really to believe.*

Washington's role as what Hamilton called "an aegis essential to

---

* Hamilton's most impressive solo flight took place shortly thereafter, when he
dominated New York's ratifying convention and persuaded that crucial but reluctant state to join the other states in the by then already established union.

me"[1] divided into two extensive phases. Hamilton's most important contributions to winning the Revolutionary War were, as we have seen, carried out when he was Washington's aide. And the totality of the achievements that have given Hamilton his greatest fame came when he was Washington's Secretary of the Treasury. Then, he brought to fruition the fiscal reforms he had for so long vainly advocated: payment of debts to the public creditors; the establishment of long-range federal funds which guaranteed that the government would stay indefinitely financially afloat; the chartering of a private national bank with federal support. He created all the institutions then needed to balance the lopsided agricultural economy, making possible a strong and permanent nation. In his *Report on Manufactures,* which was too far ahead of its time to receive Washington's sanction or pass Congress, Hamilton prophesied much of post–Civil War America. And, by a brilliant report to Washington that carried conviction eventually almost universal, he established the doctrine of "implied powers," which unshackled the Constitution from its exact wording, enabling the government that rests upon it to change with the times, satisfying needs of new generations as they come and go.

After Hamilton resigned from Washington's cabinet, he made his last major contribution, paradoxically in closer collaboration with his longtime chief than he had been since he had served as a youthful military aide. Putting on paper Washington's ideas, with which he had become so familiar through years of association, he drafted another of America's basic documents: Washington's Farewell Address.[2]

Hamilton had brought with him from the Leeward Islands an attitude that was fundamental to his thinking but not shared by any other of the founding fathers: the conviction that the human race was not only unworthy, but to him a personal enemy that must be fought and conquered. This gave rise to his basic pugnacity, his adversary turn of mind, which played such a major part in his successes, so major a part in his failures.

Hamilton had no experience of America until he was in his teens. Immigrants can fall in love with their new home, becoming more vociferous patriots than many birthright inhabitants, but this was impossible for a youth already firmly conditioned to scorn and distrust his fellowmen. Hamilton hugged to his breast the sensational opportunities offered by the environment where chance had thrown him, but he never appreciated or bothered to understand that environment. Thus, if he wished to be for once discreet and conciliatory, he did not know how to go about it. Much is explained by a statement he made when, as Secretary of the Treasury, he was at the height of his career and influence: "Though our republic has only been in existence some ten years there are already two distinct tendencies—the one democratic, the other aristocratic." The people of the United States, Hamilton continued, "are essentially businessmen. With us agriculture is of small account. Commerce is everything."[3] How wrong he was in his assessment of the primarily republican and agrarian nation was soon revealed when he and his party were submerged by the Jeffersonian tide.

Had Hamilton cared, he would undoubtedly have learned how to analyze popular opinion. But he did not care. His weapon was the sword. In his romantic dreams it was a physical sword. But neither his body nor his true gifts were martial. The sword he was born to wield was forged in the brain.

Almost all people allow their primitive drives to be suppressed by prudence. Statesmen in particular think thrice before they act. Hamilton inspired wonder and also vicarious satisfaction by the freedom with which he slashed around him. But such a champion is truly valued only on his own side of the battle line. On the far side, sharpshooters squint through their sights to bring him down.

In realizing, during the Revolution, that the difficulties of the emerging United States were increasingly financial and governmental, and in seeking apposite solutions, Hamilton was far from alone. In fact, the inexperienced and extremely busy military aide appeared on the scene later than others. But he attracted attention (particularly among historians) by adopting extreme positions and putting on paper what others considered it impolitic to disseminate. Every reform has such outriders, although rarely persons as brilliant as Hamilton. To assess their effect is difficult. They implant presently unpopular ideas in many minds, but at the same time impede the efforts of more practical reformers to proceed step by acceptable step.

Hamilton's pessimism about human nature did not extend to himself or those who demonstrated what he considered their ability and integrity by responding to his persuasion. He could thus share in the Enlightenment doctrine of progress. Where Jefferson believed in the perfectability of mankind, Hamilton believed in the perfectability of the few who were the rightful leaders of mankind. Considering himself the leader of leaders, he hated to make his visions impure by compromising with the imperfect ideas that were acceptable at the moment. Progress would demonstrate that he was altogether right. Then a new generation of the most brilliant, able at long last to carry his inspirations to fruition, would follow the torch he had lighted and kept unsullied to guide them.

The man whose youthful ambition had been for "literary pursuits" published in newspapers and often as pamphlets hundreds of political and polemical essays, almost invariably urging his compatriots to action. These sallies covered a wide range of prophetic possibilities. At their most achievable—as in such fiscal and constitutional ideas as he was in his lifetime able to put over—he was taking the van, as he had wished Washington would let him do in battle, of columns already forming that were in need of such leadership. In his practical but visionary phases—as in his *Report on Manufactures*—he was defining the future. But others of his ideas—such as his recommendation at the Constitutional Convention that the President and the senators be chosen for life by an electorate limited to the prosperous[4]—were too alien to America to have a chance of realization.

Hamilton's prophecies, whether practical or extreme, sounded together through the same eighteenth-century air, the grievously unpopular and the wild discrediting the immediately advantageous and sane. His *Report on Manufactures* seemed to the agrarian majority to reveal him as another Lucifer revolting to create a money changers' hell. And Hamilton's speech at the Constitutional Convention encouraged his opponents to diagnose monarchical scheming in his financial panacea, which, in fact, exemplified middle-class conceptions that were to prove to monarchs the greatest enemies in all history.

Hamilton enjoyed inciting contention. When Jefferson showed him portraits he owned of Francis Bacon, Isaac Newton, and John Locke, saying that these were the greatest men in history, Hamilton replied that in his opinion the greatest man who ever lived was Caesar.[5] There was no integral reason why his financial recommendations should be coupled with expressions of disdain for the common man. Nor was it necessary for the West Indian from a most dubious background to set himself up, and with him the self-made moneymen who were his followers, as an American elite in opposition to the traditional aristocracy as represented by such inheritors of land as Madison and Jefferson. In fact, the projector could hardly have sponsored necessary reforms in a manner more divisive.

In order to get his first set of financial plans through Congress, Hamilton was ultimately forced to make a concession to the South concerning the location of the national capital, but from this he learned no lesson. His plan for the Bank of the United States, the measures he proposed for fostering manufactures, flew, without any concessions, straight in the faces not only of the southerners, but of all the farmers, who formed the vast majority of the people. He tickled up Jefferson by saying to him that corruption was an essential aspect of effective rule. When Jefferson accused him of subverting the federal government through a bribed "corrupt squadon," he was only paraphrasing unfavorably one of Hamilton's often-stated contentions: federal financial institutions would stabilize the nation by cementing to the central power rich men whose prosperity would depend on federal authority.

One of Washington's greatest gifts to the founding of the United States was his perpetual concern with quelling dissension, with drawing to the national standard every individual who could be thus drawn. This had been essential to winning the Revolutionary War: in the long run, the British could only have triumphed by dividing the patriot cause. As we have seen, His Excellency so controlled his young aide that Hamilton got into no controversies of any sort, committed no indiscretions, while serving officially at headquarters. But as soon as Hamilton stepped into a private role—whether it was at a drinking party in Philadelphia, or in his recommendations for governmental reform, or in his yearning for an army revolt, or his sometimes hysterical leadership in Congress—his fierce aggressions appeared.

As the President, Washington became the head of a government completely untried, supported by only a small majority of the people, with two of the thirteen states still unconvinced and staying outside. An administration that would pull together, that would create ever mounting national unity, was the overwhelming need, and this Washington led so effectively that Jefferson wrote, on arriving to become Secretary of State: "The opposition to our new Constitution has almost totally disappeared. . . . If the President can be preserved a few more years, till habits of authority and obedience can be established generally, we have nothing to fear."[6]

Before Congress authorized the cabinet, Madison, who was in the House of Representatives, was Washington's closest adviser. To the cabinet, Washington appointed the best men he could find, including Jefferson and Hamilton. Madison was a friend of both and brought them together, intending to establish, under Washington's broad wing, a friendly and fruitful partnership between the secretaries of State and of the Treasury. Jefferson and Madison rescued Hamilton's first set of financial schemes by arranging the deal concerning the national capital.

Then came Hamilton's utterly unconciliatory recommendation for the Bank of the United States, which seemed to Jefferson's and Madison's Virginia constituency a naked power play in favor of men they saw as foreclosers of mortgages. Jefferson and Madison, still thinking in terms of cooperation, went along until the bill had passed Congress and was on the President's desk for signature. Then Madison, suddenly taking alarm and seeing no other way to prevent the signing, did an about-face on the doctrine of "implied powers," which he had supported in *The Federalist*. He tried vainly to persuade Washington to veto the bank as unconstitutional, on the grounds that the establishment of such institutions had not been specifically provided for.

The famous fight now began. Hamilton already had a newspaper, supported by Treasury advertising, that was his personal organ. With Madison's conniving, Jefferson gave Philip Freneau a job in the State Department that left him time to edit an anti-Hamiltonian newspaper. Freneau, also a born fighter, flew for Hamilton like an angry hornet. Hamilton retaliated. As the charges and countercharges went back and forth, Washington became not only upset but puzzled. Convinced that there was no fundamental basis for controversy, he could hardly believe that his two ablest cabinet ministers were at each other's throats.

Washington wrote both Hamilton and Jefferson in almost identical terms: "Without more charity for the opinions and acts of one another in governmental matters; or some more infallible criterion by which the truth of speculative opinions, before they have undergone the test of experience, are to be forejudged than has yet fallen to the lot of fallibility, I believe it will be difficult, if not impracticable, to manage the reins of government or keep the parts of it together. . . . My earnest wish and my fondest hope therefore is that, instead of wounding suspicions and irritable charges, there may be liberal allowances, mutual forbearances, and temporizing yieldings on *all sides*. Under the exercise of these, matters will go on smoothly and, if possible, more prosperously."[7]

Then came the wars of the French Revolution, during which, to vast popular tumult, Hamilton and his followers supported the British interest,* Jefferson and his followers, the French. Washington appealed to them both to support impartial neutrality.

---

* Hamilton was led by considerations of national finance and by his horror at the French Revolution into so great a sense of identity with Great Britain that he regarded a pro-British policy as "free of foreign tincture." Identification with England having remained part of the Hamiltonian syndrome, we see Hamilton praised again and again as a "nationalist," who fathered "a purely American foreign policy."[8]

Was Washington right in his belief that, with good will on both sides, the controversies that wracked his administration were unnecessary? There are reasons to think so. Despite their daily donnybrooks and their opposite brinkmanships, Hamilton and Jefferson agreed that to keep from being actually engaged in the French wars was greatly to the American advantage. And Jefferson, when he became President, continued Hamilton's financial measures, including the Bank of the United States.

Why then fight; why did not Washingtonian unity prevail? It is difficult, when the facts concerning Hamilton are in, not to see a trail leading back to the Leeward Islands.

Although Jefferson could be adept, and sometimes devious, in defending himself and what he considered the interests of the people who were his constituents, he was not a dedicated fighter. He had been a failure as the wartime governor of Virginia. When he became President, he ran the country not by controversy but by manipulation. And Madison, despite a tendency to vociferous outrage, preferred to read a book and think a thought rather than take part in a row. It was Hamilton who relished hand-to-hand fighting.

A really first-class fight requires, of course, already existing differences that can be incited. The divide along which the Hamilton-Jefferson belligerence developed had long worried Washington, whose election as commander in chief had in part grown out of it.* The South and the Northeast were naturally suspicious of each other, in part because of oppositions in economic interest. Endeavoring to seal up all cracks, Washington had hoped to hand on to his successor a profoundly united nation. He failed, and surely the major blame for this failure can be attributed to Hamilton, who exacerbated the conflicts and the suspicions that were, as the generations moved, to eventuate in the Civil War.

All myths to the contrary, President Washington was not led by his Secretary of the Treasury. Nor was he—at least until the very end of his battered second term—a partisan of the Federalists. Yet his value to Hamilton was immense.

Having suffered through the Revolutionary command (neither Jefferson nor Madison had been with the army), Washington realized how greatly the emerging nation needed, in order to be self-sufficient,

---

* Since the Revolution was then being fought in New England by an exclusively New England army, Continental rivalry required a southern commander, preferably one from Virginia.

a sound, central financial structure. His attitude towards Hamilton's innovations was thus admiring and supportive. This persuaded Hamilton's opponents that they would have to reduce Washington's prestige in order to overthrow Hamilton. The tactic boomeranged. Hamilton and his supporters were enabled to reassure the American people by claiming identity with the longtime leader who was still resolutely loved.

The seven years between Hamilton's appointment as Secretary of the Treasury and Washington's retirement from the presidency were, indeed, enchantingly fulfilling, the most fulfilling of Hamilton's career. Washington was no longer the all-controlling father he had been as commander in chief. Hamilton was now more truly self-confident; the scene was now so much larger; he now possessed his own special field of knowledge.

As when he had been commander in chief, Washington had no desire to lead Congress. Although that body was now an integral part of the process over which he presided, he was so devoted to the separation of powers that he felt that the President should not interfere with the functions of the legislators. His clear constitutional duty was to point out areas that required action and to decide, at the end of the legislative process, whether he would sign into law the bills that had been passed. Beyond that he was unwilling to go. This left a power vacuum into which Hamilton leaped, setting up, before Jefferson realized the possibility, his own bloc in Congress that became the Federalist Party. For a while, Hamilton led Congress. Throughout Washington's presidency, he was very puissant there.

That the President could only admire Hamilton's financial plans and operations, and that the Jeffersonians lacked the financial know-how to interfere with them in more than a bumbling and usually ineffectual manner, made Hamilton's accomplishments easier. A second opening was supplied by the fact that Washington thought of his cabinet as a unified body. Each secretary was given for administrative purposes his own specialty, but major decisions were made, under the President's final authority, by the cabinet as a whole. This allowed Hamilton, who was endlessly energetic, intelligent, hard-working, and full of determination, to move across the board, interfering in particular with foreign policy. When he could not operate openly, he went underground, communicating behind Washington's and Jefferson's backs with the British minister.

Even if he sometimes moved invisibly, it was part of Hamilton's satisfaction to have all eyes upon him while, as an individual

443

champion, he achieved or seemed to achieve, heroic deeds. Jefferson was at first so far behind in these lists that it was Hamilton himself who made the Virginian a public figure by selecting him as the most conspicuous target of his resounding attacks.

Those were years when Hamilton's youthful fantasies came almost altogether into being. Powerful men were his sycophants; women adored him; and if he made a flood of enemies, that was, as long as he could overcome, an integral part of his triumphant dream. Then the music stopped.

After Washington's retirement from the presidency, Hamilton's life proceeded on paths that he could not walk with true pride or even personal satisfaction. He had reached an eminence which demanded that he become the next President of the United States. Or, if he should miss at the upcoming election, he should be the leader of the opposition awaiting another chance. But his warrior approach had made him so unpopular that even his greatest admirers realized he could not hope to achieve the presidency of an elective government. To compound his plight, he had, in his determination to shine alone, failed to attract to himself followers of possible presidential stature. Whereas Jefferson, succeeded by his intimates Madison and Monroe, was to exert power in the presidency for twenty-four years, Hamilton had no surrogate. The Federalists nominated, to run against Jefferson, the archetypical New Englander John Adams, who owed nothing to Hamilton and was repelled by the West Indian's sword-waving flamboyance. After Adams had succeeded to the presidency, Hamilton was reduced to the mean expedient of plotting behind the President's back with members of the President's cabinet.

Then there arose the fascinating possibility that Hamilton might find escape from a "groveling" situation through the phenomenon he had longed for in his first known letter—a war. And from his point of view the right war—against France. The pendulum of foreign policy having swung towards England, the French were threatening to attack the United States. Congress voted to enlist a federal army. By intriguing mightily, Hamilton secured the post of second-in-command, which was in fact more than that, since Washington, the titular commander in chief, was far beyond his prime. Hamilton, who never achieved any deep satisfaction from his lucrative practice of the law, abandoned everything to live with and preside over the embryo army. He inscribed such masses of "routine and even petty and trivial" orders that the indefatigable editors of the normally exhaustive Hamilton papers

444

decided that to print more than a few samples would be a waste of time, ink, and paper.[9]

Hamilton had visions of leading the army against the Spanish Southwest and perhaps even annexing part of South America to the United States. But Adams had never really wanted the army—he thought a navy a better defense—and had been outraged at being maneuvered into appointing Hamilton, whom he deeply distrusted. The more orders Major General Hamilton sent out in a mounting frenzy, the fewer men there were to be efficiently organized. And then Adams, without consulting his cabinet, which he now realized Hamilton had infiltrated, made peaceful overtures to France, abolishing the threat of war and exploding forever Hamilton's visions of military glory.

In 1799, the Federalists renominated Adams. In pain and outrage, Hamilton wrote a voluminous attack—more than fifty printed pages—on Adams.[10] Yet he preferred his Federalist rival to his ancient enemy Jefferson; he ended by urging his readers to vote for Adams anyway. He was, indeed, so upset by the indications of a Jeffersonian victory that he suggested to John Jay, the governor of New York, a method for stealing that state's electoral votes. Jay indignantly refused.[11]

When Jefferson had won the election, a constitutional loophole opened that would permit frustrating the will of the people by seating in the presidency not Jefferson but Burr. Of the two, Hamilton more despised Burr; he opposed a Federalist drift towards using this loophole.

After Jefferson was seated, the northeastern Federalists considered his presidency so overwhelming a menace to all that was good and decent that they discussed taking their states out of the union. Now Hamilton fought for the union, helping to suppress the move towards secession. As part of this campaign, he intervened successfully to prevent Burr from becoming governor of New York.

Hamilton was no longer sailing a straight course towards stars of his own choosing. He was tacking confusedly, driven by gales and seas beyond his control. He was still powerful in his own party in his own region; he still had his law practice to fill his mind—to the extent that things which did not basically interest him could—but how limited was his volition as compared to what he had dreamed of, to what he had once achieved!

The interaction of Hamilton's temperament and his formative years had not prepared him to create or enjoy a satisfactory private life. Although he yearned to escape from his storm-tossed ambitions to a warm and peaceful home, no walls that he could build were long impermeable to outside tempests, nor, even at home, could he keep from engendering troubles. Throughout his life, he continued to write Betsey in the high style of romance and perfect love that had characterized his letters during their courtship. Again and again and again he stated that his one wish was to desert the great world to be forever at her side. Although Betsey insisted that she adored her husband, the evidence hardly points to a contented marriage.

Betsey became an extreme neurasthenic, grasping desperately, like a shipwrecked sailor, at supports she feared were not steadfast enough to keep her head above the waves. She was often sick from nerves, and she was further separated from her husband's active life by a long succession of pregnancies. Apart from miscarriages, with which she was regularly threatened, she bore eight children.

After her husband's death, Betsey's health seems to have improved: she lived to be ninety-seven, a most redoubtable old lady. During her fifty years of widowhood, her husband was all her own: he could escape from her no longer. Summoning various men to be his biographers, she repelled them all by her possessive effort to dictate what they should write. She even engaged in a lawsuit with one of her dead husband's most intimate colleagues to gain possession of papers which she believed would enhance her husband's reputation.[12] Not until she was very old and her son John C. Hamilton undertook the task, was a biography of Hamilton, now thirty-six years dead, begun. It was reverent in approach and exaggerated in claims.

That the living Hamilton had been a dedicated and accomplished pursuer of women was implied by the documents of his young manhood and became standard gossip during his years of fame. How much Betsey heard or suspected, the records do not tell, but we know that two situations were forced on her attention. The close friendship went on, for all their relations and friends to see, between her husband and her dashing sister Angelica, who wrote Betsey in 1794, "I love him very much and, if you were as generous as the old Romans, you would lend him to me for a little while." Did Betsey believe Angelica's further statement that the wife need not "be jealous" since all the sister wanted was to "promote his glory" and enjoy "a little chit-chat"?[13] In any case, the wife remained emotionally dependent on the sister.

Hamilton himself made as public as anything could possibly be what he asserted had been his affair with Maria Reynolds. His financial dealings with this lady's disreputable husband had come to the knowledge of his political enemies. They concluded that James

Angelica Schuyler Church, her son Philip, and a servant, by John Trumbull. The sister-in-law Hamilton found more fascinating than his wife. Courtesy, Mrs. Amy Olney Johnson and Professor Irma B. Jaffe

Reynolds had been serving as the Secretary of the Treasury's agent in buying up, at a low price, certificates which Treasury policy would make valuable, the owners to be swindled having been identified from Treasury records. To demonstrate that he had not been engaged in peculation but had, in fact, been paying blackmail, Hamilton published a pamphlet revealing a liaison with Reynolds's wife.[14] The accepted judgment on his behavior is that expressed by Allan Nevins in the *Dictionary of American Biography:* the revelation "had the merit of a proud bravery, for it showed him willing to endure any personal humiliation rather than a slur on his public integrity."[15]

Assuming that only sex and blackmail were involved, Nevins's explanation would be the most convincing. But overtones inevitably sound in the ears of someone who has from the start followed Hamilton's dilemmas. All that the situation required of Hamilton was that he demonstrate enough factual information about the liaison and the resulting blackmail to convince the public. But Hamilton included in his pamphlet, which ran to ninety-five pages, the entirely unnecessary statement that he had entertained Maria in his own home, and quoted entire love letters in which his paramour expressed both the extremities of passion for him and an almost suicidal despair when he neglected her. As one reads on and on, a feeling grows that there was an emotional need behind all this quoting. Was Hamilton, however subconsciously, identifying Maria with his mother? Was he trying to overcome unslaked humiliations by putting himself, as publicly in the great world as had been his disgrace in his childhood environment, triumphantly in the role of his mother's lovers who had incited his impotent jealousy and rage when he had been a child?

Not everyone, from then to now, has been convinced that Hamilton was in fact guilty of infidelity rather than of some other activity he was hiding. His contemporary tormentor James Thompson Callender wrote: "Those letters from Mrs. Reynolds are badly spelt and pointed [punctuated]. Capitals also occur in the midst of words. But waiving such excrescences, the style is pathetic and even elegant. It does not bear the marks of an illiterate writer."

When I myself was making my preliminary survey of the Hamilton material, before I took seriously the questions that had been raised about the Reynolds affair, I was struck by the resemblance between the perfervid style attributed to Maria and that authentically used by Hamilton in his love letters to Betsey, both as his fiancée and as his wife. The modern historian Julian Boyd has pointed out that, despite urgings and expressed doubts, Hamilton kept hidden from all reliable eyes the originals of the letters he was willing to publish so widely. If he did in fact write these love letters to himself, the implication of childhood fantasy is overwhelming.[16]

There is no reason to believe that whatever love affairs Hamilton did have brought him anything but temporary surcease. And his legitimate family life mounted to a double tragedy. He had brought up his eldest son, Philip, according to his own ideas. And at the age of nineteen, Philip instigated a quarrel with a political enemy of his father's and challenged him to a duel. Probably close to the spot on the Jersey Highlands where his father was to be mortally wounded, Philip himself received a mortal wound. We are assured by Hamilton's grandson, Allan McLane Hamilton, who was in his own lifetime famous as a doctor for the insane, that the shock of Philip's death drove Hamilton's second child—she was named Angelica after her aunt—over the edge into an insanity from which she never recovered, although she lived to be seventy-three.[17]

Hamilton had, of course, his circle of male admirers: politicians and businessmen of ability, wealth, and influence who accorded him all the admiration that, as a scorned and then disinherited youth, he had so passionately desired. But he could not translate this admiration into what he desired even more: power. Power not for its own sake, not for the license it gave to destroy, but for the opportunity to create order and system, to build. He had a vision of the perfect state, orderly when he could hold on to his passions, and for a time it had seemed that he could turn that vision into reality. He could not foresee that his conceptions, which he believed had been defeated, would rise again, achieving, in later generations, proportions in many ways above his most ambitious dreams. Before his living eyes the nation was dissolving into what he considered chaos—and he had lost the power effectively to intervene.

The French statesman Talleyrand had become intimate with Hamilton during two years of exile in America and then returned to France to dominate, as Napoleon's foreign minister, European international affairs. He wrote: "I consider Napoleon, Fox, and Hamilton the three greatest men of our epoch, and if I were forced to decide between the three, I would give without hesitation the first place to Hamilton. He divined Europe."[18]

Should Hamilton have settled in the Europe he had divined? Had it been an evil wind that had blown him from St. Croix to a continent where the people, those vicious clods who had been his enemy since

Hamilton as a lawyer, by John Trumbull. This full-length portrait shows the slightness of physique and the narrowness of shoulder, which explain why Hamilton was always described as a little man, although he was not short. Courtesy, Chamber of Commerce, City of New York. Photograph, Pach Brothers

childhood, could block the road, preventing a man of vision from grasping the power he needed to achieve personal glory and also to bring into being what he knew was best for everyone?

In 1802, Hamilton meditated: "Mine is an odd destiny. Perhaps no man in the United States has sacrificed or done more for the present constitution than myself; and contrary to all my anticipations of its fate . . . from the very beginning, I am still laboring to prop the frail and worthless fabric, yet I have the murmurs of its friends no less than the curses of its foes for my reward. What can I do better than withdraw from the scene? Every day proves to me more and more that the American world was not made for me."[19]

A long-envisioned way out was left to him. He had written Laurens, now dead these twenty-two years, "I have no other wish than as soon as possible to make a brilliant exit."[20] Aaron Burr had sent him a duelist's challenge. Although he admitted that dueling was the worst way of determining the justice of a quarrel, such encounters were part of the military, the ceremonial, the chivalric world. He would expose his body to Burr's bullet, but himself fire in the air.

On July 12, 1804, Alexander Hamilton died in great pain.

Appendix A

Hamilton's Arrival in North America

Hamilton's son John, who was almost always wrong concerning the early years, stated that his father arrived from St. Croix at Boston in October, 1772. Broadus Mitchell, citing only this source and expressing only a little doubt, has Hamilton disembarking at Boston in September or October, 1772.[1]

The two men who had known Hamilton during his first New York years and who wrote down their recollections a generation later, disagreed about the time of his arrival. Hercules Mulligan gives the date as October, 1773, while Robert Troup has Hamilton entering King's College, his schooldays in New Jersey already over, in the fall of 1773. Hamilton himself mentioned the matter only once, stating that he had arrived "at about the age of sixteen." According to his long-accepted and probably correct birthdate, he became sixteen on January 11, 1773.[2]

Hamilton was surely at St. Croix when he dated his hurricane letter September 6, 1772. When it was published on October 3, 1772, a note stated that "the author's modesty in long refusing to submit it to the public view is the reason for its making its appearance so late as it does now."[3] Hamilton had to be on St. Croix during his "long" period of "refusing," and, indeed, the note refers to him as "a youth of the island." At the very earliest, he could not have sailed more than a few days before October 3. If the publication, as is usually assumed, encouraged the plan to send him abroad, that would have dictated a further delay, say until mid-November. But no wise sea captain would have undertaken that late in the year the fifteen-hundred-mile trip to North America; eighteenth-century vessels did not challenge the Atlantic Ocean in midwinter.

James Lytton's executors noted payments to Hamilton on the account of Ann Venton, who was then in New York, twice in May, 1773, and again on June 3.[4] Scholars who wish Hamilton to be in North America by then infer that Hamilton had sent requisitions to St. Croix as her agent. But why should Hamilton, who was theoretically at school in New Jersey, be collecting in St. Croix for Ann Venton? Furthermore, it seems indicative that three Venton documents are grouped within a month, while there is during Hamilton's whole association with Ann only one other such notation: May 23, 1772. It seems highly probable that his cousin was helping Hamilton to get off.

Under ideal conditions, a fast sailer could go from St. Croix to New York in two weeks. Calms or contrary winds could expand the time into months. Since the chronology, once Hamilton reached North America, becomes otherwise cramped, it seems probable that his voyage was at least moderately quick. If he left St. Croix directly after June 3 he could have been in North America before the end of the month.

The statement that Hamilton landed in Boston originates with Mulligan, who asserts that the youth published in newspapers there two or three political pieces before he came on to New York. Troup, who agrees that Hamilton published his first political piece in Boston, explains that the youth had gone there from New York after the Boston Tea Party (December, 1773) to see what was going on.[5] This account is much the more probable, for three reasons: (1) when it is possible to check, Troup proves much more consistently correct than Mulligan; (2) Hamilton would surely have been unable to write acceptably about American controversies at the very instant he set foot on American soil; and (3) since traffic between New York and St. Croix was considerable and the specific route of the merchants who were supporting him, there seems no reason why Hamilton should have added to the expense of his trip and also wasted time by making necessary a second voyage: on a coasting vessel from Boston to New York.

Hamilton probably arrived in New York Harbor during June, 1773.

Appendix B

Note on the Battle of Trenton

The description, given in Chapter 13, of Hamilton's part in the march on Trenton and in the ensuing battle rests on information that cannot be proved to the hilt. In his scholarly account of the battle, Professor Thomas Jefferson Wertenbaker cautiously avoids committing himself on the question of Hamilton's presence by never mentioning Hamilton at all.

In his reminiscences already cited (page 125), Peter Cattell states that Hamilton was at the battle. Cattell's testimony is supported by his independently checkable statement that before the battle Hamilton was sick.

But the truly basic consideration is how much credence to give William Stryker's *The Battles of Trenton and Princeton,* in which Hamilton's position in the march and role in the battle are specified. Unfortunately, Stryker did not cite references, preferring to publish selected documents in an appendix. None of these documents bear directly on Hamilton during the march or battle. However, Stryker's entire work reveals so many evidences of conscientious research that I have decided, with the reservations stated in this note, to accept his statements.

Acknowledgments

The New-York Historical Society—Robert G. Goelet, president; James J. Heslin, director; James Gregory, librarian—has again made its superb facilities available to me. Every member of the library and museum staffs has assisted me on many occasions. I am particularly grateful to Sue Adele Gillies, reference librarian, and to Philip Klingle, who has helped me disentangle many a knotty problem. I also wish to thank my longtime friends Mary Black and Richard Coke; Charlotte P. Rowell, assistant to the director; Thomas J. Dunnings, Jr., curator of manuscripts; and William Asadorian, Mary Alice Kennedy, John A. Lovari, Roger N. Mohovich, and Wendy Shadwell.

I have also been assisted by the Library of the Century Association; the Free Library of Cornwall, Connecticut; the New York Public Library, which has given me access to the Frederick Lewis Allen Room; and the New York Society Library.

My gratitude to Harold C. Syrett, the editor of the *Hamilton Papers,* is expressed at the opening of my bibliography. I wish to add here my thanks for his friendship and advice. I am also indebted to Mary-Jo Kline, whose knowledge of the papers of the founding fathers is as great as her generosity in imparting that knowledge.

My investigations on the Leeward Islands were facilitated by the hospitality of Mr. and Mrs. James Pomeroy Hendrick on St. Croix and William M. Gordon on Nevis.

My wife, Beatrice Hudson Flexner, has toiled over my manuscript, in the process earning the family appellation of "werewolf" through her determination to make me use the subjunctive. My editor at Little, Brown, Llewellyn Howland III, has, although much my junior, played his usual parental role. Many improvements in the text were made at the suggestion of Jean Whitnack. Christine Coffin, also of Little, Brown, has cheerfully suffered the rigors of making an illegible manuscript legible. My daughter, Nellie Flexner, helped by doing research at the Massachusetts Historical Society.

Bibliography

Legends and special pleading have down the generations hidden the Hamilton who suffered and achieved. My desire to get back to the man who actually lived has dictated that this book be, as far as possible, based on original materials. For background, I have, of course, consulted the most reliable secondary sources, but the picture here presented was created, almost altogether, by a fresh examination of the direct evidence.

To the vast advantage of this study, the bulk of the evidence is included in the edition of Hamilton's papers being edited by Harold C. Syrett and his associates. This labor, which already extends far beyond the part of Hamilton's life dealt with in this book, is a model for documentary publications. Communications both to and from Hamilton are included, as are his other writings. The notes are accurate and informative and not inflated—kept down to the essentially useful.

The family archive of Hamilton papers, which is by far the most voluminous, is in the Library of Congress. It is available on a microfilm which, although difficult and complicated to use, contains a variety of documents, including material collected by Hamilton's widow, that are not within the scope of Syrett's volumes.

All previous compendia of Hamilton papers are being made obsolete by Syrett's publication. Mention should, however, be made here of the two most extensive: *Works*, edited by John C. Hamilton and published in seven volumes in 1851; and *Works*, edited by Henry Cabot Lodge and published in nine volumes in 1885–1886.

H. U. Ramsing made an exhaustive study of the evidence in existence concerning Hamilton's ancestry, connections, and life in the Leeward Islands. Ramsing's invaluable report, which is completely documentary, was published in Denmark in 1939. I have made use of the English translation by Solvejg Vahl in the New York Public Library.

Another important source is *The Law Practice of Alexander Hamilton: Documents and Commentary*. Two volumes out of the projected three have been published under the editorship of Julius Goebel, Jr. The lack of the third made small difference to my studies, which were concerned only with the beginnings of Hamilton's law career.

As a group, the published biographies of Hamilton are so biased, so given to exalting his character, to exaggerating his achievements, that reading them is more a study in myth than fact. There being no further scholarly need, only those biographies actually cited in my text are included in the subsequent list. The lives I have found most useful are the extensive although idolatrous works of his son John C. Hamilton; the biography by Allan McLane Hamilton who, as a professional psychologist, understood his grandfather more than his text acknowledges on the surface; Broadus Mitchell's two volumes, which, despite an overpowering admiration for Hamilton, reveal greater research than any other biography; and John C. Miller's *Hamilton*, the least prejudiced and most comprehending of character. Richard B. Morris's *Seven Who Shaped Our Destiny* contains a well-balanced, short account of Hamilton.

This book is being published more or less on the fortieth anniversary of the publication of my first book, *Doctors on Horseback*, a group of short biographies that included discussions of the medical history of the American Revolution. Many of the more than twenty volumes I have subsequently completed have also dealt, in full or in part, with the times and events in which Hamilton was embroiled. A full bibliography of the works I consulted down the long years would be both impossible and pointless to compile. No effort has here been made to document the general history of the Revolution. The citations that follow point directly at Hamilton and serve, for the most part, to supplement with fuller titles the abbreviations in the Source References. Citations for materials in Syrett's edition of the Hamilton papers are to that work. I have not encumbered this bibliography with a list of the manuscript collections directly consulted, since it seemed more useful to report the location of each document in the relevant source reference.

Adams, John, *Diary and Autobiography of John Adams,* ed. Lyman H. Butterfield, 4 vols. (Cambridge, Mass., 1961).

——, *Familiar Letters of John Adams and His Wife Abigail Adams During the Revolution,* ed. Charles Francis Adams (New York, 1876).

——, *Letters of John Adams Addressed to His Wife,* ed. Charles Francis Adams, 2 vols. (Boston, 1841).

Adams, Thomas R., *American Independence . . . : A Bibliographical Study of American Political Pamphlets Printed between 1764 and 1776* (Providence, R.I., 1965).

Alden, John Richard, *Charles Lee: Traitor or Patriot?* (Baton Rouge, 1951).

Ames, Fisher, *Works,* ed. Seth Ames, 2 vols. (Boston, 1854).

Armstrong, John, Jr., "Review of Sketches of the Life and Correspondence of Nathanael Greene . . . by William Johnson," *United States Magazine,* I (1883), 3–44.

Aspinall, Algernon E., *The Pocket Guide to the West Indies* (New York, 1911).

Atherton, Gertrude, *Adventures of a Novelist* (New York, 1932).

——, *The Conqueror* (New York, 1902).

——, *A Few Letters of Alexander Hamilton* (New York, 1913).

——, "The Hunt for Hamilton's Mother," *North American Review,* CLV (1902), 229–242.

Augier, F. R., *Sources of West Indian History* (London, 1962).

Bancroft, George, *History of the Formation of the Constitution of the United States,* Vol. I (New York, 1882).

——, *History of the United States,* Vol. VII (Boston, 1898).

Bill, Alfred Hoyt, *The Campaign of Princeton* (Princeton, 1948).

Bland, Harry MacNeill, and Northcott, Virginia W., "The Life Portraits of Alexander Hamilton," *William and Mary Quarterly,* 3rd Ser., XII (1955), 187–198.

Bliven, Bruce, Jr., *Battle for Manhattan* (New York, 1956).

——, *Under the Guns: New York, 1775–1776* (New York, 1972).

Bonsal, Stephen, *When the French Were Here* (New York, 1945).

Boudinot, Elias, *Journal or Historical Recollections of American Events during the Revolutionary War* (Philadelphia, 1894).

——, *Life, Public Services, Addresses, and Letters,* ed. by J. J. Boudinot, 2 vols. (Boston, 1896).

Boyd, George Adams, *Elias Boudinot* (Princeton, 1952).

Brant, Irving, *James Madison, the Nationalist, 1780–1787* (Indianapolis, 1948).

Brooks, Noah, *Henry Knox* (New York, 1900).

Burnett, Edmund, C., ed., *Letters of Members of the Continental Congress,* Vols. I–VII (Washington, D.C., 1921–1934).

——, "New York and the Continental Congress," in Flick, Alexander C., ed., *History of the State of New York* (New York, 1933) III, 293–325.

Burr, Aaron, *Memoirs,* Vol. I (New York, 1836).

Burns, Alan, *History of the British West Indies* (London, 1954).

Butcher, H. Bordon, *The Battle of Trenton* (Princeton, 1934).

Calendar of Historical Manuscripts in Albany: Revolutionary Papers, 2 vols. (Albany, 1868).

Callahan, North, *Henry Knox* (New York, 1958).

Caribbeana, being miscellaneous papers relating to . . . the British West Indies, ed. Vere Langford Oliver, Vols. I–V (London, 1910–1919).

Catalogue of Manuscripts and Revolutionary Relics deposited at Washington's Head Quarters [sic] (Newburgh, N.Y., 1858).

Chastellux, Marquis de, *Travels in North America in the Years 1780, 1781, and 1782*, trans. and ed. Howard C. Rice, Jr. (Chapel Hill, 1963).

Clinton, George, *Public Papers*, 10 vols. (New York and Albany, 1900–1914).

Closen, Baron Ludwig Von, *Revolutionary Journal*, trans. and ed. Evelyn A. Acomb (Chapel Hill, N.C., [1958]).

Codman, John, *Sermon Delivered at the Funeral of General Stephen Badlam* (Cambridge, Mass., 1815).

Coke, Thomas, *A History of the West Indies*, Vol. III (London, 1811).

"A Collection of Papers Relative to Half Pay and the Commutation of Half Pay," *The Remembrancer . . . for the Year 1783*, Vol. XVI, Pt. 2 (London, 1783).

Continental Congress, *Journals, 1774–1789*, 8 vols. (Washington, D.C., 1921–1926). Referred to as CCJ.

Crawford, George, *General Description of the Shire of Renfrew* (n.p., 1710).

Cunningham, Anna K., *Schuyler Mansion: A Critical Catalogue of the Furnishings and Decorations* (Albany, 1955).

Custis, George Washington Parke, *Recollections and Private Memoirs of Washington* (New York, 1860).

Davis, W. W. H., "Washington on the Banks of the Delaware," *Pennsylvania Magazine of History and Biography*, IV (1880), 133–163.

Denny, Ebenezer, "Military Journal," *Memoirs of the Historical Society of Pennsylvania*, VII (1880).

Deux-Ponts, Guillaume, *My Campaigns in America* (Boston, 1868).

Documents Relative to the Colonial History of New York, ed. by E. B. O'Callahan, Vol. VIII (Albany, New York, 1857).

Drake, Francis Samuel, *Life and Correspondence of Henry Knox* (Boston, 1873).

Duncan, James, "Diary of Colonel Moses Hazen's Regiment in the Yorktown Campaign," *Pennsylvania Archives*, 2nd ser., XV (1890), 743–752.

Eberlein, Harold D., and Hubbard, Courtland Van D., *Diary of Independence Hall* (Philadelphia, 1948).

Edward, Bryan, *The History, Civil and Commercial, of the British Colonies in the West Indies*, Vol. I (Dublin, 1793).

Feltman, William, "Journal . . . of the First Pennsylvania Regiment . . . comprising the Siege of Yorktown and the Southern Campaign," *Historical Society of Pennsylvania Collections*, I (1853), 316 ff.

Fernow, Berthold, *New York in the Revolution*, Vols. I and II (Albany, 1887).

Flexner, James Thomas, *George Washington*, 4 vols. (Boston, 1965–1972). Vol. II referred to as FR.

———, *The Traitor and the Spy* (Boston, 1975).

———, *Washington, The Indispensable Man* (Boston, 1974).

Force, Peter, comp., *American Archives*, 9 vols. (Washington, D.C., 1837–1853).

Freeman, Douglas Southall, *George Washington: A Biography*, completed by J. A. Carroll and M. W. Ashworth, 7 vols. (New York, 1948–1957).

Fuld, Leonhard Felix, *King's College Alumni* (New York, 1913).

Garden, Alexander, *Anecdotes of the American Revolution*, 3 vols. (Brooklyn, New York, 1865).

Gordon, William, *History of the Rise and Progress of the Establishment of the Independence of the United States*, Vol. IV (London, 1788).

461

Graydon, Alexander, *Memoirs of His Own Time* (Philadelphia, 1846).

Greene, George Washington, *The Life of Nathanael Greene,* 3 vols. (New York, 1867–1871).

Hamilton, Alexander, *The Law Practice of Alexander Hamilton: Documents and Commentary,* ed. Julius Goebel, Jr., 2 vols. (New York, 1964, 1969). Referred to as G.

———, *Observations on Certain Documents contained in number V and VI of the History of the United States for 1796, in which the Charge of Speculation against Alexander Hamilton . . . is Fully Refuted* (Philadelphia, 1797).

———, *Papers,* ed. Harold C. Syrett, vols. I–XXIV, all so far published (New York, 1961–1976). All documents to be found here are thus cited, and are therefore not listed separately in this bibliography. Referred to as HS.

———, *Works,* ed. John C. Hamilton, 7 vols. (New York, 1851).

———, *Works,* ed. Henry Cabot Lodge, 9 vols. (New York and London, 1885–1886).

Hamilton, Allan McLane, *The Intimate Life of Alexander Hamilton* (New York, 1910). Referred to as AMH.

Hamilton, James A., *Reminiscences of . . . Men and Events* (New York, 1869).

Hamilton, John C., *History of the Republic of the United States of America as traced in the Writings of Alexander Hamilton and his Contemporaries,* 7 vols. (1857–1864). Referred to as JCH, *History.*

———, *The Life of Alexander Hamilton,* 2 vols. (New York, 1840). Referred to as JCH, *Life.*

Hatch, Louis Clinton, *The Administration of the American Revolutionary Army* (New York, 1904).

Hazard, Samuel, ed., *The Register of Pennsylvania,* Vol. II (Philadelphia, 1828).

"Historic Keeps and Castles and Stately Homes of Ayrshire: Kerelaw House," *Kilmarnock Standard,* 4/5/1924.

Hooker, Philip, "Sketch, Description and Appraisal of the House and Property of the late General Philip Schuyler, 1/20/1818," illustrated MS, New-York Historical Society.

Humphreys, Frank Landon, *Life of David Humphreys,* Vol. I (New York, 1907).

Humphreys, Mary G., *Catherine Schuyler* (New York, 1897).

Huntington, Jedediah, "Correspondence," *Connecticut Historical Society Collections,* Vol. XX, Pt. 2 (Hartford, Conn., 1923).

Irving, Washington, *Life of Washington,* Vol. III (New York, 1858).

Jay, John, *Correspondence and Public Papers,* ed. Henry P. Johnston, 4 vols. (New York, 1890–1893).

———, *The Making of a Revolutionary: Unpublished Papers, 1745–1780,* ed. Richard B. Morris, Vol. I (New York, 1975).

Jefferson, Thomas, *Papers,* ed. Julian P. Boyd, 14 vols. (Princeton, N.J., 1950–1974).

———, *Writings,* ed. Andrew A. Lipscomb and Albert E. Burgh, 20 vols. in 10 (Washington, D.C., 1903).

Johnson, William, *Sketches of the Life and Correspondence of Nathanael Greene,* 2 vols. (Charleston, 1822).

Journals of the Provincial Congress, Provincial Convention, Committee of Safety, and Council of Safety of the State of New York, 2 vols. (Albany, 1842).

Kalm, Peter, *The America of 1750: Peter Kalm's Travels in North America*, 2 vols. (New York, 1966).

King, Charles R., *The Life and Correspondence of Rufus King*, Vol. I (New York, 1894).

Kline, Mary-Jo, *Alexander Hamilton: A Biography in His Own Words* (New York, 1973).

Kohn, Richard H., "The Inside History of the Newburgh Conspiracy," *William and Mary Quarterly*, 3rd ser., XVII (1970), 143–158.

Knollenberg, Bernhard, *Washington and the Revolution* (New York, 1940).

Knox, Hugh, *A Letter to the Rev. Mr. Jacob Green of New Jersey Pointing Out Some of the Difficulties of the Calvinistic Scheme of Divinity Respecting Free Will, Divine Decrees, Particular Redemption, etc. and Requesting a Solution of Them* (London, 1770).

Lafayette, Marquis de, *Memoirs, Correspondence, and Manuscripts . . . Published by His Family*, Vol. I (New York, 1837).

——, *The Letters of Lafayette to Washington*, ed. Louis Gottschalk (New York, 1944).

Larson, Harold, "Alexander Hamilton: The Fact and Fiction of His Early Years," *William and Mary Quarterly*, 3rd ser., IX (1952), 139–151.

——, "The Birth and Parentage of Alexander Hamilton," *American Genealogist*, XXXI (1945), 161–167.

Laurens, John, *Army Correspondence . . . in the Years 1777–1778* (New York, 1867).

Lee, Charles, *The Lee Papers*, 4 vols. (New York, 1872–1875).

Lee, Henry, *Memoirs of the War in the Southern Department of the United States*, 2 vols. (Philadelphia, 1812).

Lefferts, Charles M., *Uniforms of the American, British, French and German Armies in the War of the Revolution* (New York, 1926).

Lewinson, Florence, *Diverse Information on the Romantic History of St. Croix* (St. Croix, n.d.).

——, *St. Croix Under Seven Flags* (Hollywood, Fla., 1970).

Lodge, Henry Cabot, *Alexander Hamilton* (New York, 1898).

Lossing, Benson J., *The Life and Times of Philip Schuyler*, 2 vols. (New York, 1872–1873).

Lycan, Gilbert, *Alexander Hamilton and American Foreign Policy* (Norman, Okla., 1970).

McDonald, John MacLean, *The McDonald Papers*, ed. William S. Hadway, Vol. I (White Plains, N.Y., 1926).

MacElree, Wilmer W., *Along the Western Brandywine* (Chester, Pa., 1912).

Madison, James, *Papers*, ed. William T. Hutchinson and William M. E. Rachal, Vols. V–VII (Chicago, 1967–1971). Referred to as MP.

——, *Writings*, ed. Gaillard Hunt, Vol. I (New York, 1900).

Mailler, Marion Mackenzie, and Dempsey, Janet, *Eighteenth Century Homes in New Windsor and Vicinity as Depicted by Simeon De Witt* (Vails Gate, N.Y., 1968).

Martin, Joseph Plumb, *Private Yankee Doodle*, ed. George F. Scheer (Boston, 1962).

Mason, J. M., *An Oration Commemorative of the late Major General Hamilton Pronounced before the New York State Society of the Cincinnati* (New York, 1804).

Miers, Earl Schenck, *Blood of Freedom* (New York, 1958).

Miller, John C., *Alexander Hamilton: Portrait in Paradox* (New York, 1959).

Miller, Samuel, *Memoir of the Rev. John Rodgers* (New York, 1813).

Mintz, Max M., *Gouverneur Morris and the American Revolution* (Norman, Okla., 1970).

Mitchell, Broadus, *Alexander Hamilton*, 2 vols. (New York, 1957, 1962). Referred to as MH.

——, *Alexander Hamilton: A Concise Biography* (New York, 1976).

——, *Alexander Hamilton: The Revolutionary Years* (New York, 1970).

——,"The Man Who Discovered Hamilton (Hugh Knox)" *Proceedings New Jersey Historical Society*, LXIX (1951), 88–114.

Morris, Gouverneur, *Diary and Letters,* ed. Anne Cary Morris, 2 vols. (New York, 1888).

Morris, Richard B., *Alexander Hamilton and the Founding of the Nation: A Selection from Hamilton's Writings* (New York, 1957).

——, *Seven Who Shaped Our Destiny* (New York, 1973).

Morse, John T., *Life of Alexander Hamilton*, 2 vols. (Boston, 1876).

Mulligan, Hercules, "Narrative," *William and Mary Quarterly*, 3rd ser., IV (1947), 209–211.

Murray, John, *Jerubbaal or Tyranny Grove Destroyed. . . . A Discourse delivered at the Presbyterian Church at Newburyport* (Newburyport, 1784).

Murray, Nicholas. *Notes Historical and Biographical Concerning Elizabethtown* (New York, 1941).

Nelson, Paul, "Horatio Gates at Newburgh: a Misunderstood Role; with a Rebuttal by Richard H. Kohn," *William and Mary Quarterly*, 3rd ser., XXIX (1972), 143–158.

North Carolina, *The State Records*, ed. Walter Clark, Vol. XVI (Goldsboro, N.C., 1899).

Oberholzer, Ellis P., *Robert Morris* (New York, 1903).

O'Brien, Michael J., *Hercules Mulligan* (New York, 1937).

Oliver, Frederick Scott, *Alexander Hamilton: An Essay in American Union* (New York, 1912).

Paltsits, Victor, *Washington's Farewell Address* (New York, 1935).

Panagopoulos, E. P., ed., *Alexander Hamilton's Pay Book* (Detroit, 1964).

Patterson, Emma Little, *Peekskill in the American Revolution* (Peekskill, N.Y., 1944).

Pickering, Octavius, *The Life of Timothy Pickering*, 4 vols. (Boston, 1867–1873).

Pickering, Timothy, "Historical Index to the Pickering Papers," *Massachusetts Historical Society Collections*, 6th ser., VII (1896).

Postlethwayt, Malachy, *The Universal Dictionary of Trade and Commerce, Translated from the French by Monsieur [Jacques] Savary . . . with large Additions and Improvements* (London, 1755).

Provincial Congress of the State of New York, *Journals, 1775–1777* (Albany, N.Y., 1842).

Ramsing, H. U., "Alexander Hamilton og hans modrene Slaegt. Tidsbilleder fra Dansk Vest-Indiens Barndom," *Personalhistorik Tidsskrift,* 59 de Aargang, 10 Rekke, 6 Bind (1939). Trans. Solvejg Vahl, MS of trans. in the New York Public Library. Referred to as R.

Rochambeau, Count de, *Memoirs . . . Relative to the War of Independence in the United States,* trans. by M. W. E. Wright (Paris, 1838).

Rodney, Caesar, *Letters to and from,* ed. George Herbert Ryden (Philadelphia, 1933).

Rush, Benjamin, *Autobiography,* ed. George W. Corner (Princeton, 1948).

Ruttenberg, E. M., *History of New Windsor* (Newburgh, N.Y., 1911).

Rymer, James A., *A Description of the Island of Nevis* (London, 1775).

St. Croix Pocket Companion, or a Brief Sketch of Things to be known by the Dwellers or Traders to the Island (Copenhagen, 1780).

Schachner, Nathan, *Alexander Hamilton* (New York, 1946).

———, "Alexander Hamilton Viewed by His Friends: The Narratives of Robert Troup and Hercules Mulligan," *William and Mary Quarterly,* 3rd ser., IV (1947), 203–225.

Schuyler, George Washington, *Colonial New York: Philip Schuyler and his Family,* 2 vols. (New York, 1885).

Seabury, Samuel, *Free Thought on the Proceedings of the Continental Congress* (New York, 1774).

———, *Letters of a Westchester Farmer,* ed. Clarence H. Vance (White Plains, N.Y., 1930).

———, *A View of the Controversy between Great Britain and her Colonies* (New York, 1774).

Sedgwick, Theodore, Jr., *A Memoir of the Life of William Livingston* (New York, 1833).

Sellers, Charles Coleman, *Portraits and Miniatures by Charles Willson Peale* (Philadelphia, 1952).

Shannon, Sister Anna Magdeleine, "General Alexander McDougall," doctoral dissertation, Fordham University (New York, 1957), New-York Historical Society.

Shaw, Samuel, *Journals, with a Life of the Author,* ed. Josiah Quincy (Boston, 1847).

Shea, George, *Life and Epoch of Alexander Hamilton* (Boston, 1879).

Smith, Samuel Stelle, *The Battle of Trenton* (Monmouth Beach, N.J., 1965).

Smith, William, *A Natural History of Nevis* (Cambridge, England, 1745).

Smith, William Henry, *The St. Clair Papers,* Vol. I (Cincinnati, 1888).

Sparks, Jared, ed. *Correspondence of the American Revolution, Being Letters of Eminent Men to George Washington,* 4 vols. (Boston, 1853).

———, *Life of Gouverneur Morris, with Selections from his Correspondence and Miscellaneous Papers,* 3 vols. (Boston, 1832).

Steiner, Bernard C., *The Life and Correspondence of James McHenry* (Cleveland, 1907).

Stille, Charles J., *The Life and Times of John Dickinson* (Philadelphia, 1891).

Stokes, I. N. Phelps, *The Iconography of Manhattan Island,* 6 vols. (New York, 1915–1928).

Stourah, Gerald, *Alexander Hamilton and the Idea of Republican Government* (Stamford, Conn., 1970).

Stryker, William S., *The Battles of Trenton and Princeton* (Boston and New York, 1898).

Syrett, Harold, *Interview at Weehawken: The Burr-Hamilton Duel as Told in Original Documents* (Middletown, Conn., 1960).

Tansill, Charles C., ed., *Documents Illustrative of the Formation of the Union of the American States* (Washington, D.C., 1927).

Thacher, James, *Military Journal of the American Revolution* (Hartford, Conn., 1862).

Thomas, Milton H., "The King's College Building," *New-York Historical Society Quarterly*, XXXIX (1955), 23–61.

Tilghman, Oswald, *Memoir of Lieutenant Colonel Tench Tilghman* (Albany, N.Y., 1876).

Townsend, Barbara, *An American Soldier: The Life of John Laurens* (Raleigh, N.C., 1958).

Townsend, Joseph, *Some Account of the British Army . . . and the Battle of Brandywine* (Philadelphia, 1846).

Troup, Robert, "Narrative," *William and Mary Quarterly*, 3rd ser., IV (1947), 212–225.

Trumbull Papers, *Massachusetts Historical Society Collections*, 7th ser., III (1902).

Tuckerman, Bayard, *Life of . . . Philip Schuyler* (New York, 1903).

Valentine, Alan, *Lord Stirling* (New York, 1967).

Van Amringe, John Howard, *A History of Columbia University* (New York, 1904).

Van Rensselaer, Florence, *The Livingston Family in America* (New York, 1949).

Waldo, Albigence, "Diary, Valley Forge, 1777–1778," *Pennsylvania Magazine of History and Biography*, XXI (1897), 299–323.

Wallace, David Duncan, *The Life of Henry Laurens, with a Sketch of the Life of Lieutenant Colonel John Laurens* (New York, 1915).

Ward, Christopher, *The War of the Revolution*, ed. John Richard Alden, 2 vols. (New York, 1952).

Washington, George, *Diaries*, ed. John C. Fitzpatrick, 4 vols. (Boston and New York, 1925).

——, *Writings*, ed. John C. Fitzpatrick, 39 vols. (Washington, D.C., 1931–1944). Referred to as GW.

Wertenbaker, Thomas Jefferson, *Princeton, 1746–1896* (Princeton, N.J., 1946).

Westergaard, Waldemar, *The Danish West Indies under Company Rule, 1671–1754, with a Supplementary Chapter, 1755–1917* (New York, 1917).

Wharton, Francis, ed., *The Revolutionary Diplomatic Correspondence of the United States*, Vol. IV (Washington, D.C., 1889).

White, Philip L., *The Beekmans of New York* (New York, 1956).

Wilkinson, James, *Memoirs of My Own Times*, Vol. I (Philadelphia, 1816).

Williams, Catherine, *Biography of Revolutionary Heroes, containing the Life of Brigadier General William Barton and Captain Stephen Olney* (Providence, R.I., 1839).

Source References

Since the Bibliography gives full citations, the source references have been kept as brief as seems clear. The sources most often repeated are referred to by the following abbreviations:

AMH:	Allan McLane Hamilton, *Hamilton*
CCJ:	Continental Congress, *Journals*
FR:	Flexner, *Washington*, Vol. II
G:	*Law Practice of A. H.*, ed. Julius Goebel, Jr.
GW:	Washington, *Writings*, ed. Fitzpatrick
HS:	Hamilton, *Papers*, ed. Syrett
HSP:	*Historical Society of Pennsylvania Collections*
JCH, *History:*	John C. Hamilton, *History*
JCH, *Life:*	John C. Hamilton, *Life*
LC:	Library of Congress
MH:	Mitchell, *Hamilton*, 2 vols.
MHS:	Massachusetts Historical Society
MP:	Madison, *Papers*, ed. *Hutchinson* and *Rachal*
NYHS:	New-York Historical Society
NYPL:	New York Public Library
PMHB:	*Pennsylvania Magazine of History and Biography*
R:	Ramsing, *Hamilton*
WMQ:	*William and Mary Quarterly*

INTRODUCTION

1. Oliver, *Hamilton*, 429–430.
2. HS, III, 306.

1. SETTING A TRAUMATIC STAGE

1. MH, I, 468–469.
2. *Caribbeana*, II, 267, 269.

3. MH, I, 2–3; R, 1.
4. Atherton, *Letters*, 269–282.
5. Lewinson, *Diverse* and *Seven;* MH, I, 19 ff.; Westergaard, *Danish*
6. Augier, *Sources*, 38–44; *Gentleman's Magazine*, XXXVI (1766), 229–230.
7. Lewinson, *Diverse* and *Seven;* Westergaard.
8. Mitchell, *Knox*, 101.

9. MH, I, 14.
10. JCH, *History*, I, 41–42, and *Life*, I, 2.
11. Atherton, *Letters*, 272–273; HS, III, 84; Larsen, "Early," 142; MH, I, 5, 471–472.
12. R, 3–4.
13. R, 14.
14. MH, I, 6.
15. R, 8–9.
16. Personal visit, 1975.
17. R, 8.
18. Mitchell, *Knox*, 98; MH, I, 8; R, 6–10.
19. MH, I, 8; R, 5.
20. Atherton, "Mother," 237–238.

2. PARENTAL SHADOWS

1. AMH, 4.
2. Contract of marriage betwixt James Hamilton and Mrs. Eliz. Pollock, 6/15/1711, transcript in NYHS.
3. MH, 9.
4. "Historic Keeps"; James A. Hamilton, *Reminiscences*, 302.
5. AMH, 4.
6. AMH, 14; MH, I, 12, 476; Schachner, *Hamilton*, 9.
7. Lodge, *Hamilton*, 288–291.
8. R, 41–44.
9. Atherton, *Adventures*, 353.
10. Aspinall, *West Indies*, 217; Rymer, *Nevis*, 1; personal visit to Nevis, 1975.
11. Smith, *Nevis*, 343.
12. AMH, 6–7.
13. HS, II, 539.
14. HS, II, 350.
15. HS, I, 563.
16. MH, I, 11.
17. R, 8–9.
18. R, 11–12.
19. JCH, *Life*, 3.
20. AMH, 21n.
21. R, 15.
22. R, 8.

23. R, 16–22.
24. R, 23, 26–27, 38.
25. MH, I, 13.
26. HS, II, 418.
27. R, 27.
28. MH, I, 373.
29. MH, I, 474; R, 13–14.
30. JCH, *Life*, I, 2–3.
31. HS, II, 35.

3. THE END OF RACHEL

1. Personal visit to St. Croix, 1975; Lewinson, *St. Croix*; R, 32; Westergaard, *Danish*.
2. Atherton, "Mother," 237–238; R, 24.
3. R, 23.
4. MH, I, 13.
5. MH, I, 16–17; R, 23–26.
6. HS, I, 1–3.
7. Bancroft, *United States*, VII, 79; HS, I, 3; Lodge, *Hamilton*, 243–245.
8. R, 24, 28.
9. Personal visit; R, 25–26.
10. R, 24.
11. MH, I, 11–12.
12. R, 24–25.
13. R, 26.
14. *Caribbeana*, V, 37; R, 28.
15. R, 28–29.

4. EXPLOSION OUTWARD

1. White, *Beekmans*, 213, 222.
2. HS, I, 369–370.
3. HS, I, 4–5.
4. AMH, 14.
5. HS, I, 6–7.
6. MH, I, 22–24; White, 222.
7. JCH, *Life*, I, 6.
8. MH, I, 23.
9. HS, I, 61, 148–149; MH, I, 20.
10. Aspinall, *Pocket*, 17 ff.; Westergaard, *Danish*, 139 ff.; Smith, *Nevis*, 233.

11. Smith, 225; R, 49.
12. MH, I, 485.
13. HS, II, 18; III, 597, 654; V, 351; Miller, *Hamilton*, 294.
14. HS, I, 53.
15. Lewinson, *Diverse* and *Seven*.
16. HS, I, 28.
17. Tansill, *Documents*, 49; Miller, 226; various portraits and busts, particularly those by Giuseppe Ceracchi, Charles Willson Peale, and John Trumbull.
18. HS, I, 10; III, 373.
19. HS, I, 16.
20. HS, I, 17.
21. HS, I, 12–13, 18.
22. HS, I, 16.
23. HS, I, 14.
24. HS, I, 18.
25. HS, I, 27–28.
26. HS, I, 24.
27. HS, I, 30.
28. HS, I, 21.

5. SPRINGBOARD

1. Lodge, *Works*, VIII, 629.
2. R, 17–18, 30–32.
3. Knox, *Letter*, 7-10; Miller, *Rodgers*, 97–101; Mitchell, *Knox*.
4. R, 75.
5. JCH, *Life*, I, 6.
6. Miller, 103.
7. HS, I, 34–38.
8. JCH, *Life*, I, 6–7.
9. HS, III, 573; Mitchell, *Knox*, 100.
10. HS, I, 40–41.
11. Mulligan, "Narrative," 209; R, 51.
12. JCH, *Life*, I, 7.

6. SCHOOLBOY IN A NEW LAND

1. Hamilton, Artillery Account Book, MS in LC; Mulligan, "Narrative," 209.
2. Mulligan, 209; Troup, "Narrative," 212.
3. Kalm, *Travels*, 123.
4. *New Jersey Archives*, 1st ser., XXV (1903), 227–228, 512; MH, I, 41–43; Mitchell, *New Jersey*, 88; Murray, *Elizabethtown*, 37, 86.
5. Chastellux, *Travels*, I, 344; JCH, *Life*, I, 8; HS, I, 513.
6. JCH, *Life*, 8.
7. Schachner, *Hamilton*, 209, 212; MH, I, 41 ff.
8. HS, I, 255–257; Van Rensselaer, *Livingston*, 86.
9. HS, I, 182.
10. Mulligan, 209–210.
11. Thomas, "King's," 24.
12. Mulligan, 211.
13. Miller, *Hamilton*, 523; Thomas, 36.
14. MH, I, 57.
15. HS, I, 80; Troup, 212; MH, I, 54–55.
16. Troup, 212.
17. HS, I, 44.
18. HS, I, 43–44.
19. Troup, 211; Mulligan, 214.
20. Troup, 213.
21. Troup, 212–213.

7. A TEEN-AGED PROPAGANDIST

1. HS, I, 67; Troup, "Narrative," 213.
2. HS, I, 46, 82.
3. Troup, 213.
4. HS, I, 135.
5. JCH, *History*, I, 55–67.
6. *Documents Relative to . . .*, VIII, 571.
7. Adams, *Independence*, 88; Seabury, *Free Thought*.
8. HS, I, 67.
9. HS, I, 46.
10. HS, I, 47.
11. HS, I, 144.
12. HS, I, 155.
13. HS, I, 65.
14. HS, I, 154.
15. Seabury, *View*.
16. HS, I, 50n.

17. HS, I, 81–82.
18. HS, I, 86, 86n.
19. HS, I, 122.
20. HS, I, 86, 88, 104.
21. HS, I, 122.
22. HS, I, 87.
23. HS, I, 94–95.
24. HS, I, 159.
25. HS, I, 156–160.
26. This copy is in the NYHS.
27. Mulligan, "Narrative," 211; Troup, "Narrative," 214.
28. Seabury, *View*, 106, 145.
29. Atherton, *Conqueror*, 34.

8. THE WAR TUNES UP

1. *Documents Relative to* . . . , VIII, 580.
2. Troup, "Narrative," 218.
3. Nicholas Fish to Timothy Pickering, 12/26/1828, Columbia University Library; *Documents*, VIII, 601–602.
4. *Documents*, VIII, 297.
5. *Documents*, VIII, 581; *Gentleman's Magazine*, XLVI (1776) 326–327; Mulligan, "Narrative," 211; Troup, 219.
6. Bliven, *Under*, 2–12.
7. Bliven, 155.
8. HS, III, 141.
9. HS, I, 165–176.
10. Bliven, 34–38; Mulligan, 210; Stokes, *Iconography*, IV, 901.
11. Bliven, 39–63.
12. Mulligan, 211.
13. HS, I, 176–178.
14. John Jay to Alexander McDougall, 12/17/1775, NYHS.
15. HS, I, 178.
16. Jay to McDougall, 12/4/1775 and 12/8/1775, NYHS.
17. Troup, 214.
18. HS, I, 65.
19. HS, I, 179.
20. HS, I, 181.

9. AT LAST, A SOLDIER

1. Fernow, *New York,* 72; *Journals of the Provincial Congress,* I, 354; Troup, "Narrative," 214.
2. Elias Boudinot to Alexander Stirling, 3/10/1776, NYHS; Valentine, *Stirling,* 169.
3. Boudinot to Stirling, 3/10/1776, NYHS.
4. Nicholas Fish to Timothy Pickering, 12/26/1823, Columbia University Library; Codman, *Badlam;* Fernow, 84; *Journals of the Provincial Congress,* I, 359.
5. HS, I, 181; Mulligan, "Narrative," 210; NYHS, *Collections,* XLVIII (1915), 339–345.
6. HS, III, 13–14; *New York Journal or General Advertiser,* 6/9/1776.
7. Fernow, 79; *Journals of the Provincial Congress,* II, 72; Lefferts, *Uniforms,* 46, 121 pl. xvii; MH, I, 81, 517.
8. AMH, 204; JCH, *History,* I, 52.
9. Troup, 214.
10. GW, IV, 499–500.
11. GW, V, 44.
12. GW, V, 24.
13. GW, V, 51; *New York Journal or General Advertiser,* 6/9/1776.
14. GW, V, 25, 37, 125.
15. HS, I, 185.
16. HS, I, 183–187; *Journals of the Provincial Congress,* I, 103, 119, 550, 564.
17. HS, I, 187–188.
18. *Journals of the Provincial Congress,* I, 573–574.

10. TOWARDS DANGER
    AND OPPORTUNITY

1. Brooks, *Knox;* Callahan, *Knox;* Drake, *Knox.*
2. Stokes, *Iconography,* I, 356, pl. 146a; IV, 915–916; VI, 406–407.

3. Force, *Archives*, 3rd ser., VI, 920–921; John Montressor, *Plan of the City of New York* (London, 1776), NYHS.
4. GW, V, 134.
5. Bliven, *Under the Guns*, 318 ff.; Stokes, IV, 936 ff.
6. John Morin Scott, army orders, New York, June–July, 1776, MS in NYHS.
7. *Continental Gazette*, New York, 7/8/1776; *New York Gazette*, 7/8/1776.
8. GW, V, 244.

11. DEFEATS

1. FR, 98–99; *New York Gazette*, 7/12/1776.
2. HS, I, 188, 190; *Calendar*, I, 501, 631.
3. Ward, I, *Revolution*, 209.
4. *New York Gazette*, 7/22/1776; Stokes, *Iconography*, V, 995.
5. Stokes, V, 1002.
6. FR, 117.
7. Mulligan, "Narrative," 210–211.
8. Mulligan, 207, 210–211.
9. Hamilton, "Pay Book of the State Company of Artillery," Hamilton Papers, LC.
10. Burr, *Memoirs*, I, 100–101; Drake, *Knox*, 30.

12. BLACKNESS

1. Fernow, *New York*, II, 53.
2. GW, VI, 125.
3. Greene, *Greene*, I, 193, 333.
4. HS, II, 421, 566; V, 345–359.
5. Hamilton Papers, LC.
6. HS, II, 37.
7. HS, III, 13, 22.
8. Hamilton, "Pay Book."
9. FR, 140.
10. JCH, *History*, I, 133–134.

11. McDonald, *Papers*, I, 45–55; Rodney, *Letters*, 143.
12. Hamilton, "Pay Book."
13. HS, III, 11.
14. Stryker, *Trenton*, 308.
15. GW, VI, 321–322.
16. Custis, *Recollections*, 344–345; Wilkinson, *Memoirs*, I, 119.
17. Irving, *Washington*, III, 88n.

13. RESPLENDENT LUSTER

1. HS, I, 190, 200; Stryker, *Trenton*, 357.
2. HS, I, 200.
3. Davis, "Washington," 146–148.
4. HS, I, 484.
5. Stryker, 357.
6. Butcher, *Trenton*, 24; Stryker, 142.
7. Bill, *Princeton*, 53; Butcher, 24; Stryker, 158.
8. Bill, Butcher, Stryker, etc.
9. HS, I, 200.
10. Wilkinson, *Memoirs*, I, 139.
11. Bill, 112; Sellers, *Peale*, 235; Stryker, 290.
12. MH, I, 91.
13. HS, V, 349.
14. Hamilton, "Pay Book," Hamilton Papers, LC; HS, I, 245; Knox MSS, nos. 111, 116, 122, MHS; Rodney, *Letters*, 160.
15. HS, I, 195.

14. A DISTURBING LETTER

1. GW, VI, 487–488.
2. GW, VII, 38; HS, I, 195.
3. HS, I, 200.
4. MH, I, 527.
5. HS, I, 216, 245, 565.
6. GW, XII, 164; HS, I, 196; II, 35.
7. HS, I, 426; II, 35, 388.
8. HS, II, 35.
9. HS, I, 566.
10. FR, 40.

11. HS, I, 307; II, 566n.
12. HS, II, 566.

15. NEW FATHER, NEW FAMILY

1. GW, VII, 214, 218; MH, I, 527.
2. HS, I, 201–202, 206.
3. Tilghman, *Tilghman*, 153.
4. HS, II, 110, 517.
5. HS, I, 355.
6. HS, II, 566.
7. Flexner, *Washington*, I.
8. Chastellux, *Travels*, 343–344.
9. GW, XXXVI, 461.
10. Atherton, *Conqueror*, 161, 168.
11. GW, XXXVI, 460.
12. GW, XXXVI, 460.
13. MH, I, 110–111.
14. Chastellux, 343–344.
15. HS, I, 350; II, 304, 427, 431, etc.; Tilghman, 153.
16. JCH, *Life*, 161; HS, I, 168; II, 423.
17. Greene, *Greene*, I, 310, 333.
18. *Proceedings . . . New Jersey Historical Society*, LI (1933), 150–153.
19. Chastellux, 343–344; Graydon, *Memoirs*, 275–276.
20. Information from Mary-Jo Kline.
21. HS, I, 224–227.
22. HS, I, 258–261.

16. THOUGHTS DURING DOLDRUMS

1. HS, V, 349.
2. HS, I, 207–208; Provincial Congress, *Journal*, I, 646, 662; *Calendar*, 510, 518, 522.
3. HS, I, 209–212, 234.
4. GW, VII, 293, 317.
5. HS, I, 211.
6. GW, VII, 318.
7. HS, I, 309; V, 349.
8. HS, I, 399; II, 353.
9. HS, I, 215, 217.

10. GW, VII, 334.
11. HS, I, 220–221.
12. Chastellux, *Travels*, I, 343–344.
13. HS, I, 246–247.
14. HS, I, 233–234.
15. HS, I, 253, 255.

17. BLINDMAN'S BUFF

1. HS, I, 256.
2. FR, 205; HS, I, 252.
3. HS, I, 275–277.
4. HS, I, 270.
5. HS, I, 285–286.
6. HS, I, 286.
7. HS, I, 299–301.
8. HS, I, 200, 301.
9. HS, I, 288.
10. Chastellux, *Travels*, I, 189, 338; HS, I, 286; Pickering, *Pickering*, I, 147.
11. FR, 211.
12. FR, 212.
13. HS, I, 302.
14. HS, I, 305.
15. HS, I, 308.
16. HS, I, 304.
17. HS, I, 294, 302, 309.
18. HS, I, 314.
19. HS, I, 307.
20. HS, I, 310–312.
21. HS, I, 314–316.
22. PMHB, I (1877), 275 ff.
23. Lafayette, *Memoirs*, 19.
24. Lafayette, 24.

18. FOOLED AGAIN

1. FR, 217; Lafayette, *Memoirs*, 20.
2. HS, I, 320–321.
3. HS, I, 321.
4. FR, 220–222.
5. GW, IX, 206 ff.
6. Freeman, *Washington*, IV, 475; GW, IX, 205.

7. FR, 222–224; MacElree, *Brandywine*, 140–141; Townsend, *Account*, 30–33.
8. HS, I, 329–330.

19. A WILD WARNING

1. PMHB, XVII (1893), 430.
2. HS, I, 326–328; Lee, *Memoirs*, I, 18–21.
3. HS, I, 326.
4. HS, I, 328.
5. Lee, 21.
6. GW, IX, 235–237.
7. GW, IX, 237–238.
8. HS, I, 327–328.
9. CCJ, VIII, 754.
10. Adams, *Familiar Letters*, 314.
11. Burnett, *Letters*, II, 497; PMHB, I (1893), 3–4; LXXXII (1958), 448–449.
12. Adams, *Papers*, II, 265.
13. PMHB, LXXXII (1958), 448–449.
14. GW, IX, 227n; HS, I, 330–331.
15. GW, IX, 249–250.
16. HS, I, 332–333.
17. PMHB, I, 6; LXXXII, 448–449.
18. HS, I, 334.
19. PMHB, LXXXII, 449.
20. GW, IX, 250.

20. DESPERATE MEASURES

1. Rush, *Autobiography*, 132–133.
2. GW, IX, 276–277, 305.
3. GW, IX, 3–7.
4. Lee, *Memoirs*, I, 29.
5. Flexner, *Traitor*, 158.
6. Lee, *Memoirs*, 29–30; *North American Review*, XXII (1826), 427–428.
7. FR, 234.
8. GW, IX, 320.
9. Knollenberg, *Revolution*, 190.
10. HS, I, 342, 345–346.

11. GW, IX, 479.
12. GW, IX, 461–464.

21. THE FIRST MAJOR MISSION

1. GW, IX, 466 ff.
2. HS, I, 347–349.
3. GW, IX, 464–466.
4. Israel Putnam to Horatio Gates, 10/31/1777; Putnam to Council of War, 10/31/1777; William Malcolm to Gates, 10/31/1777; Gates to George Clinton, 11/2/1777; Gates to Putnam, 11/2/1777—all in NYHS.
5. HS, I, 349–351; MHS, *Collections*, 7th ser., II (1902), 187–188.
6. HS, I, 350.
7. Gates to his wife, 10/20/1777, NYHS.
8. HS, I, 353–355.
9. Troup, "Narrative," 224; MHS, *Collections*, 184–185.
10. Joseph Reed to Gates, 10/30/1777, NYHS; Sparks, *Correspondence*, IV, 500.
11. HS, I, 354–355.
12. HS, I, 351–352.
13. Gates to Washington, 10/2/1777, NYHS.
14. Gates to Washington, 11/7/1777, NYHS.
15. HS, I, 357–358.
16. HS, I, 358–359.
17. HS, I, 356–357.
18. HS, I, 357, 359.
19. HS, I, 358–360.
20. HS, I, 360–362.
21. HS, I, 361–363.
22. HS, I, 363; Patterson, *Peekskill*, 77.
23. HS, I, 367.
24. Clinton, *Papers*, II, 541–542, 556; Laurens, *Correspondence*, 92.
25. HS, I, 412–414; R, 25.
26. Hugh Hughes to Gates, 12/19/1777, NYHS.
27. HS, I, 368–369.

28. HS, I, 372.
29. HS, I, 414.

22. VALLEY FORGE

1. HS, I, 414–421.
2. GW, X, 362–407.
3. Waldo, "Diary," 306–307, 309.
4. HS, I, 425–428.
5. Ibid.
6. HS, I, 436–437.
7. HS, I, 428.
8. Ibid.
9. Troup, "Narrative," 222.
10. GW, X, 29.
11. Thomas Mifflin to Horatio Gates, 10/8/1777; Gates to Mifflin, 12/4/1777, both NYHS.
12. Wilkinson, Memoirs, I, 372–373.
13. Troup, 224.
14. Sparks, Correspondence, IV, 486–488, 501.
15. GW, X, 263–265; HS, I, 224.
16. Sparks, IV, 494–495.
17. GW, X, 415–416.
18. HS, I, 428.
19. Boudinot, Journal, 43.
20. HS, I, 440–441.
21. GW, X, 31.
22. Boudinot, 44; GW, X, 212–213.
23. HS, I, 452.
24. Boudinot, 45.
25. Boudinot, 47.
26. HS, I, 461, 467.
27. HS, I, 476–477.
28. Boudinot, 48.
29. HS, I, 492, 493.
30. HS, II, 566.
31. HS, II, 569.
32. FR, 269–270.
33. HS, I, 510.
34. HS, I, 428.

23. A FRENZY OF VALOR

1. GW, XII, 2.
2. GW, X, 366; Waldo, "Diary," 306–307.

3. GW, XII, 102–114; HS, I, 501.
4. James McHenry, "Journal," entries from June 18 to July 15, 1778, MS, NYPL.
5. GW, XII, 115–117; Lafayette, Memoirs, I, 50.
6. GW, V, 16–17; HS, I, 510.
7. FR, 298–299; Lafayette, Letters, 46–47.
8. HS, I, 510–511.
9. FR, 298–299; HS, I, 510–511.
10. HS, I, 503–504; Lafayette, Letters, 48.
11. HS, I, 504–506; Lafayette, Letters, 22.
12. GW, XII, 117–123; HS, I, 506.
13. Alden, Lee, 213; HS, I, 508.
14. HS, I, 511, 521.
15. Alden, 215.
16. Lee, Papers, III, 156.
17. HS, I, 517–518.
18. Lee, Papers, III, 61, 67–68, 71, 79.
19. Lee, III, 72, 79.
20. FR, 304; HS, I, 520.
21. HS, I, 518.
22. Lee, III, 114, 200–201.
23. HS, I, 521–522; Lee, III, 59–62.
24. HS, I, 519.
25. HS, I, 519–521; Lee, III, 127–128, 159.
26. Tench Tilghman to Elias Boudinot, 7/2/1778, NYPL; Lee, III, 200.
27. HS, I, 512.
28. HS, I, 513–514.

24. GRAPESHOT

1. HS, I, 516.
2. HS, I, 524–530.
3. GW, XII, 233–235.
4. HS, I, 528–529.
5. HS, I, 537–543.
6. HS, I, 545–546.
7. FR, 305.
8. HS, I, 547–548.
9. HS, I, 551–552.

10. HS, I, 562–563, 567–570, 580–582.
11. HS, III, 3.
12. HS, I, 567–568.
13. HS, I, 562–563, 580–581.
14. HS, II, 53.
15. FR, 312; HS, I, 577–578.
16. HS, I, 593.
17. HS, I, 600.
18. Graydon, *Memoirs*, 323–324; HS, I, 602–604.
19. GW, XIII, 454–502; XIV, 1–66; HS, I, 602–605; II, 1–7.

25. A DEADLY RUMOR

1. HS, II, 90–92.
2. HS, II, 99–101.
3. HS, II, 108–109.
4. HS, II, 123–126.
5. HS, II, 126–127.
6. HS, II, 127–128.
7. HS, II, 140–141.
8. HS, II, 141–143.
9. HS, II, 153–156, 169.
10. GW, XVIII, 322; HS, II, 222, 224, 313–317; MHS, *Collections*, LXIII, 434.
11. MH, I, 179–181.

26. FRUSTRATIONS

1. HS, II, 19–20; Van Rensselaer, *Livingston*, 86.
2. HS, II, 22–23.
3. HS, II, 70.
4. GW, XV, 202 ff; HS, II, 64.
5. GW, XV, 386, 396–398, 430.
6. GW, XV, 439; HS, II, 105–106.
7. HS, II, 128–130.
8. HS, II, 158–159, 199.
9. HS, II, 164, 174.
10. GW, XVI, 272–275, 409–415; HS, II, 194.
11. GW, XVI, 453–454, 483; HS, II, 199–220.

27. A ROMANTIC FRIENDSHIP

1. Townsend, *Laurens;* Wallace, *Laurens.*
2. Sellers, *Peale,* 123, 367.
3. Wallace, 449 ff.
4. HS, II, 17–18.
5. HS, II, 34–38.
6. HS, II, 102–103.
7. HS, II, 165–169.
8. HS, II, 225–226.
9. HS, II, 230–231.
10. HS, II, 226, 254–255, 509.

28. A DIM PROPHETIC VISION

1. GW, XVII, 272–273, 360–365; Sparks, *Correspondence,* IV, 144.
2. HS, I, 142 ff.
3. HS, I, 373 ff.
4. HS, I, 579.
5. HS, II, 234–251.
6. HS, II, 604–605.
7. GW, XXI, 181, 181n.
8. HS, II, 244–245; Miller, *Hamilton,* 55.

29. ENGAGED TO BE MARRIED

1. HS, II, 260–261, 263.
2. FR, 336; HS, II, 258–259.
3. HS, I, 537.
4. HS, II, 261; Humphreys, *Schuyler,* 176.
5. Tilghman, *Tilghman,* 173.
6. Philip Schuyler to Baron von Steuben, 1/10/1780, NYHS.
7. Benjamin Walker to Steuben, 2/21/1780, NYHS.
8. HS, II, 263.
9. HS, II, 269–270, 351.
10. HS, II, 271 ff.
11. HS, II, 285–287.
12. Tilghman, 90–91.
13. Tilghman, 173.
14. Collection, Museum of the City of New York.

15. Humphreys, *Schuyler.*
16. Chastellux, *Travels*, I, 198.
17. HS, II, 303–304, 348.
18. HS, II, 351.
19. HS, II, 398.
20. HS, II, 305.
21. HS, II, 543.
22. MH, I, 202.
23. HS, III, 235.
24. HS, II, 305–306.
25. HS, II, 306–307.
26. HS, II, 306.
27. HS, II, 375–376; *Royal Gazette,* New York, 10/18/1780.
28. HS, II, 350.

30. THE DARK CONFUSIONS
OF A SUMMER

1. HS, II, 303–304.
2. HS, II, 310.
3. Lafayette, *Letters*, 82.
4. HS, II, 320.
5. HS, II, 321–322.
6. HS, II, 323–324.
7. HS, II, 326–327.
8. HS, II, 322–323.
9. HS, II, 332.
10. HS, II, 336 ff.
11. Flexner, *Traitor*, 309–310; HS, II, 343.
12. HS, II, 347–348.
13. HS, II, 347.
14. HS, II, 367.
15. HS, II, 377 ff.
16. Rochambeau, *Memoirs*, 12–16.
17. HS, II, 351.
18. HS, II, 353.
19. HS, II, 361–362.
20. HS, II, 370–371.
21. HS, II, 374.
22. HS, II, 375.
23. HS, II, 397.
24. HS, II, 387–388.
25. HS, II, 397–399.
26. HS, II, 418–419.
27. GW, XVIII, 367, 382.

28. HS, II, 385–387, 420–421.
29. HS, II, 422–423.
30. HS, II, 427–428.
31. HS, II, 347, 422–423, 427.
32. HS, II, 423, 425–426.

31. THE REVERIES OF A PROJECTOR

1. JCH, *History*, II, 84.
2. HS, III, 137.
3. HS, II, 400–418.
4. Atherton, *Conqueror*, 208–209.
5. Bancroft, *Constitution*, I, 10 ff.; Burnett, *Letters*, V, 378; VI, 42; Burnett, "New York," III, 316; JCH, *History*, II, 79 ff; HS, II, 383; Lossing, Schuyler, 431 ff.
6. HS, II, 479.

32. EXTREME EMOTIONS

1. FR, 370; HS, II, 413.
2. HS, II, 391–396.
3. FR, 371–373.
4. HS, I, 512; II, 367.
5. FR, 284.
6. Flexner, *Traitor*, 366–369.
7. Flexner, 370.
8. Flexner, 371.
9. Flexner, 366–367.
10. HS, II, 440–441.
11. HS, II, 438–439.
12. HS, II, 441–442.
13. Chastellux, *Travels*, 344.
14. HS, II, 470.
15. HS, II, 467.
16. HS, II, 446–447.
17. Flexner, 386–387.
18. HS, II, 448.
19. HS, II, 448–449.
20. Flexner, 389–390; HS, II, 445–446.
21. HS, II, 649.
22. HS, II, 468.
23. HS, II, 449.

33. DISSATISFACTIONS AND MARRIAGE

1. HS, II, 475.
2. HS, II, 431.
3. HS, II, 517.
4. HS, II, 509.
5. HS, II, 483n.
6. HS, II, 509.
7. HS, II, 509.
8. HS, II, 517.
9. HS, II, 501, 508.
10. HS, II, 505–506.
11. HS, II, 509–510.
12. GW, XX, 395.
13. HS, II, 519.
14. HS, II, 517.
15. Lafayette, *Letters*, 131.
16. GW, XX, 470n; MH, I, 224.
17. Personal visit to the Schuyler mansion, 1976; Hooker, *Sketch*.
18. HS, II, 523–524.
19. HS, II, 524.
20. HS, II, 521.
21. Chastellux, *Travels*, I, 198.

34. RUMBLINGS

1. GW, XX, 470–471; HS, II, 419.
2. HS, II, 518–519.
3. CCJ, XVIII, 1138, 1141; JCH, *History*, II, 44.
4. CCJ, XVIII, 1115, 1156, 1164, 1166.
5. HS, II, 526–527.
6. HS, II, 543.
7. HS, II, 566n.
8. HS, II, 528.
9. FR, 405–407.
10. FR, 407–409; HS, II, 544, 549.
11. Closen, *Journal*, 61; Mailler, *New Windsor*, 31–34; Ruttenberg, *New Windsor*, 70–71.
12. Elizabeth Schuyler to Margarita Schuyler, 7/21/1781, LC.
13. HS, II, 539–540.
14. AMH, 73, 232; HS, V, 497.

35. THE CRACKUP

1. HS, II, 529–533, 549, 551–552, 554.
2. HS, II, 551–552.
3. GW, XXI, 181.
4. GW, XXI, 259; HS, II, 563–565; Lafayette, *Letters*, 184.
5. GW, XXI, 491.
6. HS, II, 569.
7. HS, II, 563–569; the reader should check this source for variant readings.
8. HS, II, 575–576.
9. FR, 414–416; HS, II, 573–574.
10. HS, II, 583–584, 587, 641.
11. GW, XX, 247; HS, II, 565, 587.
12. HS, II, 568.
13. GW, XXI, 488–489, 580, 593–597, 599.
14. HS, II, 594–595.

36. OLD OR NEW DIRECTIONS

1. HS, II, 589, 591, 593, 603.
2. HS, II, 600–601.
3. HS, II, 601–603.
4. HS, II, 636–638.
5. HS, II, 646.
6. HS, II, 640.
7. HS, II, 595–596, 606.
8. HS, II, 604–605.
9. HS, II, 635.
10. Robert Morris to Philip Schuyler, 5/29/1781, NYPL.
11. HS, II, 645–646.
12. HS, II, 416.
13. HS, II, 649–652, 654–657, 660–665, 669–674; III, 75–82, 99–106.
14. HS, II, 649.
15. HS, II, 650–651, 654–657.
16. HS, II, 662, 665, 670.
17. Lodge, *Hamilton*, 6–8.
18. HS, III, 106.
19. MH, I, 245.
20. HS, II, 594; III, 75.

37. ENDANGERING THE CAUSE

1. HS, II, 647.
2. HS, II, 647.
3. HS, II, 648.
4. HS, II, 652–653.
5. HS, II, 566–567.
6. GW, XXII, 424.
7. GW, XXII, 438.
8. HS, II, 255, 509; III, 3.
9. HS, II, 659–660.
10. HS, II, 665–666.
11. GW, XXIII, 19.
12. HS, II, 643.
13. Washington, *Diaries*, II, 219–220.
14. GW, XXIII, 11 ff.
15. HS, II, 667–668.
16. *Clinton-Cornwall Controversy* (London, 1888), 149, 152.
17. HS, III, 71n.
18. HS, II, 676.

38. THE ROAD TO THE BRITISH REDOUBT

1. Duncan, "Diary," 745–746; GW, XXIII, 69 ff.
2. HS, II, 675.
3. FR, 444–445.
4. Duncan, 745.
5. Feltman, "Journal," 315; GW, XXII, 134, 141–144, 146.
6. GW, XXIII, 147–148.
7. Duncan, 746.
8. Duncan, 746.
9. Duncan, 746.
10. Duncan, 748.
11. Duncan, 749.
12. Duncan, 749–750.
13. Duncan, 750–751.
14. Duncan, 751.
15. HS, II, 602.
16. Lee, *Memoirs*, II, 342n.

39. THE LONGED-FOR CONSUMMATION

1. Lee, *Memoirs*, II, 342n.
2. MH, I, 257.

3. Deux Ponts, *Campaigns*, 143.
4. Bonsal, *French*, 163.
5. *Pennsylvania Packet*, 9/27/1781.
6. Duncan, "Diary," 752; HS, II, 679–681.
7. *Magazine of American History*, VII (1881), 364.
8. Lee, II, 340; Williams, *Biography*, 276.
9. Deux Ponts, 143; Martin, *Private*, 235.
10. Williams, 276.
11. Miers, *Blood*, 152; Williams, 152–153.
12. Lee, II, 340–343.
13. HS, II, 681.
14. HS, II, 680; Williams, 277.
15. HS, II, 680; Lee, II, 342n.
16. Bonsal, 163.
17. HS, II, 681; Thacher, *Journal*, 285.
18. HS, II, 679n, 682.
19. Deux Ponts, 145–146.
20. Lee, II, 342n.
21. HS, II, 681.
22. Duncan, 522; Martin, 234–237; Williams, 277.
23. HS, II, 682.
24. GW, XXXIII, 227–229.
25. Lafayette, *Letters*, 235.
26. HS, II, 679–681.
27. HS, III, 461.
28. CCJ, XXI, 1082.

40. ENTER THE LAW

1. FR, 456–458.
2. Philip Schuyler to James Duane, 12/6/1781, NYHS; GW, XXIII, 280; HS, II, 683.
3. HS, II, 684.
4. HS, III, 71.
5. HS, III, 150–151.
6. HS, II, 684
7. HS, III, 68.
8. CCJ, XI, 1186–1187; XII, 40–41; HS, III, 6.
9. HS, III, 4–5.

10. HS, III, 70.
11. FR, 478–482; HS, III, 91–93.
12. CCJ, 651; HS, III, 71, 96–97, 120.
13. HS, II, 568.
14. HS, III, 82–83.
15. AMH, 14.
16. G, I, 5.
17. HS, III, 88.
18. HS, III, 192–193.
19. HS, III, 512.
20. HS, III, 4–5.
21. G, I, 47 ff.; HS, III, 191; Troup, "Narrative," 215.
22. G, I, 42, 49–50.
23. G, I, 28; Troup, 215.
24. HS, III, 122, 189.

41. TAX COLLECTOR

1. HS, III, 320.
2. HS, III, 85–86, 96.
3. HS, III, 86–87.
4. HS, III, 89–90.
5. HS, III, 90–91, 93–94.
6. HS, III, 98–99.
7. HS, III, 107n.
8. HS, III, 95, 106, 123, 125–126, 130–132, 143, 147, 161–162.
9. Abraham Yates to Philip Schuyler, 8/9 & 10/1, 4/1782, NYPL; HS, III, 139; MH, I, 265–266.
10. HS, III, 108.
11. HS, III, 114–116; HCH, History, II, 295–297; MH, I, 226.
12. HS, III, 114–116.
13. HS, III, 117, 145, 151.
14. HS, III, 132.
15. HS, III, 133–134, 137.
16. HS, III, 141.
17. HS, III, 135–137.
18. HS, III, 137–138.
19. HS, III, 140.
20. HS, III, 165.
21. HS, III, 171–177; JCH, History, 309–314; MH, I, 273–274.
22. HS, III, 181.
23. HS, II, 155, 191.

24. HS, III, 192.
25. HS, III, 150.
26. HS, III, 152.

42. TEMPTATION

1. HS, III, 192.
2. HS, III, 151.
3. HS, III, 145, 151.
4. GW, XXV, 121, XXVIII, 97; HS, I, 193.
5. MH, I, 280–281.
6. HS, III, 183–184.
7. Burnett, Correspondence, VI, 430, 452; HS, III, 198.
8. HS, III, 226.
9. HS, III, 238.
10. HS, III, 258, 413–414.
11. HS, III, 136, 204, 208, 212, 266–267, 275.
12. HS, III, 208.
13. HS, III, 213–223.
14. HS, III, 223n.
15. GW, XXV, 227–228, 431.
16. Shaw, Journals, 102.
17. Alexander McDougall to Henry Knox, 1/9/1783, NYHS; Bancroft, Constitution, I, 76–77.
18. John Brooks to Knox, 9/26 & 10/17/1782, MHS; Knox to John Lowell, 10/18/1782, MIIS; Hatch, Administration, 144 f.; Shaw, 98 ff.
19. HS, III, 240.

43. THE EDGE OF THE PRECIPICE

1. Alexander McDougall to Henry Knox, 1/9/1783, NYHS.
2. MP, VI, 32.
3. HS, III, 243–245.
4. HS, III, 246–247, 247n.
5. HS, III, 245, 250.
6. HS, III, 319, 319n.
7. McDougall to Knox, 2/8/1783, NYHS.
8. "Brutus" to Knox, 2/12/1783, NYHS.

9. HS, III, 263–264.
10. HS, III, 253–255.
11. HS, III, 256.
12. Knox to McDougall, 2/21/1783, NYHS.
13. "Brutus" to McDougall, 2/27/1783, NYHS.
14. HS, III, 272, 274, 319.
15. HS, III, 277–279.
16. Information from Mary-Jo Kline.
17. Kohn, "Newburgh"; Nelson, "Newburgh"; *Catalogue* [Newburgh].
18. HS, III, 286–288.
19. CCJ, XXIV, 295–297.
20. GW, XXVI, 211.
21. HS, III, 287.

44. FINANCIAL COLLAPSE

1. Burnett, *Letters*, VII, 84.
2. HS, III, 292–293.
3. GW, XXVI, 232–234.
4. HS, III, 307–309.
5. HS, III, 305–306.
6. HS, III, 315–316.
7. HS, III, 317–321.
8. HS, III, 329–331.
9. CCJ, XXIV, 253, 269–270, 364–365.
10. Walter Stewart to Horatio Gates, 6/20/1783, NYHS; GW, XXVI, 78.
11. CCJ, XXIV, 257–260, 354, 363, 377; HS, III, 367.
12. HS, III, 291, 295.
13. HS, III, 322–323, 344–345, 350.
14. GW, XXVI, 374–398; HS, III, 321.
15. HS, III, 378–397.
16. HS, III, 466–467.
17. HS, III, 312, 321, 437, 458, 464 ff.
18. HS, III, 350, 355–356, 367, 377.

45. LEADING CONGRESS ON A WILD PATH

1. Burnett, *Letters*, VII, 189; HS, III, 398n, 400n; MP, VII, 141; Pennsylvania Archives, 4th ser., III (1900), 905.
2. CCJ, XXIV, 405n.
3. Burnett, VII, 194; HS, III, 397–398.
4. Burnett, VII, 193.
5. Burnett, VII, 197; Eberlein, *Hall*, 293.
6. MH, I, 318; *Pennsylvania*, 906–907.
7. HS, III, 450; *Pennsylvania*, 906–907.
8. *Pennsylvania*, 907–908.
9. *Pennsylvania*, 908.
10. Burnett, VI, 193–195; HS, III, 401–402.
11. HS, III, 401–402.
12. HS, III, 403; *Pennsylvania*, 908–911.
13. HS, III, 402, 404–406, 442–443; *Pennsylvania*, 912–916.
14. HS, III, 404–406.
15. *Pennsylvania*, 912, 914.
16. HS, III, 447–449.
17. HS, III, 446, 480; *Pennsylvania*, 916.
18. Burnett, VII, 195–196.
19. Burnett, VII, 200n; GW, XXVII, 326; HS, III, 408, 457; MH, I, 321; *Pennsylvania*, 918 ff.
20. HS, III, 410–411.
21. Burnett, VII, 200n.
22. HS, III, 408–409, 412, 469–470.
23. HS, III, 426–430.
24. *Pennsylvania*, 905 ff.; *Pennsylvania Gazette*, 9/24/1783.
25. HS, III, 438–458.
26. HS, III, 438.
27. HS, III, 449.
28. HS, III, 455.
29. HS, III, 409.
30. HS, III, 449.
31. HS, III, 451.
32. FR, 407–409.
33. HS, III, 452–453.
34. HS, III, 454–455.
35. *Pennsylvania*, 201n–202n.

46. RETREAT TO DOMESTICITY

1. HS, III, 304.
2. HS, III, 310–311.
3. HS, III, 472.
4. HS, III, 462.
5. FR, 514–515; GW, XXVI, 482–492.
6. HS, III, 463.
7. HS, III, 420–426.
8. HS, III, 376.
9. HS, III, 292.
10. HS, III, 418, 430.
11. G, I, 47–52.
12. HS, III, 461–462.
13. HS, III, 470, 475–477.
14. G, I, 197 ff.
15. HS, III, 420–423.
16. HS, IV, 178–207.
17. HS, III, 481, 601, 609, 611.
18. HS, III, 512.
19. GW, XXVII, 58.
20. HS, III, 513–514.

47. TRAJECTORY'S END

1. HS, VI, 418.
2. Paltsits, *Farewell*.
3. AMH, 296.
4. HS, VI, 178–207.

5. Morris, 225.
6. Flexner, *Washington*, III, 226.
7. GW, XXXII, 130–133.
8. AMH, 263.
9. HS, XXII, viii.
10. Miller, *Hamilton*, 518–520.
11. MH, II, 467–468.
12. Paltsits, 84 ff.
13. AMH, 259.
14. Hamilton, *Observations*.
15. *Dictionary of American Biography*, VIII, 177.
16. HS, XXI, 121–144; Jefferson, *Papers*, Boyd, ed., XVI, 455–470; XVIII, 211–225.
17. AMH, 219.
18. Atherton, *Conqueror*, quotation on title page.
19. AMH, 280–281.
20. HS, II, 255.

APPENDIX A

1. JCH, *Life*, I, 7; MH, I, 36, 490.
2. Troup, "Narrative," 212; Mulligan, "Narrative," 208–210; AMH, 13–14.
3. HS, I, 34n–35n.
4. HS, I, 40–41.
5. Troup, 213; Mulligan, 209, 211.

Index

247, 451; farmers, 266; Jews, 24; human nature, 6, 27, 387, 396–397, 437, 438, 439; money and trade, 21, 22–23, 35, 37, 53, 65, 241, 372, 375, 376, 396, 439; slavery, 39–40, 69, 258; women, 46, 149–152, 250, 259–260, 270–271, 446, 448

POLITICAL AND FINANCIAL VIEWS: early pro-British feelings, 56, 58, 63; change to pro-Colonial sentiments, 64–65; on treatment of suspected Tories, 159; favors "representative democracy," 159–160; advocates the superiority of federal system of government, 208, 296–297; his (rumored) favoring of an army uprising against Congress, 244–248, 302, 325; on printing of paper money, 265–266, 267; plan for combatting inflation and rescuing the economy, 266–268, 298–299; favors securing foreign loan, 266–268, 298; favors taxation as anti-inflationary measure and means of funding public debt, 266, 299, 340, 400–401; advocates founding a national bank, 267, 268, 299, 340, 439–440, 441; on states' rights, 299, 302; advocates strong central government, 299–300, 301, 302, 342–345; advocates a constitutional convention, 300, 301; on efficacy of a national debt, 340; advocates new taxation system for N. Y. State, 382–383, 387; and doctrine of implied powers, 393, 416, 437, 441; on army pay issue, 394–395, 397–414; on a peacetime army, 300–301, 302, 397, 415–416; on congressional funding of public debt, 414; on French Revolution, 441, 441n

WRITINGS: assessed, 3, 439; his poetry, 36–37, 62–63; prose style, 47–48, 72, 145, 285, 343, 344; hurricane letter (1772), 48–49; *A Full Vindication of the Measures of the Congress,* etc. (1774), 67–70, 71, 76; *The Farmer Refuted* (1775), 71–75, 76, 375; "Publius" letters (1778), 239–241, 266; "Narrative of an Affair of Honor" (1779), 242–243; letter to Duane on the state of the country (1780), 298–303, 341; letter

to R. Morris, outlining plan for economic health of U.S. (1781), 340–341; "The Continentalist" (1781), 342–345, 346, 400; pen portraits of opponents (1782), 384–386; "Practice Proceedings in the Supreme Court of the State of New York" (1782), 378–379; *The Federalist* (1787–1788), 441; *Report on Manufactures* (1791), 343, 437, 439; Washington's Farewell Address (1796), 437; attack on John Adams (1799), 445

ACHIEVEMENTS: as a military leader, 90–91, 92–94, 135, 357; as a military prophet, 74–75, 156–157, 166; opposing views of, 3–4; in politics and finance, 6, 390, 397, 436–437, 438–445; as Washington's aide, 5, 141–146, 157, 219, 437

Hamilton, Alexander (grandfather), 16
Hamilton, Allan McLane (grandson), 449
Hamilton, Angelica (daughter), 449
Hamilton, Elizabeth Pollock (grandmother), 16
Hamilton, Elizabeth (Betsey) Schuyler (wife), 21, 26, 56, 276, 279, 311, 315, 321, 338, 340; AH writes about, to her sister, 271–276; AH's letters to, 276–277, 288–292, 292–293, 297, 328–329; her letters to AH, 277; her background, 277; physical appearance, 278; her neurasthenia, 278, 446; becomes engaged to AH, 278; marriage to AH approved by her father, 280, 281; marries AH, 323; with AH at New Windsor, 327, 328; AH sends news of march to Yorktown to, 351, 352; joints AH in Philadelphia, 391; returns to Albany, 416; married life of, 446; widowhood, 446
Hamilton, James (father), 15, 18, 140; family history and youth, 16–17; lives with Rachel Lavien, 21–22, 23, 24–25; separates from Rachel, 25–26; AH invites to New York, 282
Hamilton, James (brother), 16, 29, 31, 32
Hamilton, John C. (son), 12, 17, 24, 27, 47; on the "hurricane" letter, 49–50; on AH's first public address, 65–66; on AH at Battle of White Plains, 119;